CHRISTIAN HERITAGE COLLEGE
2100 Greenfield Dr.
El Cajon, CA 92021

Song of the Sky

→SONG

OF
THE SKY

by Guy Murchie, *1907—*

with illustrations by the author

New, revised edition

Ziff-Davis Publishing Company · New York

BOOKS BY GUY MURCHIE

Men on the Horizon
Song of the Sky
Music of the Spheres
The Seven Mysteries of Life

Library of Congress Catalog Number 79-53948
ISBN 0-87165-030-4

First edition published by the
Houghton Mifflin Company

The author wishes to thank the Society of
Authors and The Public Trustee for permission
to quote lines from *Saint Joan*,
by George Bernard Shaw.

TO THE MEMORY OF OUR SON

JED

Contents

Acknowledgments

I<small>N EXPLORING</small> a subject as big as the sky I have come upon so much stimulating material that I have been able to use only a small part of it in this book. And yet for even that portion I am indebted to the generosity and diligence of scores of persons during the ten years it has taken me to get it down to earth and ink.

Most difficult to put into words is my wife Kathe's share — she who labored long to remove distractions and who understood that a man may be working even when gazing dreamily at the sky.

Next I must express my profound debt to Wolfgang Langewiesche, and particularly for his published work which has been so close in subject to my own and of such excellence that it has taken much restraint for me to quote him as few as half a dozen times herein. But far beyond the quotations Mr. Langewiesche has generously allowed me to take from his book, A Flier's World, I owe much to him in inspiration and factual information on the subjects of air masses, aerodynamics, the engineering problems of long-range flight, and the mysteries of the sonic barrier.

For much further help and constructive criticism on chapters and illustrations dealing with their special fields of study I am indebted to Professor Charles Franklin Brooks of the Harvard Meteorological Observatory on Blue Hill, to Giles Greville Healey of the Institute of Navigation, to Alfred Holland of the Aeroelastic and Structures Laboratory at M.I.T., and for helpful extra information to Edwin H. Bryan Jr. of Bishop Museum in Honolulu (on South Sea navigation), to Professor Henry L. Yeagley of Pennsylvania State College (on bird navigation), to Richard Borden of the Audubon Society (on the dynamics of bird flight), to Dr. Joachim Kuettner of the Air Force Cambridge Research Center (on the mountain wave, especially material for the text and illustration on pages 195 and 196), to Frederick Billings Lee, administrator of the Civil Aeronautics Administration (on a number of elusive flying facts), to Captain Daniel L. Boone and Navigator Willie Leveen of American Airlines for the account of their modern saga in navigation, and to Letty Grierson who helped edit the galley proofs.

Inevitably I have also had to delve extensively into hundreds of published sources, among which I feel my largest debt to the following books: the *Compendium of Meteorology* published by the American Meteorological Society, *Bird Flight* by Gordon C. Aymar, *Cloud and Weather Atlas* by Hugh Duncan Grant, *The Raft Book* by Harold Gatty, *Light and Colour in the Open Air* by M. Minnaert, *Tornadoes of the United States* by Snowden D. Flora, *Great Adventures and Explorations* edited by Vilhjalmur Stefansson, *Admiral of the Ocean Sea* by Samuel Eliot Morison, *Science for the Citizen* by Launcelot Hogben, *Soul of Lodestone* by Alfred Still, *The Wright Brothers* by Fred C. Kelly, *Ballooning* by C. H. Gibbs-Smith, *Wildwood Wisdom* by Ellsworth Jaeger, *Aerodynamics of a Compressible Fluid* by Hans Wolfgang Liepmann and Allen E. Puckett, *One, Two, Three . . . Infinity* by George Gamow, and many others.

Although all facts and anecdotes in this book have been made as accurate as my limited experience and repeated checking by friendly authorities would allow, I myself must of course assume responsibility for all the boners that may still be lurking in the rhetoric. The only intentionally fictitious names used are of flight crew members in a few of the accounts of air accidents where implication of blame might otherwise (perhaps unjustly) be embarrassing to the men involved.

Last and longest I want to express my heartfelt thanks to my friends the publishers who have been so generous and patient with me these many years: to Dorothy de Santillana and Paul Brooks who first had faith in my efforts and gave me sound advice, to Anne Barrett, Austin Olney, and the many others who so skillfully edited and handled the manuscript and illustrations.

Nelson, New Hampshire   G. M.
1954

Foreword to the 1979 Edition
by Guy Murchie

A lot has happened to our skies in the quarter century since this book was written in the early 1950s. I am adding these pages to bring to *Song of the Sky* a broader, more comprehensive view, a perspective that must include the amazing developments of the jet age, our dawning space age, and an educated peek into the approaching but still scarcely imaginable succeeding centuries.

Although jets existed during World War II, by 1954, few people had seen them as more than occasional dots, as high altitude bombers drew white vapor lines across the skies. Yet the jets swiftly proliferated into the vanguard of commercial as well as military aviation, which, together, expanded in the 1950s and 1960s on a scale never dreamed of by the most optimistic prophets during the pre-war decade.

There are now at least 10,000 airliners in the world, most of them large jets, carrying some half a billion passengers each year between a thousand large, well-equipped airports on six continents. These airports do an annual business in excess of 200 billion dollars. And these airliners, lots of them gigantic, are far outnumbered by some 275,000 other aircraft, of which roughly 70,000 are military (including jumbo jet transports and armored helicopters) and more than 200,000 are private, including 2000 business jets, 6000 helicopters, and many gliders and balloons. Although most of these aircraft are American and Canadian, France displays her air-mindedness with 6000 private aircraft, as does Australia with 4000, and, in varying degree, a hundred other countries, with about 25,000 airfields. Even the newly liberated ex-colonies find supporting a national airline to be a heady extravagance but desirable just the same. For many countries, the idea of moving into space, as have the United States and the Soviet Union, is a budding temptation.

As for the world's airports, not a few of them are already cities in themselves, far bigger than the great railroad terminals of old. Some surpass large seaports in capacity. Their work forces may number more than 50,000 people, and when we include families, the total dependent populations surrounding these terminals can exceed a quarter of a million. Until recently, most cities and towns tended to be apprenhensive about building airports, fearing the public's reaction to takeoff noise and possible real estate depreciation. Now, such anxieties are noticeably fading. The increasing size of airliners means fewer takeoffs and landings and therefore reduced average noise levels, while improved aerodynamic efficiency is beginning to shrink the required lengths of runways. Airports have become so indispensable to modern life that it is virtually inconceivable that they will ever disappear or even significantly diminish in importance while humanity continues to dominate the earth. In fact, their sudden appearance in this century is potent evidence of the thousandfold increase in travel speed that has so recently occurred on this planet and that so clearly symbolizes the universal Germination principle explained in detail in my recently published *The Seven Mysteries of Life.*

The drama of aviation has continued to unfold in fantastic ways, in concepts and experiments of amazing variety. There were once flying boats, some with wingspans as long as a football field, seats planned for 700 and powered by as many as twelve 6000-horsepower engines driving contra-rotating propellers. After them came nonhelicopter vertical takeoff craft which evolved from a bare-boned "flying bedstead" into various tiltwing transports. In a great rush, a host of other craft were developed—hovercraft, piggyback planes, stratospheric U-2s, swivel-winged F-111s, highly flexible STOL planes, stowable and inflatable reconnaisance craft, the pioneering X-15, which attained Mach 6.72 (4,534 miles per hour in 1967), hang gliders in the 1970s and man-powered airplanes, among them two named the *Gossamer Condor* and the *Gossamer Albatross.* The *Condor,* which has a 96-foot wingspread but weighs only 70 pounds, won the coveted Kremer Prize by being pedaled like a bicycle through the air for 1.4 miles on a closed course. In 1979, the *Albatross,* a similar design, actually was pedaled across the English

Channel, over a distance of 23 miles, in a flight that lasted nearly three hours, as pilot Bryan Allen battled undexpected headwinds.

The challenges of flight have always been varied and sometimes bizarre. As early as World War II, the airplane had proved its versatility in performances ranging from the capture of a German submarine off the Hebrides by a lone Royal Air Force land patrol plane using two bombs and a machine gun to the victory of an R. A. F. fighter pilot who, having run out of ammunition, defeated a German Messerschmitt by ramming it, using his Hurricane's wing to knock off the enemy's elevator and send him spinning into the Channel.

An American DC-3 pilot, on the other hand, faced an entirely different situation in peacetime Alaska when flying an old Jenny through a narrow canyon and getting caught by a wind so strong he could not make headway against it. Having too little room to turn around or climb past the overhanging crags, he "just throttled the old girl down" and flew out backwards.

There was also the astonishing but well-authenticated case in 1956 of the U. S. A. F. jet fighter pilot who dove supersonically below and ahead of a subsonic volley he had just fired, only to be overtaken and shot down by his own bullets as he attempted to level off.

I mention these things to demonstrate that the problems of flying have always been varied—and often barely believable—and don't seem to be less so with the advances of recent years. Towering cumulonimbus clouds are an undiminished danger, because they harbor thunder cells containing violent shear currents and deadly hail and because they create icing. When liquid rain droplets collect and freeze on the forward edge of a wing, they can quickly destroy the wing's power to lift (as we shall see in Chapter One). Collisions remain a rare but persistent horror despite altitude and pattern discipline, with flight controllers using radar, computers and steadily improving warning instruments. Although navigation has become so easy through the perfection of inertially guided computers (which now use electromagnetically-suspended gyros) that navigators are no longer part of flight crews because the pilot can read his latitude and longitude right off the panel, the pilot's growing dependence on this miracle can become frightening when something goes wrong. As satellite navigation systems replace radio beams, loran and other nav systems, and as cruising speeds rise, the wind becomes less of a problem—in fact, in the long run, steering an airplane gets to be more and more like firing a gun: if you take proper aim, you can hardly miss. But other problems that haven't gone away involve the dangerous invisible wakes of jumbo airliners, which, without warning, can flip over small craft half a mile behind them, and the elusively persistent risks of explosive decompression at stratospheric altitudes, where any large puncture (despite oxygen masks) threatens loss of consciousness above 40,000 feet and loss of life above 50,000.

All in all, these trials of the skies are ultimately solvable and are being lived with like other problems in this finite world. Indeed, computerized electronic systems are progressively evolving to help with them, including fully automated flight patterns from takeoff to landing. Executive helicopters are likewise saving time as well as money (compared with planes) on all but the longest business trips. The ballute, a high-altitude crossbreed of parachute and balloon (instantly inflatable with a cylinder of stored gas), has proved a life saver at 110,000 feet and speeds of Mach 5. And the simpler paravulcoon, producing hot air for controllable buoyancy, does still better at lower altitudes. There are even signs that the venerable blimp (using helium) may make a comeback for low-key transport in wind-resistant, streamlined form.

I have a feeling that before the end of the century, the current space shuttle program will evolve some sort of transoceanic rocket plane, which, by efficiently attaining orbit, will transport passengers, without further use of fuel, to any spot on Earth in an hour for the same fare as is now charged for transoceanic flight. An idea in advanced dynamics that just might make this happen is called the Flying Bonfire, in which the shock wave produced by a wedge shape at 3500 mph compresses the air behind the wedge so much that, when fuel is injected into it, the air explodes, accelerating the vehicle still more, with continuous combustion of atmospheric oxygen (and perhaps no other fuel) until it is well above the air and approaching orbit.

Our outward progression into space has been unstoppable since long before Sputnik startled the world in 1957—and is absolutely certain to continue. Mankind's emergence will accelerate quickly and dramatically as the great advantages of space clarify and prove themselves. The only question is: how soon?

While no nation to date has announced a firm commitment to colonize space permanently, research to that end is increasing and, unless some world catastrophe (like nuclear war) intervenes, the step will be taken in this century—and probably sooner than most of us imagine. Indeed, the shuttle program has already proved the economic feasibility of lifting large cargoes into orbit on a regular basis—and as quickly as the Congress of the United States (or comparable authority elsewhere) is made to see that space colonization can solve the energy crisis and ease the pollution problem (including population pressure and the arms race) such colonization can be well underway in less than a single decade.

Plans for it are already quite advanced, stimulated by a grant from the N. A. S. in 1975 and by such imaginative scientists as Gerard K. O'Neill, of Princeton and M. I .T. First priority will be to assemble temporary quarters in space for a workforce whose initial job will be to set up a manufacturing industry and habitat in orbit high enough above Earth to give them continuous solar power in perpetual sun-shine. While this is going on with some 2000 men and women workers, a smaller force of 200 will land on the moon to start mining it and sending its ores and oxygen (fortunately plentiful there) to the space factory. They will do this with the aid of a wonderfully efficient invention called the mass driver, which can electromagnetically accelerate unlimited masses of material to escape velocity (from the moon's low gravity) without need for rocket vehicles, thus economically supplying most of the raw material required in the space foundries and construction operations. These will use a giant floating "catcher" to collect and deliver the ores, the slag destined for radiation shields (important in airless space).

All this will be very expensive at first, costing something like $100 billion before a powerplant (using solar mirrors to focus heat onto boiler tubes) begins to supply energy to the automated, computerized foundry and factory and before the colony's population has built up to about 10,000. By then, around the end of its first decade, the space facility (including the moon miners) should achieve "ignition," which means becoming self-sufficient not only through mining and fabricating most of its own materials but also by returning more to earth (in microwave-transmitted solar power and other valuables) than it receives from Earth.

If you find this hard to believe, remember that space has many advantages over our planetary surface as a place to live and produce. Not only does solar energy's intensity average eight times greater in space than in, say, the United States, but in three-dimensional space, a power station can be located much closer to where the power is needed. Furthermore work without gravity is obviously a lot easier and simpler, especially when zero-G automated techniques are perfected, and all major transport (except that lifted from earth) becomes much cheaper and much faster. Nor are drivers or pilots needed for most space vehicles, because events in general there are more predictable. There are no storms or winds except for the "solar wind" (which does not blow vehicles off course), and traffic problems (except local ones) would be virtually non-existent in the outer vastnesses.

Of course, there will be farms in space—agriculture being a vital part of self-sufficiency both for food and air (as vegetables inhale carbon dioxide and exhale oxygen)—but farming up there will be free of storms, droughts and floods, and probably free of stones and pests (from worms to weevils to rats), and therefore will be simpler and more predictable with sunshine or rain made to order.

After the early spherical or doughnut-shaped factories and colonies in which gravity can be imparted to the perimeter by rotation, later and larger ones are likely to take the form of double cylinders, each perhaps four miles in diameter, 20 miles long and rotating (once every two minutes) on the same axis in opposite directions. In them, all water, air and waste will be recycled (nothing will be excreted that could litter the universe) and sunshine programmed by huge mirrors.

I haven't room here to describe the delights of low-G swimming pools, space ballet, orbit gliding, waterless fish, zero crystal-growing, STAR (for Self-Testing and Repair) computers, and the *absence* of crutches and canes, but these and many more items will all be part of the humanization of space. And despite the rapid industrial development of the orbiting colonies, they will not be as concentrated as the obsolete, smoky steel mills and roaring factories of Earth, for there is plenty of room. In fact, that is what space means: room. The goals out there will be diversity, efficiency, simplicity, harmony. Moon matter will be used because it costs only one-twentieth the cost of earthly stuff. As time passes, matter from the asteroids will become more and more available, being cheaper still, not to mention more abundant and varied. Never mind the distance. Think *energy*, not *miles*, even in their hundred millions, for in space, transport, including orbital changes, is practically a gift of God. And normal space navigation assumes accuracy to 1 in 20,000,000.

Space evolution, of course, will relieve Earth of some of her worst germinal problems, will enable her to become more pastoral again with a long-range population goal of only one or two billion. But although the human population will inevitably grow in space (along with that of a few animals), its density should soon decrease, for neither pollution nor poverty will be allowed there. The 600 tons of smoke, dirt and gas now given off by the average human in his lifetime will all be absorbed and recycled.

In the unfolding centuries, almost surely the whole solar system will evolve under the organized influence of maturing man, who seems to possess the only form of life here-abouts that is capable of making such a thing happen. But as he dismantles and rearranges the asteroids, moons and perhaps ultimately whole planets, using matter-antimatter powerplants, man will also launch automated probes to other star systems,—indeed, starship engines are already on the drawing boards capable of building up velocities to 10 psol (percent of the speed of light)—and in some millenium colonists will follow. Man cannot forever be denied the full adventure of space, of fulfilling Cyclops' shy attempt to commune with other worlds and one day to join other souls.

At present, there may be wisdom in the silence of advanced worlds. For we are yet unfledged and unaware of the need for polarities in this mortal phase of life, of the function of evil, or even of the failure of material prosperity to guarantee happiness. And very few are the philosophers who have yet sensed that our local noosphere is the seed of a Soul School with Transcendent potentiality.

Still the Song of Space will increasingly be heard in our expanding sky. It will not whistle or roar but only faintly hum, then fade off, mayhap into a mystic whisper compounded of nothing but faith . . . and patience . . . patience . . . patience . . . awaiting man's hatching of the planetary egg—of Earth's inspired willingness at last, at last to reach out in spirit and spread her wings.

The Airplane
Finds Its Way

1. The Craft

SHE WAS BUILT like a whale, for cargo and comfort. Ninety-four feet long and full-bellied, with wide tail flukes that could ease her nose up or down at the merest nudge of her controls.

Her sinews and nerves were four and a half miles of steel cable and insulated copper wire. Her brain was a set of instruments tended by radio waves, inertia, magnetic force, and atmospheric pressure, and all pivoted on sapphires and crystals of rare hardness.

She was Number 896, one of the original C–54s, the famous flying freighters designed especially for ocean transport — perhaps the most widely used long-range weight-carrying airplane to appear in the decades since man taught metal to fly.

On this night of the fifth of February she floated confidently on a mantle of black air 11,000 feet deep and bottomed by the angry North Atlantic ocean. Her wings were of duralumin, styled to cut the sky at two hundred and forty miles an hour. She rolled slightly — ever so slightly, like a porpoise sighing in sleep — just enough to tick the octant bubble from Mizar by the pole.

Inside her lighted hulk the air was at twenty inches of mercury, or only two thirds the density of sea level. The temperature was

75° Fahrenheit where her crew sat in the cockpit, 52° in the fuel compartment amidships, and 8° below zero outside. Her four motors, representing the heft of 5400 horses, breathed the thin cold air with the aid of superchargers forcing the vital oxygen into their pipes at a manifold pressure of thirty-one inches. Her gross weight at this moment was 62,180 pounds — 6200 pounds of it cargo, priority 1A, battened by rope and steel rods to the cabin floor: penicillin from Chas. Pfizer & Co., New York City, destined for London, England, and oxygen cylinders, type F–2, from Firestone Steel Products, Akron, Ohio, marked for Burtonwood, England. She had taken off from Stephenville, Newfoundland, amid snow flurries in the late afternoon. She was bound for Prestwick, Scotland, 2296 miles away by the great circle.

We men of the crew sat at our stations, going through our motions, writing words and figures into flight logs, occasionally dreaming, or talking, or unbuttoning a little with caprice. From the flight deck we could not see the waves two miles below. There were dense clouds covering the sea and the sun was deep under the earth. In the western sky Orion and the gibbous moon swung downward at fifteen degrees per hour. And as the earth turned and the planets turned, the galaxy of the Milky Way moved on its inscrutable course through the black universe of which man knows not the beginning nor the end.

"What are you doing up here? Why is that octant in your hand?"

It could have been the wind asking. I was the navigator seated at my chart table in the airplane's cockpit, gazing into the darkness beyond the window. The wind — a wind which never existed before the airplane — was crying in long monosyllables like a Chinese bird-monger. "Why — wh-h-y — wh-wh-h-h-h-h-y-y?" It sprang full-born from the Plexiglas nose and exploded upon the duralumin skin, sprawling backward over the humps of the astrodome and the engines, tearing itself cruelly on each protruding edge of cowling, each pitot and spar. It was the invisible substance of which the sky is made — not just air, not just wind, but a stuff which is part of the insoluble consciousness of flight.

"Why is that octant in your hand?"

Because I am the navigator. I hold the needle that will pierce the cloud. I sing the song of the sky.

While flying the ocean I am plainly the busiest of our crew of five. I keep account of the airplane's position and track over the earth, of altitude and the passing cloud layers, of horsepower and consumption of fuel. My flight log sometimes contains scores of entries in a single hour. I work with wind, radio waves, sun and stars, with charts of many colors, with tables heavy in figures. My hands know tools of precise design. My mind is as a detective in the crime laboratory, sifting and weighing the clues of drift and speed. I winnow the meager facts, seeking to construct truth only from the clean kernels. I am a human lodestone — the homing pigeon of mankind.

Frequently I converse with the pilot who likes to know where we are, how long before we will get to such and such a place ahead on the map, or how much gas is left in our tanks. Pilot on this flight is Captain Blake Cloud who sits up front in the driver's seat, a wiry little man with pale brown eyes that blink nervously from behind his oxygen mask. He is the ranking officer of this Douglas-built C–54, this oceanwise dragon of the air.

Second in our hierarchy is Gullerman Dropford, the co-pilot or first officer who sits on Cloud's right with a duplicate set of controls. He graduated from Yale and appears to veer to the conservative.

I am third in command, followed in rank by sleek Ernie Silvers, flight radio officer, an ovate Lothario whose desk is opposite mine in the cockpit, and Ignatz Wuzienski, flight engineer, a gangling Texas lad who sleeps most of the time between his few routine check duties while in the air.

We are all serving as employees of American Airlines in this first regular transoceanic round-the-clock freight service that the world has ever seen. We sense our place in history as pioneers of a great age of air transport that will defy time and space and weather and future dangers of extreme speed and altitude of which we have hardly yet begun to learn.

I came into this exotic calling by the usual chance combination of events. Back in Chicago in March 1942 after two years in Europe as a war correspondent, I was faced with the need of either resuming my war meanderings or choosing some other brand of war activity before the draft board chose one for me. A new kind of job after nine years on a newspaper? The idea was stimulating, and the day exuberant with possibilities. The sky was the great frontier and the war an extraordinary opportunity to develop it. I only wondered where I could get in on this incomparable adventure upward and outward.

Then one afternoon: a voice out of the radio describing the urgent need for aerial navigators in the Air Transport Command. This daring transportation project was to web the earth with traffic routes of a swiftness and efficiency that would amaze friend and foe alike. The nation's airlines and flying schools had the pilots. Radio operators and engineers were in training. But where were the navigators needed for ocean and jungle flying, especially near the fighting areas and over the oceans where radio aid would be limited? The nation's airlines had no navigators, with the exception of a handful at Pan American which had cautiously pioneered a few mild weather routes over the oceans in sea planes. Domestic airline pilots of course merely flew the beam, plotting their progress by rule of thumb across the checkerboard of multiple-range stations that covered the country. They had not had to face any real problems in navigation and the whole subject was relatively unknown and undeveloped. The tough routes of the earth had not been flown except by lone pioneers and statistics concerning them were as rare as grasshoppers in Greenland.

Especially serious was the lack of instructors capable of teaching navigation for, as any natural philosopher could tell you, it takes navigators to make navigators as surely as it takes flamingos to make flamingos.

The main hope for navigation at American Airlines came to rest on a fellow named Colin McIntosh, a diminutive Scot who had somehow picked up a lot of the science and art of aerial navigation, mostly on his own. He had cornered one or two former Pan American navigators who had flown the South Atlantic and was commissioned to start a navigation school at the Chicago airport.

When I went to see him in response to the voice on the radio, the first thing he told me was that I was several inches too tall for aerial navigating. "The Air Transport Command won't accept a man over six feet two," he explained from the safe altitude of a little over five feet. But when I told him I had had a private pilot's license for six years, of my interest in mathematics, of my education, of my hitch with the merchant marine and other sea experiences, his dour eyes lighted perceptibly.

"Perhaps we could take you as an instructor," he said.

For more than a year after that I taught navigation at the Chicago school. Learning as I taught, I specialized as a flight instructor, conducting classes of both civilian and army navigators in a flying DC-3 schoolhouse which roamed the skyways of North America from Manitoba to Puerto Rico. The pilot of this winged institution bravely did his best to carry out the erratic courses specified by his fledgling mentors with their circular slide rules, rotating star finders, and curlicued minds. It was perhaps unique in being the first schoolhouse in history which tested the theories of a whole classroom of students at 150 miles per hour, dramatically proving or disproving them in a way the student could never forget, while the lives of all the classmates, the instructor, and the fate of the schoolhouse itself sometimes literally hung on the outcome.

At the end of 1943 the Navigation School folded. The government had decided that we had trained all the A.T.C. navigators they wanted for a long time. So I made the easy shift from teacher

to navigator — no one remembered the matter of the height limit
— and here I am flying the ocean with the rest of them.

The substance that is the sky still swallowed us in its roar as
Number 896 continued on her course. In my reverie I wondered
if it could make any difference whether we moved while the air
stood still or the air moved while we stood still. Whichever way
was true, the body of the airplane rested there firmly upon the
sky, and the stars shone immutably from their ancient places — and
it was only the air that showed its violence.

I put the octant back into its case and glanced at my airspeed
indicator. The needle pointed to 166 knots. My thermometer
read 6° below. The altitude was 11,000. Magic needles quivering
before me — needles of light in the darkness. Adjusting my slide-
rule computer in a familiar calculation, I read off our corrected or
true airspeed: 184 knots. That was the actual speed at which the
sky's air was passing us. Although the airspeed instrument said
166 knots, the truth was 184 knots — a difference which is one of
the navigator's first lessons in the air, a difference accounted for
by the limitations of instruments in this pioneer era of navigation.
Instruments can measure airspeed pretty accurately at a constant
altitude and temperature but the varying altitudes and temperatures
of actual flying cause errors which no improvement of the instrument has so far been able to overcome.

Jotting down the airspeed in my flight log, I glanced next at the
fuel-flow meters on the main panel to see the rate of gas consumption. Again by some familiar figuring I found the true hourly
rate and recorded it in the log.

Then for exact altitude I had to correct the altimeter needle
reading for barometric pressure and temperature, working it out
on my computer: 10,850 feet. Scores of times on every flight these
same corrections have to be understood and reckoned. And many

others like them. It is a part of life, a sort of compensation for the untamed inexactitude of nature.

While checking my compass against the pilot's compass, I noticed that Cloud and Dropford had fallen asleep. It is not unusual to find both pilots dozing in the vast stretches of the sky's ocean, and I have sometimes known this state of affairs to continue for more than an hour while the automatic pilot faithfully guides the plane, continuously correcting the controls according to the dictates of the compass and the altimeter — the needle guiding man through the sky even while man's mind is not there to see it. It is a minor miracle that this can happen. And it is also customary for the radio officer, whose instruments are of least use in mid-ocean, to sleep part time in the air, to say nothing of the engineer.

I suppose there have been times when the entire crew of a plane slept over the ocean for fairly long periods without ill effects, but the navigator is one who definitely should not sleep for it is his serious responsibility to keep constant track of progress. He must note any change of speed, direction, or any factor of temperature, altitude, or engine adjustment that might affect the speed. If he does not, he loses a clue to accurate reckoning — which would be like a detective overlooking a bloodstain at the scene of a murder.

As I watched, Blake Cloud stirred, rubbed his eyes, and ran his fingers through his hair. He put on his oxygen mask again. Extra oxygen is not essential at 11,000 feet, but a little now and then will help keep a man from sleepiness.

Blake Cloud glanced at the compasses, checking the gyro against the magnetic. He reached out to adjust the gyro-compass knob on the panel. He set it to read 113°. That was the correct compass heading. The gyro-compass does not swing from side to side like the magnetic, but it has to be set periodically from the magnetic. Being steady, it is easier to steer by.

"Wonder how long this snow's gonna keep up," said Blake, indicating the windshield with his flashlight where a crust of freezing slush was collecting as fast as the wipers could take it.

"Probably just a local storm," I said, "but anything is possible from the weather forecast."

"What about the wind for twenty-four hundred? (hrs.)" he asked.

I looked at my log. "One-twenty at thirty knots. That was a between-fix wind." (120° at 30 kts. is a fairly strong southeast wind.)

"Okay," said Blake. "I think I'll go down to six hundred horsepower. What's the r.p.m. for eleven thousand at six hundred horse?"

Checking my power table, I answered, "Nineteen twenty. One nine two 0." (1920 revolutions per minute.)

"Thanks. Do you want to hold her on one hundred and thirteen heading?" (113°)

"That's right. I'll give you a new heading in an hour."

"Okay."

Just as I had turned back to my desk and started to plot another section of my fuel-consumption graph, I heard the captain call out: "Somebody wake Woozy! We're taking on ice and the de-icers aren't working."

Wuzienski was asleep in the upper bunk of the crewroom. I stepped in there and poked the prostrate form.

"Woozy! Better get up. The skipper says we're taking on ice and the de-icers are on the fritz."

"Okay, okay."

He scrambled to the linoleum floor, all six feet two of him, rubbed his blond mop of hair, shook his coverall straight, and walked the ten feet to where the captain sat.

"Look!" said Blake Cloud. He picked up the Aldis lamp, which is something like a car headlight with a handle and a trigger, and flashed its brilliant beam out the window. Woozy and I could see the forward edge of the wing glistening white where the light struck it. The ice was already two inches thick. The air was dense with supercooled rain which streaked horizontally against the wing, the engine nacelles, and the aerial spars, rapidly forming ice.

"What's the matter with the de-icers?" asked the captain, looking at Woozy. "The switches are on but the pressure gauge reads zero."

"Don't know, sir. I'll check the fuses." Wuzienski stepped back and opened the fuse-box door behind where Silvers sat.

"Look at that airspeed," said Cloud. "God, a hundred thirty-five on the instrument. If this keeps up we'll be stalling in ten minutes. What d'you find, Woozy?"

Woozy shut the fuse box and stepped forward. "Fuses okay, sir. The trouble might be in the wiring somewhere, or the air line might have a leak."

"We're gonna get out o' here," said Blake Cloud. His jaw was tight as he pulled back gently on the wheel and adjusted the four throttle knobs. "We're goin' upstairs."

The motors took on a deeper roar, seeming to change from a major to a minor chord as the plane began a steep climb. That sinister harmony of the four great engines may have been a reflection of the crew's anxiety as we realized the growing seriousness of our burden of ice. It was a weird hum that seemed to throb through my brain with every heart beat.

I watched the airspeed indicators: 125 . . . 123 . . . 120 . . . It was natural for the airspeed to decrease in starting a climb, but it shouldn't be nearly that low with the increased horsepower, and it shouldn't keep on decreasing. Blake Cloud flashed the Aldis lamp on the wing every minute or so. By the time we got to 12,000 feet there was more than three inches of ice and it was getting ragged and irregular in form. The whole airplane had begun to vibrate strangely.

The altimeter needle crept slowly upward — more slowly than at first. The airspeed continued to fall. The airspeed was hardly enough to permit the plane to continue climbing. The needle pointed to 116 now.

"Suffering Christ!" said Cloud. He turned around in his seat. "Woozy, have you found what's wrong?"

"No sir. The boots just don't go. Must be a leak somewhere."

The gross weight of the airplane was increasing as the ice added to it. But more serious was the fact that the ice was changing the air foil, changing it from the smooth curve the Douglas engineers had designed into an irregular blunt shape that threw eddies into the slip stream, destroying the air pressure components that gave the wing its lift. As the wing lost lift Blake Cloud had to hold the wheel further back, bringing the airplane's nose higher, in order to keep flying. This adjustment temporarily restored the wing's lift but it also reduced airspeed, bringing it ever nearer the airplane's stalling speed, somewhere close to 100 m.p.h., at which it would start to mush or lose altitude no matter how much its nose might be inclined upward. If the ice kept on accumulating, the plane would sink lower and lower until eventually it would fall into the sea like a pigeon dipped in plaster.

"Say, let me see that weather folder again," called the captain suddenly. "If we don't top this stuff damned soon our only choice will be to get under it or find a space between layers. We can't thaw the ice off. The temperature is below freezing all the way down."

He grabbed the paper, unfolded it, and scrutinized the cross-section drawing of forecast cloud layers done in green and pink by the weather office in Stephenville.

"God," he muttered. "There's liable to be clouds clear to the drink according to this. I can't count on coming out with all the stuff they got on here. But of course this thing may be all wet. It's twelve hours old. I think I'll top this stuff if I can."

He flashed the lamp once more against the wing. The ice was bulging forward from the air foil in angry corrugations — in some places four or five inches thick. The airspeed indicator read 112. And still the rain streaked mercilessly against us, and we labored upward foot by foot — a creature of the air, a delicate creature for all our 62,000 pounds — a flying whale built by Man — Man who had dared that which even the birds could not do.

It was only one of the problems that must often be faced and conquered by men who climb the sky. It would not take long. It could not. Somehow it must be solved within a few minutes — by a mechanical contrivance, by a man, by God.

For my part, I sat at my table engrossed in thoughts that were by no means all to do with navigation. Your earth lubbers who have not yet flown the ocean might suppose an aerial navigator is often worried about getting lost. This is not the truth. The navigator is accustomed to threading his way through the sky. His is a long view on time and space — and his mind knows the fullness of its freedom, bounded only by navigation's prodigious outer margins of safety: the multiplicity of precision instruments, four engines, three radios, the fuel reserve, hand pumps that can duplicate hydraulic pumps, the emergency equipment, the self-reliance of five men.

Besides, what navigating can you do while flying through rain or snow? Keeping track of how you are heading by the compass, how fast you are going by the airspeed indicator, how high you are by the altimeter, and of how warm it is by the thermometer — that's about the spread of it. But that steals few minutes from the hour. Plenitudes of opportunity lie between times — if not to doze, at least to glimpse a book or ponder the metaphysical clues of the universe.

By well-grooved habit I glanced at my instrument panel for information every few minutes and added brief notations to my log. The while my frontal thoughts unlimbered freely. In common with the others I knew the danger but, more important somehow, the ice had a symbolic meaning for me.

Its whiteness, like the white aura of Coleridge's albatross or the whiteness of Melville's whale, had the pallor of doom about it. No living creature could have the intensity of ice's color, nor quite its unearthly effulgence. White is no color and yet, as a culmination of the sun's rays, it is all colors.

White is the hue of extreme heat and of extreme cold. It stands for alienness in albinos, purity in women, cleanliness in doctors and technicians. It means winter in summer, peace in war. It is the color of the baby's first food — and of the ghostly apparitions of the departed. It is the aspect of the warm wool of sheep, of the empty coolness of the cloud. It is the color of Borak, Mohammed's sacred mare, whose eyes shone like jacinths as she thundered through the streets of Mecca, drinking the wind. It is the great principle of light from the largest and farthest spiral nebula to the whirling electrons in earth's minutest atom.

All of these things were part of the whiteness of that creeping ice to me, and part of its coldness. If they argued one with another was not that part of the sinister character of the element?

Did not, in fact, the whiteness of the ice pervade the body of the airplane itself? There was the white alumina, the principal material from which the aluminum is formed. There was the light-hued magnesium, even lighter than aluminum. These two with a modicum of steel formed the skin and bones of the craft. There was the birch plywood of the partitions, from the very tree which stands whitest in the snowy forests of the north. There was also the cotton, fleecy white, of which the inner linings of the cockpit and the crew quarters was spun and woven.

Could it be that there was an unsuspected affinity between the ice and the winged craft in which we had trusted our lives? Or was it my fantasy?

Gently I pulled my mind back into the cockpit and jotted down another reading of airspeed: 108 m.p.h. How much lower could it go, I wondered. Altitude: 14,700 feet. Temperature: −18°. I noted that the compass said 114°. This was dead-reckoning data. How far off course might we be by this time? Perhaps one hundred miles. Not serious if we could get another position by the stars within an hour.

Suddenly I felt a jerk. The whole airplane lunged sickeningly. So this is it? We are going into a spin. It will be quicker than I thought.

I'd better figure our position for the S O S. My watch says 00:49. Latitude? . . . Longitude? . . . An S O S in the North Atlantic on a February night is about as practical as digging for water on the Sahara. I felt empty — strangely detached.

Then I noticed the airspeed: 115. Isn't that faster than before? I felt Cloud goosing the motors. The plane heaved itself forward, jerking violently several more times.

"They're working!" shouted the captain. "The de-icers are working!" He flashed the lamp on the wing and I could see that large sections of the ice had already been pried off by the pulsating boots.

Woozy grinned from the fuse box. Black smooches covered his face. "I did it," he announced with mock conceit. "When you need anything in engineering, just send for me."

"What was it?" I asked.

"The fuse," he said. "I had a brain wave and stuck a new one in. Old one looks okay but it must be haywire. No trouble. No trouble at all."

A few minutes later, as if in response to our feelings, little lights suddenly appeared outside the windows. Stars! We had come into the clear once more — at 16,000 feet. I breathed easier, even through my oxygen mask.

We had emerged from our shroud of doom. Number 896 had thrown off all her clothes: her white underwear of ice, her white overcoat of cloud. Regulus and the Big Dipper were almost grinning at us from their appointed stations.

"No trouble at all," Woozy had said. All part of life: problems . . . problems . . . You take them in your stride as part of the day's work and you keep going — flying — flying over the sea, flying through the clouds — under the winking stars.

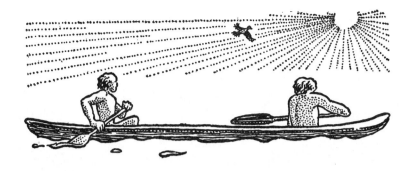

2. The Way

FROM WHERE I SIT here in the sky, the world of waves and ships and men below seems far and somehow small. Yet human history has it that this life up here sprang from that down there — that eons of blind earthbound toil and erring struggle had to pass before man hatched out the simple secrets of the birds.

I may sit here on the wing through six shades of the moon before I can inwardly realize it, but the books I've believed have told me much already of the ancient groundschool of the airplane, of man's painful stabbing of his way through the trackless oceans and forests of the earth before he could dare this gaseous realm. I know that most of it has not been written. It could not be. The years have been too hard and sharp, the pen too new, the hour too short. Truth is deeper than memory and, unlike memory, timeless, inviolable, unbounded.

This being evident, our past down there is parcel of our future here, and our new higher education will not forget the old, lowly lessons. It shall not let the soft lips of a book cover up the hard teeth of the years.

Have you heard how the ancient Arabs found their way for hundreds of miles across desert and sea? How the American Indians moved unerringly through the uncharted wilderness? How

17

the island dwellers in the South Seas sailed confidently over the entire Pacific?

These things are the thin brave seeds that we are now harvesting across the sky, the first heritage of aerial navigation.

How did he do it, the Arab?

We will put ourselves in his sandy footprints. We are on the desert — alone but for a flock of scraggly sheep and goats moving across yonder gravelly slope. Our duty: to watch the flock. Otherwise there is little to occupy thoughts as the sun goddess swings slowly overhead each day, leading her myriad star children on their nightly caravan.

We hardly need to wonder that the familiar star Alphecca passes always directly overhead, for here near El Ala it has always been so. The wise old men and the Jews all tell of it. In fact when we are many days' journey south on the desert, faithful Alphecca always shows us the way to El Ala just as surely as the famous star of Bethlehem is said to have led the wise men to the birth bed of the Christian prophet. Similarly Alpheratz points straight down on Mount Sinai, Albireo on Tebuk, Hamal on Medina, and Markab on the great southland of Sheba. Each star is a beacon showing the way to its own part of creation.

We Arabs, like most others in this early time, do not think of places in relation to a globular earth, but rather to the paths of the sun, the stars, and the wind. Our world is the fullness and breadth of Arabia with seas and mountains and cooler countries far northward and, some say, hotter countries far southward under the sun, with all around vast oceans and rivers from which no man has yet lived to return. If any of us ever saw a map it had no lines of latitude or longitude, but it may have included star paths or perhaps arrows showing the big winds: the simoom, the belat, the asifat, the zaubaat.

For on land, as at sea, in the ancient days it was the winds that told direction almost as much as the sun and the stars. The winds usually did not swing with the hours and could therefore be used as reasonably steady indications of direction, as indeed could the ripples the wind left in the sand.

The stars gave the Arabs only latitude — northness or southness — because latitude was the only thing in the motion of most stars that was constant. One star alone seemed to stand always in the same direction: a certain low star in the north. The sun was fairly trustworthy if one studied her wanderings with the seasons, but the moon was capable of almost anything and it required a man of oracular power and rare patience to fathom his inveterate waywardness.

As one might expect, it was the men who watched the flocks by night who became the most familiar with all these occult things of the heavens. They were the ones who spoke often of the Almighty and sometimes saw visions, and it was they who gave most of the stars their names, by which we know them still. Jesus, the Jew, was one of these, and he may well have tended sheep in northern Arabia in his twenties. Mohammed, an Arab traveling salesman in his youth, is also known to have been a part-time shepherd between caravans.

These men of course had other means than stars for finding their way on the desert. They knew the track of the ass and the camel and the horse. They could read many signs from afar: tall palms, smoke, habitual mirages, sometimes little clouds that lingered over oasis groves, or even a reflection on a cloud now known as a "desert blink" in which a bright-bottomed layer may indicate the presence beneath it of some known patch of unusually white sand.

As Arab navigation science grew spasmodically with the centuries one of its greatest strides came when Arab seamen first built dhows big enough to leave the coasts and brave the Sea of Oman to the Indian Ocean. It was then that they plotted the rising and setting points of fifteen stars, picked for distribution at almost equal intervals around the horizon so that, added to the true north and south, these formed the thirty-two points of the compass known today as N, N by E, NNE, NE by N, NE, NE by E, ENE, E by N, E, E by S . . .

The Arab compass points of course had Arab names and were associated with specific winds so that ships could be steered at angles relative to the wind when the stars or the sun were out of sight. The northeast trade wind was one of the most reliable of these. Like the other winds, it could be recognized by its individual and seasonal qualities of dryness or dampness, by its temperature, swiftness, and temperament, thus giving the Arab helmsman an easily verifiable wind bearing.

Another early navigation device much used by ancient seafarers was the shore-sighting bird. This was a preview of our dimension, for the bird's vision in flight gave man one of his first means of obtaining bearings at sea in stormy weather, a time when bearings are most welcome. Indeed ravens, cormorants, doves, and many other species of land birds in cages were customarily taken along on ocean voyages. When in doubt about the direction of the nearest coast, the navigator could release a bird and watch it circle for altitude. If it eventually flew in a definite direction the assumption could be reasonably made that it had seen land that way. If it did not find land, a bird which could not rest on the sea would have no choice but to return to the ship.

The earliest of known navigators, Noah, is reported in the Book of Genesis to have used exactly this system in guiding the ark. Having had the benefit of a weather forecast from God Himself, to say nothing of fine specimens of all the birds on earth, Noah was well equipped by the standards of the day and watched with unruffled calm as "the fountains of the great deep were broken up, and the windows of heaven were opened."

His huge craft, said to have been built of gopher wood (probably cypress), took off and rode the face of the deluge for "fifteen cubits upward," even over the mountains. For forty days and forty nights the downpour continued without let — a record. On the forty-first day the sky at last looked so much cheerier that the great navigator confidently opened his hatch and "sent forth a raven" which flew searching "to and fro." No land in sight.

Next Noah tried a dove. "But the dove found no rest for the sole of her foot, and she returned unto him into the ark . . ." Seven days later again Navigator Noah "sent forth the dove . . . And the dove came in to him in the evening: and, lo, in her mouth was an olive leaf, pluckt off: so Noah knew that the waters were abated from off the earth." He also saw the direction (NNE) from which the dove returned.

After still another wait of the customary seven days, Noah dispatched the dove for the third time "which returned not again unto him any more." But he had noted the course (E by S) of its flight to shore and, reassured by his double bearing, safely brought the big ark in and made a perfect landing.

Peoples in forested countries of course had a different problem in navigation. Since it was easier to find food, shelter, and fuel in the woods, most of them neither kept herds like the Arabs nor often traveled great distances. Judging latitude by the stars does not appear to have been a widespread accomplishment of the American Indian, though he certainly learned to take bearings by the North Star and probably could tell time by the circling Dipper.

Rather did the Indian navigate the wilderness by little clues of direction found in trees and plants, by deer or buffalo trails, by observing waterways and mountains, sometimes by a signal thread of distant smoke. He was taught in childhood to notice that the tips of evergreen trees inclined slightly to eastward, bowed by the prevailing west wind; that moss and bark are slightly thicker on the moist north and northeast side of trees, and tree rings consequently wider there; that the gum oozing from the spruce is clear amber on the south side but dull gray on the north; that compass goldenrod tips bend gently northward, and the leaves of prickly lettuce, rosin weed, and prairie dock all lean more north or south than east or west.

Stalking proved to him that the north side of a hill is the quiet side — because the ground stays damper there and thereby deadens sounds, while the dry south slope is often treacherous with rustling leaves and hidden crackly sticks. The loon and the duck, he observed, prefer to breed on the western shores of lakes and rivers. The flying squirrel and the pileated woodpecker dig their holes on the east side of trees. But the spider spins her web on the south side, the favorite resting place of the sun-loving moth and the fly.

In tracking, he spotted the sparest spoor of man or beast. The Osage Indians, noting that their enemies the Pawnees tied their moccasins by a thong under their soles, made it a rule never to do the same — the better to divine whose the footprints in the dust. Ability to identify the prints of many tribes was definitely a navi-gational accomplishment, as was skill in tracking deer, bear, or other beasts whose known habits and habitats might thus yield clues of location or direction.

Though probably the world's best tracker, the Indian neverthe-less often blazed his trail as a navigation aid, bending saplings, stripping bark, planting forked sticks in streams, or piling cairns of rock on cliff paths above the timber. On the prairie he used simple grass signs to indicate direction, such as knotting the grass into bunches and pointing the top right or left to show the way. For long-range broadcasting when smoke signals were too tem-porary, he used the famous "lop stick" sign, many examples of which are preserved to this day in ancient virgin trees of former Indian country. This signal was made by precise lopping off of branches of these prominent trees on ridges where their coded pattern messages could be read for many miles.

It would be only natural for the South Sea Islanders, who grew up close to the thundering surf and ate and slept with its sound and smell in their ears and noses, to be masters of ocean naviga-tion. Obviously if their ancestors had not already successfully sailed the sea they would not have been there in the first place.

So one need not be surprised to learn that these "Vikings of the sunrise" regarded a third of the earth's surface as their private lake across which they could go in any direction and at any time.

If they had only a dim idea of the shape of the whole Pacific — dimmer still of the earth — that must have given an aspect of infinity to their spiritual outlook, so limitless was the unknown. What was the sun or the moon to them? What was the earth, and how big? Was there any end to the islands and atolls, dispersed remotely across the waters like stars in the vacant heavens? A people virile enough to create the great idols of lonely Easter Island hardly needed await death to find the things of God. Was there not opportunity aplenty to hunt Kingdom Come on earth?

Finding out about Polynesian and Micronesian navigation has not been easy, because not only was there no written language to record it but this pristine science was for millenniums jealously guarded by the island navigators, who developed a kind of hereditary priesthood and attained power and rank for themselves second only to their kings. Even today, ferreting out the details of this ancient sacred navigation walled in by mortal tabus has been a task in detective work requiring a navigator's needle nose for direction, not to mention his craft and patience. Indeed a man who fairly accomplished the feat is actually a flying navigator as well as a native of the southern ocean: Harold Gatty, the New Zealander who navigated Wiley Post on his famous first flight around the world.

As a result of Gatty's research, and that of some earlier "navigators" ranging back to Captain Winkler of the nineteenth-century German navy, we know that the first of the Polynesians' tools of navigation was the wave. To the islander the wave was like a tool, for it was studied and measured to a degree not to be exceeded anywhere until the latter days of oceanography. In fact, as we use radio and radar today so did the South Sea navigator a thousand years ago use the ocean wave. He did not merely steer by the angle of the wave, but he observed the whole pattern it made around an island, and the swells and eddies — affecting the very shape of the atolls and the coral reefs and the channels through them.

He recognized the differences between the ripple, the wave, and the swell — how the tiny ripple changes with each puff of breeze as it laces the greeny slope of the wave, how the wave keeps on rolling despite a momentary lull or sideways gust until the wind as a whole shifts to another quarter, and how the great swell may persist in one direction all day or night against wind and even waves which have swung around the compass to oppose it, sometimes outrunning the wind altogether to give warning of the unseen typhoon like a dog before his master.

This wonderful stability of the swell gave the navigator a system of sea marks around an island almost as reliable as the complex radio pattern around a modern airport, including two narrow fixed beams of eddies equipped with direction finders, and a special pointed swell aiming precisely at the safe lagoon channel. The extent of this telltale swell pattern, he observed, went far beyond the sight of land, for the nature of the swell was to bend itself invariably around each piece of shore, shaping its contour to the smallest reef, sending a counterswell in to the land against the wind from the leeward side, its shape transmitting itself backward revealingly, betrayingly, suggestively in all directions — ever fainter but ever farther — detectable under ideal conditions perhaps twenty miles at sea.

The South Sea people who advanced this particular study to its greatest perfection were the Marshall Islanders, who inhabit one of the more northeasterly groups of atolls fought over in World War II. These black-haired Micronesian navigators made elaborate charts out of ribs of coconut palms tied with fiber to form a meaningful framework indicating winds, swell systems, and the eddying junction lines where swells meet. Shells on these rib charts represented islands, and sticks were placed to show how far offshore the coconut palms could be seen, or how far out one could detect the indentations on swells made by the ebb of a lagoon tide.

Most of the charts represented the conditions around single islands or small groups, each being a kind of cryptic notation made by an individual navigator to aid his memory and to instruct his heirs in a particular oceanographic situation. But some charts have been found which represented large sections of the Pacific and

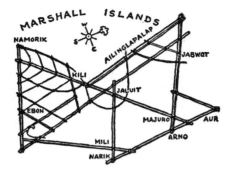

showed on a grand scale the interlacing patterns between one island group and another — lines of swell eddies in some places stretching in series for a hundred miles, forming cross-wind bearings on each island, each peninsula, each reef.

It will never cease to amaze me that at night as in daylight these eddy bearings can actually be followed like radio beams or lighted runways because the eddies stir the microorganisms of the sea into clear paths of luminescence. And the beams even have a direction finder to show which of the two opposite directions they point to is toward the nearest land, for the shining eddies move continuously with the swells toward the shore. Should a navigator lose his way and miss an island he would thus still have a good chance of picking up one of these eddy lines and homing in on the beam, sailing before the beam wind without even needing to tack.

Not only that, but the navigator has at his command a kind of primordial radar: the faint swell echoes reflecting outward from all shores, riding right over the larger incoming swells and giving him an indication of distance as well as direction. And should he be approaching a lee shore the navigator may judge shore distance also by the reduction of the waves in proportion to the shelter of the coast, an effect noticeable off a high lee, well beyond the sight of land.

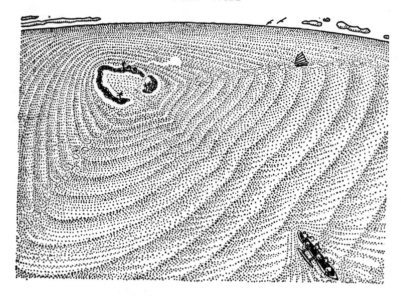

The full significance of all these subtle manifestations of wind and wave is almost impossible for modern man to appreciate until he flies over an island archipelago in one of the calmer seas, knowing in advance just what to look for. The great primary swells are almost always quite visible as seen thus from the air, their lines revealed in moving shades of green and blue according to the changing angle between surface and the light. So too may the eddy beams be seen, and if you look sharp you can usually pick out the fainter echo swells in gentle weather. Tuning in on them all from a sailing canoe on the surface a thousand years ago was of course navigational sleuthing of the highest order.

The South Sea Islanders naturally used much more than wind or waves for compass and bearings. In mid-ocean the sky was for them a compass, clock, and map, all in one — and it had the advantage of being permanently built in, at least most of the time.

They regarded the sky as a sort of great scallop shell in which the stars followed the scallop grooves from horizon to horizon each night. From their Arab contacts in the East Indies they had inherited some knowledge of stars and constellations, and this they developed until the more advanced of their navigators are said to have been able to call 150 stars by name. They knew as well the time and position of each star, seasonal changes, and exactly when and what islands that star would pass over so that their courses could be set by it in the open sea: Sirius in the third watch for the Fijis, Dschubba in the fifth for Rarotonga . . .

Time by the sky clock was highly developed in the South Seas, for the navigators had long recorded the stars' custom of rising earlier each night (by about four minutes in our modern way of measuring), and of course the regular nightly and seasonal rotation of the Southern Cross. The Tahitian day was divided into six watches (each of two hours by a modern clock), and the night the same.

Distance was a vaguer dimension to these men, for it was geared to human effort, not merely to the earth or the heavens. The Polynesian had no word for distance, no thought of space apart. Time and direction were his important measurements. Funafuti was not 450 miles away but five days' sail toward Rigel. The tops of palms could be seen not from nine miles but from two watches of paddling into the wind.

As for compass direction when stars were not visible, the sun and the trade winds were among the best guides, though obviously not to be relied upon everywhere or everywhen. It has been said that the "sacred" or "wind" calabash was used by the ocean people for measuring points of direction, sighting through regularly spaced holes around the hard hemisphere of the gourd, or using it as a sextant of the pole; but modern research indicates that the calabash holes were filled instead only with root thongs for fastening on a lid — that this natural container was really the Polynesian jug or keg, and many and sundry calabashes were taken on all long voyages for holding fresh water, food, dry clothing, or any other valuables that needed shelter from the spray or storm.

Shore-sighting birds, however, perhaps another heritage from the Arabs, were used in navigation by the Pacific islanders, as by the Phoenicians and Vikings in the Atlantic. The island navigators kept the frigate (man o' war) bird for this purpose, for this forked-tailed sea bird does not normally land on water but heads for the nearest land. It is still a common pet on Ocean and Nauru Islands in the central Pacific.

And careful records of bird migration from island to island, of bird nesting places and feeding and roosting habits, undoubtedly gave many a handy bearing in the lonely reaches of the great deep. If boobies and gannets are seen flying in the late afternoon the navigator can safely follow them toward land for they are commuting home from their fishing grounds to feed the family. In the remote Galapagos area of the Pacific, cormorants and pelicans indicate shore, being rarely found as much as twenty-five miles from land. And if at night or day he hears the cries of sea birds of any sort the South Sea Islander can be sure land is near, for these must be gulls and no true gull but the northern kittiwake strays far from his low-tide hunting grounds along the coast. The sea birds that follow ocean vessels many days out from land are usually terns, fulmars, petrels, shearwaters, skuas, jaegers, or one of the great southern family of albatrosses — all of which keep peaceful tongues at sea.

When seafaring Polynesians in Tahiti sought new land for their privacy further southwest in the ocean, what could have been more natural than to observe the repeated yearly migrations of land birds in that direction, and follow them? Did not the long-tailed cuckoo fly always southwest from their islands? Knowing that the cuckoo cannot rest at sea, the Tahitians could follow it with confidence in their great double canoes, spaced wide apart in a long file for visibility. And, like the cuckoo, they actually landed in New Zealand 2500 miles away.

When Kanaka traders in semi-precious greenstone plied their cargoes between Tahiti and Hawaii, a similar distance, what easier way than to track the straggling flocks of golden plover which unerringly cover that route on their yearly flights to Alaska? Or the shining cuckoo from the Solomons?

Even butterflies can give vital bearings to ocean navigators, often migrating thousands of miles across the sea. They fly low and are easily seen, but since their flights are commonly suicidal in result, the direction they came from is a better indication of land than the way they are headed.

Undersea creatures and fish likewise give important clues, since the numerous coastal species rarely venture out with the few oceanic kinds like the blue shark, bonito, sunfish, and flying fish, the air-breathing porpoise and whale.

Land-smelling mammals have at times served the function of shore-sighting birds, and it is known that the Tahitians carried pigs for this purpose, because the sensitive snout of the sea-weary pig would sometimes show excitement at approaching land long before it was visible even to a flying bird. In the same way the odor of burning peat may reveal the unseen Falkland Islands to this day, as the scent of orange groves the Cape Verdes, or the ammoniac fumes the Guano Isles of Peru.

As the clouds serve as beacons, hovering over unseen atolls beyond the horizon, reflecting the pale green of the lagoon or the white of sand, as dawn thunder may hint of a mountainous coast, so does the color and temperature of the sea also yield its clue to the navigator's ocean store. Blue water is salty, warm, and deep and speaks of the tropics where evaporation is great and dilution small — the Sulu Sea, the Indian Ocean, the Gulf Stream. Green water is cool, pale with particles, thin with river and rain, often shallow. In the tropics it means land, just as in the north with white jigsaw ice it means a frozen bay is close.

When water is reddish, organisms abound. And brown or yellow water tells of a river mouth and nearby civilization. I remember my surprise on first seeing the Yellow Sea which is indeed intensely yellow far out of sight of the estuaries of the Yangtze, the Whangpoo, and the Whang Ho. And they say one can spot the effects of the muddy River Plate more than a thousand miles off Argentina.

Along with the finer shades of ocean color drawn by the keen Pacific navigators, it is known that they noted the drifting weeds, the fronds, and the paths of currents which could be told by temperature. As Benjamin Franklin was to do centuries later, to the plaudits of the academies, using a thermometer, the island seafarers did with their fingers and toes — feeling the ocean's warmth to test where the hot New Zealand Current ended and the cold West Wind Drift began — plotting a bearing line where the South Equatorial bowed to the Tuamotu.

To those of us who were brought up on western history it may be an effort of mind to accept this early eminence of the brown men of the Pacific in a branch of science as important as navigation. But there is ponderable evidence in that Captain Cook and other explorers found one people and one language presiding over the four thousand miles of ocean from New Zealand to Easter Island, and the last great colonizing voyages of Tahitians to Hawaii in the thirteenth century and to New Zealand in the fourteenth are so well recorded in story and song that they are used today by genealogists in tracing family relationships between these islands.

Of course most of the great early feats of navigation have been lost to human memory by now, and in the unwritten millenniums great discoveries had to be made many times to overcome intervening ages of forgetfulness until finally they came to be recorded.

The bark boats of Australia and America must have been plied in the pleistocene days of Talgai and Sandia men, as the pirogues and kayaks and curraghs move still on the less-known rivers and seas of the world, flowing and ebbing with their sweating paddlers, their unlisted cargoes down the dreamy blank pages of history.

Where and how they went in the animal days of Eden is hard to prove, but it could not have been long afterward that the voyagers finally girded their loins against adversity and rubbed their brains and set about inventing the knife, the hoe, the sundial, the harp.

Of these primary works the sundial was almost as important in navigation as it was in astronomy. Making a calendar and navigating a ship depend, in fact, on the same kind of knowledge and are hard to keep apart, which is something to be remembered if you would clear up the mystery of the fourth dimension.

As man learned to herd as well as hunt, to mine as well as forge, to sow as well as reap, the seasons became more important to him and he studied how to measure them, how to keep records. His first true writings: the score and tally. His first god: the sun.

Stonehenge in Britain and the sixteen Inca towers in Cuzco were elaborate early models of the sundial. Being large of dimension they could measure accurately the sightings of the sunrise at the solstices and the equinoxes, the polar point, the zeniths, the months, the days, the hours.

The medicine men, the priests — astrologers, navigators, alchemists — these wise men of science of their day did their best to bring order and sense into the discordant life of earth. In Babylon they measured and decreed a neat year of 360 days, which seemed too wonderful to be wrong. To match it, they apportioned their circle into 360 parts — ancestors of the 360 degrees we still use.

The Mayans did a closer job of measuring. They made a god of the planet we call Venus and adopted a Venus year. They clocked the planet's circling of the sun to the second decimal: 583.92 earth days of time. To even out the earth days in a Venus calendar year the Mayans dropped four days at the end of every sixty-one Venus years, and an additional eight days after every three hundred Venus years. This unique calendar used for many centuries by a people who had no telescope was so accurate that had the Mayans continued it to the present, the accumulated error over this period of more than a thousand years would have amounted to only a day.

The Eskimos, who had a rare sense of place and made good maps, easily measured the midnight sun and the noonday dawn and forecast the exact dates of the solstices. So did the Hawaiians, who called the northern limit of the sun at Cancer "the black, shining road of Kane" and the southern tropic at Capricorn "the black, shining road of Kanaloa." The equator they named "the road to the navel of Wakea," the center of the world.

Fat priestesses of Borneo used to sit in the bowl of a big stone at Batu Sala in the river bed of the upper Mahakam to watch when the sun would set behind a certain mountain tip to fix the first day of sowing.

Some people did less well, like the Dakota tribes who were known to dispute hotly in their powwows over what moon it really was. Yet the Egyptians who let Sirius, the Dog Star, take the chief place in their year, timed it at 365 days as long ago as 4241 B.C. It is well known that their pyramids were super sundials and star dials of great precision, which broadcast by reflection off their polished surfaces the sowing and harvesting dates to distant farmers.

The pyramids of Cheops and of Sneferu, for example, were both built on a common geometric plan, their four sides facing exactly north, south, east, and west, and their combined base lengths being exactly as great in proportion to each pyramid's height as the circumference of a circle is greater than its radius: 2π. According to Flinders Petrie: "The squareness and level of the base is brilliantly true, the average error being less than a ten-thousandth of the side in equality, squareness, and level." And the rays of Sirius in transit were perpendicular to the south face and shone precisely down the long slender ventilating shaft to the royal chamber.

These early morsels of astronomical knowledge naturally brought conjecture about the shape and nature of the earth and of how far one might go upon it, but often created more fear than confidence. A widespread and logical idea developed that the equator land directly under the sun was so hot that eternal fires burned there, hopelessly cutting off a strange southern temperate zone, comparable to the northern, where mysterious nether people must exist. These imaginary creatures seemed as unapproachable at the time as men of Mars do to us today, and of course there probably are planets somewhere in the sky on which roasting tropics actually do divide the population in twain.

In any case, this concept did not prevent ambitious kings of the earth like Necho II in Egypt from sending out expeditions to explore the matter, as he seems to have done around 600 B.C. According to the great historian Herodotus, Necho hired several crews of adventurous Phoenician seamen to set out from the Red Sea in a small fleet. And these men evidently circumnavigated the whole of Africa in a three-year voyage, stopping each year to raise grain for food until at last they arrived unbelievably at the delta of the Nile with tales of a sun that shone from the north and stars and birds and people that had never been known in the world before. It was probably the first great voyage of purposeful exploration to be recorded in history.

In Necho's time of course navigation was not just a matter of finding one's way. Foremost it was a matter of finding out whether there was any way and, if so, what sort of way. It was a job of exploring more than piloting, of map making more than map reading. It was a calling for men who dared follow the footsteps of Jason and Perseus and Ulysses — for giants, for heroes. Every ship's captain was a king at sea; every sailor a god to the natives of new discovered lands.

The Minoans of Crete, like the Arabs, were pioneers at sea and dominated the Mediterranean from their island ports of Cydonia and Hierapytna, trading in linen and precious stones with the Pharaohs, stealing youths and maidens for slaves and concubines and sacrifices from barbarian villages in Greece and Asia Minor.

By the time of Necho, however, the Minoans had been excelled on the sea by the long-nosed Phoenicians who also laid their keels in island ports, Tyre and Sidon, expanding westward to build the great North African cities of Utica and Carthage protected on

the south by the Sahara desert, on the north by the vast Mediterranean. These bronze-skinned people, named after the legendary
fire-red phoenix, were probably the most ambitious traders of all
history, sailing their famous Tarshish ships through the Pillars of
Hercules and into the Green Sea of Darkness, north to the tin
isles, to Königsberg in the Baltic for amber, to the Red Sea for
henna to dye Babylonian beards and the toes of Hophra's queen,
around the remote tropics to Ophir for Solomon's gold, for silver
and peacocks.

They built lighthouse towers on prominent capes which showed
smoke signals by day, blazing bonfires by night. They used sea-
conch foghorns to outscream the storms, later long trumpets of
silver and brass. With Lebanon cedars they stepped their masts,
of Egyptian linen their sails were spun, their planking of fir from
Senir, their oars of Bashan oak.

Little is known of their explorations, less of their navigation
methods, for the Phoenicians, like the Polynesians and most others
in ancient days, kept their secrets of courses and currents well — for
military security, for business advantage, for prestige for their
nation, their company, and themselves. A commander who gave
away the truth of how and where he had been or of what he had
seen committed high treason. He was regarded as a man would
be regarded today who betrayed the vitals of the hydrogen bomb.
Strabo tells how a Phoenician captain who had just filled his hold
with tin in the Cassiterides purposely went off course and wrecked
his vessel because he thought he was being followed by a Roman.
When he finally got home he was fêted and honored for his deed
by the city of Tyre.

As the Phoenicians began to grow fat, their glory to wane, the
newly civilized Greeks took up where they left off. Thales and
Anaxagoras and Pythagoras, all Greeks of Phoenician parentage,
brought the latest in astronomy to Greece: Thales the secret of the
polar point in the Little Dipper called Arktos Minor; Anaxagoras
forty new calculations of latitude from the Ionian navigators of
Miletus; Pythagoras the plotted courses of Venus and Mercury in
the sky, and all the Egyptians could tell of the ecliptic. Pythagoras

was also the first navigator ever reported to have used what may have been the magnetic compass, when he "took from Albaris the Hyperborean his Golden Dart without which it was impossible to find the road."

Some of the Greeks were only armchair navigators, like famous Plato who wrote a Dialogue on Nature describing legendary Atlantis: an island continent beyond the Pillars of Hercules, larger than all Asia and Africa together and divided by Neptune into kingdoms for each of his ten sons. Instead of actually exploring the facts of the material world, which seemed to him too superficial to be important, Plato sought truth in contemplation like an Oriental sage, but splurging his great logic on untested axioms of postulated science. In his Republic he wrote: "It makes no difference whether a person stares stupidly at the sky, or looks with half-open eyes upon the ground. So long as he is only trying to study a perceivable object, I deny that he can ever learn anything, because no objects perceivable to the senses admit the scientific treatment."

Yet from the Greek port of Phocaea in Asia Minor emerged a multitude of practical navigators who colonized much of the Black Sea and the northern Mediterranean coast, founding the first settlement of France at Massilia (Marseille). And out of Massilia arose the philosopher-scientist Pytheas who would make his name as the greatest navigator of all the ancients, and one of the very great figures in human history.

Pytheas might be considered to have discovered America, for he certainly went to Thule (Iceland) and to the Greenland pack ice beyond it. As Greenland can be seen from Iceland — mountaintop to mountaintop on a clear day — and as it is easy to walk from Greenland over the ice to Ellesmere Island and thence to the rest of America, the discovery of Thule was tantamount to revealing the beginning of the New World — if the Europeans had only been capable of realizing it.

Pytheas also discovered the effect of the moon on the tides, and worked out a method of applying astronomy to geography so as to get precise latitude which, combined with approximate longitude, made possible great improvements in map making. This of course was long before the golden age of Polynesian navigation, even before the great Greek scientists Eratosthenes and Hipparchus.

Before setting forth on his most famous voyage, Pytheas carefully established the latitude of Massilia as his point of departure. Up to that time the Greeks had measured latitude principally by observing the length of the longest and shortest days of the year, which obviously vary with one's distance from the equator. They had divided the earth into parallel zones of latitude called "climates," from the Greek word *klima* (incline), each of which was characterized by longest and shortest days of within an hour of the same duration. It was a crude system and the more northern "climates" turned out to be much narrower than the more southern, but Pytheas, who probably had been to Egypt, erected for himself a large gnomon graduated vertically into one hundred and twenty parts. With this he caught the sun's shadow at noon on the solstice at 41⅘ parts in length, showing the sun's altitude to be 70° 47' 50" and giving him Massilia's latitude with remarkable accuracy.

Pytheas also determined in advance the exact polar point, which was different in relation to the stars in those days, so that he could check the true north at any time. This would be of special importance in case he actually reached the North Pole.

It was around 330 B.C. when Pytheas embarked in his large Massilian vessel, probably twice as long as Columbus' little *Santa María*.

He kept careful track of his latitude as he went northward up the coasts of Iberia (Spain) and Celtica or Gaul, observing the height of the pole at night and sometimes of the sun at noon. He noticed of course that the farther north he went, the more the southern constellations of stars slipped out of sight into the southern horizon, strong evidence of the sphericity of the earth.

Undoubtedly Pytheas accepted the concept of the earth being round, for it was far from a new idea even in his day. Had not his countryman, Bion, taught the doctrine of the midnight sun in a supposed Arctic Circle under the pole? The Arctic was named for the Greek bear (arktos) which is the real name for the northern constellation we generally call the Big Dipper. Perhaps it looked more like a bear in those days. At any rate the old people used to say that those stars were a great bear prowling among the northern lights who darkened the northern earth with his shadow and froze its waters with his icy breath.

Little is known of Pytheas' remarkable voyage to the arctic ice because his great book *The Ocean* is lost, and no one of his contemporaries considered his tale about Iceland believable enough to be worth much discussion. Cleomedes mentions only that Pytheas of Massilia said that north of Thule "the entire circle described by the sun at the summer solstice is above the horizon, so that it coincides in these places with the Arctic Circle. In these regions, when the sun is in Cancer the day lasts one month . . ."

Strabo three hundred years later reflected the skepticism of Greece and Rome when he reported that Pytheas had "undertaken investigations concerning Thule and those regions in which there was no longer any distinction of land or sea or air, but a mixture of the three like sea lung, in which he says that everything floats, and the mixture binds all together, and can be travelled neither on foot nor by boat. The substance resembling lung he had seen himself, as he says . . . This is Pytheas' story."

Such tall tales of Pytheas become fact of course when one visits the northeast coast of Greenland, as I have, to see the crunching floes of sea sludge in dense fog when everything is wet and cold and gray and you can scarce tell up from down.

Although Pytheas evidently judged longitude — eastness or westness — only by estimating the speed of his ship and figuring how far west or east it traveled in a day, there were a few attempts by later Greeks to solve longitude by astronomy. Hipparchus worked it out in principle, suggesting that eclipses be clocked in different localities to establish their time relationship or longitude, thus making possible an accurate map of the world. Marinus of Tyre actually drew such a map, within the limits of available knowledge, with lines for the first time to show longitude as well as latitude. He got his longitude by checking events like the eclipse of 331 B.C. which gave evidence of the distance between Carthage and Arbela, and an eclipse of the sun seen in Campania between the seventh and eighth hours and in Armenia between the eleventh and twelfth, indicating a difference in longitude of four hours or 60° — much exaggerated but passable as a starter.

Ptolemy of Alexandria soon made an improved latitude and longitude map of the world, which was to confuse Columbus more than thirteen hundred years later; and Eratosthenes, also of Alexandria, undertook to measure the entire earth. One June 21 he checked the solstice sun at noon in Alexandria at 7½° south of the zenith while it was known to be exactly overhead at the same hour at Syene on the Tropic of Cancer just below the first cataract of the Nile. Having measured the distance from Syene to Alexandria at 5000 stadia or 500 miles (a standard stadium being a tenth of a mile long) Eratosthenes judged that 500 miles must be one forty-eighth of the earth's circumference, since 7½° is one forty-eighth of 360°. Thus he reached the remarkable conclusion that the earth is about 24,000 miles around, which is less than 4 per cent off the truth, and that "if the extent of the Atlantic Ocean were not an obstacle we might easily pass by sea from Iberia (Spain) to India, still keeping the same parallel ..."

This prophetic logic does not seem, however, to have aroused new excitement as to what might be on the other side of the earth, perhaps for the same good reason that we do not get easily worked up today over what may be on the other side of the moon.

From the time of the Alexandrian school of astronomy to the Renaissance the science of navigation appears to have made very little progress in most of the so-called civilized world. Many important advances in fact were forgotten and had to be discovered all over again by the successors of Columbus.

Yet all this time the seafarers and explorers were navigating the Pacific and Atlantic and Indian Oceans and probably Eskimos the Arctic, as they may well have been doing for very many thousands of years without bothering to make any record of it at all. Most of these people were primitive and illiterate — the Polynesians, the Norsemen, the Eskimos, the men of Britain and Ireland, the early Arabs, the Hindus, the Malays — yet sagas and legends were remembered for a while and, as writing spread, a few stories got into print.

The more literate Chinese, who looked to the past of China as the highest possible earthly attainment, naturally had little interest in exploring the unworthy barbarian world that surrounded them. One of the very few foreign expeditions attributed to a Chinese in this period is the easterly journey of an eccentric missionary monk named Hoei Sin in A.D. 499 to bring the gospel of Buddha to the barbarians of the far land of Fusang, which has been identified as somewhere in America — perhaps British Columbia or California, perhaps even as far south as Peru. Hoei Sin described the "marked men" of Fusang who were likely either tattooed Eskimos or painted Indians.

Iceland's earliest known permanent colonists were brought by Floki the Norse in A.D. 865. Floki undoubtedly used one of the open boats common to the Vikings and he is reported to have navigated by the Little Dipper and by carrying "sea ravens" (cormorants) for getting bearings on the land. Much in the manner of the Polynesians, it is said that two days west of the Shetlands he released a sea raven which, after circling high, flew astern — giving Floki a bearing on his last point of departure. A few days later a second bird rose high over the ship but returned without seeing land. While eventually one of the birds, flying forward to Iceland, gave Floki a conclusive bearing on his destination.

The Norsemen were in their great age of exploration at this time and their sagas tell of Gunnbjörn who saw Greenland's icy coast in 877, while others like Ottar passed the north cape to tell King Alfred of England in 890 about the Finns and Russians. It was Erik the Red, as hot tempered as his hair was carroty, who was exiled from Iceland for murder and sailed west to colonize Greenland in 982. And his carefree son Leif who, on an intended voyage from Norway direct to Greenland in 1000, somehow muffed his latitude and missed Cape Farewell, coming instead to Labrador (possibly Newfoundland or Nova Scotia). This pleasant but unexpected landfall in a country of "self-sown wheat, and wine berries . . . and maples big enough for house building" he called Vineland, but it remained somewhat legendary for a time when Erik and Lief's brother Thorbjörn tried to locate it again but lost their way in a terrible storm.

Meanwhile Cheng Ho, the great Ming admiral, was coasting the Pacific in his broad-beamed junks, his lorchas, while Richard the Lion-Hearted with his crusade fleet the Atlantic. And the Flemish and the Portuguese sailed the new luggers, the ballingers, the cogs, carracks, corvettes, and caravels, while the dhows of Mombasa plied the Indian Ocean, the praus of Samarang the corner seas.

And in far Persia a famous mathematician, Omar Khayyam, son of the tent maker, measured more of the wandering stars (the planets) and discarded the Greek alphabet system of pictorial mathematics, adopting the Hindu sunya or zero to equip us with a better arithmetic. He wrote his great new algebra in Arabic, the language of learning, and his quatrains in poetry eternal:

> *With them the seed of Wisdom did I sow,*
> *And with mine own hand wrought to make it grow;*
> *And this was all the Harvest that I reap'd —*
> *"I came like Water, and like Wind I go."*

And presently Roger Bacon in thirteenth-century England sounded the knell of the dark ages and of Plato's subjectivity when he shouted to mankind: "Experiment, experiment! Cease to be ruled by dogmas and authorities; look at the world! . . . Machines for navigating are possible without rowers . . . Likewise cars may be made so that without a draught animal they may be moved . . . And flying machines are possible, so that a man may sit in the middle turning some device by which artificial wings may beat the air . . ."

If this spirit did not immediately rouse all the thinkers of the earth it was at least an overture to the astonishing doings two centuries later of Prince Henry the Navigator, the Infante Dom Henrique of Lusitania, son of King João I of Portugal. There had been a good deal of hit-or-miss discovery in the world throughout the millenniums, but Prince Henry organized discovery on a month-to-month basis and got consistent results that led directly to the first Mediterranean-to-India sea route as well as to Columbus' eye-opening demonstration that the earth was bigger and more potential than anybody had ever dared believe.

Prince Henry built himself a town on strategic Cape St. Vincent, the extreme southwestern tip of Europe which in Pytheas' day had been the sacred limit of the known world and which was still a place where northbound ships anchored in the last lee of sunny

Portugal under the brown cliffs of Sagres Roads, awaiting a respite from the prevailing northwest wind before rounding the corner. It was a natural supply base and exchange headquarters for maritime information and it rapidly developed into the world's first naval college, hydrographic office, and marine observatory, where soft-spoken mathematicians mingled with fat ship chandlers and bearded astronomers and Arab cartographers and squint-eyed young ship masters out of Amsterdam and Bristol and Amalfi. It was the spawning spot of America unknown, the dawning door of mobility undreamed.

Prince Henry found that some of his maps from Catalan and Majorca showed a string of mysterious islands far out in the Atlantic, evidently based on nothing more definite than the legend of Saint Brendan, or the propensity of wind-blown eyes to see distant shores at twilight. And when he promoted a search for them in that fearful area of darkness, one of his ships discovered some actual islands which are now known as the Azores and are still populated by the descendants of the Portuguese colonists Henry sent out there five hundred years ago.

His next discovery was the Cape Verde Islands off Africa. And then the equatorial regions which still terrified a world that had never heard of King Necho or Hanno but listened instead to the continuing yarns of boiling tropic whirlpools and downhill one-way oceans permitting no return. Ship after ship had failed to pass Cape Nun on one pretext or another, probably superstitious about such punning proverbs as

> Quem passar o Cabo de Não
> Ou voltera ou não.

> When old Cape Nun heaves into sight
> Turn back, me lad, or else — good night!

But at last in mid-fifteenth century Prince Henry's ships junked the jinx for fair, figuratively thumbing their anchors at the capes, and soon were in the Gulf of Guinea, debunking the terror tales and searching for Prester John and his mythical Christian kingdom which was supposed to lie somewhere nearer than the land of the Great Khan. In 1487 Bartholomew Diaz announced the Cape of Good Hope, and from then on the way was clear around Africa for Vasco da Gama in 1497 and the hosts of other Portuguese and Spaniards who sailed to India and colonized the East Indies in the century to come.

This age of course was tremendous in history, but especially in the history of navigation, for it brought the great sailings of Columbus and Magellan, proving the size and shape of the earth beyond question. It was the fulfillment of Seneca's prophecy of A.D. 50 that "an age will come after many years when the Ocean will loose the chains of things, and a huge land lie revealed; when Tiphys [Jason's pilot] will disclose new worlds and Thule no longer be the ultimate."

Had the Portuguese or the English had the technique of the Polynesians they could have lighted up the Sea of Darkness centuries earlier — in fact a single Tahitian navigator on Theodoric's staff might have made the entire Dark Ages a full shade lighter. But the shadow of Plato was still among "the chains of things" and its influence had cut deep into the mind of Europe and its breaking up was painful in her soul.

Columbus fortunately had been too busy at sea all his life to read much of Plato. He had probably hardly more than glanced even into Ptolemy's great Almagest, the ancient treatise on astronomy which, translated into Arabic, became a pillar of Moslem science and was still the handbook of the Jewish astronomers who sailed on Prince Henry's ships. Book-larnin' was not strong in Columbus except for looking up authorities to back his arguments for royal patronage.

Of Cipangu (Japan) Columbus had heard from the current tales of his compatriot, Marco Polo, and he figured it as far east of

Hangchow as Marco's wild judgment could reasonably allow (30° of longitude) even as he had mentally stretched China eastward from Europe to make its discovery westward from Spain the more plausible an enterprise. With understandable prejudice he also ignored the precision of Eratosthenes for the more favorable guesses of Alfragan, Marinus, Ptolemy, Toscanelli, and Martin Behaim as to the small size of the earth, eventually outdoing them all to plump for only seventy-five per cent of the actual. Coupling this with his claim to Ferdinand and Isabella that Japan was 283° east of Cape St. Vincent, he could rationalize that he would have a mere sixty "degrees" (2700 miles) to sail westward from the Canaries to reach the gold and pearls of the Indies, so soon to be proven actually 200° (13,750 miles) away. His diagnosis of a degree in miles has been declared by his biographer Samuel Eliot Morison to have been literally "the shortest ever made."

It may seem surprising that Columbus, who was an educated man by the standards of his day, should not have known more of the accumulated navigational science of the world, especially since he had navigated widely — including "in 1477 in the month of February a voyage a hundred leagues beyond the island of Thule called Frislanda [Iceland]" where he had noted the long winter nights caused by "the narrowing of the sphere." The fact is that by no means all the world's navigational knowledge had been collected even by Prince Henry's endowed institution, and Columbus was a devout Catholic — a man with a mission, guided more by spirit than mind — a redhead who had learned the ropes the hard way and would not trade his "arte de marear" for all the fancy tabulations and astrolabes and brass scrimshaw in Christendom.

The things that were known in 1492 to some men but not to Columbus, the things he might have known but evidently didn't, make an impressive list:

That the earth is nearly 25,000 miles around, approximately as Eratosthenes announced in 250 B.C.

That the earth circles about the sun, as Aristarchus of Samos explained in 270 B.C. and would soon be demonstrated anew by Copernicus in his *De Revolutionibus*.

That it is possible to sail around Africa to the Indian Ocean, as Necho's fleet proved in 600 B.C. and da Gama was about to rediscover.

That it had long been possible to navigate with precision across four thousand miles of ocean, as the Polynesians had done for many centuries in the Pacific and the Norsemen had almost equaled in the Atlantic.

That a great unmapped land lay west of Iceland and Greenland, as discovered by Leif Erikson, Karlsefni, Snorri, Bjarni, Thorhall, Hoei Sin the monk, of course the Indians, and probably the Polynesians.

That the true polar point in the northern sky was then 3° 27' from the star Polaris, as the best of the astronomers knew, and that failure to correct for the discrepancy might cause an error in figuring latitude of two hundred miles.

That latitude may be found also by observing the sun's altitude at noon, as long used by Moslems in their "camel navigation" on the desert.

That longitude may be found by observing the moon's exact declination (distance from the celestial equator), as theorized and developed in Alexandria at the time of Ptolemy and referred to by the monk Gerard of Cremona in the twelfth century.

That a ship's speed at sea may be measured by a waterwheel and tally pot into which a pea is dropped at each revolution, as perfected by the Romans more than a thousand years earlier.

That direction and nearness to land can often be detected by careful observation of swells and eddies in the sea, as practiced by the Polynesians for untold centuries.

That land can be spotted by releasing a land bird at sea, as known to navigators at least as early as Noah.

The truth seems to be that Columbus was not particularly well equipped for his great ocean voyage of discovery, not even as well provided in respect to navigation as Prince Henry's ships coasting down West Africa way forty years earlier with their astronomers, their bronze peloruses, their astrolabes decorated with the zodiac, their Regiment of the Pole Star, their pilot books and tables of lunar distances. Columbus had only the usual things taken on Mediterranean and coastal sailings. He had no astronomer aboard any of his three ships, nor sufficient knowledge or means at hand to get any aid from the stars except a simple visual indication of north from Polaris, which his compass could do as well, and a vague judgment of latitude by guessing the altitude of the pole.

He had a primitive nonreflecting quadrant only fit for use in a flat calm, a few lead lines for sounding, and a ruler and dividers for plotting courses on his sheepskin charts which showed nothing west of the Canary Islands except a hypothetical Antillia Island laid down by hunch. His printed material consisted of an ordinary traverse table, a multiplication table, a Bible, an Imago Mundi, and a copy of *Ephemerides* of Johannes Müller intended for astrologers (evidently not looked into by anyone on any of Columbus' voyages). The tricky astrolabe that he took on his first voyage was left behind during all the others because he couldn't see any sense in it. It could not have been used effectively at sea anyway even by an astronomer, for it was meant to hang on something solid like a tree.

Columbus must have known of maps showing lines of latitude and longitude such as Ptolemy's. He had in fact once been a chartmaker himself, like his younger brother Bartholemew. But none of the charts he used at sea contained these markings. Instead rhumb lines to steer by radiated out from elaborate wind roses placed at convenient intervals. To him, as to every European navigator of his day, all directions were wind directions. He did not think of points of the compass but of *los vientos*. The Portuguese in fact still call their compass card *la rosa dos ventos*, the wind rose.

Latitude in Columbus' mind was not a whit more advanced than it had been in Pytheas' eighteen hundred years before. He still thought in terms of climates, arbitrary belts running parallel to the equator. Longitude was merely so many "hours" west of Cadiz.

How then did the Admiral of the Ocean Sea, appointed by their imperial majesties of Castile, get across the Atlantic? How did he navigate?

It was by simple dead reckoning, some good breaks, plenty of old-fashioned courage and skill, and co-operation from the Almighty.

They used to call it deduced reckoning, shortened it to ded. reckoning, then punned it: dead reckoning. We now usually call it just D.R. It was a good ninety-eight per cent of the navigator's art in 1492, especially in the narrower "climates" of the north where stormy weather often hid the sun and stars for days at a time. It is still the plinth of navigational science used on every steamer, battleship, submarine, and air liner on earth. It is simply the process of keeping track of how fast you are going, in what direction, and of when you change to other speeds or directions. It means plotting your hourly and daily positions on your chart as you go, and being able to deduce the net result of your various tackings into a definite position for any moment of time.

This required Columbus to convert the zigs and zags of his ship's daily track into so many net miles of easting or westing (departure) and so many miles of northing or southing (difference of latitude). He had traverse tables to do much of the mathematics of this for him. In effect traverse tables do the same mathematically as translating the southwesterly course from Grand Central Station to Pennsylvania Station in New York into eight blocks of south and four blocks of west.

It was a simple computation and each day Columbus would figure out where his tacking had brought him in miles east and west, north and south from his previous day's position. We navigators still sometimes use traverse tables for this general purpose, but mainly in calculating the mileages of long obtuse courses before actually flying them.

As a former map maker Columbus of course knew how to plot positions and draw his own charts of new lands. If he had had better ways of telling direction and speed, and better maps, he could have gotten more accurate results. If he had known how to check his dead reckoning with the stars or with known land positions, he could have been more accurate still. Or if he had had a sonar sounding device, he could have kept constant track of the bottom and known when to expect land. Or a radio, or a chronometer. . . . All in all, things of mind and matter being what they were, Columbus solved his navigation problems extremely well and his biographer, Samuel Eliot Morison, says categorically that "no man alive, limited to the instruments and means at Columbus' disposal, could obtain anything near the accuracy of his results."

The fact that Columbus had almost no knowledge or faith in celestial navigation does not make him a bad navigator. Few sea captains knew any more about the stars than he in 1492 and he largely made up for his celestial deficiency by extraordinary attention to D.R. and by liberal use of the lead line in strange waters.

Columbus always carried several lead lines for sounding, and frequently used them. Besides the standard forty-fathom lines on each vessel he had a few deep-sea lines of a hundred fathoms. On at least one occasion he was known to bend two of these together to make a 200-fathom sounding. This was probably in the mysterious Sargasso Sea which appeared to presage land or shallow water. If the Admiral was worried about running on a reef while plowing through the weed nothing could be more reassuring than the splash of the plunging 200 fathom line and oft-repeated cry, "No bottom, sir."

Yet even Columbus grew negligent about sounding when he got used to the steep shores of Cuba, and on Christmas Eve 1492 his flagship ran aground and was hopelessly stove in before the next tide.

How did he keep track of speed? Did he have some primitive kind of speedometer? No, his system was nothing more advanced than spitting over the side and watching the spit float by, or tossing in a chip, or simply watching a fleck of foam go the length of the vessel — judging its speed by guess and by gosh, perhaps counting out the time or pacing the deck abreast a wave. A good sailor can judge speed that way within about ten per cent — perhaps half a knot on a sailing vessel. Columbus actually overestimated his average speed by nine per cent on his epic voyage as reconstructed by Morison. A century or so later a more accurate system was devised of heaving a small log of wood overboard attached to a long line with knots tied in it every fifty feet. The log was allowed to drift aft for half a minute, timed by a special log glass; meanwhile someone counted the number of knots paid over the rail — which equaled the number of nautical miles per hour (knots) the ship was making. But Columbus never heard of knots. He just made a good guess and translated it into Roman miles per hour. That was that, and no arguing with the captain.

What about time? How did Columbus keep track of his tacks or changes of course in the sea? The medieval ship's clock was the half-hour sand glass, known to Columbus as the *ampolleta* — and which remained in general use in the British navy as late as 1839. The gromet or ship's boy in each watch had the duty of minding the ampolleta, reversing it promptly when the sand ran out. Eight ampolletas or glasses (later: eight bells) made up the four-hour watch that is still standard on ships all over the world.

Of course the ampolleta was not a precision clock for, even though it may have averaged within fifteen seconds correct per half hour in its test run in the glass factory in Venice, a heavy sea could slow it up a couple of minutes each turn, or a sleepy gromet much more between turns. Modern ships correct their clocks daily by wireless, as we do more frequently in the air, but Columbus could only check the time on sunny days by sticking a pin into the center of his compass card to watch for local noon, the theoretical moment when the pin's shadow kissed the fleur-de-lis of north — accurate perhaps within half an hour in a moving sea with the compass swinging this way and that and the magnetic north seldom equal to the true.

Columbus appears to have rarely bothered with this performance if he had any faith in it at all, probably preferring to guess at time from the angle of the Dipper — or perhaps from sunrise or sunset, the proper intervals of which he knew approximately by memory for each month, making a slight allowance for latitude. The half-hour ampolletas were all that really mattered to Columbus anyway, for they framed the discipline and religious ritual that was the custom of the sea — the soprano gromet calling out each turning of the glass, chirping a special ditty at daybreak — "Blessed be the light of day . . ." — with a Pater Noster or an Ave Maria at the end of each watch; a chant at prayer time, at tierce, vespers, and compline; a pious ditty even at the morning scrubbing of decks: "Good is that which passeth, better that which cometh, seven is past and eight floweth, more shall flow if God willeth, count and pass makes voyage fast . . ."

The course sailed in each watch was chalked up on a slate hanging against a bulkhead on the poop deck — "W" (west) — repeated aloud from helmsman to pilot to helmsman — "West — nothing to the northward — nothing to the southward — West" — and recorded in the log book by the captain with time and estimated daily distance. From the log again the captain daily made points on his chart to show his position, measuring off the scale distance with his dividers, lining up the course with his ruler against the nearest wind rose, pricking the new point at the new position — *faciendo punto* (making the point) as the Spaniards used to say — or the English: "pricking her off."

It is well known that Columbus kept two charts: an accurate but secret one for himself and a false-front chart to keep his worried shipmates from thinking they were so very far from home. This double play was quite understandable under the circumstances but the Admiral might just as well have saved himself the trouble. Ironically his "phony" chart was nearer the truth than his nine per cent overestimated "accurate" reckoning. That was the way of God and of dead reckoning in the fifteenth century.

Of course Columbus would have liked to have been able to check on his D.R. with a star shot or by any other means. He realized in particular that longitude was an important problem on a westerly ocean voyage like his — more vital and difficult to establish than it had ever been for Pytheas or any other of the early navigators who sailed mainly north or south or along known coasts. But Columbus appears not to have succeeded in checking his longitude at all, and his latitude only very crudely. He tried only ɔnce on his first voyage to observe Polaris with his quadrant but the ship lurched so much and the plumb line swung so hard that it was impossible to take a reading. Another time Columbus observed the North Star with his bloodshot naked eye as appearing "very high as on Cape St. Vincent." He was on the 35th parallel at the time, while Cape St. Vincent is on the 37th — so he was only about 120 nautical miles off. It was as close as he came to a latitude check and for a guess pretty fair at that.

The only way Columbus knew of checking his longitude was by timing an eclipse and later comparing it with the astronomers' records at St. Vincent. One can imagine him grooming his wide-eyed gromets to precision glass-turning as the fateful day approached and talking of azimuths, zeniths, and of "taking the sun" to impress his shipmates, as is said to have been his wont. In fact, he had two good opportunities to clock eclipses for longitude, in 1494 and 1503, but he muffed both. It is to his credit as a navigator that he had the sense afterward not to take his celestial work too seriously, to throw out the eclipses in favor of his D.R.

How the geographical globe looked to Columbus is hard for us to imagine, flying along here in one hour over as much ocean as it took him a week to cross, looking down from a factual perspective that he could never have conceived. But in his journal of his third voyage he gives us a good clue. He allows that the actual earth seems much more irregular to him than the smooth ball described by Ptolemy and the philosophers. Rather, he thinks, "it is the shape of a pear which is everywhere very round except where the stalk is, for there it is very protruding. Or it is like a very round ball, and on one part of it is placed something like a woman's breast, and this part is the highest and nearest to the sky, and it is beneath the equinoctial line and in this Ocean Sea at the end of the East . . . where end all the land and islands."

Seamen as a class in the old days of surface ships, in the slow mysterious days before man grew his present confidence in gadgets, were probably the most God-fearing of men. They knew they were at His mercy every hour, and their pious ritual and frequent prayers are evidence of their state of mind while undergoing the rigors of the wind aloft, of the forecastle below, of the plank bunk, the bugs, the venerable plum duff spiced with blubber. Even my own brief adventures in youth before the masts of schooner and barque bring back to mind the horror of having to choose between an icy drenching at the wheel and the sickening delirium below of nauseous fish fumes riled up from the bilge. Small wonder that the white lips of the common sailor so often responded to the sympathy of the One Hundred and Seventh Psalm, which so eloquently expressed his helplessness: "They that go down to the sea in ships, that do business in great waters; these see the works of the Lord, and his wonders in the deep. For he commandeth and raiseth the stormy wind, which lifteth up the waves thereof. They mount up to the heaven, they go down again to the depths: their soul is melted because of trouble. They reel to and fro, and stagger like a drunken man, and are at their wit's end. Then they cry unto the Lord in their trouble, and he bringeth them out of their distresses. He maketh the storm a calm, so that the waves are still. Then are they glad because they be quiet; so he bringeth them unto their desired haven. Oh that men would praise the Lord for his goodness, and for his wonderful works to the children of men!"

And the men of the sea who believed in these things took to heart the injunction of the psalmist and raised their eyes to the mast top and beyond the mast to the moving sky in praise. And of these, after Columbus, were skillful John Cabot (Zuam Gabota), a Genoese in British service out of Bristol, whose discovery in 1497 of a continent south of Greenland was almost forgotten because England did not then consider the wilderness of North America important. And there was gentle Balboa who reported in 1513 a great South Sea (El Mar del Sur) on the other side of America. And noble Ferdinand Magellan who proved the roundness and size of the earth, sailing to find the south strait in 1519. And Francisco de Orellana who first crossed South America in 1541, down the Amazon in a brigantine. And Sir Martin Frobisher to Baffinland in 1576, to debunk the impassable cold of the arctic. Willem Barents to Nova Zembla in 1596, and Torres and Janszoon in 1606 to Australia, and Henry Hudson the next year to the north tip of Greenland, and Baffin and Tasman to Baffinland and Tasmania, and the great Yorkshire farmer, James Cook, a hundred years later to the Antarctic Circle, the first human in history to reach a zone of the earth to which no human had ever been before.

It was Captain Cook who brought the reckoning of longitude in navigation to important practical use for the first time. The reflecting sextant had long since made it possible to take accurate celestial readings at sea by eliminating the swaying plumb line, thus solving the simple problem of latitude by the pole star or the noon sun. But longitude was another matter, and England's growing commerce across the Atlantic and her whalers and her East Indiamen were being seriously hampered by the impracticability of the known methods. The old system of timing eclipses depended on impossibly long waits for the eclipses, to say nothing of the moods of clouds. Occultation of stars by the moon (commemorated in the Turkish flag) was almost as unreliable. Fixing a co-ordinate of longitude by the dip of the magnetic needle never could be agreed on by either the needle or the navigators. Newton's new method of lunar distances was too laborious and complicated for anyone but a magician. And Galileo's trick of clocking the peekaboo moons of Jupiter required the use of a telescope and in any kind of a sea was about as precise as billiards on horseback.

Surveying all these efforts with a long face, the British government by the Act of 1714 offered a reward of £20,000 "for any method to enable a ship to get its longitude with an error not exceeding thirty miles at the end of a voyage to the West Indies."

This offer not only provoked tantalizing dreams among the inventors but a flurry among the clockmakers, some of whom had heard that finding longitude at sea was no harder than finding a peacock's egg on the thirty-first of June. Weights and water gave way to pendulums and springs, springs became hair springs, balance wheels and cycloidal suspension were added, and centrifuge governors led to verge escapement which turned to anchor escapement. And still the clock would not keep good time at sea — especially, be it noted, during changes of temperature. Whereupon came a Yorkshire carpenter named Harrison, who instinctively knew it was the peahen who lays the eggs, and he made expansion-compensated pendulums and compensated balance wheels — and behold, his fourth model chronometer in a test voyage to Jamaica in 1761 produced a longitude error of only one mile.

While Harrison was still trying to get His Majesty's exchequer to come across with the £20,000, fellow northcountryman Cook sailed south and west with a Harrison chronometer aboard, set to Greenwich, and eastward around the antarctic barrier — and he always knew the time in Greenwich, therefore the difference between Greenwich time and his own local sun time, therefore his longitude — in hours and minutes, in degrees of arc. And that is part of why Australia is British today: because King George's lieutenants were first to know their longitude.

Arctic navigation presented some different problems: the compass was unusable near the magnetic pole and during the equinoctial twilight neither sun nor stars could be seen for months of the year. However Shackleton almost reached the south pole in 1908 and Peary, traveling Eskimo-style in the cold season to avoid the dangerous thaws, attained the north pole in April 1909. Within three years the south pole too was reached independently by Amundsen and Scott — and the bigger exploratory navigation jobs of the planet Earth were at last complete.

This did not mean that all of the world was yet known or understood, nor that the science of navigation had much more than started. Islands continued to appear and disappear in the sea. Brazil Rock, last of Prince Henry's phantom islands of the Atlantic, had only been removed from Admiralty charts in 1873. In 1915 the

Belcher Islands were suddenly rediscovered sprawling smugly in southern Hudson Bay — one of them fifty miles long and their total area some 4700 square miles, yet apparently all unnoticed and forgotten for three centuries of continuous traffic through the bay.

The opposite happened to the Aurora Islands in the South Atlantic east of the Falklands. Discovered in 1762 by the Spanish ship *Aurora*, sighted again by the ship *Princess* in 1790, they were finally "surveyed" by the crew of the hydrographic corvette *Atrevida* in 1794. Yet despite a vivid description and detailed scientific reports by the Royal Hydrographical Society in Madrid in 1809, the Auroras have never been seen since and recently were officially disowned as purely imaginary.

The long roster of pioneers in navigation includes forgotten men of many tongues, many tastes, many beliefs. Some of these have inevitably been technical in their outlook, grimly unsnarling celestial snags like the precessions of equinoxes and the moon's nodes, which long were a confusion to astronomers trying to tidy up God's helter-skelter heavens with their feeble telescopes. Some have contented themselves with more psychological enlightenment like persuading the susceptible public that tides and clouds are no longer open to bribes, that it is already possible to talk back to the astrologers. Others have just wanted to get a private kick out of life, perhaps like Fridtjof Nansen of whom Oliver Wendell Holmes Jr. liked to think that he didn't really try to reach the north pole for science but "simply because he wanted to stand on the top and feel the earth turn round under him."

Navigation devices have often had to wait for earlier inventions or discoveries to clear the way, just as in the other sciences, in the arts, in life itself. While the printing press led to reading, and reading to eyestrain, eyestrain created a demand for spectacles, spectacles led through optics to the invention of the telescope, and the telescope revealed the planets as being round, revolving, earthlike bodies with nights and days and moons and motion about the sun. Thus the printing press not only gave the navigator printed handbooks and almanacs but spectacles to read them with, and new observations from the heavens with which to devise better navigation and write better books. Its by-product techniques of cutting type went hand in hand with better methods of cutting balance wheels for watches, thus accelerating still other interdependent technologies and steadily creating a whole new philosophy of progress.

The idea of progress of course became a core of vitality in the world, and it was apparently new. The Greeks had not had it. The Chinese are still unconvinced. But the Westerners of recent centuries recognized it in the cumulative advantages attained by their sudden storing and pooling of knowledge. Out of it they spawned the principles of bold exploration and daring postulation, of observation and experiment, of trial and error — especially error as a method of learning — error as a humble but inspired tool, the key to invention's second phase: invention not of mere tools but of tools for making tools, invention of inventions to invent inventions, faster and bigger and better and better still — on land, sea, in air — more potential, more dangerous, more beautiful, more . . . more . . .

So on the earth below I see the trail of men and ideas leading upward in our wake. I remember the patient ploddings behind us: the oxcarts, the rickshaws, the steam engines, the horseless carriages, the balloons, the gliders. And their music is in my ears: the singsong of the palanquin bearers, the *chansons de canot* of the French voyageurs as they dip their paddles in the Wabigoon, the endless rhythm of the rivermen paddling with the current, ever singing in the wilderness, drifting down with the waters — down to the forgetful sea: "Allouet-te, gentil Allouet-te — Allouet-te, je te plumerai — Je te plumerai le bec — Et le bec, et le bec . . ."

It will be part of us always. It is our past — the airplane's past — in a way of thinking, the past of all air and wind and sky.

3. The Needle

I TURNED my table lamp low so that I could see the stars better. The window glass was clear as air. Moving my head to different positions I feasted my eyes on the cosmopolis of sparks that lit up the entire vault of space.

It was a friendly cosmopolis and familiar by now, like the lights of greater New York as seen by a pilot from Jackson Heights. And I had a warm feeling for those little sparkling stars — the same glow the artist feels on entering his esoteric studio, the maestro on rehearsing his favorite fugue. I could look that way and that, with conscious abandon, taking in hundreds of stars and thousands of light-years with each sweep of vision. I could see Alphard off to the south of Regulus, and old Kochab near the pole. I could remember when I first learned their names and breathe in pleasure from each as a housewife sniffs flowers in the garden of her own planting.

But it was high time I got a celestial fix. With a head wind and the intermezzo of the ice in the log, we might be half an hour behind flight plan by now. Accurate navigation was getting more important with every minute.

I moved my stool under the astrodome and climbed upon it. It was my angel footstool, my stepway to the stars. I never have quite gotten used to this function, this measuring of stars. It always seems a kind of rite or worship, a tuning in on something of God, something unapproachable and unknowable.

When you glance casually at the moon or see a star twinkling at you through a treetop it seems far-fetched to think that those remote celestial objects could be put to any practical earthly advantage such as earning your living or bringing you closer to a full and happy life.

Yet here I find myself harnessing the moon and stars to these very ends. My mind is opened to the fullness of many continents through star-guided travel. My pay check is in large measure a practical result of this same exploitation of the celestial spheres.

And if I earn my daily bread by the stars, may I not also take professional inspiration from the patron saint of navigators, Saint Christopher, the blest? He is feasted every year when the sun is north. It was he for whom a weaver's baby of Genoa was christened Christopher of the Columboes. It is he who is the legendary guardian of the weary traveler, the erring pilot. His hand is on the throttle and the wheel. He is the saviour of cargoes, the divine of navigators.

But whereof does the navigator think as he threads his way across the sky? Of what is the needle that guides the thread?

Navigating is not higher mathematics. Contrary to a general impression, you do not have to be a chess champion to understand it — even though a liking for chess might suggest a certain aptitude. What you need most is the kind of mind a good secretary has, or an efficient switchboard operator, or a natural born paperhanger. You have to be accurate.

There was a time, in the nineteenth century, when a good navigator had to be a whiz at spherical trigonometry in order to solve the celestial triangle. In those days he might spend a couple of hours working out a fix by the stars. On a slow-moving ship he usually had plenty of time — so it didn't make much difference.

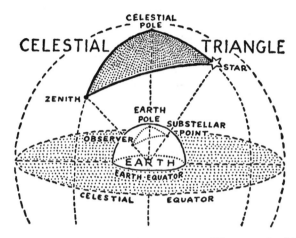

Nowadays spherical trig isn't necessary. All sorts of tables have been worked out to cut corners. Now a navigator can get a star fix in fifteen minutes by a process not much more complicated than playing a couple of hands of bridge or figuring out a route through the narrow one-way streets of downtown London.

It may seem like magic to the pedestrian, but the art is really compounded of simple logical ingredients, seasoned with experience and cool reason, spiced with courage as needed. Literally billions of miles are being flown yearly and the fabulous navigation exploits of the Lindberghs and the Wiley Posts are become common: the precision landfalls after transoceanic flights through blind overcast, the exactly timed interception of ships and bombers and pregnant clouds, the errands of mercy continued to the extreme limit of fuel ranges.

These are the achievements of navigators, this the knowledge barned from navigation's harvests in the millenniums of Pytheas and Prince Henry and Bowditch and Weems.

The simplest form of aerial navigation is pilotage: point-to-point flying by following a succession of landmarks on the ground. That is how the pedestrian navigates. It is the easy introduction to the needle. It is simplest in fair weather and daylight, more difficult at night, and impossible over the open sea or clouds.

They used to call it navigating by the seat of your pants, because early pilots used to judge the degree of skid in a turn by the tightness of their pants. It means just following railroad tracks or highways or rivers or coastlines and acting on plain hunches in the pinches. But a trained navigator need not rely on hunches in pilotage. He plans his course in advance and crystallizes it in his mind by drawing it on a map, with small circles around towns or other recognizable check points along the way. The trick then is to visualize the landscape below the airplane as a second bigger map and follow the two maps as one. As long as you can keep them synchronized, you can read your position right off the smaller map — if not off a railroad station or a roof sign down below. You should not have to navigate by television aerials as did one lost flyer I know, figuring his way to a metropolitan area by noting in what direction the aluminum cross arms were oriented.

Of course you can use your compass to keep flying on a straight course. That is the needle, the most ancient and basic among modern instruments of navigation after the map itself. The lesser needles of other indicators and clocks and gauges follow it, but it is the compass that naturally leads the way.

As you see yourself drifting off course to right or left, perhaps the wind is blowing you sideways or something else is in error. You must judge the needed correction and see that the pilot applies it, and then check again and apply further corrections, and still further ones.

When you first fly over the earth, map in hand, you may feel like a fish out of water. The earth does not look much like the map unless you happen to be over some dramatic feature like a lake or coastline. You may be so confused by the checkerboard of fields and woods and farms down there that you don't notice the more permanent details that really count. Map makers seldom put woods and fields on their maps because these things are only the window dressing of the earth, the fleeting smile on the face of the world: too often these touches of make-up change overnight as the loggers' chain saws, the bulldozers, and the farm tractors do their work. Instead you must train your eye to catch the patterns of more permanent things: river beds and canyons and hills and lakes and railroad lines and the towns and larger highways, which are, relatively speaking, part of the flesh of the earth. These also of course may be altered by dams and great new projects of man but usually slowly enough for the map makers to keep up with them.

Good pilotage is an art and to be learned only by flying and looking and seeing, by cultivating a sure eye for permanent pattern and indestructible detail, and a sense of north and south, a thoroughness in checking canals and stadiums, quarries, airports, and reservoirs. That it can be treacherous is well known to any experienced pilot and there are innumerable examples of this.

One that comes to mind is the predicament of a veteran navigator I know who was flying up a Greenland fiord in a C-47 in 1942. It was broad daylight and there seemed to be almost no problem in navigation. He knew he was in the right fiord and it was simply a matter of following it up to the landing field — or so he thought.

With the mountains all around dazzling white in the sunlight between moving cloud shadows, the navigator felt at ease as he listened to the hum of the two big engines. Now and then he gazed down upon the deep blue of the salt water with here and there a chunk of greeny-white iceberg floating. It was a fascinating scene and it did things to the mind. While one mountain seemed to be trying to lunge out at the plane, another appeared to crouch as if to spring into the clouds. And then the moving plane stood still while the mountains drifted by like arctic demigods breathing and sighing in the sun.

He couldn't say when he first noticed it but he found himself conscious of a great mass of mountain wall ahead of him. Behind it, somewhere around a bend in the fiord, was the sloping field of

Bluie West One set on a gravelly bar underneath a glacier. He did not look at the mountain wall very closely. It was just another white mass flecked with cloud shadows and it was several miles away. For the moment he was basking in the glow of a massive ridge ribbed with snow soaring over his right wing tip. The ridge was bedecked with hanging gardens of ice that appeared to float through space from one precipice to the next.

Then as the navigator noticed that some of the snow on the mountain was moving faster than the rest of the mountain, suddenly Whisssssh! The plane shuddered and the mountains were gone. The sky was gone. The sea and the icebergs were gone. Everything outside the window was white — blinding, dazzling white.

The navigator was confused. He gasped. The co-pilot had been flying but the pilot now looked up from the pile of A.T.C. forms he had been filling out and quickly grabbed the wheel.

"I'll take her," he said, dipping his left wing and turning sharply.

The navigator now realized they had run into a cloud in the fiord, a white cloud unseen against white snow.

The pilot intensely watched the compass and the artificial horizon, made a 180° instrument turn in the fiord, straightened out and — Whisssssh! — the curtain was away and there were the mountains and the sea again.

It is not pleasant to have to make that kind of maneuver blind in such a narrow spot. The strain is severe on the needle in the cloud. But such a slip in observation is one of the ever lurking hazards of pilotage and sometimes even experience and care are hardly enough to avoid it.

However it is when the ground becomes continuously invisible in fog or gloaming, or the course leads over the sea, or the map shows no detail, that pilotage must definitely give place to instrument navigation, to the elemental mathematics of dead reckoning aided, if God is willing, by the radio or the stars.

What are the instruments of dead reckoning in the sky? The tools of the flying navigator's trade, his needles of light, his dials of truth and salvation? They are the compasses, magnetic and radio and gyroscopic, that point the way, the peloruses and the computers and sextants, the altimeters, thermometers, airspeed indicators, fuel-flow meters, and driftmeters, and the various radios for navigation by ear and eye. The story of these will be unfolded little by little as we go onward, treading lightly on the technical, dwelling on things mathematical only for illustration or when they are the essence of the subject. Mastery of these instruments is vital to the modern flying navigator, and to the degree that he trusts them and himself he will keep from getting lost. To the extent that he develops a fierce faith in the needle quivering before him in the dark storm, letting it guide his mind and heart, will he be able to thread body to soul for all on board.

The basic form of navigation beyond simple pilotage is, as we have said, dead reckoning. It uses almost all the navigator's current tools of trade. As in Columbus' day, it is still the backbone of navigation, and it is still done by pricking off points on a chart with dividers. The main difference is that now we have more and better ways of keeping track. Instead of Columbian saliva on the sea, we have pitot and static tubes that work by pressure differences to measure speed through the air; we have new and better compasses, and systems to correct the notorious old errors that used to make things come out wrong.

Dead reckoning in the sky is similar in main principles to the ancient sailor's art but different in emphasis, in detail. We in the air have to think of such things as our sideways drift before the wind, even as did Columbus. That is part of keeping track of our direction. And of course we must measure our speed. But in the air we can overcome some of the inaccuracies that might be fatal in a surface ship because of our much greater vision: if we are aiming for a small atoll we can usually see it even if we are thirty or forty miles off course. On the sea we might miss it from five miles.

However, we must work faster in the air because we are moving so much faster. For every minute we take in figuring out our position, our position moves several miles ahead. And the factor of altitude is something new that was added when we took to the sky, the third dimension.

These then are the main distinctions of aerial navigation: working speed must be increased even at some sacrifice of precision, and altitude must be considered (including climb, let-down, and the effect of air density on speed).

Instead of the old lead line for sounding the sea bottom, for instance, we have altimeters to sound the sky bottom as we float above it. The basic purpose is much the same. The altimeter is not always thought of as a navigation instrument but it can do a fair job on its own in a pinch, even as the ancient sounding line. Some old-time mariners used to claim they could navigate with nothing but a lead line, and one swore he could tell where he was in any of the seven seas simply by sampling the mud brought up on the anchor — that is, until one day his mate primed his hook with a dollop of Missouri night soil and badly bolluxed his bearings.

Altimeters are of two kinds: the pressure altimeter, which is really a barometer and works on the principle that air pressure decreases with altitude; and the radio altimeter, which is a radar instrument and measures the actual distance to the ground below by timing the echoes of radio waves. Both of these are modern counterparts of the old lead line.

The pressure altimeter tells you your height above sea level if you set it for the sea level pressure of that time and place. The radio altimeter tells you your height above sea level if you are over the sea or add correctly the height of the land below you.

Thus each altimeter has its limitations and it is the combination of the two that gives the best results. In flight we get reports of sea-level pressure as often as practicable by radio so we can set the pressure altimeter correctly, and we read a map to keep track of the height of the ground below us so that we can use the radio altimeter effectively. The two in combination do some wonderful things for the flying navigator, including telling him (with barometric clues) which way the wind is blowing — often the most baffling of all the variable factors he has to cope with.

In some ways, however, flying is still more like Columbus' voyages than like modern sea navigation, for flying is riding the wind, and sailing ships are much more affected by the wind than modern steamers which need hardly notice anything short of a gale. As a sailing vessel skids a little sideways in the sea so even more does an airplane drift sideways in the air. There are modern ways of measuring the sea slip of a surface ship, and even better ways of measuring the side drift of an airplane.

Did you ever meet that basic instrument of aerial navigation, the driftmeter? It is something like a submarine's periscope but, being in an airplane and above the surface instead of below it, it points downward instead of upward. As you press your eye into the rubber eyepiece and gaze down the shaft through the floor of the airplane toward the earth you see objects or clouds or waves of the sea moving steadily rearward under you. You also see a set of luminous grid lines which are built into the instrument to help you measure the drift. As you watch the trees or the whitecaps on the waves steadily moving back, you twirl a knob which turns the whole driftmeter shaft including the grid lines until you line them up parallel to the motion of the things you see. Once that is done you can read off your drift in degrees to right or left on a scale attached to the instrument.

A normal drift for a large modern airplane is something between zero and ten degrees, but the faster the airplane the less the drift because the weaker the wind will be in proportion to the speed of the craft itself. A supersonic plane or a rocket, for instance, will seldom have a drift of more than a couple of degrees. In fact future drift readings aboard the very fast sky craft now being dreamed up will undoubtedly be measured in minutes if not even smaller subdivisions of the degree.

When you catch the concept of drift you already have caught the idea of the wind triangle, which is fundamental to dead reckoning in the sky. The three sides of this triangle represent: (1) the heading of the airplane or the direction and distance that would be flown during a unit of time if there were no wind, (2) the actual track of the airplane or the direction and distance it flies during that time with the help or hindrance of the wind, (3) the wind itself or the direction and distance the air moves in that same length of time.

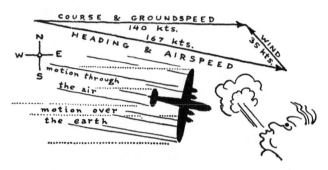

As you can see in the illustration, the difference between where the airplane would be without wind and where it actually is with wind is exactly what the wind did during the time under consideration. Thus if you know exactly what the airplane is doing you can tell the wind, or if you know the wind you can tell what the airplane is doing.

This is the basis for predicting drift ahead of time (by wind forecast) and thus figuring out what heading to fly: what point of the compass to aim the nose of the airplane at. Naturally the airplane will seldom travel in exactly the same direction it is heading, but you still have to know which way to head it.

This is elementary trigonometry and, along with the celestial triangle, is the basic mathematics of navigation. As any high school student knows, if you have any side and any two angles of a triangle you can find the other two sides and the third angle. And also if you know only one angle and two sides you can solve for the rest.

In actual flying of course the navigator's computer does the donkey work of trigonometry. You just give it the known factors and it gives you back the unknown. The computer is a kind of combined movable wind triangle and rotating slide rule: it relieves the mind for more abstruse considerations. As you fly along you set your drift reading into it and your airspeed reading and what other clues you have, especially any concerning the wind, and when you have put in enough ingredients, out comes the answer: usually your groundspeed.

Groundspeed is one of the things you are constantly seeking or checking. Groundspeed is your speed over the earth (land or sea) as distinct from your airspeed or speed through the air. Airspeed can be read off the airspeed indicator, but groundspeed usually has to be calculated from clues. Without it you can't possibly know how long it will take you to get to where you are going. With it you can figure your E.T.A. (estimated time of arrival). The E.T.A. is one of the end-products of navigation. It has to be checked and rechecked as you continue your flight for on its accuracy depends the safety of the flight, the security of fuel reserve, the whole plan and basis on which you are flying. If you are optimistic as to your E.T.A., you are optimistic as to how many miles you are getting from each gallon of gas. And that in flying is optimism that doesn't live long.

Navigation is a pursuit of truth. Since the keeping of records is an obvious boon to verity, navigators are trained in meticulous log keeping, in writing down every scrap of factual information they have at frequent and regular intervals. These bits of fact come from the needles of the altimeter, the compass, the chronometer, the fuel-flow meter and all the other navigation instruments and they form the threads of evidence that the navigator weaves together into the strong fabric of truth.

By thus keeping track of where he has been, the navigator is sure of where he is going. And by knowing when he got to places behind him he can tell when he will get to places ahead of him.

His records are not entirely in written log form, however. He also keeps records in the form of graphic charts, which give him a whole vivid picture at a glance. This is particularly important in regard to the very vital matter of fuel supply in relation to distance flown and distance to be flown. So the navigator always keeps a graph showing miles flown on the horizontal co-ordinate and gal-

lons of gas consumed on the vertical, with a slanting black line
or curve indicating the planned fuel consumption (each point on
the line being as far to the right in miles as is correct for its height
in gallons). In addition to this line of planned fuel consumption
plotted before the start of the flight, the navigator draws a red
line showing his actual fuel consumption as he flies. And there
are other lines on the graph showing what to expect in fuel consumption if the plane should have to turn back, if one of the
engines should quit, if two engines should quit . . . And a point is
plotted beyond which there wouldn't be enough fuel to turn back:
the point of no return.

This graph is universally known as the Howgozit, for its one big
purpose is to answer the eternal navigation question: "How goes
it?" Are we doing all right? It is the flyer's version of "To be or
not to be." No matter what the emergency, therefore, the navigator has his basic navigation answers all ready for instant decision.
He can see at a glance whether his red line of actual performance
is better or worse than his various black lines of planned performance — and he can decide, like any good business executive,
on the basis of facts, not guesses.

An interesting case is the terrible forced landing of the Bermuda
Sky Queen in the North Atlantic on October 14, 1947. The giant
flying boat had taken off from Foynes, Eire, the afternoon before
bound for Gander, Newfoundland, with a crew of seven and the
largest number of passengers ever yet booked for a transatlantic
flight: sixty-two, including twenty women and twelve children.

This was not a regular airline flight and evidently no Howgozit
graph was kept. When the big plane had winged its way half across
the ocean the crew reported they were "well satisfied with the
progress of the flight and expected no difficulty." But not long
after that the navigator suddenly discovered the head wind was
stronger than he had thought and the plane was not as far along
as it should be. Just then the engineer inexplicably "missed a
couple of hundred gallons he thought he had." The crew checked
as best they could and figured out they had already passed their
point of no return and still had not enough gas to reach land

ahead. They had gone bankrupt without realizing it. They would have to ditch the plane at sea.

Luckily there was a weather ship still within range, Ocean Station Charlie where the U.S. Coast Guard cutter *George M. Bibb* was watchfully riding the gale about one hundred miles west of mid-Atlantic. The *Sky Queen's* young pilot, Charles Martin, headed for it, homing in on its radio, and with great skill landed in the dangerous cross-seas close to the *Bibb*.

It took more than twenty-four hours of heroic effort before the rescue was completed, almost miraculously amid torn life rafts and stove-in surfboats crashing up and down in the thirty-foot waves, women and children and men being fished out of the icy sea and hauled painfully aboard the heaving cutter by long ropes looped under their armpits. The plane itself was a total loss.

Besides knowing his point of no return before every ocean flight the navigator must figure out alternate places where he can land in case his destination socks in with fog or closes for some other reason. This happens not too rarely in the moody North Atlantic region and even when blind-landing systems are operating, an airport may be closed on account of high wind, heavy snow, flood, fire, or accident.

If there are plenty of alternates near the destination the problem may be easy, but if, as in the British Isles, everything within hundreds of miles can fold up at once in dense fog, the situation may be tough. When the only sure alternate is a long way off, the navigator may have to calculate how far he can go and still have a choice of landing places. In other words, after he has passed his "point of no return," he may yet have a "point of no alternate" ahead of him before which he must either turn toward the alternate or forfeit his chance to do so. Or he may have multiple points of no alternate. The calculation of these is a nice geometric problem, as are others of the navigator's emergency problems, like the pattern of the "square search" designed for most efficient location of a known point when you are lost in its general vicinity.

Almost anything can happen in navigating the ocean. Not long ago a plane was flying a load of passengers from Casablanca to New York. After stopping at the Azores it took off for Newfoundland, but less than two hours later a report came that all landing fields on Newfoundland were closing on account of fog.

As the point of no return was still a long way ahead, the crew turned the plane around and headed back for the Azores. But before they got there they were stunned to hear by radio that fog had folded up every Azores airport also.

Hastily scanning his maps in all directions the navigator now discovered that his only possible alternate was in Africa. So back they flew and had just enough gas to land once more in Casablanca to the exasperation of the passengers who had confidently expected by this time to be coming into New York.

That's the way of navigation. Factors must be weighed on factors, some fixed, some variable. Contingencies on contingencies. Decisions on decisions.

How many ifs are under our control? Is the point of no return known? What about the alternates and the points of no alternates? What if Greenland folds, if Goose Bay folds, if . . . ? It is time to decide. To wait is to die. Shall we wrap up the bundle? Can we pay for the package?

Most flights are uneventful only because someone planned every detail carefully — someone who, like a chess player, knew the game and could see several moves ahead. In other words, it behooves one to imagine the worst things that can possibly happen and think around six corners. If the gyro-compass fails, use the magnetic or the radio. If the radio fails, fly by the sun or the stars. If you can't see the sun, use the driftmeter. If you have to land at sea, radio your exact position and have your emergency gear ready.

That is the way fear is conquered: not by thinking of pleasanter things, by letting George worry about it — but by facing the worst, becoming familiar with disaster and death until you've got it licked at every turn.

One of Confucius' most famous sayings is that "a man who has made a mistake and doesn't correct it is making another mistake." That comes close to being the ideal slogan for a navigator. Everybody makes mistakes; but a navigator must be a fellow who keeps mistakes and their consequences at a minimum by checking them continually, not only allowing for errors but correcting them as fast as they are discovered. It is specifically to safeguard against the danger of errors that he writes out a flight plan before take-off and checks it on the ground with his pilot and the flight operations office. That is standard practice and it has saved a lot of lives. It previews the composition for the critics before the first performance. It makes it likely that any serious mistake in figuring the course, the groundspeed, the E.T.A., or the fuel load will be spotted by someone and corrected in time. It means that the basic decisions concerning any important flight are made before leaving the ground.

That is the thrill in flight planning. It is the hour of decision, the time when the big bets are placed. It is when fuel is weighed against payload, and much hinges on the calculations of the navigator.

Again and again I've seen it happen. A long ocean hop is being planned, say from Ireland to Newfoundland, against a strong headwind. We are due to take off in half an hour. I have been figuring hard at the Operations counter, calibrating the forecast winds and temperatures, working my computer till it almost smokes, checking mileages and protracting courses and drifts, moving zone by zone across the ocean, and above all rechecking my groundspeeds and fuel figures.

And around me are my pilot captain and maybe the first officer, leaning over my shoulder to see how much fuel reserve there will be, balancing the load against the risk.

Perhaps another crew or two scheduled for succeeding flights are also present, the navigators awaiting clues for their own flight plans, the captains trying to make up their minds from my figures. Then is the moment when the weight of responsibility is large.

The final decision as to whether to fly or stay of course is not mine. It is up to the captain. The navigator only stands on his navigation, on his flight and fuel figures, his professional contribution to flying.

The captain and the operations officer must decide whether the flight is worth making on the basis of the figures given. While the captain naturally holds out for his fuel reserve, the operations man holds out for his payload, and they try to cram as much of both as they can into the maximum weight permitted. It is a squeeze and a compromise, and is mixed up with all sorts of other factors and problems. Some old, some new ones — all challenging.

Did you ever wonder why planes even today seldom fly non-stop from New York to London, or from Istanbul to Madrid? It is strictly a matter of business. They don't land at way stations like the Azores and Newfoundland just to take a breather or to let off passengers. The crew gets a rest there, it is true, while another crew takes over — but the real reason is to save gas, to reduce weight for other things.

It is easy enough for a plane to fly all the way from New York to Rome without stopping once, and it is faster and safer than having to land at various intermediate points. But how many passengers is there room for? How much freight?

Saving gas is important in the air because gas is expensive. This is almost as true of kerosene or crude oil as of the highest octane gasoline. It isn't the manufacturing cost; it's the transportation. Since it is being carried by air express its cost is a lot higher than you'd think: somewhere around $10 a gallon. So pause and consider. If you want to play it a little safer by taking a hundred extra gallons, that will cost you $1000 more. It would be much cheaper to take out some more insurance, say a mere $100 worth, and swallow your apprehension. If it was your airline what would you do?

Once in the air of course such questions become only academic. Then the navigator replaces plan with performance. He uses his experience, his aids in navigation, to get there as intended.

It is interesting to consider just what his navigation aids are, their order of importance or relative value. This is one of the fundamental sequences of nature. By general consensus of opinion the basic order of navigation aids is: (1) human brain and body — for thinking, seeing, and doing, (2) map — for knowing what's on the earth beyond your sight, (3) pencil — for marking your course, for checking, recording, calculating, (4) compass — for finding direction, (5) watch — for keeping time. These aids are in the right order for Columbus as well as for the most up-to-date modern navigation of sea or air. Of course one could add flying instruments: (6) airspeed indicator, (7) altimeter; and then a long list of more minor aids: radio, sextant, almanac and tables, driftmeter, directional gyro, computer, protractor, straight edge, dividers . . .

That's the way we navigators think of it. But many a man who flies without navigation doesn't know these relative values until he learns the hard way.

I remember one, an airline pilot flying to Amsterdam, who got into trouble because he relied on his radio more than on the elementary navigational aids. He had all the basic tools with him except a trained navigator. It was undercast and he suddenly discovered his radio wouldn't work. He didn't do his dead reckoning very well and went mostly on hopes and hunches that the undercast would clear away. Catching a glimpse of Utrecht down below, he mistook it for Amsterdam and had a very anxious hour until by great good luck he found an airport.

Another pilot, somewhat less lucky, took off in an SNJ one afternoon on a quick "easy" flight from Norfolk, Virginia, to Washington, D.C. He left so fast that he didn't even think of checking his radio. His passenger had an urgent appointment.

As they took off into the setting sun he discovered he couldn't contact the tower. But that didn't worry him. He thought the frequency must be a little off, and he would fiddle with it in the air at leisure.

For navigation he drew a straight course on his map, estimated a correction for the wind, and worked out a compass heading. He planned to tune in on a Washington range station as soon as he had the radio going right, and then come in on the beam.

But as he worked at the radio, he soon realized that it was seriously out of order. He couldn't get anything but a gentle whine: no recognizable signals at all.

It was now dark and there were lights down below. Towns drifted by. What towns? Was that Dunbrooke or Dunnsville? Or maybe Tappahannock? He didn't know.

He veered to the right. Surely he would find the shore of Chesapeake Bay, or the Potomac, or something. But thick clouds appeared and it was very dark and he couldn't see anything that looked familiar.

When he had flown as far as Washington but saw no sign of any big city he thought of starting a square search. But he had no plotting board and, as he said later, "I didn't see how we could be far off anyway." So he just kept on flying and hoping.

With throttle and mixture controls set for "maximum endurance" he zigzagged back and forth looking for some clue and was increasingly amazed that none showed up. When his gas got down to five minutes flying time he looked for a place to land. Seeing none, he told his passenger to get ready to bail out. And then the plane sputtered and started to descend. Both men jumped.

The pilot's chute opened nicely but let him down at the same rate as the circling pilotless plane which kept going around and around him, twice missing him by what seemed like a few feet. His passenger landed in a big tree and broke off branches all the way to the ground. Almost miraculously both men were unhurt, and even the empty plane made a passable landing. It was found later undamaged in a field.

Putting it mildly, this adventure is a fine example of how not to navigate an airplane, and yet that pilot probably had been flying his way for years without mishap. Maybe he still is. It would be interesting to know how many other flyers Saint Christopher has pulled strings for, how many have said, "I don't see how we could be far off anyway," and lived to tell it.

We all get our share of breaks, good or bad, but experience shows it not wise to lean on the old boy too hard, trying his patience with our "famous last words." I can see him now in my mind's eye holding starry-eyed figures up above the waves as their mortal lips roll out the familiar death-tickling remarks: "It's over in that direction somewhere."

"Don't worry. I've been flying through them mountains all my life."

"Two hundred feet? Hell, it'll be two thousand easy by the time we get there."

"Only scattered thunderstorms. Let's go."

"All we gotta do is fly half contact and half instruments."

"What did he say the altimeter setting was?"

"Never mind the check list now. We'll have plenty of time in the air."

"We don't need a log this trip. I could navigate this one with my eyes shut."

"My D.R. must be wrong. I just know we couldn't be that far off course."

"Why go back? We can always land at that emergency field if we have to."

"We've got plenty of gas. I'm sure Joe must've filled her up."

Even after the navigator has learned not to utter any of these famous last words, nor to think them, he must somehow get along with his pilot. The lives of all depend on a certain minimum degree of co-operation.

I once flew with a pilot captain who distrusted me, and things were difficult. I found out afterward that he distrusted all navigators. On one occasion he refused to fly the ocean by day even with both sun and moon in shooting position because he believed only the stars were sufficiently reliable for a celestial check. Another time on a westward crossing he mistook Newfoundland for Labrador and we got in safely only because he had a saving grace: he distrusted himself even more than he distrusted me.

A navigator friend of mine solved a somewhat similar problem by diplomacy. When his pilot refused to make a correction of 30° in heading because "we couldn't be that far off," he got him to change 10°. Twenty minutes later he asked for another 5° and got it. Half an hour later, some more. Thus, little by little in inconspicuous doses he accomplished his purpose and finally brought the plane safely home.

That is the kind of adaptability a good navigator needs to have. He must sometimes outthink his own fellow crew members and, in a modern stratoliner, that can mean three pilots, two engineers, a radio operator, a purser-cook, and two stewardesses. His job is less glamorous than the pilot's, but in the crises it is apt to be a key position.

A tragedy that resulted in part from lack of co-operation between navigator and pilot was the case of the Transocean C–54 that wound up in the drink off Ireland in August 1949. I had been a navigator with Transocean Airlines only eight months earlier but didn't happen to know Tim Gruber, the navigator involved.

Transocean is an unscheduled airline that grew up rapidly after World War II. In 1949 it was carrying mostly freight to Europe and returning with DP's and other emigrants it had contracted to fly to South America. On the ill-fated flight the four-engined N–79998 took off from Rome at 4:08 P.M. with a load of forty-seven Italian émigrés who were to settle in Venezuela. There was a crew of eight and a guest pilot: the famous woman flyer, Ruth Nichols. The immediate destination was Shannon Airport near Limerick, Eire.

Until it got dark at about half past seven Gruber kept track of his position largely by pilotage, for he could plainly see the earth: the mountains and coastlines of Corsica, the blue Mediterranean, the great waterfront at Marseille where Pytheas embarked, and then the Rhone valley and the green patchwork of southern France.

At 8:50 he was over Rennes by dead reckoning but it was dark and undercast and he had no check on his position. In this particular airplane the navigator's desk was not equipped with head phones nor any sort of radio direction-finding device and Gruber had to rely on the others. First Officer Ball, who was acting as pilot while Captain Edward Lessey rested in the crew's quarters, told the navigator he had not taken a radio bearing on Rennes on account of bad static.

Nearly an hour later Gruber saw lights that looked like the northern coast of Brittany below and thought he recognized where he was. To be absolutely sure, he shot a three-star fix just afterward, which approximately verified the position.

By this time Captain Lessey was back on the flight deck and Ball in his pilot's seat was still trying to get a radio bearing. As the static had quieted down somewhat he presently managed to get a signal from Brest coming from a direction about twenty-five degrees to the left of his tail.

Lessey, perhaps a little sleepy, guessed that the plane must now be just southwest of the Cherbourg peninsula and asked Gruber if that were so: "Aren't those the Channel Islands off to the right there?"

Gruber agreed that that must be correct. And he concluded that the plane must be about on course even if a little behind time. He was sure enough of this not to check further for the time being. He relaxed, perhaps copying a little data into his log or conversing with one of the radio men. He may have passed a few minutes in talking with the celebrated Ruth Nichols who occasionally stepped into the cockpit to see what was going on, or to try her hand at the wheel of a 54.

This, incidentally, was to have been the final leg of Miss Nichols' flight around the world. Years earlier Amelia Earhart died while trying to be the first woman to fly completely around the globe and at this moment Mrs. Richard Morrow-Tait was nearing completion of a somewhat similar feat, but Ruth Nichols was bent on nosing her out in the stretch.

Tim Gruber had calculated his groundspeed from Marseille to his celestial fix to be 138 knots, a suspiciously low figure under the existing conditions. But a little later when he saw land again off to the right, land which had to be England if the last land had been Normandy, he refigured his groundspeed on that basis and it came out 160 knots, a much more reasonable amount. He felt reassured more than ever now in his identification of those lights which must surely be the towns of Penzance and St. Ives at Land's End.

So he handed a slip of paper to the radio operator and the report was flashed to Shannon Radio that the plane was over Land's End at 10:27 and the E.T.A. was 11:45.

Shortly after this Lessey let down from 8500 feet to 3500 feet which was just over a layer of broken clouds. Gruber stowed his navigation equipment preparatory to landing, and perfunctorily drew on his chart the courses of the Shannon radio range which was being received, the signal being that of an "A" quadrant. He had no feeling of impending disaster. The radio was now practically free of static and the weather was clear except for the cumulus cloud layer below which was becoming more and more scattered. About the only thing Tim Gruber felt a little unsure of was his E.T.A. Thinking it over, 11:45 seemed a bit too soon to make Shannon in view of his earlier slow groundspeed, so he averaged out his groundspeeds and got what appeared a more conservative figure: 12:10. This he gave to Captain Lessey as his final estimated time of arrival.

When 12:10 had come and gone, Gruber did not feel alarmed at first. Perhaps his estimate was a few minutes too early. As was customary he had left the final approach and landing to the pilots. After all, hadn't the main navigating job been done by then? Even if it hadn't, an entire flight from Rome should have been possible for any experienced pilot without a navigator at all. There were several radio range stations along the way, almost as many as in parts of the United States where pilots have always done all their own navigating.

Furthermore, it could be argued, a navigator deserves some respite near the end of a trip for he is the only man in a flight crew whose work becomes harder and more important as the airplane leaves the vicinity of places to land. After take-off, as the crew settles down to a long flight, the pilots can relax or sleep most of the time, the engineer has almost nothing to do except in emergency, and the radio officer usually soon finds himself within effective range of fewer and fewer radio stations — particularly on an ocean flight. But the navigator must keep track constantly, and the further away from a place to land the more vital his work.

It was only natural then that Gruber would relax when the airplane seemed to have reached its destination and was approximately over the airport. And it was natural that he should be surprised at about 12:15 to hear Lessey throttle down the engines but then suddenly turn to him with a demand as to where in hell is Shannon anyhow.

When Gruber admitted he was confused, Lessey asked him to get a quick fix on the loran visual radio. He tried but, as has often been the case in this area, no satisfactory result could be obtained. On the audio radio a faint "N" signal could be heard on the Shannon range, but which one of the "N" quadrants was it and what part of the quadrant? None of the crew could be sure.

Meanwhile Lessey continued flying at a fuel-conserving pace to the northwest, hoping that somehow Shannon would still show up ahead. Gruber, now abandoning both D.R. and radio as a solution to the mystery, hastily unpacked his octant again and shot another three-star fix. By 12:45 he had it plotted and it showed the airplane's position 175 miles northwest of Shannon. On this evidence Gruber suggested turning around and flying a southeasterly course back to Shannon.

Lessey, however, flew almost due south for a few minutes, then southeasterly, aiming to intercept the westerly leg of the Shannon range. This he hit at 01:14, whereupon he turned due eastward to follow the beam straight to Shannon.

By this time all the crew were fully alert to danger and were calculating as carefully as possible exactly how much gasoline was left and how much longer they could stay in the air. Some thought they might just be able to make Shannon, but it was obviously very doubtful. The airplane had been in the air a total of nine hours and six minutes, and only an hour and a half of fuel remained. Captain Lessey sent a distress signal to Air-Sea Rescue facilities at Shannon, giving his estimated position and course.

Some of the origins of the dilemma were by now apparent even to the crew of the doomed plane. They remembered that they had arrived a half hour late at Ciampino Airport before take-off in Rome. To make up for lost time Captain Lessey had divided preflight duties among the crew. He and Gruber and Second Officer Davis got the weather forecast from the local weather office. Davis then prepared the flight clearance and filed it with Rome Air Traffic Control. First Officer Ball made out the weight and balance manifest. Captain Lessey went to the aircraft, while Gruber computed his flight plan based on a route to Shannon via airways and over both Marseille and Paris. As the investigation revealed afterward: "the navigator and the first and second officers did not confer, nor did either the navigator or second officer have knowledge of the correct aircraft weight and fuel load until after the flight documents were completed and they had reported to the aircraft. Captain Lessey (who was responsible for all) did not examine any of the documents before take-off."

As an example of what this lack of co-ordination could produce, Second Officer Davis had indicated on the flight clearance that the airplane carried sixteen hours of fuel, but Gruber based his flight plan on twelve hours. Different as these figures were, if either one had been correct the disaster would have been averted. In actuality when these two men got aboard the plane they discovered that only 2260 gallons, or 11⅓ hours, of gasoline were on board.

At a consumption rate of 200 gallons per hour (a standard estimate of the company) 2260 gallons was less than the legal minimum required by Civil Air Regulations. But Lessey had then decided that in view of the predicted good weather some distance could be eliminated by flying straight from Marseille to Shannon, leaving out Paris, and also by changing the alternate destination from Paris to Dublin, which he did but without reporting it to Rome Air Traffic Control. With these changes there seemed to be enough reserve gasoline, enough at least to satisfy regulations.

So it was not necessary to waste time putting any more in.

As the woeful plane flew eastward, her throttles now set to stretch every remaining gallon to its maximum, some of the other errors that combined into calamity also became evident to the crew. There were of course obvious errors in navigation. Not only was Gruber's celestial fix off the French coast wrong by several scores of miles, causing him seriously to underestimate his ground-speed, but he was several degrees off course to the left for some still undetermined reason. He also plotted his bearing on Brest incorrectly and, perhaps partly influenced by Lessey's misjudgment as well as his own errors, mistook Land's End for the Cherbourg peninsula and later thought the southwest tip of Ireland was Land's End.

This double error in recognition of coasts that look somewhat similar at night is understandable, but less excusable was the sequence of errors combined with it, such as Gruber's admitted carelessness in copying down the "A" quadrant of the Shannon range as "N" and the "N" quadrant as "A." This final slip diabolically fitted in with the earlier errors to create a fairly plausible illusion, which escaped detection by anyone on the plane until too late.

The pilots too had their customary share in the navigating, especially in listening to range signals, and they should have kept track of which quadrant of the Shannon range they were in. But evidently they relied entirely on Gruber, while he in turn left the supposedly easy homing in on Shannon largely to them. Thus as each casually assumed the other was doing more than he actually did, there was a considerable gap of error and misconception between them.

And so, her fate sealed from hours past, the big plane with fifty-eight persons aboard finally faltered less than fifteen minutes from her destination. Her engines sputtered and stopped one by one and she glided rapidly downward to the sea just seven miles off Lurga Point, Eire.

The landing was good and the aircraft came to rest in the water

without serious injury to anyone. The rubber life rafts were
launched satisfactorily, but the panicky Italian émigrés who didn't
understand English jumped into the water instead of waiting their
turns to climb into the rafts, and seven of them drowned before
they could be picked up in the confusion and darkness. Also Jack
Haskell, one of the radio men, was hit by a piece of the tail assembly
as it broke apart in the waves and he fell from his perch on the
fuselage into the black water and drowned.

By the time the airplane sank, fifteen minutes after the ditching,
rescue planes were overhead and flares and additional life rafts had
been dropped close to the scene. A couple of hours later the British
trawler *Stalberg* arrived and by sunrise had picked up everyone,
including all eight bodies of the drowned. Even Ruth Nichols,
little daunted by her adventure, soon managed to board another
plane and was still able to beat Mrs. Morrow-Tait to be the first
aviatrix to fly around the world.

Curiosity is a kind of lust of the mind, and it can extend into mathematical logic as much as anywhere else. If you are a navigator it is vital that your appetite for graphic and deductive problems have a keen edge, for flying across the world is in a real sense almost a continuous geometric "brain teaser."

To test whether sky puzzles are a challenge or a menace to you (probably the best single indication of your aptitude for navigation) here is a sample problem. Imagine an airline route from New York to Rio de Janeiro that is divided into three zones of equal length, the northern zone having nothing but variable winds of random direction and velocity, the middle zone entirely trade winds of constant direction and strength, and the southern zone nothing but doldrums of still air. Three men, Norman, Midfield, and Sunderland, are assigned to fly the three respective zones, each taking the controls only in his own zone in flights both ways between the two cities.

The airline manager had announced that, owing to unfortunate business conditions, the man who makes the poorest average zone time for the ensuing year must be dropped from the payroll. Which man has the most future security in his job?

Almost immediately the trained navigator will know that Sunderland is the man because wind is not helpful on a two-way flight. Of course if the wind chanced to reverse itself at the right time and became a tail wind both ways, it would help momentarily, but it wouldn't average out that way over a year. Winds in general just cannot help, for the reason that tail winds never save as much time as equal head winds lose. Example: if an airplane's speed in still air is 100 m.p.h., a 50 m.p.h. tail wind will speed it up 20 minutes per 100 miles, but a 50 m.p.h. head wind will slow it down 60 minutes per 100 miles. In other words, a wind of half your airspeed will help you from behind only a third as much as it will hinder you from in front. That's obviously not a fair wind.

It is seldom that a man is permitted the official rating of navigator without some aptitude for the work, but on rare occasions it turns out that a persistent person manages to squeak by all tests on some combination of memorized formulas, bluff, and luck. This of course is all too apt to lead to disaster, as actually happened on May 25, 1952, when a lost British Overseas Airways airliner crashed in French West Africa 1300 miles off course!

Both captain and navigator in this astonishing scheduled flight held second-class navigator's licenses, but the captain had earned his only on the third attempt while the navigator had barely made the grade on his fifth try. Among their unique combination of errors was mistakenly setting the variation control on the gyrosyn compass at 60° West instead of 6° West, which resulted in a heading of 54° off course during much of the six-hour flight. Although several star shots were taken neither captain nor navigator was alert enough to notice that the wrong stars had been used and when the magnetic compass disagreed with the gyrosyn the captain unaccountably pronounced it "unserviceable." Obviously several optimistic assumptions were made and accepted without checking.

Navigational boners of this order of magnitude are fortunately very rare, but all through history their occasional appearance seems to have stemmed from the same brand of slipshod thinking — as their avoidance has come through development of an appetite for accurate deduction and frequent checking. No doubt in the time of Ptolemy a conscientious navigator with an aptitude for wind angles and traverse calculation did better than most. Then, even more than now, he must have had a great advantage over his astrology-minded competitors. Indeed Ptolemy himself must have been a demon at puzzles, for he tackled some of the greatest in the world, and his work on the foundations of trigonometry and on star movements was so good that no man surpassed it for 1400 years. The Moslem prime meridian at the Fortunate Islands (now called Canary Islands) originated from Ptolemy and, as the western end of the known world, that meridian was the jumping-off place for Columbus.

However, the most remarkable thing about Ptolemy's work is that so much of it is still standard today, especially in elementary celestial navigation. Inevitably Ptolemaic astronomy is archaic, provincial and very limited in perspective. It is astronomy as looked at by the earth lubber who has not yet journeyed in his imagination to the sun or beyond. Ptolemy had almost no idea of where or what or how big the sun is. Yet his basic calculations are the most convenient ever devised for navigation. They are a representation of the apparent movements of the sun, moon, planets, and "fixed" stars. And they make practical sense too, for even after you learn the larger, simpler view that the earth and planets revolve around the sun, it is still true (relatively speaking) that all the celestial bodies revolve around the earth. To a practical navigator remaining on the earth, it is a lot easier to let it go at that and keep the old simple earth view, the view expounded in Leonardo da Vinci's down-to-earth advice that "small rooms or dwellings set the mind in the right path, large ones cause it to go astray."

With this thought I stand in the astrodome and shoot the stars. This is the highest branch of the navigator's art, the most reliable check he has on his dead reckoning once he is out beyond the sight of pilotage points and the hearing of radio beacons. It is nearly absolute. Although based on the earth view it is otherwise independent of the earth or anyone on earth beyond the airplane. It taps the cosmic relationship between earth and heavens, between the finite and the infinite.

How does it work? How can the navigator pick two or three stars, then take up his octant and in fifteen minutes fix his position within a radius of ten miles? How does knowing his way among the stars enable him to find his way to anywhere on earth?

A three-star fix is really three separate clues which, put together, give the navigator a pretty definite idea of where he is —

or, more exactly, where he was when he did the "shooting." That means that a flying navigator is seldom as sure of where he is as of where he was about a hundred miles back. This relative sureness is a kind of function of the speed of modern life itself.

It is occasionally possible in celestial navigating to do most of your calculating ahead of time by a process known as precomputation (computing on the basis of forecast assumptions), thus enabling you to know where you were a shorter distance back. But a disadvantage in this method is that you must first compute how long it is going to take you to compute. And if you should compute longer than you'd computed you'd compute, you must compute all over again.

A three-star fix is similar to taking your bearings in a city park at night from three tall lampposts. If you "shoot" one of the lamps with your octant and discover its light is 60° above the horizontal ground level, you know that you must be somewhere on the circle around the lamp from every point of which the light appears at that same 60° altitude. Thus, even if it is too dark to recognize paths, trees, or other landmarks around you in the park, if you can identify the lamp on a map of the park, you can figure out your distance from it and draw a circle with that distance as radius around the position of the lamp.

If you now shoot another lamp, you can plot yourself a second "circle of equal altitude" around the second lamp. Since you must be somewhere on both circles, your only possible position is at one of the points where the two circles meet, the point that is consistent with your dead reckoning.

The third lamp's circle is not usually essential, but if it also passes through the same point, you can be that much surer of exactly where you are.

So I swing my octant in the direction of Regulus and set it to the height of the star. I have wound up the instrument's averaging mechanism and now I press lever number three with the little finger of my right hand. The clockwork starts recording the altitude of Regulus' image in my eyepiece, balanced at exactly the same level as the luminescent bubble floating in kerosene in the octant's bubble chamber.

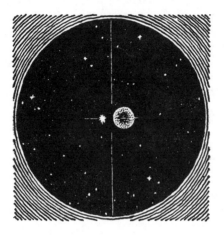

This bubble theoretically remains level, acting as an artificial horizon from which to measure the star's altitude. It would of course be possible to use the real horizon if that were visible, but the aerial navigator so seldom sees any real horizon while flying that the bubble has been found more practical. Besides, it saves having to make correction for one's height above the earth, which would influence the angle between a star and the real horizon.

It is not a hard trick to pick up, this star shooting. Once you have learned your stars you should be able to use the octant satisfactorily in a week. You just stand in the astrodome on your stool, choose a star, set your instrument to what you estimate its altitude to be, aim it, adjust it, and then start shooting: balancing bubble and star together.

When two minutes are up, this type of octant drops a screen across the field of vision, which tells you that the averaging mechanism has stopped. Immediately you observe the exact time by your hack watch and calculate the time of the middle of your period of observation: one minute ago.

Exactitude of time is of the essence of celestial navigation, be-cause every four seconds' error in time causes about a mile error in fixing your position. So it behooves you to reset your hack watch frequently by your pocket chronometer, which can be checked at least daily by radio time tick. The reason for the averaging mechan-ism in the octant is of course that the bubble is not as steady as the real horizon. It inevitably lurches about as the airplane yaws and porpoises in the sky, thereby making it necessary to observe a star over a period of time to average out the bubble's caprices.

Once you have recorded the exact heights of the three stars, you have some calculating to do. The principle of this is that you assume a position near where you think you actually are. You pick some spot in latitude and longitude that is handy to figure from and, using your air almanac and celestial tables, calculate what the heights of the three stars would have to be if you had observed them from this assumed place at the exact time you did your shooting.

Then, noting what differences there are between your computed heights and your actual observed heights, you can easily correct your assumed position into a real position, plotting on your map the circle of equal altitude for each star. Of course you don't need to draw the complete circles, which might go around the earth, but only the parts of them near where you are. For practical purposes these short pieces come out as straight lines, and the three of them form a triangle. The smaller the triangle the more accurate the fix and the center of the triangle can be considered your most prob-able true position.

It is easier to see the resemblance between this and the lamppost fix if you visualize the center of each circle of equal altitude as being exactly under its star. That center is called the substellar point and is the spot on earth nearest the star. It corresponds to the base of the lamppost, in this case a lamppost so high that, prac-tically speaking, it can be considered infinite.

Thus sitting at night in the black sky beneath the stars I see the heavens harnessed according to the mind of Ptolemy, all the stars at the same (infinite) distance from the earth. The sky is a

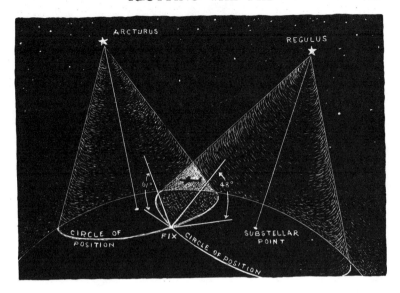

hollow sphere around me, studded with stars. It seems a kind of greater earth turned inside out.

Except for the sun and its satellites, which move along the general line of the ecliptic, all the stars are fixed in relation to the celestial co-ordinates just as islands and cities on earth are fixed on the terrestrial co-ordinates of latitude and longitude. As the earth rotates, the celestial sphere of Ptolemy with axis through the North Star appears to revolve toward the west around the earth — with the earth seemingly motionless at the hub of creation.

Once you grasp this ancient concept of the universe, celestial navigation becomes simple. Beneath every star at any given moment is a point on earth, as the Polynesian navigators well knew, and these substellar points move with their stars parallel to the lines of latitude, ever westward in a pattern so constant that its zodiacal forms of three thousand years ago are still recognizable today. You can find about fifty of the brighter stars thus listed in the air almanac, with their latitudes, and their longitudes in relation to Aries, the prime meridian of the sky, just as places on earth are listed in geography books in relation to the earth's prime meridian that runs through Greenwich, England.

So when I peek at the upper limb of the moon above my wing I remember that this very moon, which Ptolemy could almost touch, is in truth even now serving mankind as surely as a clock or a beacon. Along with radio and pilotage and dead reckoning it marks our fleeting furrow in the sky. It is a signpost for the postilion of a new age. It is still his who rides the near horse of the leaders — whose hands now grip the reins of space, whose feet fill the swinging stirrups of time.

Through
Wind and Cloud

4. Ocean of the Sky

A̲S THE AIRPLANE floated snugly in its dark fold of air I relaxed to my work with the confidence of thorough training. The mighty night wind moved by me like a shadow in a tunnel. I sensed the flecks of unseen cloud curving in to meet our wings, the mist slanting up to whet our blades.

The sky was a being and I a physician testing its health for the sake of my own. With my airspeed indicator I felt its pulse; I took its temperature, I read its altitudinal blood pressure, and timed the breathing of its wind.

In a realer sense it is quite easy to look upon the sky as a kind of greater ocean, the cities of Earth being on its sea floor looking up toward the nebulous surface somewhere above. If you think of the cirrus cloud level as the surface, and of birds and airplanes as fish swimming in these depths, the illusion is complete.

If we lived in the ocean of water we would drown. If we lived in the ocean of mud and earth and stone we would be buried. But instead we are in the third and highest ocean — the greatest of the three: the ocean of air.

The sky begins at our feet. We breathe it. We are actually crawling on the sea bottom of the heavens. We are the crabs of the airy depths.

Did you ever live near a large city airport and go to sleep at night hearing the airliners taking off one after another like a great wind blowing in consecutive gusts? Indeed it is a great wind, if man made, and it is more stirring than the intermittent thunder of a railroad line, for the roar is almost continuous.

It is a conscious introduction to time-space continuum: the yielding of the one-track earth thought of Newton to the multidimension relativity of Einstein. The planes all take off along the same runway into the same breeze, yet are bound for Chicago, Berlin, Cairo, and Karachi. Mysteriously, like corpuscles in the blood stream, they sort themselves out in flight and find their appointed ways.

Yes, the sky is more primitive, elemental, and somehow fiercer than the earth below. In the sky you cannot stop: to stop is to die. Even the helicopter and the hummingbird must spin and hover lest they fall. Even the balloon must drift with the wind, rising like a bubble, sinking like a sponge, moving as part of the volatile air itself — floating, drifting, gliding, sliding — ever given to the unseen power of air, air which is not the empty waste it seems but more ancient in its gaseousness, more vast and wild and wanton than anything the solid or liquid worlds ever knew.

Is it not significant that the last major exploratory goal of the earth to be gained was the summit of the highest mountain — that long after the great oceans and deserts and jungle had been crossed and even the poles conquered, the most skyward land remained stubbornly virgin to the foot of man? Indeed man lives in a sort of incubated schoolhouse: incubated because he is nicely balanced between the white-hot metal of subterranean layers below and the scorching vacuums of the ionosphere above, and a schoolhouse because it is divinely arranged to offer the maximum of educational experience. Most of this habitable stratum of learning is actually in the sky which is, to my thinking, the open book of knowledge, of revelation. And the more I live and fly, the more opportunities

I find in the sky — the more lessons and beauty and drama undreamed.

Islands sometimes literally pop up out of the wet sea, and volcanoes out of the earth, but these things are too rare for practical learning. And the gentle betweentime lessons of erosion, of slow-moving stones and ice and trees and sand do not compare with the drama of the heavens where mountains burst out of sweeping cloud oceans every day and ruthless thunderstorms and whirlwinds are ever aprowl looking for new places to vent their spleen.

As I sit on my stool, marking down the scant available data in my log — temperature —4°, airspeed 168, time 02:00 — I remember the year long ago when I went to sea as an A.B. seaman in the merchant marine. I had been in another dimension then. I had worked in the element of water, of water's creatures, and of sea air that is laden with water.

That was the past — my own past, but in a larger sense the past of man on earth. By taking to the air I have really only caught up with my own generation. It is what all the ocean-flying airmen of today have done. They are the ancient mariners in a new ocean, a much bigger and more potential ocean. If I had lived a generation earlier and had been of an age and occupation comparable to what I am at present, I would almost certainly be pacing the bridge of some sea-going surface vessel with a sextant in my hand. I would have been happy to touch a home port every two months and draw forty dollars in fortnightly wages instead of passing over the same ocean as I do today at twenty times the speed and ten times the wage.

The conquest of the new ocean of air has accelerated man's tempo of transport more in one generation than all his efforts of the previous thousand generations. Literally it is so. The schooner and the tramp steamer have shaken off their ancient crust of salt to sprout duralumin wings.

Less than a century ago the golden age of sailing ships was at its height and in 1865 there was staged a great deep-water race between five of the fastest tea clippers ever built: the Taeping, the Ariel, the Fiery Cross, the Taitsing, and the Serica. All cleared from Foo Chow, China, within two days of each other at the end of May. And ninety-nine days later the Taeping, the Ariel, and the Serica docked in London on the same tide, the other two only two days behind. They had all sailed 16,000 miles at an average speed of about six knots.

Two centuries earlier the heavy-laden Mayflower averaged only 2½ knots on her 95-day voyage to America, not even as fast as medieval Columbus on his 70-day voyage or Captain Bligh in the ill-fated Bounty at the end of the eighteenth century.

Our present-day antiquated flying boxcars are only a little bit longer than most of the old sailing ships — the C–54 ninety-four feet nose to tail as against ninety-three feet over all for the Santa María, ninety for the Bounty, and about the same for the Mayflower — but the difference between these two mediums of travel is actually so great that no man could appreciate it who has not traveled by both methods. As the salt sailor, wiping the rust from his chisel on the forecastle head, can hardly know the feel of the flying pilot whom he hears droning above the overcast — so the pilot, viewing the sunlit cloud meadows below him from his winged workshop, can little appreciate the wallowing struggles of the sailor. The two oceans — of water and of air — are verily oceans apart.

From an airplane the salt ocean of water is half legendary and often remains unseen during an entire crossing. It might as well be a desert or a forest for all it affects the aerial navigator. To him it is but an imaginary obstacle, a problem of a few hours to be solved. It is like a map on the classroom wall. He does not go to bed and sleep over it, nor does he eat over it but a sandwich and an orange. It is gone in an afternoon. It is so fleeting and remote that he forgets the rough hands that pull the ropes below, heaving up or down to every mood of blue Neptune. Their little ocean is no concern of his. His own ocean — the ocean of air carpeted with fleecy clouds — is the real, the great ocean.

If the sailor sees substance in his dark waves which the pale air has not, it must be attributed to his lowly view. For whence comes the wet sea's strength, its moods, its shape, its very color? Which really is the master, which the slave?

To those who have lived in both oceans the answer leaves small question. In the end it is the sky that holds the reins to Neptune's harness. Do not the waves get their actual form, their heft and hulk from the sky's winds? Is not the sea's blue face a reflection of the fathomless blue of the heavens? Is not the salty petulance of the lower ocean, its ensuing calm, its sudden towering fury but ultimate obedience to the sovereignty of the sky?

Important of course in the habitudes of the lower sea are its currents: the Gulf Stream, the Labrador, the Humboldt and Kuro Siwo, the West Wind Drift, the Northeast Monsoon Drift, the Guinea, Agulhas, Benguela, Brazil, Australian and Mozambique currents and all the smaller charted arteries that carry warm or cold water to many parts of the world, stabilizing the climates of the maritime nations. These currents are staid, orderly flows that are marked on conservative charts and are predictable in temperature, direction, and speed. They seem to the flyer as reliable as plow horses. And about as dull.

But what of the sky's currents? If any mystery remains to the wanderings of the slow waters below, how much more mysterious are the airy channels of the upper ocean — so incomparably the mightier, the moodier, the more inspiring. The wind byways of our great sky ocean are in fact so violent and capricious that they are unchartable to all practical purposes. They are wont to reverse their direction without warning and may change in velocity from 100 knots to dead calm in the space of two hours or drop their temperature from a comfortable 50° F. above zero to a biting 20° F. below in the course of an evening. Nor are these air currents less extravagant in dryness and wetness. And they are three dimensional: they blow straight up and straight down as wantonly as north or south or west. Can Neptune beneath show anything

to match? Anything so vital, so stirring to the spine?

It is an old argument but an interesting one, and it can bear modern elaboration. Some physicists the other day were studying Krakatoa Volcano, near Java, which had its famous explosion in 1883. They checked the British Royal Society's records and found that this mighty eruption not only blew up the whole mountaintop but sent air waves seven times around the earth. And also sea waves at least a few times around.

The scientists had at first supposed that the sea waves, traveling slower and by more roundabout routes, would not keep up with the air waves. But oddly enough both waves were reported to have arrived simultaneously at Panama, at San Francisco, and the English Channel.

Careful further study of the perplexing evidence showed that only the air waves could be a direct effect of the volcano's explosion, and that the sea waves recorded on tide gauges in such distant places as England must have been mainly induced by the air disturbance. In other words, Krakatoa had given the world dramatic proof that invisible events in the sky do definitely change the face of the deep below.

The view of earth from the sky is of course significantly different from the opposite and more provincial upward view from the surface. As you gaze down upon the earth from the high air you can see fine lines drawn on the ground, complex cross-hatches, circles, networks, and even tiny corpuscular dots flowing along some of the larger arterial ways. Were it not that you yourself were so recently part of that strange little world down there, how could you know that those lines are roads, those dots machines on wheels that move like living creatures yet are only tools of a still smaller life?

It is just as though the driftmeter were a microscope and you looking through it upon amoebae in a drop of water or a slice of air. How fantastic that those specks of cars could really be made up of thousands of parts not grown from seeds but carefully manufactured and assembled by remote inscrutable creatures who also do such things as write poetry, watch television screens, fall in love, domesticate birds, study atoms a billion times smaller than themselves, ride horses, play violins, worship God!

Looking upon the sky's own littler beings is very similar and no less pregnant in mystery, for who can yet begin to know their true story? There are the flying beetles, the itinerant moths and flies, the tiny gnats. These may cap the highest mountains in their airy wanderings, and some have been found twelve miles above the earth. A few species are actually more active when a mile high than when close to the ground, and even to the limitations of their size they are parasites of the sky.

Why indeed are butterflies so much smaller than buzzards? Why all insects so small — a smallness that enables them to move safely anywhere in the sky's ocean without danger from falling? It is a limitation imposed by the very substance of the air itself, by the need of all living cells, all beings to partake of sky chemicals. Insects are small because they have never learned to circulate their "blood" or to breathe with lungs. Therefore none of their body cells can be more than about a quarter of an inch from the surface since oxygen cannot be absorbed fast enough to a greater depth. In effect an insect's whole body surface is a kind of lung — the air around it a kind of blood.

Human breath, like the earth's breath, the wind, was once called *anima* or spirits. But that was before the time of one Evangelista Torricelli, Galileo's pupil who helped invent the airplane by proving the existence of air. The young Torricelli could not swallow the then prevailing idea that the wind is ghost stuff, a kind of spiritual manifestation. Neither did he have to fear the sky would fall down. He believed it already was down.

After great labor he demonstrated in 1643 that air has weight and substance, thus removing much of the popular terror of the sky, and emancipating the whole idea of flying.

Though we still use the expression "light as air," it is something of a deceptive phrase in view of the now known fact that the atmosphere of the earth is like a great drift of snow five hundred miles deep and weighing more than 5,000,000,000,000,000 tons. Gravity thus holds the airy sky to the earth with such a fierce hug that very few of its molecules can hope to escape. In order to do so, it has been calculated, an air molecule would have to attain an upward speed of seven miles a second, rather a lot more than even the rocket makers have so far achieved. On the moon, by contrast, a mere 1¼ m.p.s. is considered escape velocity — which largely explains why the moon has less atmosphere than the earth.

Besides packing plenty of weight, however, the more tangible part of the earth's sky turns out to be rich in unseen substance. It is jam-packed with life and adventure, with collision and things beyond the dreams of seagulls and stewardesses. In an ounce of air there are more than 1,000,000,000,000,000,000,000,000 molecules boiling and moiling about, each pulsing with electron orbits, buttoned with mesons, figuratively bursting with excitement. Most of them might be visualized as occupying the shapes of cigars or dumbbells or eggs, but so small and moving at such terrific speed that they are invisible even to an electron microscope.

Their violence of course is basic to the sky and actually makes it blue by scattering the correspondingly short light waves at the blue-violet end of the spectrum, while the longer, steadier red waves refuse to reflect back to our eyes.

An idea of the potency of air molecules can be gleaned from the fact that as they move in suspension, three-dimensionally, they continually collide with each other at ordinary temperatures some billions of times a second. They move on the average about as fast as today's swiftest air transport planes, yet in vibrating, zigzag courses, ramming each other every one hundred millionth of an inch of the way.

Most of these molecules are named nitrogen or oxygen, elemental vibrant beings. A few are sleepy argon, lungy carbon dioxide, wet hydrogen, with an occasional odd duck of neon, krypton, helium, xenon, or pungent ozone out of the wake of lightning. They are much and sundry, these molecules of air, for air is not a chemical compound. It is a mixture of gases, a blend of volatile liquors, stirred by the tireless spoon of wind.

The resulting perpetual diffusion of variegated molecules is of course not only basic nature in the sky but part of the worldwide law of entropy or tendency toward ultimate disorder. This is just as definite a law as the law of relativity or gravity or inertia or any other orderly law. But it is the law of disorder and it says in effect that any spontaneous changes in air, water, gravy, gravel, or any other physical medium must naturally be in the direction of disorder or mixture, final equilibrium being reached when the disorder is complete, so complete in disorderliness that it is statistically perfect, a grand impeccable homogeneous hash spread out everywhere possible with not a trace of orderliness to be found anywhere in it.

The motion of any single molecule thus is said to be similar to the random staggering of a drunkard who doesn't know whether he is coming or going. It might seem hopeless at first to predict where the drunkard is actually going to wind up, but if you are a statistician or understand the law of probability you can see at least a chance of figuring out where, if there were a thousand drunks, the average of them would end up. Taking it statistically the composite drunkard walks zigzaggily from his starting point on the average a number (D) of feet (measured in one straight line) equal to the average length (d) of each approximate course that he walks times the square root of their number (n). Thus $D = d\sqrt{n}$. Beautiful stuff, mathematics! And this goes for staggering molecules too — and probably for stars. It is the equation of disorder behind all diffusion. It explains the definite rate at which a drop of ink diffuses through still water, or a puff of soft coal smoke in a lazy sky.

If your housekeeping seems more heroic when it is put in the light of conquest over the universal law of entropy, remember that there are undoubtedly other things about the sky that will give you new appreciation of some of the common ingredients of the household. Dust, for instance, is one of the most important forms assumed by the sky's molecules. The housewife is not trained to approve of dust yet she actually could not live without it. Nor is there such a thing as dust-free air in nature. Without some sort of dust to serve as nuclei for condensation the sky would always be cloudless, it would never rain, and the earth would soon be parched for lack of fresh water. Even the tiny particles of salt dust tossed aloft by ocean waves are invaluable in condensing rain, which takes this means of returning salt to the sea refreshed with the wind's blessing.

One need not think of dust as necessarily dirty or something that needs to be cleaned up. The reverse may be true, for dust-laden air can be about as pure as anything else in this finite world and even has been used for soap. Air in fact has about as much purifying power as the sea, if less concentrated, and many a shirt gets more of a cleansing on the line than in the tub. Next time your hands are dirty just try washing them in air instead of water. Take a good strong breeze if there's one around: it dispatches the dirt faster. Mohammed taught his followers to wash in sand storms or plain sand or dust when water was scarce. Straight still air is slower in effect but will do the job if you give it time.

The viruses are kinds of molecules found everywhere in air, and their varieties and shapes are legion. They look under the electron microscope like string, caviar, beads, boats, and popcorn. They are the smallest, most elusive form of life, and bring to mankind epidemics, problems, and benefits mysterious. They usually reproduce their own kind, yet their mutations in offspring make them ever unpredictable, perhaps a tool of God to keep doctors and humanity unrutted in their thinking.

And there are the protozoa, more complex, higher creatures of the empty sky. Some of these are ancient prototypes of the airplane, having microscopic propellers which start to spin when they make contact with the starter force of moist air. Humidity is their fuel. When they go dry these unicellular animals enclose themselves in hangarlike sheaths or cysts and remain dormant in the dust — dust which is now part of the earth, now caught up by the wind and blown around the world, the life still within it, floating, flying, sleeping. When at last the winged dust is dissolved in rain or water the cysts open again, allowing the protozoa to emerge, awake, say "contact," and resume their errant spinning lives — riding upward in the clouds, swimming downward in the rain.

Some of these creatures are fourteen-pointed stars, some pulsing hexahedrons, some shaped like spaghetti, honeycombs, doughnuts, pretzels, hourglasses, seahorses, roulette wheels, pyramids, boomerangs — everything and more than the molecules they are made of — some bubbles within bubbles, the inner bubbles the offspring of the outer, so that when they grow to be as big as Mother they automatically burst out of her to venture abroad on their own, minutes later becoming bubble mothers themselves with new inner bubble babies in their turn — thus, by inner-to-outer bubble leapfrog, throbbing the generative rhythm of the sky.

Nor less remarkable among the air dwellers are the flying lichen seedlings built of fungi and algae in the form of tiny globular farms, the fungi farmers actually herding the algae livestock on which they live, sometimes riding irregular masses of inert dust for months on end, again blowing free, intermittently changing in magnetic polarity, occasionally getting doused in the floating droplet of a cloud.

Beyond such superficial details of air and moisture, science has not yet illumined much of the hidden life of the upper kingdom. Although air has been "duplicated" chemically in a laboratory retort, no one so far has been able to make sky life grow in artificial air until at least a tiny portion of natural air was added. The real sky thus still holds the secret of life — a secret not difficult for it to keep while man knows hardly the first thing about it.

To the denizens of the deep sea, the hazard of buoyancy is probably as real and ever present as the hazard of falling in the sky. Once a deep-sea fish ventures so high that his internal pressure begins to inflate him there may be some real danger of his falling upwards to the surface, which would be like having a bomb explode in his stomach — surely no easier fate than that in store for the boy who falls off a cliff.

This brings up the question of which way is down, or which way is the better: up or down? These are moot questions in the sky.

To the earth lubber it is easy: "Down is down. Down is toward the earth." To the man in the moon, down is toward the moon. Out in space the choice is more a matter of viewpoint, of taste. Even in the near sky, flying in clouds, men cannot tell up from down without gyroscopic instruments which it took long years to devise. Even some of the birds dread blind-flying and have been known to get upset when caught in dense clouds.

You have probably heard the classic "incident" of the army pilot who early in World War I overtook an enemy flying a single-seater in a cloud. In a flash of inspiration he rolled over upside down before he was seen and thus inverted flew right on by the enemy as if nothing were abnormal. The startled enemy pilot, having neither instruments nor much confidence, quite naturally concluded that he himself must be upside down, and so rolled over also — whereupon his seat belt broke and he fell to his death.

The story illustrates a very real problem in the sky where it is well known that any airliner in the fog can fly in steeply banked circles around and around in one spot without detection by its passengers, simply by replacing down-pulling gravity by an equivalent amount of sideways-pulling inertia which, as Einstein postulates, is basically the same thing. That is the why of the artificial horizons, the bank and turn indicators, that are part of every modern airliner's instrument panel. If you still don't understand them just ask a bird, or join the air force.

In the long run the indispensable criterion of down is the direction of gravity force. It is the seemingly gentle force that we overcome every time we take a step or throw a ball or fly an airplane, but it is relentless and universal and knows no compromise with clocks or calendars or gravestones. It is the builder of suns and planets, it propels the wind and the rain, and it decides the rate of settling in the sea, in the sky, even in the solid earth.

The rate of settling is another of the fundamental factors determining the behavior of objects or creatures floating in any fluid or semi-fluid whether it is a body sinking through water or an airplane flying in air. A grain of coarse sand may fall a foot through sea water in about a second, while a very fine particle of clay may take half a year to settle the same distance. It is a matter of weight in relation to resistance. At the rate of the fine particle of clay some materials have taken 15,000 years to sink from the ocean's surface to its deepest bottom. Old sailors say that the corpses of men drowned at sea sink more and more slowly as they reach great depths until eventually they cease their downward motion altogether and float to eternity in some eerie intermediate level presided over by Davy Jones. Although neither gravediggers nor scientists subscribe to this fascinating idea, something of the sort really happens in the case of the sinking shells of tiny dead coccoliths, spent plankton, and many of the semi-microscopic sea creatures whose myriad remains descend like slow-motion snowflakes, steadily, ever so gradually yet perpetually, toward the ooze-covered sink holes of the deep. The ordinary sea bottoms are covered with this pelagic sediment, a creamy colorful paste of limy disintegration, but they say there is little of it in the very deepest areas of the ocean floor for the reason that the tiny descending skeletons have time to dissolve completely before arrival, thus becoming part of the very sea water itself.

Something of the same obviously must occur in the ocean of the sky though it is less easily observed owing to the highly turbulent nature of the medium. The "glow stratum" emitted by Krakatoa in 1883, for example, traveled many times around the world, completing one circuit in thirteen days. It rose some twenty miles, then settled down at the rate of a mile a fortnight (two inches a minute), for about five months, gradually slowing as the larger particles were sieved out by weight, the last of the innumerable microscopic bits never reaching earth at all.

Likewise, aerobiologists speak of the "biologic stratification" of microbes in the sky, of visible spore ceilings, of the fall of bacteria at cold fronts, discontinuity surfaces of tropospheric life, pollen counts of air masses, a flat cloud of alternaria spores at nearly 5000 feet, resting on a definite ragweed haze at 4000 feet. Some of the crusts and corpses of the smallest flying insects must float on the winds for decades, slowly dissolving into the actual chemistry of the air — perhaps adding that magic touch of life which has ever escaped analysis. Yet larger bodies and wishbones and dust, feathers and engine oil and aluminum rivets fall finally to earth, each at its appointed speed through the air levels to return once more to the great body of our solid planet.

Indeed as the sea has its graveyards, its debris of bones and sunken hulls on the bottom seldom seen by men, so has the sky its graves. And these are almost as little seen. Flying about the country and across the world you may occasionally notice a slight scar on some hilltop where an erring pilot met his fate in 1952, but you more likely did not recognize it for what it was. The twisted metal had been carted off and the weeds and trees had begun to heal the scorched earth.

The sky has its Davy Jones too. He is Icarus, the ghost son of Daedalus, the mythical Greek architect who built the labyrinth for King Minos of Crete. Ever since his fabulous ditching in the Icarian Sea east of Sicily, they say he has been grumping about the sky-swept earth, ever yearning to ease his loneliness in upper limbo by snagging fresh victims from out the blue.

Thinking of air travel, the idea of paths in the sky comes naturally to mind. It is intriguing, the thought of aerial high roads, trailways in the trackless void of air. Fish in the sea of course often leave wakes, and not only the defensive ink or luminesence of the sea robin and the squid. The faintly oily trail of the whale is known as glip, a word from whaling days which should not be allowed to die. And there is a kind of meteoric glip in the sky too, the almost invisible trail of dust and ash behind a blazing metallic visitor to the earth. Any moving body in air makes its wake of turbulence just like the water eddies behind a sea vessel. Although this air wake is normally invisible it is quite tangible and all pilots feel it at times — either when crossing close behind another plane or when turning around on their own track. If you have ever put one wing straight down in a vertical turn and made a complete circle back to your starting place you would remember the bump that came when you ran through your wake. It's as definite as a thank-ye-ma'am on a wagon road and gives you a new understanding of the sky.

If you think I am exaggerating, you should have been at the Indianapolis airport two years ago when a small Beechcraft made the mistake of coming in to land too close behind a big multi-engined plane. When about seventy-five feet above the ground, the smooth-gliding Beechcraft was suddenly flipped into a right vertical bank by no apparent force, and started to fall. Though the astonished pilot prevented a complete overturn, he could not keep his plane from sideslipping quickly to the ground, where it cartwheeled into a crumpled heap with serious injury to all three persons aboard.

Sound and smell are other things of which air paths may be formed, and some of the sky's creatures have probably learned to follow them: an owl tracing the young bat's vibrant flit, a virus threading the sleazy wing prints of a thrip.

When one thinks on it, the sky is as scarred with crisscross tracks and trails as a city park, and much deeper — for the sky has many skins. It is in fact a kind of volatile onion. It sheathes the solid earth in global layers, mainly invisible but as real as rocks, and every bit as interesting in its topographical features.

Like the land and sea the sky has numb spots of poorer circulation, roughly similar to the Black Sea below it which is stagnant but for its feeble trickle through the Bosporus and understandably flavored with hydrogen sulphide, the gaseous harbinger of decay. Of such the sky's Sahara High and the Indian Dome, areas of tropical stagnation, might be examples. Here a lost balloon could wander for days like a bottle drifting on the Sargasso Sea before it entered a more vital part of the vast flux of the sky like the blustery North Atlantic Low or the great Antarctic Trough that extends completely around the globe above the endless graybeard seas.

The inconstancy of air pressure and unevenness of wind of course mold similar patterns of pressure and motion in the responsive water below them, an inch of drop in the barometer signalling a corresponding rise of a foot in sea level.

Where high land masses add an extra pull to gravity the air and sea may both be drawn shoreward as happens in the upper Bay of Bengal where the ocean level has been found to be several feet higher than normal because of the Himalaya Mountains and the Plateau of Tibet. Again where winds are long and strong the water always moves passively with them, partly from direct wind pressure, partly because both air and sea respond to the same great forces of the turning earth. And thus perpetually the solid mass of the globe spins on, while the moiling gases of the sky struggle to keep up with it in trade winds and prevailing westerlies (which we will look at next chapter as a natural circulation of energy) and the more sluggish currents of the wet ocean below trail forlornly after, dragging their dark depths ever hopelessly over the primeval ooze of the drain bottom of the world.

As we go upward through the air's onion layers of course the temperature drops for a few miles. But then about eight miles up it stops getting cooler and stays around 67° F. below zero. That level where the temperature ceases falling is known as the tropopause. It marks the bottom of the cold, clear, cloudless part of the stratosphere, which is the stable level of future flight, the place where you can forget thunderstorms and turbulence and blind flying, the height where your flight plan practically ceases to be a gamble. The stratosphere, extending up to sixty miles, includes a level around fifteen to twenty miles so rich in ozone it is sometimes called the ozonosphere. By about thirty miles, because of ozone absorption of sun rays, the temperature has risen to plus

170° F. There lies the land of twilight which is really nothing but sunshine reflected off the scarce molecules of the upper sky at a reputed average height of thirty-seven miles.

Some fifteen miles higher comes the colder level where radio waves mysteriously begin to bounce fifty-odd miles back down to earth. All the atmosphere above this is called ionosphere, a strange hot, etheric habitat of meteors and auroras. This raw outer skin of the onion is the earth's front-line insulation against the scorching blast of the sun and the never ending hail of charged particles and objects from outer space. Little is yet known of the ionosphere but the evidence is that it gets hotter again as you go farther from the earth out into our unseen sun shield — some think as hot as 2000° F. a few hundred miles up, an onion sheath of fire completely encasing the earth and visible only on occasions of auroras and the rarer phenomena of the heavens.

Here there is so little air that it does not behave like air at all and temperature has a different meaning. The molecules of nitrogen and oxygen no longer bounce off one another every ten thousandth of an inch of their way, but move several feet between collisions. Any solid body in this giddy layer therefore can move at terrific speed almost without resistance, as if running through a room containing a couple of random bouncing ping-pong balls instead of the familiar sea-level condition of air molecules packed solid to the ceiling like bricks.

The sky from the ionosphere looks black and the stars are brighter by day than you have ever seen them from earth by night. Looking down from up there the earth is strangely lighter in color than its surrounding sky, and so far below you that all the clouds seem to be lying belly to ground. The roundness of the planet is very apparent too, and details like cities and rivers scarcely discernible in the hazy depths. If no man has yet actually been up that high there is food for imagination aplenty in photographs snapped from rockets careering a hundred miles above the earth, and sundry other evidence and practical comparisons.

Looking down from lower levels is of course more meedful if you want to see the real earth, for as even the mighty long-range telescopes of the present have not unveiled the first mysteries of shrouded Venus nor the second secrets of naked Mars so it behooves us to read the book of life from range befitting it. The earth is an open page to the seeing eye and its fabric from the near sky can reveal the mysteries of the magic carpet.

I was raised to think the magic carpet a planing rug, a vehicle of Arabian nights to wing fancy on its way. Yet now I see — as was not given to story tellers of old — that the real magic carpet lies spread out beneath my feet. In short it is the earth itself, its magic revealed beyond ancient ken — the homespun weave of reality.

Indeed the warp of the world drifts along to slake my eyes — valleys with low wisps of fog, skeleton bones of mountains rising out of their forest blanket folds — farm patterns and quilted gardens, the contours of cultivated hills, the radial avenues of cities — woof of life on earth.

Here is a perfect volcano cone rising out of a flat sea of clouds. What does it mean? Its graceful beauty of line tells of Oriental calm, of hidden activity within. Yes — Fujiyama, the flyer's first glimpse of Japan.

As one hums in over the coast to Tokyo Bay the crowded narrow valleys below with their tight-packed paddy fields speak plainly of the Japanese rice farmers who created them — of their small stature, their economy, and the narrow competition of their lives. Even their rows of drying rice straw are visible as tiny rodlike bacteria ranged along the borders, epitome of hand industry, minute, traditional, inexorable.

There is a cloud of dust rising into the hot sky. Many dots move across the flat earth a mile below, dodging among the scattered low trees. Even had I not been here before I must recognize it as Africa — the bush country of the central south — herds of wildebeest and hartebeest migrating for pasturage — a picture of the hot, the dry, the untamed.

Now I see a green, matted mass down under lazy puff cumulus clouds, here a wide calm band of blue water. No need to check the map: it is the Amazon jungle, the endless green mattress of vine-clad trees, alive with army ants, anteaters, iguanas, wild pigs, voracious piranhas. The great river has no shore: it just flows in under the trees. Small rivers in turn flow into it but you can't see them, for the jungle folds together over their heads. This is expressive country, expressive of mystery, impenetrable, sultry, feverish.

Here we are above a gray-blue ocean. Microscopic gulls circle over the whitecaps. Long streamers of white spindrift lace the moving surface, revealing the direction and strength of the wind. Eloquently the scene speaks of the North Atlantic — the Viking seas.

And near by a rugged coastline, bleak shores — a barren, volcanic land without trees, only here and there a tiny patch of man-kept green: Iceland, like a piece of the moon come out of the deep.

Of such are the riches of the earth as given to those who fly.

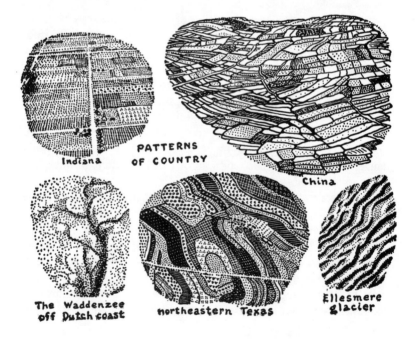

Indiana

PATTERNS
OF COUNTRY

China

The Waddenzee
off Dutch coast

northeastern Texas

Ellesmere
glacier

There is no end to it. It goes on and on — nor is it monotonous like a tiresome book or a dull movie. It packs the wallop of reality. It is the itching world beneath your feet.

You soon grow to know cities like a raven, from above. Some are a haphazard jumble of streets, like Boston or London. Some are built on circles, like Moscow, Paris, Washington. Some are squared off methodically into thousands of rectangular blocks like Chicago. Some have huge wharves sticking out toothlike into the harbors and rivers — San Francisco, New York, New Orleans — city teeth for biting shipload crumbs of sustenance from the ocean.

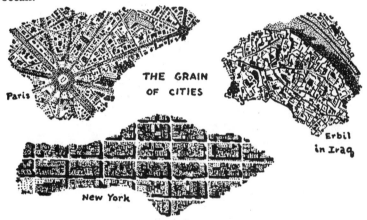

THE GRAIN OF CITIES

Paris

Erbil in Iraq

New York

A new meaning of architecture comes from flying. The little towns of the western plains, which farmers see dominated by a grain elevator standing head and shoulders over them, look from the air like nothing but flat grid patches along a railroad track — for all buildings to the flyer tend to fade into the larger pattern of streets.

The swimming pools of the Hollywood Hills, tucked away behind high walls, are so hidden from earthview that Los Angeles pedestrians know of them only by reputation — yet the secret has no chance against the airplane, for they are the outstanding feature from the sky: dazzling gems of pale blue set against the dark brown and green of the earth, sapphires in their hundreds sparkling under the sun.

New England towns by contrast, though plain to see on earth, are virtually invisible from the air when the trees are in leaf. They are nothing but slender white church spires peeking up out of a verdant sea of elms. In fact the whole of New England is a wilderness from the air with only rare little clearings here and there. I remember the remark made by an Englishman coming to New York for the first time. We had flown down from Newfoundland across Maine and Massachusetts and were only fifteen minutes from LaGuardia Airport. Gazing out the window upon the perpetual woods of Connecticut he frowned and said, "I say, when do we get to civilization?"

Perspective from the air is sometimes confusing even when you should be used to it. The skyscape seems to be continuously revolving on both sides, up and down, the stars remaining still while the near clouds swing by on invisible hinges of space. Another airplane at a great distance moves with jerks, even twinkles like a star or lunges like the setting sun. The curved paths of snowflakes upward then outward across the windshield conform more to inscrutable eddies than to textbook logic. Sometimes it is almost impossible to tell which way smoke is blowing when we are flying close above it, because our own motion is an uncertain factor in the apparent motion of the smoke. The same with blowing trees, with small planes that seem to go sideways or backward, with wild animals running in circles, clouds whizzing against the wind, or the moon swooping past your shoulder. Once I saw a pigmy two feet high pushing a toy wheelbarrow along a foot path toward a shack in the woods. But as I got a second look I saw a horse and some chickens, just as small in proportion as the pigmy, and I realized that the shack was really a large barn with huge trees around it and the pigmy a six-foot man pushing a full-sized wheelbarrow along a road. I was flying three times higher than I had realized.

It is surprising how much can be seen from the air, how much more territory is within practical eye-shot than when you stand on the ground, even on a hilltop. Which may shed light on the phenomenal hunting ability of the falcon and the eagle.

Thinking of the eagle brings to mind the time I flew alone over Chicago in a tiny Aeronca, two and a half miles up, and looked for my own house in that teeming metropolis below. It was like reading a map. At last I picked out the house, and behold — a flashing speck of white in one small back yard, my back yard! As I found out afterward, my wife had recognized my tailwag signal and was waving a sheet at me. I had picked out one woman while in plain view of a city of three million people. I was an eagle spotting a mouse or a drop of blood in the snow, a dot of warmth — visual response, a function of verticality.

New meanings of cosmic events also come to you at high altitudes — events like the turning of the earth in relation to the sun. Suddenly you notice that the "shades of night" rise at dusk instead of falling as the poets used to think. A little after sunset you can see it: the earth's shadow rising in the east and steadily mounting the sky. You can see it from 15,000 feet as easily as looking at a cloud shadow from a hill. Against the hazy lavender of afterglow over the eastern horizon it rises in blue, a slightly lighter blue than the sea, the great mammose hood of night looming upward to reveal again the timeless truth of the stars.

One can get this fresh sense of the sphericity of the earth even from lower flight levels, I find, and without requiring much imagination. When crossing the Pacific you can count the longitude meridians, a degree every twenty minutes, going east or west, watching an atoll pop up over the edge ahead, pass, and fade over the rim behind. It's almost like running your finger around a globe.

After looking at flat maps one is apt to think of a country like the United States as flat, forgetting it is part of a sphere, that when New Englanders look straight up they look at an angle 40° different from Californians. If you think that is not much of an angle, try walking up a 40° hill and remember that's the angle of the other end of the country. To visualize it right you have to think of the piece of earth's crust that is the United States as a great curved hunk of fender off a car, a wide gabbock of watermelon rind.

It is a surprisingly empty country too, considering it is the home of the most powerful nation on earth: hundreds of miles of deserts and plains and mountains with scarcely a shack in sight. It makes one pause and consider: whereof is America's strength? It reminds me of the famous Battle of the Atlantic fought during World War II. I sailed and flew over that battleground literally scores of times during the height of the fighting yet my remembrance of it is nothing but a great calm of emptiness, a thousand miles of blue ocean and neither a ship nor a soul in sight.

But truth is seldom so simple for despite the seeming emptiness, the life scattered so thinly down there holds its fast grip on the planet and even the remote bits of it turn out to be knit together with a mental and spiritual webbing the like of which no earthly agent of destruction has been able to approach.

See the chips that are boats in that harbor there, the bugs that are cows in yon field, the delicate planned geometry of the corn and the rye. Notice the rippled dunes of the desert, the paths among them, the wandering arroyos like veins on the withered arm of earth. What is that distant spark? A spangle of human hope that turns out to be sunshine reflected off an aluminum barn. See the matchstick rows of telephone poles bearing invisible dendrites of enlightenment and love. Behold the windmill reaching up to draw fresh strength from out the sky!

Can't you see the oneness of it all? The lonely specks of Diesel trucks a mile apart filing across the great Mohave — a hundred minds, a hundred miles, with a single purpose — parading on Highway 66, spouting their long palls of smoke like sternwheelers on the Mississippi.

From the sky we see all this — the work, the service, the faith. And there is beauty there for the eye that sees it. The three-step combine that draws a line of light buff across the dark wheat field is man's brash paintbrush at work on the canvas God loaned him for his first lesson in art. That pipeline crew has a piece of red chalk. That highway gang draws in charcoal. That team clearing fire lanes marks in crayon green. See them draw their little lines of wit across the breathing blackboard of the world.

Life is like that down there. The living map is a moving picture being continuously redrawn by man, sometimes by beast or insect — or accident of flood or fire. It is a sighing, stirring thing — a chalky talky world.

Contour plowing for instance — a relatively new idea to many — is fast changing the look of the earth in rolling country of the United States, in parts of India and Europe. In the steep hills it has long been there — as in the graceful terraced rice fields of Malaya and Japan that reflect the hues of sunlight like stained-glass windows in a cathedral. But the gentler country is getting it now, as a woman adopting a more becoming hairdo. Straight or slant lines, each farm for itself, have quietly become whole counties with a single scheme — beautiful curves and whorls of line, a permanent wave, a living contour map etching each hill, each gentle grade in hachures of human footprints and sweat.

I can see it everywhere, this new face of topographic grace. I can see where neighbors got together on it. The ideas met right there, a warm blend of line. And I see even plainer where they failed. Sometimes there is an obvious argument — a clash of line, an explosive discord where everything is broken at the fence. Like a gypsy reading family fortunes off their washlines before she knocks on the door, the flying man has insight into more than you'd think of the inner workings of his kind.

He feels the conservatism in the much settled look of the neat farmland of England, the canny caution of tight Scottish stone-walls, the economy of well-preserved French dairy farms, the industry of smoky German factories. He feels melancholy in the gray-blue of the Hell Stretch across grizzled western Pennsylvania — relaxation in the easy cattle plains of Texas — gaiety in the salad colors of Hawaiian shores. In his eyes are "all the corners of the earth, and the strength of the hills is his also."

And he looks on the earth below with much more than a tourist interest. He is not an amateur. He has business with the country.

He must look at the landscape for landing possibilities: would that
field do? Or that dirt road in a pinch? His eyes are restless for
clues of wind and whereabouts: that smoke is blowing southward,
it will be cold tonight . . . Guess I could follow that railroad
to Springfield. He reads the clouds and the river for weather and
considers the visibility in the smog.

The country from the air is a face, and the plain a palm. Its
character is revealed in every wrinkle, every twinkle. The expression is the mood of the people, of cattle nature, of tree nature
— in its whole, of God Himself.

You can even see underground and undersea. So many aerial
photographs have exposed the outlines of long buried ruins that
archeologists are taking to flying as a standard technique of discovery. And geologists and prospectors now take off to look for
the telltale yellow streaks of uranium deposits from the sky, as they
looked yesterday for the subtle clues of diamonds and gold. Engineers aloft can better check the advance of erosion, or spot the
slight greenth that may be their only tip to water in the desert.
Fishermen use the sky to spot schools of tuna, and the tropical
maritime chartmakers to keep track of the beautiful undersea dunes
of shifting sand, the valleys in blue and the hills in green that
have always been so treacherous to ships.

The easiest country of all to fly is probably the flat American
Midwest where not only can you land in almost any field if necessary but the section lines laid off in roads on the earth are a living
page from a geography book, actual latitude and longitude lines
breathing there beneath you. The farms were surveyed on the
exact dimensions of the quarter section, 160 acres, the historic
pioneer homestead. It is a true-life blueprint based on the equator
and the Greenwich meridian, a plan of living drawn first on paper,
second on the earth — a theory devised before much of the
country was seen — an idea made flesh to dwell among us.

If you want to fly exactly west just follow any road or fence.
Duck soup. If you want to know how fast you're going, count the
seconds between crossroads: 10 seconds means 180 m.p.h. Groundspeed on a platter. Not like the picturesque but puzzling east where

the road map is as capricious as spaghetti, where you practically skin your elbows on power poles running slantwise and scrape your belly getting off the fields.

Ever westward march the towns — grid patch after grid patch like footprints creeping over the map by day, like trays of twinkling jewels by night — beads on that string of railroad, tiaras crowning the hills, necklaces curving through the valleys. Many western towns are symmetrically cut gems: square, diamond-shaped, octagonal. At night they stand out joyfully amid the dark cold stretches of the plains, each a brave statement of faith, an inscription out of the void, a spiritual symbol like the Christmas tree in the poor man's house.

The daintiness of those tiny street lights arranged down there is enchantment incarnate. At first glance you see a child's toy town on the nursery floor: chalk lines for roads and tracks, sugarlump houses. But when you look again and remember that it is all several miles below you and peopled by hundreds and thousands like yourself — that those sparks are moving cars with men and women in them — that those little squares of bluish light are roaring factories, those white rectangles large buildings — this a hospital, that a hotel — that there is pain and anger and laughter there, babies being born and people dying and words of suspicion uttered, looks of love, deeds of tenderness, prayers reaching like glass girders unseen to God, it takes on meaning like the water drop under the microscope.

It is perhaps a first glimpse of what the sky may hold in all directions, upward as well as downward — for up here there are worlds and worlds, and we are flying not by human flight plan alone. Our destinations are not only of the earth, our cargoes not wholly earthly goods.

Even as Thoreau with his plow in Concord, we fly a broader pathway than you see. Indeed where the off engine roars it is not: it is further off. And where the nigh blade turns it will not be, for it is nigher still.

5. The Wind

WHAT IS THAT MOANING outside my window — that rising and falling voice of feeling — that rended wail of unseen doing? Whose voice? The gale's?

Yes, our slipstream is calling — the invisible wind that lifts our wings and forms the moving body of the sky — who now drifts us off our course, now wantonly blows us on our way. He is the flying navigator's most constant and inconstant host, that "fellow called the Wind, with mystery before and reticence behind." His wings are less than gossamer, yet he minds not the cold nor the blistering sun. Neither does he blench before gold nor might nor death.

The greatest corrections I have had to make in my navigating are written in Aeolus' book, in a breezy trailing scrawl — carefree, whimsical, yet etched beyond recall. It is largely for the wind's sake that we carry an extra two or three hours' supply of fuel. And many's the time when it has held body to soul — more times than the weather prophet wants to hear.

I remember that autumn day when Frank Lake had to return to Iceland after three hours of flying toward Newfoundland — while it became more and more evident that there had been a grave error in wind forecast. To his growing bewilderment, Navigator Frank found he was making almost no headway despite an airspeed of two hundred knots against a reported headwind of fifty-five.

"I thought I was barmy," he said when he landed. "I took four fixes and every one of 'em showed us practically standing still. No wind ever blew that hard. When we finally gave up and turned around we got back here in twenty minutes."

It evolved that that planeload of forty-two humans in a DC-4 had all unknowingly been flying slap in the eye of a 150-knot howler. Had the navigator not done his job, accumulating overwhelming evidence of the incredible, the pilot could well have flown doggedly on, to the doom of all on board.

What is the nature of this flighty spirit, the wind? Have ever men by any thrust of austromancy divined the secret of his being, his rule of life?

Men have tried since their first forest homes were uprooted by the tempest and their sea rafts battered by the squall, since the time of the flood when "God made a wind to pass over the earth, and the waters assuaged." Homer called the four winds by name: Boreas, the north wind, later immortalized in the Tower of the Winds at the Acropolis as a muffled-up old man with a conch to blow the bitter threnody of winter; Euros, the grizzled east wind, holding high his cloak to huff the storm; Notos the virile south wind, emptying his jar of warm rain; and Zephyros, the beautiful young west wind, bearing fruits in his careless mantle.

The mountains of Thrace were the poetic home of these ancient Greek winds, whom Hesiod called "the children of the morning." Aeolus dwelt there in the howling wind tunnel of a cave which was his palace. He studied the heavens, invented the sail, and wore his billowing robes as the great moody god of all the winds of the earth. It was he who tied up in a bag and presented to Ulysses Boreas, Euros, and every wind that could blow his ship. When Ulysses' men untied the the bag they unwittingly gave all the winds their irrevocable freedom.

Some of the legends of Aeolus are being repeated in real life today, for aerodynamic engineers again are locking up winds in wind tunnels large and small, training them to their bidding, sometimes torturing them. And weather officers are tying winds into packages so they can be put into bags (the flight bags of navigators) and carried out across the world. Even our wind-plotting instruments and computers for figuring the wind and catching its drift have a windy, Aeolian look about them these days, their wind-swept lines reminding me of graceful cirrus clouds: mare's tails of calculus, mackerel mathematics.

Another charming myth from the *Iliad* is the tale of the twelve colts sired by Boreas out of the Mares of Erichthonios "which galloped over the tops of the flowers and brake them not, and over the crest of the ocean wave." The wind also knew a high place among the gods of the ancient Chinese who called it "fung" and titled it "the envoy of heaven and earth." Their written word "wind" means "breath" as well, the giver of life. And they must have spoken of the wind often, for they have many words such as sao, "the sound of the wind"; tiu, "to move with the wind like a tree"; chiam, "waves blown by the wind"; and yao, "floating in the air as down carried on a breeze." The Japanese named their wind god Fujin and the Hindoos called theirs Indra. The Egyptians and the Arabs and the South Sea peoples had their winds and wind gods too.

But what did these men really know of the wind's way? Was there no more in wind than divine whim or mortal magic?

Let Theophrastus of Eresus speak. He is the first meteorologist in recorded history. He went to school in 366 B.C. with a number of smart youths including Alexander the Great, and his teacher, Aristotle, spoke of him as his favorite pupil. He was brought up of course on the Aristotelian theory that the four elemental principles of nature are heat, cold, dryness, and dampness. "Of these,"

Aristotle had carefully explained, "the mixture of heat and dryness makes fire, heat and dampness combine into air, cold and dryness produce the earth, and cold and dampness make the sea."

This was neat background material for theorizing on many manner of mysteries of the world, including the wind. Theophrastus accepted the prevailing idea that the initial principle of wind is fire. Wasn't it an observable fact that the leaping flames sent forth their sparks and smoke and airy ashes on a hot draft upwards to the sky? Was it not clear also that such violent upcurrents disturbed the air and, like fire itself, spread rapidly outwards? If so, then the wind must be a kind of flame of the atmosphere — a hidden airy conflagration.

But what was the effect of wind on the weather? On beasts and apples and mountains and men? No philosopher had attempted a scientific answer before, so Theophrastus studied and dreamed and analyzed the winds for years, scriving down Greek notes with his quill on sheepskin until he had worked out a general code of wind laws to fit all normal situations.

"Wherever any particular wind blows from," wrote Theophrastus, "there it is accompanied by clear weather; but to whatever place it impels the air, there it is accompanied by cloudy weather." Reason: "It propels before it only a little air at the beginning, but more as it advances; and the air, by being gathered together, becomes cloudy and, by condensation, moist."

Again: "Whenever winds attack each other before they have blown themselves out, it should cause a storm." And "if clouds settle down on the back of a mountain, the wind will blow from behind it also."

To sailing men he warned: "If much acanthus down is borne along on the sea, there will be a great wind." And "if the land appears dark from the sea, the wind will be from the north; if light it will be from the south." But of southerly winds he cautioned: "When dry and not rainy they produce fevers."

Some of his warnings were astronomical: "Red spots on the sun or moon mean wind . . ." "When many stars shoot from one quarter, it is a sign of wind from that quarter . . ." "If the crescent moon stands upright with a north wind blowing, west winds usually follow, and the months will continue stormy until the end."

And some were of living creatures: "A heron flying from the sea and crying is a sign of wind . . ." "Many spider's webs borne in the air presage wind or a storm . . ." "Divers and ducks, both wild and tame, foretell rain by diving, but wind by flapping their wings."

Others were rhyming apothegms: "A north wind rising in the night never sees the third day's light." "After frost hoar southern winds roar."

In Theophrastus' profluent science each wind had its distinctive qualities: "Zephyros, the west wind, is the most gentle of all the winds and it blows in the afternoon and towards the land, and is cold." He listed the fruits Zephyros would ripen, and the fruits it would spoil.

"Kaikias, the east-northeast wind, moves in a curved line with concave side toward the sky, because it blows from below . . .

"Lips, the west-southwest wind, makes quick clouds and quick sunshine . . .

"Clouds follow Argestes, the west-northwest wind, all the way to its end . . ."

And there followed descriptions of Mese, the north-northeast wind, Apeliotes from the east, Phoenikias or Euronotos from the southeast, Libonotos of the south-southwest, Iapyx, Skiron, Olympias, Thraskias, and cool Aparctias, some moving with lightning, some with rain, some bringing bright skies in their wake, or calm or snow or hail.

The Roman winds came to be known centuries after in their turn: Septentrio or Aquilo, the north wind, Solanus of the east, Auster of the south, Favonius (nominal ancestor of all foehn winds) of the west, and Caecias, Vulturnus, Euroauster, Austroafricus, Africus, Corus, and Circius between. And Derkias of Sicily, Karba of Phoenicia, Berekyntias of Pontus, and strong Dyris of the Gulf of Pamphylia blowing from the river Idyrus.

As the millenniums passed, new meteorologists and austromancers and prophets altered and added to wind lore. In medieval Germany the *luft-mensch* appeared, a man reputedly willing to "buy a bag of smoke, trade it for two bags of wind, and lose them both in a gale." In medieval Scotland the more progressive witches got to raising wind by dipping a rag in water and beating it thrice on a stone, chanting:

> *"I knok this rag upone this stane*
> *To raise the wind in the divellis name,*
> *It sall not lye till I please againe."*

And the ocean navigators of the great age of exploration made new advances upon all the main winds of the world — traveling, eating, living by the wind, loving as the wind allowed, dying as the wind forbade. Columbus sailed westward before the northeast trade to the dismay of his sailors who feared its awesome constancy, thinking they could never bat their way back home against it. He was fortunate in skirting the West Indies in the hurricane season without a mishap, then returned eastward by a more northerly route, aided by the prevailing westerlies, proving that the wind may change the course of history, as has happened before and since.

The wind is kinder indeed than some of nature's mysterious forces, and has more often than not shown itself the friend of the wise. Cryptic it is to the pedestrian mind, but it freely offers clues of itself to the seer, the thinker, and the believer. As when the dry leaves fill the air of October or the winter wood smoke outlines his

transparent being to our feeble eyes, so can perspective reveal
something of the earth's total scheme of wind.

To see the whole, one must stand back in the sky a piece and
view the full sphere, look well at its mountains and seas and at
that faint envelope of air that wraps it round like cellophane about
a pumpkin. It is plain to see that this globe has wanted neither
fare nor favor, for its form is that of the intemperate friar or his
gassy horse. It bulges at the waistline. And this is more true of
the air than of land or sea.

There is more than one equator at the earth's fat middle, you
see. Beside the well-known fixed equator of rotation there is the
moody heat equator which is the equator of the winds. Unlike the
rigid former, familiar on every world map, the subtle equator of
the winds drifts with the seasons and bends strangely about the
continents and seas. It is known also as the doldrums, the famous
belt of equatorial calms where olden sailing ships would drift for
weeks with limp sails and blistering planks, "ghosting through."
It is the band of greatest sun heat, where the warm air rises fastest,
leaving a low pressure girdle of lazy light air about the earth, forever bulging upward, forever sucking toward it the more temperate airs from north and south: the trade winds.

As the trade winds carry cooler air toward the wind equator, the
air already there, warmed and rising, flows back northward and
southward again at a higher level forming opposite and less-known
antitrade winds.

At the poles a different sort of circulation holds sway, calm
cooling air descending and fanning intermittently outwards in great
bursts. The bursts do not move symmetrically from the poles, but
in curving irregular waves or fingers, while warm air to replace
the cold flows poleward between and above the fingers. And now
again the pole of the winds is not the axis pole of earth's rotation

for, as wind is thermodynamic air, the polar circulation naturally centers around the poles of cold — in Antarctica and Siberia.

Although the warm air in general flows toward the poles and the cool air toward the equator, the winds keeping a kind of balance of energy in the atmosphere, the total flux and flood of air is far from mannerly or simple. The warmed air in its poleward flow is not content to remain aloft as would seem reasonable. Instead it cools, contracts, increases in pressure, and presently descends to earth, meteorologically itching for trouble — behaving as only prescient nature could conscionably permit.

Great wreaths of this clear, heavy settling air are found girdling the subtropical earth north and south of the equator where the fitful Calms of Cancer and Capricorn prevail, commonly known as the horse latitudes. These zones have always rivaled the doldrums as a bane to shipping and are the breeding grounds of many of the world's strange winds.

Some say they were named after Ross, a British explorer. In German atlases Ross Latitudes appeared as *Ross Breiten*, but *Ross* is an old German word for horse and when retranslated into English they may mistakenly have become the horse latitudes.

Others insist they were named for the equestrian ghosts of ill-fated cargoes of the horse transports which much too often on voyages to the Indies found themselves helpless victims of calms or fickle variables, eventually having to dump their dead and dying horses overboard, a pathetic contribution to the nightmares of Davy Jones.

Beyond the horse latitudes on the pole sides lie cooler regions of swirling uneasy winds which blow predominantly from the west. In our northern hemisphere this broad sash of winds covering the United States and Europe and most of Asia is known as the prevailing westerlies and they are characterized by the shifting of the northward moving air which, approaching the earth's axis, speeds up like a shortened pendulum, racing eastward ahead of the turning earth.

In the south temperate zone the corresponding air currents are the "brave west winds" which sweep unobstructed by any land around the empty southern oceans encircling the whole earth. These are the motive force of the famous "graybeards," the grim waves thirty to fifty feet high that roll endlessly eastward off the Horn, around and around the gray, watery world.

It is written that the old-time whalers who battled those endless seas last century dubbed the successive southern latitudes: the roaring forties, the howling fifties, and the screeching sixties. Not without reason either: one of the outposts of the sixties, 1200 miles below Tasmania, Adelie Land (RFD 1, Antarctica) has recorded the world's most relentless winds, with an average velocity of more than fifty miles per hour day in day out the whole year round. Subzero Adelie gusts often measured around two hundred m.p.h. and it is understandable that Sir Douglas Mawson who wintered there early in the century was heard to mutter through his teeth on his homeward voyage that a long and happy life somewhere else could hardly make up for a single year spent in Adelie Land.

On the poleward edges of the westerlies, around latitude 45° N. and 50° S., are the great mixing belts where warmed humid air from the tropics meets clear polar bear's breath from the poles in wavy shifting "polar fronts" of variable and veering winds. These zones cover the northern United States and most of Europe and well account for the fickle moody weather familiar to so much of the world's population. Beyond them: the comparative quiet of the arctic and antarctic.

Fortunate it is for densely settled America, Europe, China, and Japan that this north temperate region provides enough mountain barriers and continental distractions to break up its prevailing westerlies into a somewhat tamer team than the brave west ruffians of the south. But since the north's geographic pole lies on the crust of a liquid ocean, which is as a hot stove compared with the dry rigor of the Antarctic plateau, the northern pole of cold is found far from the Arctic Sea in dry Siberia. Hence our capricious north pole of pressure and of the winds is wont to hover in this forbidding region of the last pages of the gazetteer, far beyond Yakutsk where bitter Verkhoyansk lies by the hiemal vice of the Yana between Zashiversk and zesty Zhigansk.

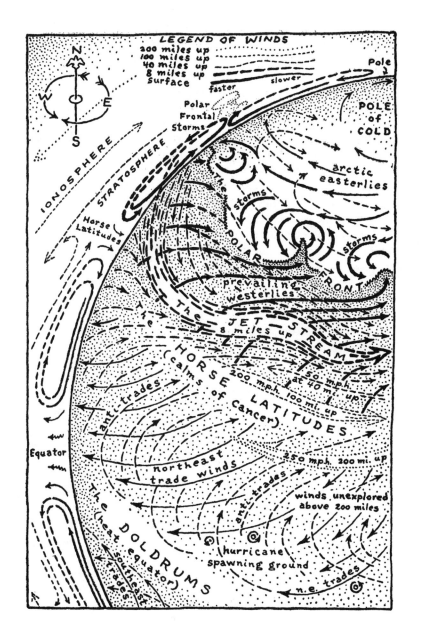

This eccentricity of our wind pole inevitably abets the wayward-ness of the winds in our northern ocean of air, and gives insight into their great variety. For there are a hundred local winds known in the inhabited north to each score of winds of the tropics and the south — and their names express the wonder of human imagi-nation in every age.

Have you heard the wind names of the world, which are among the least known and most beautiful of words? They are truly the heritage of all men for they reflect the tongues of history from ancient Cathay to the slang of the United States Army. Consider the dry khamsin of Egypt, reputed to blow sand unceasingly for fifty days; the westerly datoo of the Straits of Gibraltar; the misty waimea of Hawaii; the cool pontias from the Rhone gorges; the chinook of the dry American plains; the sudden violent williwaw of Alaska and Magellan's Strait; the biting black buran of Russia; the great typhoon of the China Sea; the whispering matsukaze which shifts through Japanese pine groves; the mild shamal that descends the twin valleys of the Tigris and Euphrates; the warm brickfelder of southern Australia; the playful vento coado which whistles through crannies in the hillside hovels of Portugal; the snorting sonora which crosses Arizona from Mexico to California each summer; the dainty feh of Shanghai; the whirling tsumuji of Japan; the vindictive rok of Iceland; the refreshing imbat off the blue Mediterranean; the ruthless helm wind of Cumberland which uproots turnips in the field.

Can you feel the rhythm of the wind in human memory? It is music in the sky and in men's souls. I cannot refrain from listing them, even at risk of being encyclopedic. It has taken years to snare some of them, and the evidence is that no real wind roster has ever before been assembled.

Faring further into the sky then, it becomes obvious that the winds of the world are of distinct kinds. There are the hot, dry winds like the simoom or "burning wind" which are said to wreak great hardship on all living creatures and the moving parts of all machines. Wagon wheels have to be tarred in a desert wind to prevent a fatal brittleness. A wooden flute must be dipped in cool water or oil to prevent it from splitting end to end. And sometimes men are driven to desperation by the parching of their skins, and their throats and noses. Herodotus tells of the ancient people of Psylli (Tripoli) who became so hysterical when their wells dried up that they actually declared war on the simoom and marched into the Sahara with clashing cymbals and beating drums until they disappeared forever into a red cloud of whirling sand.

Herewith the desert winds:

Simoom — of Arabia, Syria, and probably Libya
Samiel — Turkish version of Simoom off Arabian desert
Brickfelder — of Australia
Zonda — of Argentine pampas
Ghibli — dry, southerly wind of the eastern Mediterranean
Leste — warm easterly wind of January in the Madeiras
Black roller — duststorm of the western United States
Naalehu — of Hawaii, blowing from the arid interior areas
Soo-oop-wa — bitter sand-laden wind of Southwest Africa
Harmattan — parching wind of Algeria and Morocco
Haboob — of the Sudan, the black roller of the upper Nile
Chergui — sand-laden wind of Morocco
Khamsin — of Egypt

The khamsin blows in summer from Aden to Cairo carrying so much sand that it is the obvious modern explanation for the "darkness that could be felt" of the ninth plague of Egypt.

Then there are the stormy northeasterly winds of passing low pressure:

Koshava — of Yugoslavia, bearing snow from Russia
Steppenwind — of Germany blowing from the steppes
Crivetz — of Rumania, like a blizzard
Buran — of Russia, usually with snow
Viuga — of southern Siberia
Myatel — of northern Russia
Purga — of Russia
Seistan — of Iran

Fung chiao hsueh — of China
Bise — cold wind of France
Euroclydon or Euraquilo — of the Levant
Tegenwind — of Holland
Hokuto no Kaze — of Japan
Blizzard — of northern America, a howling snowstorm
Nor'easter — of New England, a variant of the blizzard

Suestada — of the Rio de la Plata
Black southeaster — of South Africa
Southerly burster — of Australia, preceded by an eerie lull
(these three are southern hemisphere counterparts of northern
NE winds)

Of the true north winds there are:

Gallego — of Spain
Tramontana — Alpine blast of the Italian east coast
Leung — of the China coast
Pei fung — of China
Erh chi chih fung — of northern China
Hawa shimali — of Arabia
Belat — of Arabian coast in winter
Etesian — of cool summer afternoons in Greece and
    Levant
Sarsar — of Arabia
Narai — of Japan
Norther — of the Pacific coast and of the Texas pan-
    handle plains
Canadian north wind — wintry wind of northern America

The last-mentioned wind helped Benedict Arnold's fleet stop
the first British invasion from Canada in the American Revolution.
This was at the Battle of Valcour Island on Lake Champlain,
October 11, 1776, where, by taking a northerly upwind position for
his ambush of the superior British fleet, Arnold gained the indispensable advantage.

The non-simoom south winds are fewer but no less fraught with character:

Siffanto — up from the hot heel of Italy
Kona — of Hawaii, sultry and petulant with many varieties
Kai — balmy south wind of China
Hawa janubi — of Arabia
Vendavales — out of Morocco and blowing over Spain

This last is the gentle breeze which, at the Battle of Trafalgar, influenced Nelson to risk attack in two columns instead of the traditional line.

Of plain east and west winds like the helm, the haur, and the datoo, the most famous in history is the east wind that blew at the Siege of Orleans. As Joan of Arc on the west bank of the Loire prayed to Saint Catherine to help her men cross on their gun rafts to attack the English fort, it miraculously changed into a west wind. Cried Dunois, in the words of Shaw: "West wind, west wind, west wind. Strumpet: steadfast when you should be wanton, wanton when you should be steadfast . . . west wind, wanton wind, wilful wind, womanish wind, false wind from over the water, will you never blow again?"

Trade winds cover vast areas, and the best known ones are the northeast trades that extend around most of the earth from the wind equator to the north horse latitudes, while corresponding southeast winds blow trade over the equivalent Capricorn belt. Some special trade winds are:

Eliseos — of Spain
Moncao — of Portugal
Boekifu — of Japan
Maoi fung — of China
Tung shang fung — of China
Shih ling fung — of China

Of more local type are the treacherous down-blowing or fall winds, warm and cold, of the ice slopes of mountains — particularly the gusty foehn winds of the high Alps, the Rockies, Andes, and the deep fiords of Norway and Greenland which blow savagely down from the lee heights, becoming drier as they warm under the pressure of lower altitude. This family of down-blowing winds, which sometimes move with boiling turbulence and form local jets in narrow valleys, has undoubtedly brought disaster to more unwary fliers crossing high mountain ranges than any other type of wind there is. The foehn has been estimated to throw pressure altimeters into error by as much as 1000 feet on the optimistic side near high peaks, and even though it is a fall wind the effect of its wave motion has been observed to reach twenty-five times the height of the mountains. Fall winds include:

Maloja — from the lofty Maloja Pass in Switzerland
Yamo oroshi — foehn of the steep valleys of Japan
Chinook — widespread foehn wind in the lee of the Rockies that in winter warms the sheepherders of Montana
Zonda — foehn of the Andes in Argentina
Papagayos — of Costa Rica
Santa Ana — of southern California
Klod — Balinese wind that blows "downwards to the sea"
Reshabar — lusty and black, out of the high Caucasus
Gregale — a Maltese wind off the Balkan highlands
Taku — off Taku glacier in southern Alaska
Berg — hot wind off the South African plateau
Shirkshire — out of the Green Mountains of Vermont

and these northerly winds which bring cold air masses down from continental plateaus to balmy coasts:

Mistral — down from the Cevennes to the Riviera
Bora — the dry, blustery, katabatic wind that cools the Dalmatian coast and freshens Naples before the dawn
Monsoon — off the Tibetan plateau to India in winter
Tehuantepecer — the mistral of Mexico, down from the central plateau

Sometimes the lesser lee downdrafts are poetically referred to as air falls, while their counterparts to windward are air fountains. Akin to these gravity winds are the squally kind:

Galerna — of the Bay of Biscay
Pampero — of Argentina
Norther — of Texas
Chocolatero — of the Gulf of Mexico
Blaast — of Scotland
Bull's Eye Squall — off the Cape of Good Hope
Ghost of Gouda — local gust on a calm night, South Africa
Kawaihae — of Hawaii
Sumatra — westerly squall of the Indies
Vinds-gnyr — ancient blustery wind of Iceland
Reffoli — wild gusts associated with the Adriatic bora
Naf Hat — blast of Arabia
Wisper — whistling through narrow Rhine valleys
Briza Carabinera — of Spain
Om — of Canton
Line squall — grumbling frontal wind of the United States
Tapayagua — of western Central America
Kwat — of Amoy
Chubasco — thunderous wind of Pacific Mexico
Williwaw or Williewaught — of Alaska and Magellan's
    Strait which sometimes puffs for only a few seconds
    at a time

The sea breeze has several poetic names, particularly on the Mediterranean coasts:

Imbat — refreshing North African shores
Datoo — blowing from the west across Gibraltar
Vento de baixo — of Portugal
Solano — of Spain
Levanter — blowing over Italy and Spain from the east
Virazon — cooling Montevideo on summer afternoons
Soldier's wind — named by Cape Town yachtsmen
Ponente or Ponentino — westerly Italian breeze

Libeccio — southwesterly wind also of Italy and, like the
Ponente, mentioned by Milton in *Paradise Lost*

In other places it is known by other names:

Monsoon — of summer in India
Kadja — of Bali, blowing "upwards to the mountain"
The Doctor — of English-speaking shores
Kaus — of the Persian Gulf
Kapalilua — of Hawaii

And there are the very gentle breezes:

Feh — of Shanghai
Kohilo — of Hawaii
Flakt — of Sweden
Creithleag — of Ireland
Waff — of Scotland
Aura — breath of dawn in ancient days
Soyo kaze — of Japan
Vyeterok — of Russia
Sveszhest — of Russia
Ch'ing fung — of China
Sz — first faint breeze of the Chinese autumn
Cat's paw — which barely ripples mill ponds in America
Thalwind — of German valleys
Flauwewind — of Holland
Nasim — of Arabia
Vind-blaer — of Icelandic sagas
Chwa — of Wales
I tien tien fung — a sigh in the sky of China

In contrast the mightiest of winds, the great West Indian hurricane (from the Taino word "huracan" or "evil spirit") dominates
the Caribbean as the typhoon (from "ty fung," "great wind") the
China Seas. But this elephant among the winds has many names
for his many haunts, among them:

Mauritius hurricane, or cyclone — of the Indian Ocean
Baguio — of the Philippines
Reppu or Kamikaze ("Divine Wind") — of Japan
Willy-willy — blasting Australia from the Timor Sea
Asifa-t — of Arabia

Of his lesser cousins, the high gales, there remain:

Orkan — of Norway
Landlash — of Scotland
Doinionn — "wild weather" of Ireland
Colla — of the Philippines
Frisk vind — of Sweden
Ventania — of Portugal
Elephanta — of the Malabar coast
Bofu — of Japan
Yuh — of Shanghai
Kohala — of Hawaii
Dromi — blowing from Syria to the Aegean Sea

Most of the true tropical hurricanes are born mysteriously and unattended in the giddy heat of the doldrums. Little is definitely yet proven about the dynamics of their origin. But their initial power is widely conjectured to come from a rising vortex of heat over water that "must be at least 82° F." and surrounded by a certain amount of atmospheric instability.

Hurricanes are mainly a late-summer phenomenon, and this suggests that the instability associated with them is derived from the cumulative effect of the sun's nearly vertical rays throughout the summer. When air begins to rise in any area the surrounding air must move inward to replace that which has risen and unless it is almost exactly at the equator it is bound to acquire some rotation from the effect of the turning of the earth. As it rushes inward it inevitably spins faster like a shortened pendulum, taking on more and more of the characteristics of a young hurricane.

In bygone times sailors had great superstitions about this fearful incurving of the wind which was sometimes strong enough to send ships sailing in circles day after day. Usually the vortex dies out again before too long, but near the time of the autumnal equinox in the Caribbean when the heat has attained its peak one occasionally becomes a monster of violence.

With conditions just so, it may be a menace for weeks, steadily growing in size and speed of turning. At first the hurricane child spins leisurely westward with the sun, here hovering in one spot for a day or two like a blind dervish pondering his path, there meandering onward — dragged by the major wind streams of the upper air like a tail after a kite — terrible in its whirling contrast of pressures — unstoppable until its sultry fuel is cut off by a continent or the quenching cold of the north.

The approach of a tropical hurricane is signaled usually days ahead by changes in the normal rhythm of the tides, not only the sea tides but the air tides which on the average affect the barometers about one tenth of an inch daily. Along with a slow, steady drop in air pressure and a rise in temperature, a reduction in frequency of sea swells is noticeable — swells that radiate outward from the spinning giant in all directions. Eight per minute is considered the normal swell frequency under the trade wind in the open tropical Atlantic, but when the frequency has dropped as low as five or four, the islanders know a real storm is on its way. If the big waves continue coming from one direction, the storm can be expected head on, while a change in direction indicates it will pass to one side, the distance away being inversely proportionate to the acceleration of change.

The first visible signs of warning in the sky are gay streamers of high cirrus clouds, usually radiating from one point on the southeastern horizon, followed by a thickening hood of milky cirro-stratus, perhaps revealing a halo around the sun or moon; then grayer and lower clouds, alto-stratus, alto-cumulus, darkening, sometimes turning to copper in color, with dense ragged clouds scudding low overhead in a different direction from the higher ones.

The finale of this ominous overture is a heavy black wall of cumulo-nimbus, closing down from above like a curtain of doom. Sometimes it is called the bar cloud, approaching in the form of a

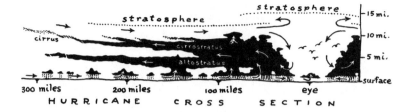

HURRICANE CROSS SECTION

massive bar from two to five miles up, and extending as far as the
eye can see — while just before it the visibility is crystal clear,
and the trade wind gives way to fitful scherzo breezes.

The passage of the bar itself leaves no mistake that it is the start
of the hurricane proper, for violent squalls now begin and lashing
rain increases in a moody intermittent rhythm as successive arm-
like banks of clouds march overhead, sometimes ten minutes apart,
sometimes more than an hour, with violent thunder squalls often
punctuating the spells of howling mist-strewn gales.

Seen by a hurricane scout flying at 50,000 feet, the great sprawling
disturbance would look like a series of concentric cumulus mountain chains, peaked with towering thunderheads — each rising
higher than the last as he approaches the dramatic center of the
system. The valleys are sometimes so deep and dark they seem to
extend down under the sea but are really miles above the worst
squalls, for the soaring ridges can rise as high as ten and twelve
miles, possibly higher if we only had sufficient records to know.

Of course even a pilot in the stratosphere could hardly see all
of a mature hurricane, which might be four or five hundred miles
in diameter, but if he were thirty miles higher in a rocket he could
undoubtedly take in the whole, noticing the spiral pattern of the
encircling thundery ridges that spread further apart and get more
irregular as they reach outward from the center, finally dissipating
into ragged patches and dainty streaks of cirrus perhaps two hundred and fifty miles out.

The central eye is plainly the most fascinating hurricane part,
being often a bowl of clear blue sky 25 miles in diameter reaching
right down to the sea. Intense young hurricanes may have little
eyes only three or four miles across, but the average eye diameter

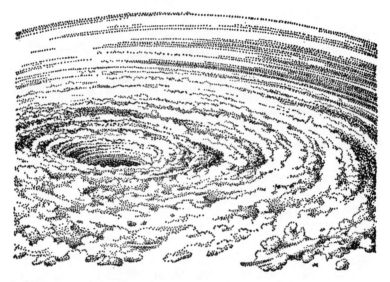

is fourteen miles and in many cases covered with a white eyelid of
broken or solid strato-cumulus blanketing the surface at an altitude of a few thousand feet while the spiral thunder ridges rise all
around it like tiers of a Roman amphitheatre.

   The heat of the eye is usually quite noticeable even at low altitudes and its center has been found to be as much as 32° F.
warmer than the outer storm at 18,000 feet. The eye's calm is
proverbial but so real that flocks of sea birds have been seen
there on several occasions, wheeling endlessly and understandably
anxious to keep out of the encircling fury as long as they are able.
Airplanes can fly there with relative safety too, but surface ships
avoid the eye with well-founded dread, preferring the areas of
swiftest wind. For the surrounding hundred-mile blasts blow the
waves topless and decimate the crested seas to reasonable, trun-
cated proportions, while in the eye the great swells and waves
seem to run wantonly, beyond control or order, often clashing
from opposite directions in such wild collisions as to rear up jagged
pyramids of water high enough to buckle a 10,000-ton ship in two
or stave in her decks by toppling upon them.

The extreme low pressure near the center of a hurricane, by the way, causes the sea level to be sucked up abnormally high under it, especially on its dangerous side of forward spin (the right side of a hurricane north of the equator). This elevation of several feet, furiously lashed by the winds around it, builds up a heavy swell which may travel as fast as eighty miles an hour, outrunning the storm itself and sometimes even its remotest barometric indications — the dog before his master. Though such a swell can be dangerous when it arrives at high tide, at least it forewarns of something even more dangerous to follow.

From recent observations, meteorologists have hypothesized that the warm low-pressure air in the eye flows continuously straight downward to within a couple of thousand feet of the surface, thence curving and spiraling outward and upward inside the surrounding thunderheads, while all the lower clouds for more than a hundred miles around edge gradually inward, circling the eye many times before they are finally swept upward near the dark inner face of its bowl, upward through the black chimney of whistling rain. From here they sometimes blossom forth again into clear air as they approach the top, so that the alto clouds are spiraling slightly outward at 15,000 feet and the lacy cirrus flying almost straight out at 40,000 feet or better, while cumulus tops show themselves at all levels above a couple of miles.

The hurricane is rather similar in structure to a thunderstorm cell enlarged a hundred times, or a tornado multiplied by several thousand. In fact, both thunderstorms and tornadoes are spawned by hurricanes as tornadoes in turn have been born of thunder. And all three storms are now believed to follow behind advancing invisible tongues of slightly warmer air which, in the case of the hurricane, extend about a thousand miles before it, a real boon to forecasters engaged in trying to predict its path.

The unblinking clarity of its eye, of course, is a distinctive feature not often visible in the smaller vortex storms, and to many of us who have never seen a hurricane eye to eye, its full significance requires an effort of appreciation. The eye's deceptiveness, for example, is a clue as to why the Tainos named this wind the "Evil

Spirit" — for the low-pressure calmness in the center of the fury often leads the uninitiated to assume the whole hurricane has passed — to their undoing.

On September 18, 1926, when a hurricane whirled spang through Miami, everybody huddled in the safest spots, especially during the wild pre-dawn hours of hundred-mile easterly winds just before the eye. When it suddenly grew dead calm and a beautiful sunrise appeared, hundreds of people came out to go to work or to see the night's devastation. Scores of adventurous young people crossed the long causeway to Miami Beach for the thrill of swimming in the great surf. But after only an hour of lull, an abrupt opposite gale from the west arose, reaching full hurricane force so quickly that the surge of water out of Biscayne Bay washed over the causeway, sweeping many astonished bathers to their deaths. Miami Beach virtually disappeared under the rising wind-whipped tide, drowning additional hundreds.

There is always something to be learned from a new hurricane, for it is never quite like any you ever saw before. The one that hit Florida on Labor Day 1935 was only thirty-five miles in outside diameter, yet the barometer fell to 26.35 inches, and weathermen later called it "the most intense hurricane in United States history." After two weeks of development, hurricanes usually begin to get weaker, sprawlier, and more erratic. Some nearly a month old have been known to develop two eyes and rotating arms hundreds of miles long, probably appearing from space almost like an octopus. In October 1951 two hurricanes collided near Bermuda and the North Atlantic was in wild confusion for a week. The smaller one lost strength while the larger one gear-wheeled itself around it to the right, losing forty per cent of its force before careering off on a new slant.

There are nearly always some such storms meandering about the world's oceans, like the almost unannounced typhoon that flattened Wake Island just after I last flew there in 1952, or the baguio (Philippine hurricane) that in 1927 made the lowest barometric reading ever officially accepted: 26.185 inches.

Several have left their mark on history too — perhaps never more dramatically than when Kublai Khan's fleet set sail from the Asiatic mainland in A.D. 1281 to invade Japan. There appears little doubt that the then primitive Japanese would have fallen easy prey to the Golden Horde which had conquered the world from the Mediterranean to the China Sea had it not been for a great typhoon which swept without warning upon the overloaded wooden transports, scattering and foundering them to an almost total loss. After this single awe-inspiring blow from Fujin, the wind god, the great Khan lost all appetite for pressing his designs on the Land of the Rising Sun.

Strange to relate, Fujin arose again in Japan's defense in mid-December 1944 and actually gave her a modern naval victory about as devastating (if not so decisive) as the triumph of 1281. When Admiral Halsey's Third Fleet retired from striking Mindoro to refuel five hundred miles eastward in the Pacific, such huge seas came up that all oil lines broke before fuel could be pumped through them. Nor had Navy weather officers sufficient information to locate the typhoon's center or course in time, and it struck Halsey with full ferocity, sinking three U.S. ships and damaging twenty-eight others, demolishing or blowing overboard 146 planes, killing 790 men, and forcing the indefinite postponement of the then planned American invasion of Luzon.

Devastating as is the hurricane in its vast strength, however, it is far behind the tiny tornado in concentrated velocity. Named from the Latin tornare, "to turn," and variously described by Pliny the Elder, Seneca, and Lucretius, this frenzied whirlwind plays hornet to the hurricane's elephant. It has its corresponding local names from the tourbillon of France to the piao of China, its waterspout variants from the dancing trompa of the Black Sea to the descriptive skypompe of the Baltic.

While the hurricane, cutting a swath two or three hundred miles wide and sometimes ten thousand miles long during its fortnight to a month of rampage, blows with a velocity known to have exceeded 200 m.p.h. at its highest fury, the little tornado's path is rarely as much as half a mile wide, usually less than a couple of dozen miles long, and it seldom outlives the hour. Yet the air whizzing around the tornado's vacuous center moves with a speed estimated at from 200 to 800 m.p.h. More accurate determination of tornado velocity has not been made at this writing, for the good reason that on the rare occasions when anemometers have happened to be in its path, they have been wrecked by the wind itself — committing a kind of meteorological suicide.

Like the hurricane, the tornado is conceived in heat and turmoil. It may appear in almost any country, and has been reported in every one of the United States. Statistically, the most likely place in the world to meet one is in eastern Kansas late in the afternoon of a sultry day around the end of May, and they are fairly common any place east of the Rocky Mountains, where the cold dry winds from the north or west meet the warm moist airs from the Gulf.

Thunderstorm weather is ideal for tornado breeding, with violent heat rivers bearing the air upward like a giant drain in reverse, the black thunderheads serving as the inverted bottom of the tropospheric bathtub out of which the air is being sucked aloft in a swirling effusion.

The dynamics of it is not really so simple, however, and W. J. Humphreys, authority on physics of the air, has listed "twenty-six conditions normally associated with the occurrence of tornadoes." Although there is always open season on interpretation of tornado statistics, the checking of which in the field is usually as haphazard as it is hair-raising, meteorologists are largely agreed on the basic nature of this wind gone wild.

In general terms, they consider the tornado as a small focal point in a large turbulence — an eddy stirred by the clash and mixing of two opposite kinds of air: (1) warm, buoyant, expanded, humid air that tries to rise up from the lower levels and, (2) cool, heavy, dry air that prefers to sink down from the shifting heights. When a polar air mass is drifting along from the northwest, for instance, tornadoes sometimes appear from fifty to a hundred miles ahead of it while the lower wind is still blowing warmly from the southwest, because the over-reaching "upper cold front" of advance dry air creates top-heaviness, manifesting itself usually as a squall line of thunderstorms where the hot lower air tries to chimney its way up through the unstable roof — where any persistent updraft may be caught (like the baby hurricane) between conflicting winds and set whirling before the lash law of angular momentum.

Of course this is by no means the only birthway of the tornado, which can sprout directly from a giant typhoon or grow out of the updraft of a man-made fire. The hot black smoke from a burning oil field in California in 1923 generated "hundreds of whirlwinds, one of which was violent enough to kill two people and wreck a house," and during that same year in Japan four full-fledged tornadoes were reported to have emerged like phoenixes out of the fires that followed the great Tokyo earthquake on September first.

While small in horizontal area as compared to a hurricane, the tornado can be just as tall, and the great twister that smashed through Worcester, Massachusetts, in 1953 was fourteen miles high at the cirrus top of its overriding thunderhead. The relationship between these two classic forms of cyclonic wind is shown more particularly by the fact that the tornado has an eye at its center also, and some meteorologists think there is a proportionate downdraft of relatively warm air in the eye's middle (although none has yet aspired to prove it). In a few cases cool-headed observers have noticed the momentary calm and the clear air inside a large tornado eye (sometimes more than a mile in diameter), and several have remarked on the chill (not entirely psychological) felt during its passing. The coolth at the base of the vortex seems to be a generally accepted fact and is in accord with the well-known cooling effect of expansion (as in air released from a tire). Outside the vacuous vortex, conversely, the air is denser, warmer and there has been observed a surrounding downdraft that spirals inward near the ground just as definitely as the ferocious updraft spirals outward into the sky, the two forming counterbalancing parts of an integral circulation as in the hurricane, in hot and cold currents of the sea, even as in the two-way flow of our human blood.

A glider pilot flying near a huge dust devil over a desert recently proved this to his own satisfaction, clocking the outer downdraft at 1800 feet a minute, the air getting warmer (by adiabatic compression) as it descended. Near the ground a few hundred feet outside another whirlwind some ardent weather scout felt "hot puffs" of air moving inward toward the twister and measured them with his pocket thermometer at "about 20° F. warmer than the prevailing air."

That sort of evidence is almost all that Science has to go on with tornadoes, but by putting together hundreds of bits into the meteorological mosaic, the weathermen have learned a good part of the over-all picture. They know that tornadoes need not be expected until there are signs of thunder about, for the pendant funnel always hangs down from a towering cumulo-nimbus cloudbank, often one showing turbulence all over its under surface in the form of drooping eddy pouches called *mammatus* because they resemble breasts. But it is not the funnel itself that is to be feared. Rather it is the fast wind whirling around its base, the tornado's outer collar that is usually black with raised dust and in which debris is continuously being sucked aloft, then inevitably hurled outward again in a wild fountain of nigritude.

So powerful is the terrific updraft that it has been known to lift tons of steel in its overwhelming spiral that at times must develop a vertical velocity of several hundred miles an hour! Although a tornado's base is normally dragged along behind its more dynamic top, like a vacuum-cleaner hose behind its motor, Meteorologist Edward M. Brooks of St. Louis University cites one overeager twister that somehow ran ahead of its thundercloud, then immediately created a new one that shot up to "35,000 feet in one minute."

Sometimes the dark funnel grows so fat in its upper turbination it has been described as balloon-shaped. Sometimes it is thicker at the bottom than the top, like a tree, or it may become waspwaisted with the narrowest part halfway up the trunk, a virago in a pirouette. At other times it dwindles to a snakelike thinness,

now black as tar, now fading into ghostlike transparency.

There is something weird about an invisible tornado descending upon a town, like the unseen angel of death, but exactly that has been known to happen when the vortex was passing through unusually dry air — too dry for condensation. Sometimes the clouds above the tornado show a faint greenish or yellowish reflection from the earth, and when the funnel is well off the ground it usually remains a steamy gray, now and then turning almost as pale as milk. On rare occasions, in winter, it may dip low and become suddenly pure white, as the time a tornado passed over a snow field on the east slope of the Wasatch Mountains in plain sight of Salt Lake City airport, sucking tons of snow up into its dazzling maw like some kind of rotary snowplow, releasing an intense miniature blizzard in its wake.

Most witnesses of tornadoes do not remember them as having any particular smell other than that of the raised dust, yet a few reliable and sensitive observers have reported a distinct odor of sulphur and ozone — perhaps the chemical consequences of vacuous air and electrical discharge. Certainly tornadoes are associated with a special lightning of very delicate lacelike texture and of almost continuous flickering frequency. Pilots flying blind through thunderstorms have been known to take evasive action after recognizing this tornadic trademark, usually climbing above 15,000 feet to avoid the risk of running into a hidden vortex at its level of greatest frenzy.

What can happen in a blind collision between an airliner and a tornado ambushed in a cloud is suggested by the fate of the DC–6 that is thought to have run into a "stormspout" off Mobile, Alabama, on February 14, 1953. All that is definitely known is that the big plane was suddenly and mysteriously thrown out of control and spun or dove into the Gulf, killing all forty-six persons aboard.

As to the sound of a tornado, the memories of all witnesses are usually quite definite. It has the roar of a thousand trains passing in the night. If more distant, the prolonged whine of a swarm of bees. Even from twenty-five miles away, the persistent bellow of a mature tornado has been noticed, and for as long as an hour before the storm's arrival keen ears have warned a population of the danger. The final roar is frequently augmented by nearly continuous thunder and often as not by a rattling obbligato of large hail mixed with shingles, nails, and assorted splintering boards.

The average recorded duration of the tornado's passage over one spot is but 15 seconds, and its average total endurance along the ground about 8 minutes. But many tornadoes are far from average. One midwestern twister was recorded as dawdling along in a continuous path for "seven hours." Although the average swath cut by tornadoes, according to statistics, is thirteen miles long, this amazing storm started in Missouri at noon and meandered eastward across the middle of Illinois and southern Indiana, stopping only at sunset close to the Ohio border, having traveled 293 miles, "the longest continuous path of a tornado of which there is any authentic record." An unusual but not unique feature of this one also was that no funnel of any sort was visible after the first hour, but just "a boiling mass of clouds" in which individual clouds "seemed to roll towards each other and downward, like the meshing of a pair of huge cogwheels," no doubt sucked inward by the central vortex hidden somewhere in the very low cumulo-nimbus confusion.

In general, tornadoes last their longest over flat open country and travel fairly steadily in a northeasterly direction. Rough terrain, large buildings, or high hills are apt to change their course or bounce them back into the sky, but such wind barriers also have been known to spawn entirely new twisters. You might think that houses on hilltops or windward slopes would be more vulnerable to tornadoes than those in secluded valleys, but statistics do not bear this out. Instead, the record indicates that leeward slopes actually have suffered more destruction than windward ones, and that tornadoes have almost as great a propensity for dipping into valleys as an elephant has for groping into peanut bags.

A Kansas whirler on June 5, 1917, after barreling over the wheatfields for thirty-five miles, "swept down the face of a steep bluff sheltering the town of Elmont and demolished every house but one." Others frequently have bored deep enough into river beds to suck them completely dry. One extracted all the water from a well thirty-six feet deep.

Tornadoes can be indecisive to the point of uncanniness too, and a few have been known to move in circles, make U-turns, figure-eights, and even to stand spinning in one spot for nearly twenty minutes.

The best description of a close look at a tornado I have run across is the account of Will Keller, a Kansas farmer, who told it thus to Alonzo A. Justice of the Dodge City Weather Bureau:

On the afternoon of June 22, 1928, between three and four o'clock, I noticed an umbrella-shaped cloud in the west and southwest and from its appearance suspected there was a tornado in it. The air had that peculiar oppressiveness which nearly always precedes a tornado.

I saw at once my suspicions were correct. Hanging from the greenish black base of the cloud were three tornadoes. One was perilously near and apparently headed directly for my place. I lost no time hurrying with my family to our cyclone cellar.

The family had entered the cellar and I was in the doorway just about to enter and close the door when I decided I would take a last look at the approaching cloud. I have seen a number of these and did not lose my head, though the approaching tornado was an impressive sight.

The surrounding country is level and there was nothing to obscure the view. There was little or no rain falling from the cloud. Two of the tornadoes were some distance away and looked like great ropes dangling from the parent cloud, but the one nearest was shaped more like a funnel, with ragged clouds surrounding it. It appeared larger than the others and occupied the central position, with the great cumulus dome directly over it.

Steadily the cloud came on, the end gradually rising above the ground. I probably stood there only a few seconds, but was so impressed with the sight it seemed like a long time. At last the great shaggy end of the funnel hung directly overhead. Everything was still as death. There was a strong, gassy odor, and it seemed as though I could not breathe. There was a screaming, hissing sound coming directly from the end of the funnel. I looked up, and to my astonishment I saw right into the heart of the tornado. There was a circular opening in the center of the funnel, about fifty to one hundred feet in diameter and extending straight upward for a distance of at least half a mile, as best I could judge under the circumstances. The walls of this opening were rotating clouds and the whole was brilliantly lighted with constant flashes of lightning, which zig-zagged from side to side.

Had it not been for the lightning, I could not have seen the opening, or any distance into it.

Around the rim of the great vortex small tornadoes were constantly forming and breaking away. These looked like tails as they writhed their way around the funnel. It was these that made the hissing sound. I noticed the rotation of the great whirl was anticlockwise, but some of the small twisters rotated clockwise. The opening was entirely hollow, except for something I could not exactly make out but suppose it was a detached wind cloud (perhaps a tornadic counterpart of the hurricane's eyelid.) This thing kept moving up and down. The tornado was not traveling at a great speed. I had plenty of time to get a good view of the whole thing, inside and out.

Although the spinning speed of the vortex in such a storm has never been measured, plenty of indirect evidence has accumulated: the burnt look of trees stripped bare in the tornado's wake, the imbedding of grass stems in wooden fence posts, even a case of a bean discovered "one inch deep in an egg without having cracked the shell." The element of personal whimsy is of course proverbial with tornadoes, in the way they will pick out one house yet leave the next untouched; or whisk one member of a family into the sky like magic; perhaps carry a cupboard full of crockery for a quarter of a mile and set it down without breaking a dish.

One twister whooshed a horse into the air among debris, horse flies, horse shoes and barn, allowing the terrified animal to alight unharmed half a mile distant. In another case a woman milking a cow saw the cow swept into a black funnel, leaving her sitting with a pail — but no cow. At Harleyville, Kansas, a whirler passing close to a farmhouse sucked the bedding and mattress from under a sleeping boy without so much as giving him a scratch. Another blew a lighted kerosene lamp for several hundred yards, leaving it still burning and undamaged though with a smoky chimney.

An exceptional account of tornadic violence as viewed from the sky is the report of an Air Force lieutenant who happened to be flying over Waco, Texas, when that city of 90,000 people was struck on May 11, 1953. As the twister bore down Main Street, he saw plate-glass windows on both sides burst outward into the street in progressive waves, then opposing brick walls met each other as they crashed on top of the lanes of slow-moving cars, roofs falling into the wall-less interiors of the stores. A theater and a six-story furniture mart burst at the seams like slow bombs, both immediately collapsing into twisted heaps of wreckage.

The explosive tendency of an enclosed building when enveloped in a tornado vortex is obviously the result of the sudden decrease in pressure outside the building relative to its normal interior atmosphere of about fifteen pounds per square inch. When the barometer drops to twenty-three inches, as was unofficially recorded for the U.S. Weather Bureau in the eye of a tornado at Minneapolis on August 20, 1904, the pressure inside a closed house suddenly finds itself almost four pounds per square inch higher than outside. That means that the force of a ton is immediately exerted against every section of wall two feet square, several tons upon an average window, and nearly a thousand tons throughout the typical small house.

One of the statistics about tornado damage that used to puzzle the pious was the fact that so many churches were completely blasted, while the more numerous barrooms and taverns rarely suffered even minor damage. Only recently have church dignitaries come to realize the meteorological importance of the swinging door as a safety valve of pressure distribution. In the Midwest, I hear, a few of the more enlightened ministers, sensing the moral of this tornadic bias for Bacchus, are taking to opening up their churches to the air and incidentally to the people all week long, day and night. This kind of church, to my weather eye, is likely to live longer not only in the secular gales but in some of the even less measurable flowings of the human heart.

If explosive air pressures can blow up buildings, of course the same principle must apply proportionately to air and gas encased in living bodies, and it is known that persons killed by tornadoes are sometimes so swollen up they look "like pigs" just after the passage of the vortex. This naturally applies to farm animals as well, and it is a common sight to see chickens not only blown up but plucked clean by a tornado. The fact that their feathers come off so readily even when the bird is unharmed has led some meteorologists to speculate that the air sealed into the feather quills actually explodes under the sudden provocation of the vacuum.

How significant the whirlwind is in the world, is hard to comprehend without checking its incidence in places near and far, looking at its lesser cousins, even perhaps glancing back from the perspective of time. Did you know that Washington, D.C., has seen four tornadoes, all since Calvin Coolidge took the presidential oath? And that a dozen American cities have been struck at least five times each: Chicago, Cincinnati, Fort Smith, Indianapolis, Little Rock, Minneapolis, Oklahoma City, New Orleans, St. Louis, Terre Haute, Topeka, and Wichita?

England has had its share of tornadoes too, including one that romped through the heart of London from Victoria Station to Euston on October 26, 1928, hurling chimney pots and cornices into the streets by the hundred. Others have struck such unlikely places as Moscow, Naples, Bourges, Delhi, the outskirts of Tientsin, Bermuda, many parts of Australia, even the Fiji Islands.

Although a good deal has been discovered recently about tornadoes, man has not learned to outwit them. In fact their nature seems to have the curious effect of making them increasingly dangerous and destructive as populations grow. This seems to be because cities are a tornado's natural prey, and effective warning systems very difficult to organize. People who would telephone an alarm of fire forget to give the more important (and more unselfish) alarm of tornado, and the storm wreaks its worst havoc in cities where anyone caught in the streets is in mortal danger of being buried under flying debris. This is in striking contrast with hurricanes, which are mainly maritime, are progressively being disarmed through systems of warnings several days ahead (including a new balloon that automatically floats in a hurricane's eye and continuously broadcasts its position), and which in any case sel-

dom develop the wind force for collapsing buildings more substantial than cheap hangars, barns, and cottages.

The dust devil can be distinguished from the tornado mainly by
its smaller size and by the fact that it is dancing upon the earth
rather than hanging from a cloud. To a meteorologist it is the
trunk without the elephant.

Nonetheless, these small vortexes of sand are a common sight
on the desert, and derive their power from updrafts of sun-baked
air caught in natural eddies of the wind. Their average height has
been estimated as 600 feet, maximum diameter about 100 feet,
and they seldom last an hour. The biggest one on record was seen
on the Egyptian desert near Cairo. It stood a mile high, and spun
along for five and a half hours, obeying the general rule of thumb
that a dust devil will stay alive as many hours as it has thousands
of feet in altitude.

The centrifugal action of the devil's vortex has the interesting
effect of keeping the larger grains of dust or sand to the outside,
making a gradation of progressively smaller particles toward the
center where there is a suggestion of an eye of calmness, a fitful
navel of cousinship with all the greater vortex storms of the world.
Although the central updraft has been conservatively estimated to
exceed thirty miles an hour vertically, the circumferential swirl
must sometimes attain several times that speed in horizontal component. And the spinning devil has a curious predilection for
higher ground — so much so that it will work its way uphill even
if this means bucking a 3 m.p.h. prevailing down-slope breeze.

When the surrounding wind fields are turbulent, dust devils
often contort themselves into curves, corkscrews, or leaning angular
figures, sometimes scores of them in one apparently co-ordinated
ballet. I have seen a chorus of brown wind dervishes that lay
nearly horizontal, steamrollering across the Mexican desert, now
bounding over the hillocks, now tilting vertically to rise a thousand feet, now leaning downward again before the dry hot wind.

It is rare for a dust devil to grow into a real tornado, but it has
been known to happen "in special cases" (according to Edward N.

Brooks), and this sun-heated desert vortex still holds its reputation for mystery dating from ancient times.

The most epic whirlwind in history, I believe, was the one that miraculously arose during Mohammed's first battle in the little valley of Badr near Medina in A.D. 624. Awakening from a brief spiritual trance just at the critical turn of the fighting, Mohammed impulsively picked up a handful of dirt and flung it toward his enemies with a holy curse. Whether or not he intended literal fulfillment of the ancient prophecy that he who sows the wind shall reap the whirlwind, he mounted a horse and charged like a madman into the midst of the fray, followed by a very small dust devil that had curiously sprung to life from his cast handful of earth. As the wrathful prophet dashed forward it is said that the whirling spiral of dust behind him grew rapidly in size and speed until it drew abreast of Mohammed and swept with full fury into the masses of Koreishite swordsmen opposing him. In a few minutes the enemy were so blinded and confused by the unexpected storm that most of them turned in headlong retreat and the first Moslem victory was assured.

Waterspouts are basically similar to tornadoes and dust devils, yet have a cleaner, smoother look both because of the dearth of dust at sea and the seascape's relative lack of friction. They also depend proportionately more on humidity for power, less on heat.

The commonest kind are what weather men call "storm spouts" or maritime tornadoes which, like all tornadoes, have their roots in cumulo-nimbus clouds. They often come in flocks. One ship saw thirty big ones in one day. The Gulf knows many of them in summer and they appear on the Great Lakes and most of the tropic and not-too-temperate seas. They often turn out when the sky is sultry and sullen, when there may be a bluish haze and surface suggestions of the moodier air currents. Suddenly a dark elephantine cloud with a hanging trunk is noticed, usually lengthening rapidly from the stubby tornadic funnel to the scrawnier, snakelike stem of the typical waterspout. As the winds carry it along, the thin whirling stalk may bow forward ahead of its cloud, dragging its spinning base after it willy-nilly, like a celestial vine goddess borne by her torso.

In most cases you can look right through the transparent bole of the vortex as it dips down to draw up what superheated air and spray it can collect just over the water. But it has enough condensed moisture to be not invisible, and occasionally even appears with an outer cylinder of falling mist descending around it like a fountain after being lifted in the inner whirl.

Although the amount of suction, of inward and upward flow, is not so great in a full, sea-going waterspout, the basic tornado nature of this wind is obvious from the fact that in many cases it starts as a land whirler, and may change from a waterspout to a tornado and back several times in crossing isthmuses, gulfs, capes, and straits, impartially demolishing houses one minute and boats the next. Few of them last long enough in one spot to be reliably measured, but a spout destined for particular renown happened to appear one day in August 1896 between Martha's Vineyard and the Massachusetts mainland just as summer boarders were relaxing from lunch. As there were many trained observers on hand and the spectacle lasted thirty-five minutes, it became perhaps the best photographed and documented waterspout in history. It turned out to be "3600 feet high, 840 ft. in diameter at the top, 140 ft. in the middle, 240 ft. at the base." Its "cascade" was "420 ft. high" and showered the spray outward "to a diameter of 720 ft."

The maritime equivalent of the dust devil is the "fair-weather waterspout," which depends on a spontaneous local updraft of hot air over water strong enough to develop a durable and recognizable vortex — something that does not happen easily. However, in tropical sultry seas these spray devils, as they might be called, have been known to appear in impressive numbers — dancing over the shining waves like the colts of Erichthonios, lifting a salty mist many hundreds of feet into the sky, often assuming the forms of genii, dragons of the nether rainbow, or birds with fluttering wings. I read of one seen off the coast of New South Wales which became "very long, swaying and coiling like a serpent," until "all at once it made a complete coil and vanished."

The smaller ones are, like picture-book houris, more fascinating than dangerous, and I have not known of any modern ocean ship to suffer serious damage in encountering them — though flags have been torn, barrels and light gear whipped around, and fresh spray lashed against the captain's door (indicating most water in a waterspout is condensed aloft rather than picked up below).

The most recently discovered of the world's important winds is a gigantic, elusive torrent of thin air that howls perpetually around the base of the stratosphere somewhere eight miles above the middle latitudes. It is shaped like a tape worm, follows the course of a shaken rope, and moves invisibly at a speed varying from 100 to 500 m.p.h.

Respectfully known as the jet stream, it is really a double whirlwind nearly as much bigger than the hurricane, as the hurricane is bigger than the tornado. In fact, each of the earth's two jet streams averages about 22,000 miles in circumference, and the Arctic and Antarctic circles form but the irises of their oppositely staring eyes, one looking perpetually at the North Star, the other gazing forever upon the Southern Cross.

Almost too tremendous for human conception, this lofty wind was first suspected by the navigators of the B–29 bombers flying to southern Japan near the end of World War II. The flight crews were amazed to find that north of the horse latitudes at 35,000 feet they regularly met west winds of more than 250 m.p.h., three times as swift as the average hurricane. Sometimes they found themselves actually flying backwards at 40,000 feet in 400-m.p.h. headwinds! They could not account for it nor find even a mention of it in the meteorology books. When the weather engineers heard the reports and collected all the information at hand, it was evident that something big was up. An entirely new kind of wind had been discovered, a sort of by-product of the age of jet, a supercharged Gulf Stream of the upper sky.

Special projects of exploration were immediately launched to investigate it thoroughly. This was not easy, for an invisible river eight miles straight up is something even the Air Force was not organized to handle, especially when its unknown course is constantly shifting both horizontally and vertically, sometimes by as much as a thousand miles in a day.

Gradually however, as data accumulated in quantity, the jet stream began to take shape as a predictable wind. Some meteorologists started referring to it as the circumpolar vortex. It turned out to be the actual nerve center of the prevailing westerlies, the core of maximum speed, the volatile backbone of that greatest of wind systems on earth, blowing completely around the world between the polar fronts and the tropics. Thus obviously there are two jet streams, one howling over Argentina and around the watery southern temperate zone, the other sizzling through the skies over China, the United States, and the Mediterranean area, weaving about in conformity with the changing pressure contours of the great waves of the northern polar front, easing further northward in spring with the sun (as do the polar fronts, horse latitudes, and doldrums alike), working south again in fall.

The jet stream is shaped just as a river is supposed to be, wide and relatively shallow. But besides being a hundred times faster, it is also a hundred times bigger than any river you ever saw on earth, far bigger even than the Gulf Stream which would exceed all the continental rivers put together. Thus the jet stream of air is by all odds the world's greatest river — a twin river flowing continuously sometimes for nearly twenty-five thousand miles around each hemisphere, only a few miles deep but its volume amounting to five thousand cubic miles of air per minute past every point on its banks (if it had any banks) — its total course in both hemispheres: more than forty-five thousand miles, or a fifth of the way to the moon.

Yet while it is undeniably the super-Amazon of the heavens and far aloof from all lower circulations of sky, the jet vortex, no less than the lumbering hurricane and the fleeting earthbound tornado, springs from deducible dynamic sources — from the cyclonic clash of conflicting bodies of wind, from the inherent shear of crisp polar cold against sultry tropical heat. It is thus whipped to its frenzy by an uneasy pressure gradient that, like the slopes of the Alps, steepens with height, that, like boiling liquid, is made turbulent by disparate temperature.

The jet stream has also a rhythmic wave motion which sometimes follows the phases of the moon with an almost feminine fatality. Its cyclic month or longer starts with a straight west wind that very gradually begins to undulate in the manner of a snake coming out of hibernation. After ten days of continuous increase in amplitude, the wave curves are describing moving S shapes two or three thousand miles apart that presently develop signs of instability, actually breaking apart by the end of the second or third week into loose wheels and kidney whorls that fly off as separate circulations and may roll on, for all now known, as far as the equator and the poles.

After a wild week of such wanton discontinuity, the discordant waves have usually canceled each other out enough to permit new frontal pressures to oil the turbulence. Thus the trend turns again toward order and in another week the jet stream has notably ironed out its curves so it can stiffen back into the simple western component of its beginning.

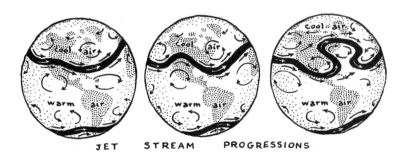

JET   STREAM   PROGRESSIONS

Naturally this great wind offers wonderful possibilities for saving time and fuel on long easterly flights — especially where it has been rechecked as most virile in winter off southern Japan, over the southeastern United States, and in the clear skies of Egypt and Arabia. Since 1953 some of the trans-Pacific airliners have been regularly hopping the jet for free rides between Tokyo and Honolulu, a stretch that used to be a dog-legged 4320 miles by way of Wake Island for refueling, but is now less than 3900 via direct jet stream — the trimming of time even more striking from the former 17 hours to 11 hours, or 10, sometimes 9, depending on the mood and favor of the river of winds.

Of course the jet current is of no help going the other way. Indeed it can be a serious hindrance, as the B–29 boys found out. But in midwinter eastward bound, it is almost invariably worth "2200 gallons of gas" ($20,000 in air freight), even at present cruising levels miles below the stratum of full jet strength. At 40,000 feet it will be the bonanza of the blue, a golden Rio de Janeiro ever waiting to be claimed, and the airline meteorologists are already perfecting techniques of adjusting payload to tailwind for the optimum exploitation of whatever a great wind can give that they can take. The fact that the jet core was clocked at 490 m.p.h. a few days ago over Spokane is more than a hint of the future, for any old B–47 that had troubled to climb into it would have looked a cinch to make New York in two hours and a half!

Such interesting problems in calculus as to how far it is worthwhile to go out of one's way in pursuit of the jet stream, how late in the spring it can be used despite the seasonal slump, exactly where the efficient navigator should cut into it or veer out for his optimum course — these will occupy our minds in the coming years and should well fill the gap left by the tedious spherical trigonometry of old. And although we are learning more every day of this upper world, it still holds ample mysteries like the sudden turbulence that besets airplanes threading the jet rivers, the abrupt sequence of "short, sharp, hammering repercussions" that remind pilots of a speedboat battering choppy seas. These vibrations often begin with startling suddenness in clear air around 35,000 ft. without warning, nor obvious cause. They may be an aerial form of tide rip or cross current of conflict between opposing oscillations of air striking each other at discordant angles to the lee of mountains. Or might they possibly be a pressure counterpart of the cloud streaks that linger on the equator side of jet streams so often that they are getting to be officially associated with them — the bouncing breath of Argestes — mackerel spindrift upon the timeless river of wind?

The murderous bomb wind, born of the atomic age, is one of the strangest of all the world's winds. Even with the earliest "model T" atomic bombs the outward blast at a thousand feet from "zero" (directly under the bomb) blows at 800 m.p.h., or faster than sound. Two miles away the wind is still whooshing out at 70 m.p.h. But this vast expanding puff is exhausted in a couple of seconds and is followed by an instant of stillness as in the eye of a hurricane. Then immediately it reverses itself, the wind literally bouncing back into the vacuum at about half its outward velocity but lasting longer. This double-action wind is what causes most structural damage in an atomic explosion, and many buildings which are only weakened by the initial outward blow are collapsed by the rebounding blast. H-bomb winds and bigger and worse blasts from successively more powerful explosions can be expected to behave in similar patterns but with velocities and distances proportionately increased.

And don't imagine that winds are only out there in the sky or blown by special instruments. Winds are everywhere. Winds are moving air. That draft down the hall — that's a wind. That sneeze. That's a wind. That rise of warmth over the stove. That's the kid brother of the same wind that starts thunderstorms to growling. Some have names. Some have not. But in God's eye every one is a wind, however small — and any one of them somehow may grow into a whirlwind, even as the handful of dust that Mohammed threw at Badr.

It must be understood of course that all the winds man discovered up to the day he cracked the ancient chain that held his wings were those felt close to earth. They had to be, for till then he knew no way to probe the upper sky except with the vicarious aid of his friend the bird or an occasional kite or balloon. His precarious eighteenth-century balloon, though it carried the dauntless adventurer high in the air, was a poor ambassador to the wind because it was swallowed so completely by the wind itself that it put him in a position similar to Jonah on his introduction to the whale — a position hardly conducive to intelligent discourse.

Old balloonist Monc Mason's famous *Aeronautica* tells of the "awful silence" of the sky as known from a free balloon. It is the silence of gastronomic equilibrium, of absence of the wind sounds made by the friction of air against the alien earth, against the ear, against houses and trees. For the well-ballasted free balloon riding the wind comes to rest in the wind's body until it is in perfect frictionless balance. As Mason expressed it, "The greatest storm is, in respect to its influence upon this condition of the balloon, as utterly powerless as the most unruffled calm . . . [A man] might look down from his airborne car and behold houses levelled, trees uprooted, rocks hurled into the sea, and all the various signs of desolation by which the path of the storm is marked, and yet he might hold in his hand a lighted taper without extinguishing the flame, or even indicating by its inclination to one side or the other the direction of the mighty agent by which such awful ravages had been created."

Monc Mason, if you'll recall, first won fame as one of three intrepid Englishmen who boarded the west wind by balloon in 1836, riding from London to a place five hundred miles away in the little Duchy of Nassau, Germany, a record flight of eighteen hours that amazed the world.

But it was to take man another century to plumb the real dimensions of the wind — a century of experimenting with theodolites and wings in which he demonstrated that wind extends as high as air, gradually thinning for hundreds of miles. The swiftest wind level, he found, is above the cirrus layer of six miles up where mackerel bones and mare's tails ride unreined around the world. It is the haunt of the jet stream and of less-known stratospheric gales, yet meteor trails up to twenty times higher have been clocked to prove that winds blow about as swiftly at even two hundred miles up, frequently from the opposite direction — for the direction of prevailing winds is reversed several times at different high altitudes according to the major circulations of ionic heat.

The wind's strength does not keep up with its speed all the way to the top, it must be remembered. Wind is a spineless ghost above ten miles, for the upper air becomes too thin to feel. In fact if any bird could fly that high it would flap helplessly in the eerie nothingness like a fish out of water.

Another wind discovery of importance was the vast tropospheric scope of our traffic rule: keep to the right. When you are flying around a thunderstorm or a tornado it may be the difference between life and death to go right instead of left. To right you're with the wind, to left against it. This is because all storms and low pressure areas in the northern hemisphere are surrounded by counterclockwise winds. The cause is the motion of the earth itself: the veering geostrophic, gyroscopic force known as coriolis. It is the reason why an east wind spells trouble, being part of a storm from the west. It is why the right side of a north-moving hurricane is the dangerous side of forward spin. It is why an airplane flying east (turning faster than the earth) is lighter than the same airplane flying west, or why an airplane flying over the equator (where centrifugal force is greatest) is lighter than one flying elsewhere. It is why a pendulum clock, taken to a northern country, will run fast. It is the secret of the gyroscopic compass: the ever present centrifugal component of net gravity.

A Dutch physicist, oddly named Professor Buys Ballot, discovered this basic wind principle in 1860. His law says: "Stand with your back to the wind and pressure is lower on your left hand than on your right in the northern hemisphere. South of the Equator the reverse is true." And that is why Australian flyers go to the left of storms while Americans go to the right.

A mighty planetary force is obviously at work here, causing everything from spinning tops to draining bathtubs to turn one way more easily than the other in each hemisphere. This is because the earth beneath the sky is forever turning "out from under" whatever is upon it, whether air or water or solid moving object. It is why arctic rivers cut faster into their right banks than their left ones, why the Trans-Siberian Railroad has to replace more right than left rails on each stretch of one-way track. It is why the Germans' Big Bertha gun in World War I, firing on Paris from seventy miles away, had to aim a mile to the left of target so the three-minute trajectory of its shells would be corrected. It is why a rocket missile aimed at New York today from the North Pole would, unless artificially guided en route, land near Chicago after an hour's flight. It is because the earth is constantly moving Chicago to where New York was an hour ago.

Coriolis is not so simple as this may seem, however, for it is complicated by the earth's spherical shape and by eddy effects which, like adjoining gear wheels, must turn in opposite directions. A hurricane, for example, is an eddy in relation to larger higher-pressure masses revolving clockwise north of the equator, yet it has slow-turning thunderstorms and sometimes eddying tornadoes within it, which may spin in both directions. Even large tornadoes often are surrounded by smaller reverse-spinning pilot twisters which have a tendency to act like ball bearings around a shaft, the prevalence of such subvortexes being suggested by the fact that about five per cent of 550 tornadoes investigated in North America are known to have turned clockwise despite the general coriolis law of counterclockwise for all northern low-pressure systems.

Could it be possible that something like the same majority of northern nations order their traffic to the right for the same sub-conscious reason that the edges of northern high pressure air masses naturally swing to the right, forcing their eddying low

pressure vortexes to turn away from them to the left, counterclockwise, in the manner of rotary traffic around the "eye" of a "Keep
to the Right" intersection — or aircraft spiraling into an airfield?

Could this also be why our northern merry-go-rounds turn
counterclockwise, and our horse races and auto races counterclockwise around the track? Is it the reason why timber wolves in the
north usually range counterclockwise around the territory they
claim as theirs? Does it affect also pirouetting ballerinas, whirling
dervishes, the spin of boomerangs, cowboys' lassos, circling seagulls,
roulette wheels, and lazy Susans? Does it subconsciously influence
you when you take a turn around the block? Does it guide the
sensitive brown creeper as he spirals upward about the trunk of
the tree? And what of the screw bean and the turning worm?

Curious consequences come to mind. If the trudging of the ox
about the wheel is affected by the spinning of the earth, no matter
how slightly, is not the earth's turning influenced in return by the
motion of the ox — though more slightly still? Action and reaction. Broadside and recoil. The horses racing around the bend
hurl themselves forward, their flying hoofs heeding not that
they also kick the great earth out behind them — subtly but
surely.

Possibilities do not tire. If it could be arranged that all the
cooks and bathers of the hemisphere should stir their pots and
tubs the other way, and all the dogs chase their tails but clockwise,
and traffic circles and dynamos and windmills reverse themselves,
would not the cumulative force noticeably retard the spinning of
the earth?

The velocity of the wind has long been a spicy topic of argument,
especially among sailors, and many have sought ways of measuring
and classifying it. One Charles Tomlinson worked out a sailing-
wind scale which gave the olden skipper a kind of standard. Force
zero in the Tomlinson scale was "dead calm"; force one: "steerage

way." Increasing from there a few knots at a time, force 5 was "with royals"; 6, "three reefs in topsails"; 9, "close-reefed main topsail and courses"; 10, "close-reefed topsails and reefed foresail"; 11, "storm staysails"; 12, "hurricane" (or, likely, "hove to with sea anchor").

For a time they printed "wind stars" on sailing charts as a means of giving wind information at a glance. Added to the compass rose these irregular wind stars gave the old charts a fine artistic flavor. Each star had eight points, representing by their lengths the average wind force from the eight principal directions of the compass, with other graphic weather data between.

The old Admiral Sir Francis Beaufort devised the wind scale that is still used today in modern form, sorting the breezes from the gales, and defining the hurricane anew as a wind force of 75 m.p.h. or over. Though seventy-five is rarely exceeded in normal experience in the densely settled parts of the earth, it is commonplace in some mountainous regions. The blue ribbon for highest precisely measured wind speed is now held by the observatory on Mount Washington in New Hampshire which recorded a full hour's average of 173 m.p.h. on April 12, 1934, with brief gusts up to 231 m.p.h. The chief danger in such hurricane wind force is in the fact that air moving squarely against any surface creates pressure "proportional to the square of its velocity" — so that even a wind of 120 m.p.h. hits your house 144 times as hard as a ten-mile breeze.

The whirling cups of the anemometer, by the way, reveal things about the wind that no other instrument can. They show that a high wind is actually not a steady flow of air like a river but irregular like a tidal surge from the ocean when uneven surf is rushing into a shallow estuary. It is broken into multiform gusts and eddies and its average velocity ebbs and flows with the passing hours. Specifically, its main but invisible eddies vary from two to ten miles in diameter and fill most of the sky as "local circulation" cells up to 20,000 feet. These are almost constantly if slowly bubbling and boiling past any given point on the earth. Their effect has been measured also as a fluctuation of about two knots of average wind velocity in a cycle of approximately ten minutes. This is the wind's basic rhythm.

It is what science is learning of the local shape of wind — wind that is the transport of air masses viewed from human perspective — wind whose differences at various sky levels are indicated by the leanings of clouds, whose smaller wave frequencies can be seen in the size of circles carved by the soaring hawks or perhaps in higher reaches by the bone patterns of herring cumulus or the scales of cirrus mackerel.

Have you ever noticed how sometimes on a calm day a sudden huff of wind will come out of nowhere? Just a momentary whoosh of breeze, a flaw in the blue ointment followed again by tranquillity for a long time? Such a solitary gust always makes me feel as though a great stone had been tossed off some distant mountain into the ocean of air and that this brief breeze is the ripple expanding outward from the splash — traveling slower than sound, as surely as sight, and insolubly part of the little-sensed adagio of the sky.

At other times when the wind blows over rough wooded country interspersed with ravines and sharp ridges, I think it takes on the character of a babbling mountain brook with breeze bubbles of lighter air pouring and wimpling over the crested hills much as a brook's fingers purl over the rocks on the way to the valley.

Both moods are familiar degrees of what is known to science as the phenomenon of turbulence — in this case turbulence of free air, which means wind and cellular motion, backwash, large eddies that dissipate into smaller ones: ofttimes eddies within eddies within eddies.

Little is yet known about the seemingly interminable subject of turbulence, but it is now being actively studied from the gyrations of electrons to the motions of galaxies and it is considered vital to the future of flying. It is one key to the friction that lets propellers grab and grip the air in pulling the airplane forward. It is responsible in part for rain and weather — cells of motion in the sky. It promotes effective human breathing and digestion — local winds of torsion in the torso. It is what makes "big whirls have little whirls that feed on their velocity; and little whirls have lesser whirls — and so on to viscosity."

In the sky you can sometimes see the wind bouncing off the ground again and again after being stirred up by a high ridge. Dr. Charles F. Brooks of Blue Hill Observatory near Boston tells me he once counted twenty such bounces in the lee of Mount Washington, each bounce about five miles from the next and visible from the clouds that formed at each crest of the air waves.

It takes quite a while for such turbulence to get ironed out of the wind. When I owned a windmill I used to wish it could happen quicker, for an air flow that is steady as well as strong is important to a windmill's average output of power. In England they figure a wind averaging 20 m.p.h. or higher can produce cheaper power than coal. And I hear that some English windmills on hills enjoy average winds as high as 30 m.p.h. day and night, month after month. The best spots have turned out to be the tops of very smooth bare hills where the wind is speeded up "about five per cent" by its upward aerodynamic flow, where the slipstream is naturally tailored to a human purpose almost as by the precisely engineered surface of a man-made flying wing.

Tibet of all the inhabited lands is probably where the wind feels most at home. There it is free to scythe across "the roof of the world" three miles up bearing the full heft of an unobstructed sweep around the middle of the earth. A young American, Frank Bessac, who recently crossed Tibet in flight before the Reds, wrote: "The thing I will remember most about the Tibetan mountains was the wind . . . a howling, skin-blasting roar which never died for a moment throughout the day. So bad was it that if anyone had anything to say he got it said before midmorning. After that there was no conversation: it was impossible to do anything but hide our heads in our coat collars."

The Tsang Po winds are indeed so heady with altitude up there at 16,000 feet in the little city of the big winds that they say that on nights when the wind has been known to stop completely, the sky is so startled it feels dizzy with emptiness — "like an empty box."

Fortunate it is for the Tibetans that this drastic phenomenon is rare, for almost always it is accompanied with unaccountable illness and death. Perhaps life in that wind-lorn land is as mystically dependent on the wind as a candle flame is dependent on calmness. While the wind blows, the crust of life holds on, but when the wind dies a vital fuel valve seems to close and life quietly softens and ebbs away.

With its almost timeless devotion, the wind has shaped and colored much of the earth — and the task continues hourly. Wind deposits called loess or eolation blanket wide areas of the continents and the sea bottoms. Wind erosion carves lofty rocks and lowly knolls, small swales of grass and rolling dunes that creep like waves in largo.

One such wave of sand swallowed the whole village of Kunzen on the Baltic, then in a few years flowed on to uncover it again — leaving it little the worse for wear. Yet in the Sudan a sand haboob is known to have rasped down wooden telegraph poles in a night, and roughened windowpanes to intransparency in an hour.

Inexplicable indeed the moods and deeds of the wind, countless the mountain trees warped to its will, the whistling towers, the chimneys of stone sculped by its sightless chisel, the buttes and the graceful monoliths. Atolls in the Pacific are said to be designed entire by the steadfast tradewinds. Even the scope of great windward rain jungles in the tropics are architectured by the wind, and vast leeward deserts across Africa, Australia, Asia, and the Americas.

In May 1937 during a southwest gale yellow sand fell in Canton Basle, Switzerland, so heavily that the countryside appeared swathed in a strange sulphuric fog. The sand was later proved to be from the Sahara Desert a thousand miles away and it must have been picked up by a simoom to be blown over the Alps at above 12,000 feet.

At the same time in the Engadine valley, also in Switzerland, a mysterious fall of red sand occurred, the origin of which has not yet been discovered. At other times and places pebbles, shells, and seaweed, even living frogs and fishes, have rained upon the earth, perhaps after being sucked aloft in a vortex, then carried inexplicably on the wind for great distances.

Can anyone ever say what shall not serve as grist for the wind?

And what of the wind's song — so familiar yet never quite repeated? The wind has a hundred voices, which have awed and lured and terrified mankind from his beginning. Have you heard the whine of the hound that grew from the wail of the wind, pleading at first, howling with rage as it freshened? Have you listened to the thresh of needled boughs in a gale when "that grand old harper smote his thunder-harp of pines?" Hark the warm sigh of the salt breeze sprawled in the bellying sail, the flutey trickle of air from the knothole in the fence, the limp flutter of shirts and aprons on the line.

Did you ever take pencil and book to scrib down the sounds the wind makes as it sifts and soughs through trees? Each kind of tree is a sort of musical instrument: the apple a cello, the old oak a bass viol, the cypress a harp, the willow a flute, the young pine a muted violin. Put your ear close to the whispering branch and you may catch what it is saying: the brittle twitter of dry oak leaves in winter, the faint breathing of the junipers, the whirring of hickory twigs, the thrumming of slender birch clumps, the sibilant souffle of the cedars, the mild murmuring of the sugar maple, and behind them all the trafficky thunder of whole bare trees torn in a headlong tide of air.

Inclining your accustomed ear downward you may even tune in on the soft purring of pussy willow buds, the burr of the wild cranberry, and the swish of swamp grass barely rising above the clicking of reeds and cattails, blending again into the over-all cataract of sound.

The humming telephone wires along the road seem to have a further significance in the language of the wind. Is it the harmonics of those aeolian strands or the mumbling gossip of the breezes as they eavesdrop on the long-distance calls? Sometimes martins and swallows sit by hundreds on those vibrant wires — listening in — perhaps divining more than we know of the business and hope and love that pulse mile on mile within the clasp of their tiny toes.

In Ireland they say that of all the barnyard creatures the pig is the most gifted for he alone can see the wind. If it's true, pilots should not stint on their breakfast bacon, even before a stratosphere flight, for you really have to see the wind to fly well. You have to think wind too, and feel it as a bird feels it on his wings and through the barbules of his feathers.

As you fly, the wind comes to you little by little, more every day, every week, depending on how sensitive you are. On your first flight you are puzzled as to where the wind is — like old Monc Mason in his balloon — but presently you begin to feel it and it grows apace.

Is it intuition? Is it your subconscious mind? Through little clues it comes — clues everywhere: that nodding tree down there with the leaves always appearing lighter on the windward side, that dust behind the wagon, the rippling grass, the flag, the little waves on the lake, the girl burning leaves with blowing hair and skirt, and the smoke from her fire. Even the drifting of your plane itself. Can't you smell the wind? Can't you feel it?

The whole air becomes at last a fluid mass that you can see moving, that you can understand and trust and lean against. Your wings now grip it surely and hold you steadfast in the sky as firmly as your feet hold you above the ground.

No longer need you find yourself in the bone-chilling situation of a young lady pilot I know who hadn't learned to know the wind. Flying cross country in a small plane she saw ahead of her a range of hills and a dark cloud about two hundred feet above it. Thinking to pass easily between the hills and the cloud she continued dreamily on her course at an altitude slightly higher than the hills. It simply didn't occur to her to consider the wind. When she noticed that the plane was settling she just advanced the throttle and pulled into a climb to regain altitude. But for some reason, instead of rising the plane continued to settle. The girl naturally kept advancing the throttle, still trying to climb over the hill which didn't yet seem too much to her.

By the time she realized that the nearer she was getting to the hill the faster the plane was settling, it was too late to turn back. The situation suddenly looked hopeless. She was headed straight for a rocky ledge just below the top and she braced herself for the crash. But in the final instant an amazing wind hit her, supporting the plane so firmly that she neatly cleared the ridge and no sooner passed it than a violent upsurge lifted her high into the sky.

The close call left the girl shaky for days but she had learned a lesson she never forgot: there has to be a downdraft somewhere on the lee side of a hill. Observation will soon show where it is, and it is elementary in flying to know whether you are going with or against the wind and which is the lee side of any elevation.

A famous illustration of the consequences of not thoroughly learning this lesson is the tragic crash of the British dirigible R101. Seven hundred and seventy-five feet long, the R101 was in her day the largest airship in the world. She had taken off from Cardington, Britain, the afternoon of October 4, 1930, on her maiden voyage, bound for Egypt and the Orient with most of England's leading airmen on board. Considered, like the *Titanic*, the latest thing in comfort and safety, there was no quiver or qualm among the eager and prominent passengers who filed up her gangway only seven hours before the unimagined holocaust in a French sugar-beet field. Most of them had relaxed in the wide cabin for a smoke after dinner while cruising at sixty knots across the south coast and all retired early as the luxurious sky giant hummed reassuringly over the channel.

It was only on encountering a severe rain squall near Beauvais that an inkling of serious trouble came to the pilot's mind. As he recalled it afterward: "We got into a terrific storm with high winds. The dirigible simply would not rise. I gave her more gas to get her up in the air, but she did not respond.

"Rain was falling in such torrents that our ship was blown down to earth. She bumped twice, slightly, and then with a terrible impact buried her nose into the ground. Immediately came a terrific explosion followed by two lesser ones.

"Flames instantly engulfed the airship. I was shot outside my pilot window and found myself on the ground. At the moment of the catastrophe everybody aboard except myself and assistant navigators was asleep. The motors were turning to perfection. It was the tempest which caused our destruction."

Fire shot through the entire length of the R101, and the bewildered passengers screamed in agony as they fought to escape the confusion of bedclothes, scorching heat, and smoke while flames leaped hundreds of feet above them, feeding on twenty-five tons of fuel oil as well as the huge mass of hydrogen. Only eight of the fifty-four persons managed to get out, each by his individual miracle — such as being doused under the water ballast tank, blown out a window, diving through a fire-rent hole in the hull.

The committee of investigation at first largely blamed the rain for the accident, though it was admittedly something of a mystery why the fast-moving airship could not have overcome the slight added weight of the downpour. Many months were to pass before some sleuth finally tracked down the real guilty element: the wind.

For in truth the culprit was one of those air falls or down-blowing eddies over the lee slope of a hill. The particular hill was about 500 feet high, near Beauvais, and the configuration of the ground there was found to affect the air up to a height of nearly 2000 feet. Although the minimum safe altitude for dirigibles had been de-declared to be two and one half times their length, or about 1900 feet for the R101, the great airship had approached Beauvais at only 1500 feet of altitude.

Obviously that had seemed safe enough to the pilot but, even though he was foreman and engineer of the Royal Airship Works, admittedly he had not sufficiently reckoned on the wind. Caught suddenly by her nose in the treacherous downdraft, the R101 tilted earthward. Some free hydrogen in her huge envelope floated aft to the stern, giving it so much lift that although her elevators were put up at once she could not answer but plunged helplessly to her doom.

Yet it is possible, with knowledge and care, to avoid going against the wind's grain. It can be profitable too, for there is an ancient saying that "the wind is not in your debt though it fill your sail." The flying navigator is therefore always seeking ways to cash in on his wind acquaintanceship, to fill his sail for nothing.

One of his newest ways (besides the sporadic jet stream) is

pressure-pattern flying. In the early World War II days we used to fly by the great circle as ocean steamers do. That is the shortest geographical distance across the earth's curved surface. But now again we have found it worthwhile to go out of our way looking for favorable winds, as did the sailing ships, and on a daily routine basis. By going a hundred miles off the great circle we can sometimes get such a wind boost that we arrive an hour earlier. Some days we gain almost nothing. But in the long run it averages out. As it costs more than $1000 an hour to fly a modern four-engined airplane it is big money in the pocket to put a steady average following breeze on the payroll along with the crew.

To find the right wind at the right time for the daily job of course may not be as easy as you think. The aerial navigator cannot depend, like a sailing ship captain, on the average wind direction over weeks or months — which is usually well enough known to be a reasonable bet. He flies too fast for that. A strong head wind lasting only five hours may set him back as much as if it kept blowing for weeks.

The map of air pressures offers the basic answer. If you can find out the exact pattern of weather pressures, you have the dope on the important winds that will blow many hours and many hundred miles ahead. What is more: you can harness them to your craft.

Dr. Hugo Eckener of the Graf Zeppelin first proved this. The old Graf naturally couldn't fly very fast: perhaps seventy m.p.h. at cruising speed. On his westward crossing of the Atlantic if he had stubbornly tried to buck westerly headwinds he might have spent days going backward. Instead he closely studied pressure and wind conditions and zigzagged all over the ocean hitchhiking on tail winds wherever they could be reached on time. He went extra miles over the water, but less miles through the air: a vitally important saving.

As pressure-pattern flying became common practice shortly after the war, various ways were worked out to help navigators keep track of the winds. Weather reports were radioed from planes in flight every hour, co-ordinated and edited at central stations and the information rebroadcast at half-hour intervals. Besides that, planes now carry barometers which can be accurately corrected for altitude so that navigators can tell independently whether they are approaching a lower pressure area or higher pressure, therefore whether the best winds are to the right or the left. Coming into lower pressure north of the equator you must of course veer to the right to find tail winds, as coming into higher pressure you turn to the left.

If you want to learn the most intimate of all the secrets of the wind you must of course take up gliding. For in a glider or sail plane every movement — often your life — depends on the wind. You feel the wind in your fingers, on your cheek, in your bones. It is the bird's way — soaring — catching the rising thermal air over the sun-baked hayfield by day, over the sultry pond by night, coasting up the windward slopes of hills, spiraling over factory chimneys, searching for "cloud streets" marked by the cumulus coiffure of rising air.

Prince of the soaring birds is the albatross — that wandering ghost of the nether seas who is so truly the wind's child that he cannot even fold his great wings comfortably but, after an hour on the mast, must slump back into the sky again, like a club man into an armchair, in order to relax.

If there is another of God's creatures so attuned to the wind's world it must be the tiny gossamer spider whose web is almost the very essence of wind. More trusting than the able albatross, he throws his pliant being literally to the winds to do with what they will, retaining not even a free balloonist's control over the ups or downs of fate.

Did you ever see a gossamer spider on an October afternoon, standing on a tree limb or a gatepost preparing for take-off? With his tiny head to windward he spins out into the sky a fine silken thread from the spinneret at the end of his body. It's a "run-up" of a special kind. When this spider spinnaker is long enough to hold some real wind and he feels the halyard tugging hard, the spider lets go and sails away on the breeze.

Where to? That is a matter for the wind to decide. However, the gossamer spider has his slight measure of control. If the wind rises he can reef in his thread to "shorten sail." If the wind drops he can pay it out again like a yachtsman in a tight race. His own body is his craft and crew. He may sail thus on the wind for hundreds of miles, even across continents or seas if the wind wills it so, rising as high as 60,000 feet and remaining aloft for weeks. In proportion to his size he can cruise to the moon with ease, literally riding on a cushion of molecules tuned to the inscrutable marrow of the sky.

As windmills upon the earth turn and turn again so upon the sea sails fill and fulfill while the mysteries of the wind blow ever as they list. Rabbinical tradition whispers betimes of wind angels who die as soon as born, and it is said old hags still hawk winds on knotted strings for superstitious sailors on the wharves of Norway.

Even as He did in the days of Job, "God thundereth marvellously with his voice; great things doeth he, which we cannot comprehend . . . Out of the south cometh the whirlwind: and cold out of the north . . . Dost thou know the balancings of the clouds, the wondrous works of him which is perfect in knowledge? How thy garments are warm when he quieteth the earth by the south wind? . . . By what way is the light parted which scattereth the east wind upon the earth? . . . "

6. The Cloud

PERHAPS IT IS the sheer exuberance of the moving shapes I see from my work window up here. Or perhaps it is what naturally happens to thoughts that have too long been grazing in the pasture of the clouds. But every now and then I think I sense a maidenly wile in the way some passing nimbus form waves at us as we thunder by — our four engines coolly roaring.

A few of these buoyant wisps of cloud will only tentatively sway aside to let us pass, so awed are they by our slipstream, half turning to gaze wistfully after our virile hulk until we leave their view. And some cling to each other self-consciously — now giving way to timorous mirth, now raining a silent tear.

For through their sky we play the dominant, the active role. We are their hero, their goer of the go. And as the plow lusts after the gentle body of earth, so our flashing propeller blades yearn for the tender mists, whirling apart the coy veils of cloud. Our airspeed pitot tubes and loop antennae are the stamens of the sky — our phallic fuselage with its powerful driving action into the passive softness of the cloud as wonderful a symbol of ravishment as can be known.

In fact, it is scarcely less overwhelming than the complete penetration of the wind itself, which can go through the densest cloud like a thought through the mind, perhaps bearing the same relation to it as the soul to the body. For indeed if the wind is the spirit of the sky's ocean, the clouds are its texture. They are embodied imagination, the sheet music of the heavens, the architecture of moving air. Theirs is easily the most uninhibited dominion of the earth. Nothing in physical shape is too fantastic for them. They can be round as apples or as fine as string, as dense as a jungle, as wispy as a whiff of down, as mild as puddle water, or as potent as the belch of a volcano. Some are thunderous anvils formed by violent updrafts from the warm earth. Some are the ragged coattails of storms that have passed. Some are stagnant blankets of warm air resting on cold. Some are mare's-tails made of ice crystals floating like whispers in the chill upper sky. Some are herringbones, sheets, cream puffs, ox-bends, veils, hammerheads, lenses, spangled mantillas, sponges, black shrouds.

Did you ever think how unbelievable clouds would be if you had been born blind and no one had ever told you about them? Some of us born with eyes, on the contrary, must guard against letting them become a perfunctory backdrop to our imagination. Yet here float the clouds in their unignorable glory! So much so that when I fly over the common cumulus meadows of the seven-thousand-foot level, it is sometimes hard to keep from visually tending the sheep down there or looking for paths among the flowering groves of cotton. In the dawn, I would sometimes have to look the other way to miss the fat pink sultan disporting with his harem, his yellow slob of eunuch lolling impotent in the background. In the shadow of thunder, could I possibly avoid the sleepy forms that suddenly stand erect, casting their white bedclothes aside, then bulging into titanic genii to the bidding of the gale?

Frequently our sky wagon takes us literally through halls of air — long corridors built of clouds that make me feel I am flying down a gray tunnel with ever changing walls — here an open vista or an alcove, sometimes a shaft upward or down or slanting — perhaps a series of veils to be penetrated. Sometimes for hours we get no glimpse of earth nor sun nor stars, but simply grind our way onward and onward by faith in instruments in our private world of cloud, relying on chance for what we see — which, often as not, turns out to amaze us.

The other day, for instance, flying for an hour through a great gray banquet hall of cloud, an inter-layer plain, I suddenly beheld a glowing red and gold sunset straight down! The direct sun in the west was blocked from view by cloud walls at our level, but a hole had opened in the floor out of which the reflected solar glory, after passing underneath, bounced up from the nether clouds — a sort of twentieth-century Dante's Inferno!

As we see them from above, all clouds are in a sense the earth's outer face, her expression of mood, her veil of confidence. They are the dress that covers her nakedness, the coiffure that adorns her head. They are the realm of gaseous speed, of fantasy incarnate — the arena of dramatic change, of meteoric smiles and grimaces that come and go, cubic mile for cubic mile.

Some flyers no doubt regard clouds as little better than a menace, something to be avoided, the complexion of evil weather which they must combat and conquer. Yet to the more sensitive, even the blandest of clouds can be symbolic of great unseen forces which winged man is just now beginning to comprehend. Obviously all clouds mean something, and even though their Rosetta stone may be undiscovered we can already sense that they tell of the contours and temperatures of continents and seas — letting some of the form of the earth show through.

If it is true that clothes do not make the man, at least they can give the discerning eye something of his nature. That is how it is with the clothing of the atmosphere. In the sky's wardrobe there is a dress for every occasion: white cumulus plumes for a fine spring day, gay cirrus feathers for summer, or a sporty fall mantle of high lamb's-wool — a costume inimitable for each page of history.

By the close of the nineteenth century, clouds had been pretty well cataloged and classified — both by shape and behavior, and their hidden natures were beginning to be understood. The basic types were four: the *cirrus* which comes from the Latin word for "curl" because these clouds often look like wisps of curly hair as they float in the upper sky; the *stratus* type from the Latin for "spread out" because they are like great soft blankets spread out across the light of day; the *nimbus* from the Latin "rain," being the spongy, wet, low-scudding kind of clouds that characteristically dowse us with their rainy contents; and the *cumulus* meaning "heap" in Latin, which are the common fair-weather clouds that heap themselves upward into beautiful mountainlike shapes, sometimes turning into tremendous thunderheads that fill the sky.

Of course there are innumerable variations and combinations of these clouds and a few special extra ones which make up the unlimited panoply of the actual skyscape, but these four types remain the foundation of cloud classification today.

The cirrus are the highest of the regular workaday clouds, which seems to give them something of a special ethereal nature. They are the wing feathers of the wind and have been seen from two hundred miles away. They have neither the thunderous voice of the cumulus nor the wet cargo of nimbus, but silently flick their horse tails and their dainty plumes like a kind of elite fairy cavalry that no ordinary earthlings can hope to approach. Because of their height they seem to move slowly even though their real speed is commonly more than a hundred miles an hour. They are calm in aspect and very cool. In actuality they are the birthplace of snow — fine powdery snow that floats six miles up in summer and winter alike, seldom relaxing its steadfast grip on the sky to let a handful of Heaven's purity flutter its way to earth.

The cirrus are the only common clouds which seldom grow heavy or show a dark side. They are the silver eyelashes of the sun, their whole surface being nothing but silver lining, silver that I have seen up close as tiny dazzling ice crystals or, if you prefer, newborn snowflakes. Sometimes in tropical latitudes a cirrus canopy will rise eight or ten miles up, tilting into a giddy fish-scale staircase to the moon. And sometimes its silvery scales become shells and take on a pearly iridescence in the twilight, holding the warm colors of the sunset long after the lower clouds have turned to gray.

The actual material of the cirrus is tenuous indeed: ice crystals spread out about 5000 to the cubic foot, which is only 3 per cubic inch and much less dense than the substance of ordinary clouds. Cirrus wisps and tufts sometimes become almost invisible when you fly close to them, revealing a kind of unearthly, optic shyness like that of the rainbow.

Yet they are completely real and they perform a strange but natural drama that meteorology has hardly begun to understand. At medium range many look more like frozen cascades than strands of hair, and this is exactly what they turn out to be. A German cloud pioneer called them *Fallstreifen*, or "fall streaks," having

cirrus crystals found at 26,000 ft. and 40°F. below zero

particle from a vapor trail four minutes old at 30,000 ft.

all magnified X 50

discovered that, when visible, this type of cirrus is actually composed of slowly falling ice trails. It is similar in dynamic principle to spindrift on the sea, the streaks of spume blown off the crests of breaking waves.

As the sky's wind almost always decreases in speed with a decrease in height, the crystals that fall soon get left behind the cloud they fell from. Evaporating and shrinking as they descend, they drift behind in visible curved streaks like handfuls of fine seed sown by angels upon a fallow sky, there left on the wind to blossom into some future life still hidden from our little view.

This beautiful cascading of snow goes on continuously before our eyes in mare's-tails, in the simple hook-shaped cirrus-uncinus, and in cirrus of more complicated form. You have to look for a long time to see any trace of motion, but that at least is now well established by much patient photography. The falling may happen several times in one long wavy tail too, for the tail can become a river of infant snow with a whole series of cascades in it, the crystals growing as they fall through humid layers of sky, decaying as they pass into drier layers, alternately moving vertically and horizontally fast and slow, according to the actual folds of air — their maneuvers revealing their adventures like a bat-winged parachutist stunting over the fairgrounds. The writing of the wind gets into the script also, of course, for the actual paths of the floating snow crystals depend not only on their weight in relation to surface friction but on the complex stirrings of the air itself, on the strange shearings and outer turbulences of the jet stream, on the circling highs and lows of the polar front.

The fluffy tops of some cirrus forms are made of water droplets as well as tiny snow, but these are not truly cirrus yet and they seldom last long, for their snow is growing as their water dries and

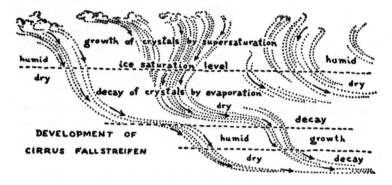

DEVELOPMENT OF
CIRRUS FALLSTREIFEN

they too soon fall transformed into the graceful fibrous curves that are their priceless contribution to beauty in the sky.

Other examples of cirrus are born of the slipstreams of passing airplanes, sired by exhaust fumes, mothered in the womb of wind, slowly growing from vapor trails into great shimmering stripes, half a mile wide, perhaps eventually descending into the largo ripples of mackerel scales. And sometimes you see natural cirrus arranged uncannily into endless radiating bands that cover the sky like the meridians of the celestial globe from horizon to horizon in straight lines which, like railroad tracks, appear to meet at one point in the distance. Still other cirrus clouds are the living ghosts of thunderheads, coattails of Thor, having been torn by the winds from the fibrillated tops of thunder anvils as the fury dissipated below — some of these still slowly churning after days in the invisible grinding wheels at 30,000 feet — some drifting like silver birds with symmetrical rows of feathers in eerie stateliness across the sky.

When cirrus clouds begin to thicken and compromise with lower clouds, naturally they are given different names. First after cirrus in the usual sequence comes the gauzelike stratified form known as cirro-stratus, the milk cloud, a high milky cobweb veil made of ice crystals that barely dims the sun and moon yet creates halos around both, sometimes rainbow halos when the film is curdling still further into cirro-cumulus, the mackerel sky.

As the milk cloud is flattening and descending toward stratus, it normally soon warms up, its crystals melt into droplets, and it develops into the low dense blanket of that name, a change that is definitely a sign of approaching rain.

The stratus cloud bears no resemblance to the ethereal cirrus. It is by contrast earthy, homespun, often shapeless. It is the great-plains country of the sky, the broad aerial valley floor. It is the conservative member, the stable personality, the wet blanket of the heavens that poets seldom write about and few people definitely remember. It does not transmit sunshine nor does it completely blot out the sun, usually permitting just a dim spot of light to reach its underside.

It tends to seem the drabber because it is undynamic: neither high nor brushing the ground, neither dry nor wet enough for an exciting shower. It is a kind of Tory fog of the lower levels (about two thousand feet up). It is the Scottish mist, its brightest color a dour bluish gray, its strongest rain a slow steady drizzle.

But the circumstance of perhaps greatest significance in the stratus is the fact that it represents a temperature inversion — or nearly so. That means that the stratus is born when the normal condition of warmer air near the ground and cooler higher up is reversed or reduced. It is exactly the opposite of the cumulus which appears when that condition is accentuated, when hot air below bursts through the cold, condensing into visible vertical form. The stratus by contrast is an utterly horizontal cloud and kept so by complete absence of vertical currents. It is the epitome of equilibrium, the stolid envoy of peace.

Sometimes the stratus cousin called alto-stratus at around 10,000 feet becomes so thin it is semi-transparent like the surface of a calm sea — silent and still as you fly over it, yet arranged in slight waves like a sheet of gauze lying on the beach. Through this veil you can look down on the colorful anatomy of the landscape, green and yellow fields and glistening ribbons of roads and white streams and purple hills crouching, appearing through the thin cloud like the gaudy bottom of a tropic lagoon.

At other times this same cloud becomes fibrous like a great cobweb and floats in beautiful silky whorls or, having thickened, may look from above like nothing in the world but a field of snow as you skim above it in your winged toboggan — league upon league of it — a kind of subjective arctic plain, a glacier of the mind.

From below, alto-stratus is often dark enough to blot out the sun's outline completely though sometimes it seems illumined from inside like a frosted bulb. It is the same thing as ground fog raised a few thousand feet into the air and drifting along on the breeze in tattered spongy blotches.

When the stratus or alto-stratus evolves into a real rain cloud it is called the nimbo-stratus. Then it becomes heavy and low and ragged, sometimes mixed with soggy cumulus, and it emits a steady pattering rain.

In modern meteorology there is no longer any such cloud as the pure nimbus of old, it being recognized that this ancient drencher is really the rain-producing development of two of the other main kinds of cloud: stratus and cumulus. The nimbo-stratus, already described, is the rainy aspect of the low-strung well-tempered stratus breed. It forms a ceiling at 3000 feet on the average, though often much lower, and has been found to produce rain or snow within four hours in seventy-three per cent of all cases, this precipitation averaging eight hours' duration in winter, but varying widely in individual cases.

The cumulo-nimbus on the other hand is the big rainy brother of the rough, radical cumulus cloud and he heaves into being as the cumulus grows into a thunderhead and starts tossing his weight around to his favorite accompaniment of thunder and lightning. Cumulo-nimbus is probably the most violent and dangerous of all clouds, and we will come to its details presently. The straight nimbus aspect, indistinct as it is, might be summed up as the soggy, scudding bottom parts of clouds that come stampeding low over the hills like rampant mustangs, tossing their soft manes about them, their bodies passing darkly before the east wind and kicking out behind not dust but drenching rain.

The cumulus, on the other hand, the last of the basic clouds, is of course the most dynamic and dramatic of all. It is the head end of a wind that blows straight up. It is the vertical cloud which grows high as much as wide or handsome. It is the healthy, heaping helping of normal fair weather. It is the white woolly sheep cloud that looks like a puff of steam cut off square at the bottom.

That, in fact, is just about what a cumulus cloud is: a puff of steam or hot humid air. And it is cut off square at the bottom by the horizontal condensation level below which the air is warm enough to hold its moisture unseen. So to visualize a cumulus cloud correctly you need to see it as only the visible capital of a tall transparent column of hot air. Or perhaps it would be more exact to describe the column as shaped like a tree, for it is strong and steady and narrow near the base, spreading and branching and tossing about in the breeze as it goes upward. It is by nature almost exactly like the rising column of smoke over a campfire, but so much bigger that it seems to be standing still and, being mostly clear air instead of smoke, its main body is invisible.

It is thus a kind of unseeable fire tree, a rising stream of bubbling hot air whose foot is a heat source: a plowed field baking in the sun, a town, or perhaps a lake at night whose waters are warmer than the surrounding country because of their better conservation of the day's heat. And remember, it is only the tip top of the tree, above the cool, condensation level, that is visible as a cumulus cloud. The rest, like eight ninths of an iceberg, is out of sight.

One reason so little of the heat tree can normally be seen is that the upward flow of warm air has a kind of anchor that usually stops its rise shortly after it condenses into visible form, thus strictly limiting the cloud. This anchor is the cooling and weighting down of the cloud as it expands in the thin upper air. Expansion has a cooling effect on any gas — you have noticed the coldness of the air hissing out of a deflating tire — and when the cloud gets as cool as the surrounding air it is not light and buoyant enough to rise any higher.

That is the way it usually happens — on a normal sunny day. And it is just as well, else the sky would be one great perpetual thunderstorm and life on earth would be far wetter and noisier and

more dangerous than it is already.

Cumulus clouds usually appear around ten o'clock on a sunny morning as the ground heats up and starts those columns of hot air bubbling upwards. Quite suddenly you notice them springing to eye all over the sky and all at the same altitude, perhaps three or four thousand feet up. From then on they grow slowly larger until late afternoon when their sources of heat are cut off.

Along a coastline you can often see these cumulus sheep grazing **high over the** sunbaked land while over the cooler sea the sky remains an empty blue because updrafts of air are too feeble there to give clouds birth. This observable fact, by the way, was very important to the ancient South Sea navigators, for even a small sunny atoll will usually puff up enough heat to produce a lone fleecy cloud which may float all day a mile above it like a cosmic lighthouse, pointing the way to land from ten times as far out at sea as the island itself can be seen. What better could a Micronesian helmsman wish to steer by?

A cumulus cloud is by no means a static passive thing, however. It has a metabolism all its own that may completely renew its body every few minutes, the time depending on its size. It has been proven to be rolling and changing constantly, growing on the windward or rising side, decaying on the leeward sinking side. A large cumulus cloud is also normally a corporation of smaller clouds that were born separately and grew together into working partnership. We often find one hollow or full of holes and shifting crevices, perhaps doughnut-shaped. And though its roots of rising heat are usually quite definite over land, they may become so dissipated over the sea that even the gulls do not feel them. The Caribbean project of the Woods Hole Oceanographic Institution investigating the dynamics of trade-wind clouds, for example, reports the clouds down there usually "seemed to arise from random bunches of air, or eddies, that had reached the condensation level."

Of course on some days the cumulus clouds don't show up at all, even over land. Maybe the air gets too dry to condense, or an inversion warms things so much up high that any heat bubbles stop before they get there. On other days the cumulus clouds form so close together that they make a solid horizontal woolly blanket. On still others they wax vertical until they grow thunderheads. There are in fact as many varieties of cumulus clouds as of vegetables in your garden, even a degree of similarity. Cumulus humilis, the fair-weather cumulus, pops out daily like cabbages in the spring; cumulo-nimbus first appears as a cauliflower head; altocumulus often lines up in neat compact rows like brussels sprouts.

In the alto-cumulus family alone there are more cloud species than you could shake a weathervane at: the handsome turreted a.-c. *castellatus*, the strange lens-shaped a.-c. *lenticularis*, the sheep-like a.-c. *floccus*, the thin a.-c. *translucidus*, the dense a.-c. *opacus*, the wavy a.-c. *undulatus*, the twilight a.-c. *vesperalis*, the sundry alto-cumulus bands, ripples, and rolls, the dainty herringbones. And both cumulus and cumulo-nimbus have varieties like the bridged *arcus*, the thready *calvus*, or the bosomy *mammatus* which is as temperamental as it is female and deservedly feared as an occasional breeder of tornadoes. Cirro-cumulus and strato-cumulus clouds have each their own variations also, as has the broken-up fracto-cumulus or the stuffy *cumulus congestus*. All are born of rising heat, all hankering to billow upward like a puff of steam.

Something every glider pilot needs do is study these cumulus forms, and especially the unseen heat streams that create them. They are his propellor, his spark, his gasoline. Except perhaps for windward hillsides they are his main staircase to altitude. He knows them as thermals or "cloud streets" and one of his favorite tactics is gliding from one to another of these unseen elevators across the country, spiraling upward in each to gain what height he lost between.

That is how the hawks and eagles fly: the easy way, hitchhiking on the heat currents, riding the fire bubbles like the fledgling phoenix of old. Theirs not to fuss or flap, but just to ease onto a warm shelf of air and ride it up the sky. Man might have done it centuries ago if he had had the imagination to visualize air and heat and speed as they really are. He certainly had the materials and tools at hand to build a glider — all but the ken that would make it work — and that knowledge, simple as it now seems, was enough to stump everyone from Leonardo da Vinci to Tom Edison.

Nowadays the glider pilot already has a wealth of experience behind him. He knows all the signs. He has delicate instruments for reading temperature and altitude too. Sometimes he even outsoars the birds, as recently happened to one of the crack glider men of Southern California. This pilot was soaring across the desert, thermal by thermal, minding his own business when he picked himself such a powerful updraft that he began spiraling skyward so fast he attracted the attention of an eagle, a hawk, and three buzzards which joined in behind him, evidently doing their best to follow his example. And the rising wind even picked up pieces of dead sagebrush and tumbleweed and carried this and other debris swirling aloft among the birds and around the plane — up and up for nineteen thousand feet, ending inside and near the top of a large cumulus thunderhead! When he finally emerged none of the birds were to be seen anywhere.

This kind of updraft of course becomes partially visible through its flotsam and indeed impresses itself on the mind as the true power at the bottom of every cumulus cloud. But its strength does not always originate with heat alone, for another source of uplift can also create cumulus clouds and in fact was discovered much earlier by the very first glider pioneers as a good booster to get you off the ground. This is the air rise created as the wind blows toward a hill or mountain, climbing to get over it. Not necessarily as warm in the first place, this kind of air stream is just about as readily condensed into visible cloud by expansion and on contact with the coolth of the upper levels. And it also spawns a number of cloud types somewhat related to the cumulus family.

The manner of cloudbirth incidentally is something well worth investigating, as it is beautifully revealing of the way God creates His material world. Try climbing a high hill on a humid windy day and watch the air pouring over the crest. If there are vertical cliffs there and the relative humidity is close to 100 per cent, you are almost sure to see steamy exhalations drifting off from the highest points — infant clouds that squirm happily as they nestle in the cradle wind of heaven — misty fledglings that may grow in an hour into a sea of vapor so dense it shrouds the mountains from top to toe, blacking out the sun.

That is how clouds are born, but it is only one of many ways. The process is practically continuous and almost universal. Cumulus nurslings emerge from their hot-air eggs over warm fields and towns often only to blow along on the wind for a few minutes to cooler regions where, mixing with drier air, they fade and die. But meanwhile their hot-air mothers have been giving birth to new brothers and sisters who march through life behind them in an intermittent, ever changing file, that grows at one end while decaying at the other, keeping condensation up with evaporation — a perpetual process without which clouds cannot live.

And so, under genetic conditions apparently remote but actually closely related, clouds come into the world wherever air is cooled too low to hold its moisture unseen — on stifling, sultry summer afternoons; on clear, crisp winter nights; on soft October dawns; on windward mountain slopes; even miles above mountain ridges where eddies of humid wind spiral into the chill reaches and are literally cooled into sight.

Of course there must be some dust particles in the air (at least 200 nuclei per cubic centimeter, they say) for moisture to condense around, or else no cloud can be born — but no need to worry that air near the earth will ever become too pure for condensation. Meteorologists say that the purest natural air rarely gets much below a dust count of 300 or 400 particles per cubic centimeter at sea level, and then only when there is a strong downdraft of crystal clean air from high altitudes. Even in mid-Pacific where it is cleanest, air averages about 1000 particles per cubic centimeter, sometimes rising to 40,000. Over forest land the average count is 50,000, and over cities 150,000, increasing into the millions at times of smog.

Cloudbirth begins when the humidity is high enough to supersaturate the largest and flakiest of whatever nuclei are in the air. Some of these hygroscopic particles are several hundred thousandths of an inch in diameter. Only two or three out of each hundred of them collect sufficient moisture to produce the droplets that make the cloud, but the total number is plenty large enough and, once these chosen particles are activated by their coating of moisture, they alone take on all the additional moisture condensed while their smaller, drier fellow dust particles swarm about them like flies around pots of molasses. Only when the relative sizes reach the disparity of flies buzzing about a horse does the condensation become visible or can it be said that a cloud has been born.

The birth of mountain clouds brings to mind a special kind of cloud not ordinarily classified among the four basic types: the cloud that stands still. Most ordinary clouds, as you've noticed if you have ever lain on your back in the grass, drift slowly along on the wind, eventually disappearing below the horizon. But they have some strange cousins that behave very differently, defying the winds as if literally tied to the earth. You see these generally near mountain peaks and they are in fact tied to the earth by invisible thongs of humid air that spring from solid ground, that may reach up from any orographic configuration bold enough to deflect moist currents up into the cold. The island lighthouse cloud mentioned earlier is sometimes in this category though usually created more by heat than a hill.

The best known of fixed clouds is probably the banner cloud which streams like a flag from a high peak — continuously gaining new substance as valley air, riding up a mountainside on the wind's back, condenses near the crest — continuously evaporating old substance at its tattered flagtail end perhaps a mile to leeward as the air mixes with drier air or subsides to a warmer level. Thus the wind blows right through the banner cloud instead of carrying it along — just as if it were a flag of cloth.

Another stand-still cloud familiar to mountaineers is the crest or cap cloud, a kind of tablecloth of fog that drapes itself snugly upon summits. Like the banner cloud it lets the wind blow through it, eating condensation on the one side, voiding evaporation on the other. It is also called the helm cloud or foehn wall through which the foehn winds blow.

The third stay-put cloud is the strangest and loveliest of all, the lenticular or lens cloud. It is usually shaped like an almond or a surreal convex lens with tapering pointed edges and, like a lens, often shows iridescent colors around its circumference. It looks as if it might have been painted by Dali. As with the last two clouds, it remains stationary in the windy sky, balancing condensation with evaporation, often miles from a hill so that its air leash from earth is hard to trace. Yet it is anchored securely by a standing wave of air that billows up from some irregularity of ground to windward. It may be high enough to mark the beginning of the stratosphere or it may float close to the low stratus level. Wherever it is found it is a living graph of the wind's true path, the fixed white cap of a standing billow of air — as real as a stopped clock, as graceful as the flying tresses of Aura — cool, beautiful, unearthly.

A special form of the lenticular in mountain skies is the moazagotl cloud or "foe's beard," so called because of its reputation as an omen of trouble. This dangerous cloud, part of the complex condensation in standing air waves to leeward of high mountain ranges, was recently explored with its associated violent winds in a special "Mountain Wave Project" of the Geophysics Research Directorate of the United States Air Force. The objective was to discover the full pattern of the wave and the causes of its most violent disturbances which have so often led pilots to disaster, particularly in sudden turbulent downdrafts that dropped them from apparently safe altitudes to the crags below.

Flying sail planes that are too slow to be seriously buffeted by rough air, the research men gradually accumulated facts. They found that the many waves of wind in the lee of the Sierras near Bishop, California, flow up and down in almost regular rhythm between two layers of rotating, eddying air, the upper moving invisibly in the stratosphere, the lower outlined by a long succession of revolving moazagotl clouds, now better known to meteorologists as rotor clouds because of their roller-bearing action under the leaping wind. At the base of each of a long series of multiple lenticular clouds arranged like stacks of airplane wings in a factory, the rotor clouds are the focal points of the wild lower turbulence that extends to the ground and includes treacherous jetlike downdrafts in the lee of each roller.

More mysterious but of a similar ilk are the shy nacreous or mother-of-pearl clouds that stand still at an altitude of from fourteen to twenty miles: three times the height of cirrus. These rare clouds that are seldom seen except in polar regions when a foehn wind is blowing at ground level are now known to be lenticular in nature and normally composed of ice crystals which by refraction create the pearly iridescence observed. They are perhaps best known to Norwegian weather men in Oslo who see them in the clear evening skies as the dry west wind descends from the mountains in the wake of a storm. They show up at night almost as plainly as by day, sometimes remaining luminous three hours after sunset. Might they be more than the remote spoondrift of a mountain wave stirred by the passing jet stream? What significance that "an exceptionally lovely development of mother-of-pearl clouds was seen on May 19, 1910, the day when the earth passed through the tail of Halley's comet?"

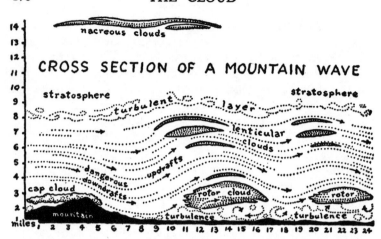

I know of only one kind of earth cloud loftier and rarer than the nacreous, and that is the very aloof one called noctilucent. Measured at more than fifty miles above the ground and illumined by the sun virtually all night, it is believed to be composed of very fine, dry volcanic dust, or perhaps the faint, powdery ash of meteors. It is seen in the north only from the latitude of Canada and northern Europe, mysteriously lingering close to the horizon, seldom observed as high as 10°. Few noctilucent clouds have been reported since World War I, although they were frequently seen on summer nights for a few years after the 1883 explosion of Krakatoa, the Siberian meteor of 1908, and the lesser blowup of Katmai in 1912. They are silvery white at the top, yellowish gold nearer the bottom, rarely faintly bluish but never iridescent. And sometimes among them at the same low angle lurk darker clouds which, curiously enough, are not lucent at all.

The opposite extreme from noctilucent in the cloud hierarchy is the ground cloud, fog, which is actually nothing more than an ordinary stratus resting on the earth. When you encounter it while driving along a mountain road you could as well call it cloud as fog. Then would be a good time to take careful note of the cloud's intimate texture at first hand, its living flesh. Some clouds are juicier than others, some of coarser grain. There is just as much variation in cloud substance as in that of meats, cloths, or stones.

Most stratus clouds, especially of the nimbus affiliation, are spongy and rather fleshy of body with porous tatters hanging at the bottom. The microscopic droplets that compose them are relatively large. But cumulus clouds are more solid and well defined with a finer, denser grain, becoming cottony and fibrous as they get drier and cooler usually at their frayed tops. Cirrus are the most silky and fibrillated of all, but you could hardly get near enough to see their very delicate diamond dust texture except in an airplane.

Fog is generally divided into two main kinds: radiation fog and advection fog. They are similar in substance but are created differently. Radiation fog is the stay-at-home type that forms usually on clear summer nights when the humid air loses heat by radiating it into the sky, resulting in condensation as it becomes too cool to hold its moisture invisibly. It is rarely 500 feet thick and clears soon after sunrise. Its droplets are orderly and uniform in size.

Advection fog, however, is the traveling type such as often rolls in from the sea, sometimes a mile thick, its droplets assorted, having formed when the moist salt air condensed under varying conditions in passing over relatively cool parts of the sea or land.

Radiation fog is a kind of dew of the whole air for, just as dew is air moisture condensed on cooling objects like grass and trees, fog is air moisture condensed throughout cooling air as a whole. It saturates the surfaces of trees, houses, or anything the air touches, leaving what is known as fog drip, which is not dew but a kind of fog gravy as different from dew as tears are from sweat.

Advection fog is formed horizontally almost exactly as cumulus clouds are formed vertically. It is what pours through the Golden

Gate upon San Francisco on humid afternoons, or creeps in from the Grand Banks and down the coast of Nova Scotia. It condenses as it cools by advection, by motion over cool surfaces. It may last for days.

Fog of course is not at all the same thing as haze, which is formed of dust rather than mere moisture and has a bluish tinge. But in these days of rapidly multiplying factories when so much smoke is spewed upforth, fog is commonly combined with various amounts of haze and smoke — even unto the sulphurous smog of the industrial metropolis, or the blinding four-foot visibility of the "London pertickular." Formerly almost pure white, fog today is often streaked with gray, sometimes with an overlayer close to black.

There are occasions also when fogs or smogs have a high enough percentage of waste industrial gases to be dangerous. There have been fogs in Europe that killed people in their sleep. And in our own day the "Big Smog" of Donora, Pennsylvania, near Pittsburgh, that accounted for 2500 illnesses, 1440 serious cases, and 20 deaths. One Donora woman first felt the sickening effect of the acrid fumes while talking to her daughter on the telephone after supper. She died the next day. The husband of another heard her coughing when he went to bed on the fourth night of the smog. She did not last until morning. Plants and flowers withered on all sides. Both the Donora hospitals were filled with the stricken and dying and the Red Cross had to send emergency equipment to handle the disaster.

The most deadly smog of the past century was undoubtedly the one that hit London early in December 1952, and is now credited with 4000 deaths and millions of dollars worth of property destroyed. It started as a white fog on Thursday, December 4, turned dark gray by the week end, and ended almost black from the soft-coal smoke of a million fires. While the warm layer above the city called an "inversion roof" kept the fog droplets from rising and dispersing, the microscopic flakes of soot kept the numbers of smoke particles per cubic centimeter extremely high and the interjacent air abnormally dry. By the third day, old people with asthma or bronchitis began to get frightened, and oxygen tents were in great demand. Blondes were turning into brunettes. An airplane that managed to make an instrument landing at Croydon got lost between the runway and the ramp. Blind men were helping as street guides in the city, firemen groped in front of their engines, while dock police were busy trying to rescue those who had walked off wharves into the Thames and could be heard calling and blubbering hopelessly somewhere in the filmy water. People in theaters could not see the stage from the sixth row and projected moving pictures could not penetrate to the screens. Sounds of choking could be heard everywhere, mingled with distant church bells and the muffled clanging of ambulances. The whole city seemed to be suspended in the sky, floating in a cloud — cool, dank, inviolate.

I am in a different world of course when I fly over such a weather clot in an airplane, and it is hard to remember how it can feel to be submerged in the sea of particles below; the whole thing looks so different from outside. Streaky, sooty fogs from the sky can be as beautiful as the purest marble. They are slow-moving seas or fast-flowing glaciers — rivers of vapor that reveal the wimpling and snurling of air as plainly as brooks show the rippling of water — by day their whorls gray and brown, sometimes with interfolds of yellow, lavender, or red — by night the lights of cities pulsing dimly through this glowing flesh of the weary brow of earth.

Once I saw San Francisco blinking up at me through such a mottled shroud that it seemed the hidden heart of a strange planet. Car and street lights of every color flashed on and off in weird contrapuntal rhythm through holes and thin spots of the moving fog. If one had descended upon Saturn or Pluto to behold a similar sight I can imagine the awe it would inspire.

Although fog and higher clouds can be compared in beauty to fields of snow or patches of effervescent sea foam, the clouds have the advantage in range of color. As they are of vapor they can transmit light as well as reflect it, which gives them not only the striking contrasts of blue shadow, dazzling illumination and the refractive reds, but also all the subtle grays and lavenders of translucency.

Have you noticed which clouds have silver linings, which are solid white, which edged in glowering blue? Did you know that it is when you are between a cumulus cloud and the sun that the cloud reflects all colors together to your eye, therefore looks most nearly white? And when the same cloud is overhead or toward the sun you will see mostly its shadow side — dark with a bright edge — the cloud from this angle often appearing plain gray, sometimes dark yellow or reddish, its color changing with dust and the height of the sun, its shade with its own thickening or thinning, its mood with the unpredictable surrounding reflections.

Why do lenticular clouds stand out in the far sky like purple splinters against the white of the cumulus? Have you ever wondered that the one is so dark, the other so light? Could it not be that lens clouds, like flat roofs, show only their undersides to the earth, while cumulus clouds, like tower walls, show much of their upper reflecting surfaces, and catch all the hues of the sunset?

The high cirrus clouds naturally reflect the vesper reds and plums of dusk the longest, unfurling the sultan's nightmare, fading slowly off after sunset in gentle streaks from pink to yellow to green to blue. What others could assume so becomingly the crimsons of rippling flame in the late afternoon or flash the fire opal light of warning before a tropical hurricane?

I cannot wonder that these spectacular cirrus displays are considered omens of disaster for I will never forget a Polish musician's description of the blood-red sheets of cirrus that filled the whole heavens over his village at three o'clock the afternoon before World War I began. All the Poles who saw it, he told me, regarded it as a supernatural warning — and subsequent events did nothing to alter their interpretation.

And are not blue clouds that toss their dark skirts before us a warning of strong winds? And well-fed clouds of yellowish complexion whispering of the snow? Pale yellow indeed is the reflected light from these fat January clouds that are composed of the largest snowflakes fluttering earthward from three miles up — the sallow lining of the winter overcoat of Pennsylvania, of Argentina, of far Shantung.

Thus from the frosty cobweb of the cirrus noon to the cumulus apricot sunset we have reviewed the shapes and colors of clouds of the modern earth: clouds that in the dawn look like purple shoulders of the distant mountains floating above them — frilly feminine clouds like wads of tissue out of a celestial hatbox — scud clouds that skim above us sneezing at our wings — alto-cumulus shadows weaving across cotton stratus sheets loosely featherstitched with sun — cirrus brushstrokes like Chinese script upon the ceiling — full many a passage of suspense and meaning to those who read the writing of the sky.

A noted psychologist said, "There is nothing in imagination that
was not previously in sense." The clouds of the world are ever
trying to prove him right, dramatizing before our innocence all
the art of the millenniums, bestowing upon us the shape of
the divine manifestation that we may have material for our learning.

They are of subtle material, the clouds — don't mistake. They
are not to be appreciated except from the remotest perspective in
space and thought. Beside them the trafficking of our little orb will
appear quite mad when any of us becomes detached enough to
see it.

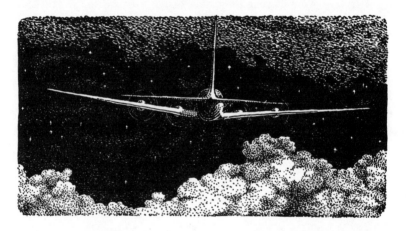

And still the clouds will march — an army of mists behind a
lone scout riding down the horizon — nubians on the pilgrimage
— cirrus goat's hair and the devil's tablecloth — elusive Flyaway,
the seagoing Dutchman's cape that drifts on the wind. And beyond
the Himalayas the Tibetan will wag his wrinkled head again and
sigh his ancient adage to the sky: "Even the mountains cannot
stop the progress of the clouds."

7. Thunder, Hail, and Rain

ERNIE SILVERS lay asleep in the top bunk, snoring gently, with his head phones on and connected by an extension wire to his radio. I had just been trying to get a bearing on the same set but had put the phones aside in disgust. All I could hear was the wail of a discordant sky, the sizzle of electron collisions in continuous ionic frustration.

Yet this harsh sound was as peaceful as the kettle on the stove to Ernie. He slept on and on — until suddenly there came into his subconsciousness a faint pattern of meaning: ". . . whooew-meeeee — dah — di — dah — dimoueeeei — didi — di — dit — deeommm — di — di — dah — aaehooumm — dah — dit — mmmmmmeeeoo — dah — di — dah — dit — eeooo — di — di-di-dit — 000000 — di — di — dah — 0000emmm . . ."

Ernie opened his eyes instantly. C — H — U — N, he thought. Those were our own call letters. In ten seconds he was at his desk responding to the call, which came from another plane half an hour behind us. It was a routine check, but to me seemed a significant demonstration of human adaptability to radio waves — response of the human mind to something a hundred miles away in the sky — if not beyond the horizon at least hidden behind an ocean flowing with quadrillions of molecules. It was a tuning in on part of the great mystery of the total electric forces of nature — forces that have scarcely begun to be resolved even in the limited pragmatic understandings of industry.

It made me think of the time the big flash came a few years ago when we were flying out of Miami to Puerto Rico. It was my first personal acquaintance with a stroke of lightning. Had I not been in an airplane — one of the safest places to be when lightning comes your way — it might also have been my last.

We were in a C–87 and had just ridden through three minutes of the most violent turbulence I think I ever experienced. As I was beginning to wonder how much longer our wing spars could stand the terrific bouncing — up — down — up — slantwise — skewways — down — up — up — down, suddenly it happened! The cockpit lit up like a neon tube. It lasted less than a thousandth of a second, yet huge pale green sparks jumped all over the room, including one to the pilot's pedestal. The radio man was knocked to the floor and the hairs on the back of my head stood as stiff as bristles.

The lightning bolt had evidently struck our trailing antenna and followed it to the tail of the airplane — then on into the radio itself, which was severely damaged. From the radio it had branched out into the skin of the airplane by way of several score of little aluminum rivets, most of which were blasted completely out of the ship, leaving empty holes.

What is the strange power behind such a bolt out of the seeming unsubstantial sky — such a ruthless stabbing of the darkling air? Is it something in the dynamic of the particular cloud?

The thunderstorm comes to our attention as the culminating drama of all clouds. More precisely is thunder the natural temper of the great cumulo-nimbus, the free expression of runaway heat turned explosive.

Men have long made obeisance to Thor, the thunder god. They have not understood him, even those who visited him in his ancient home of Buitenzorg in Java where thunder has been heard during 322 of the 365 days of the year, more than anywhere else on earth. But they have recognized him as a major god. They have trembled even to see his "messengers," those small cumulus clouds that precede him in the sky, for they remember well the mighty wrath that follows.

The natural causes of the thunderstorm were probably not systematically investigated until Benjamin Franklin tried to catch a few particles of lightning through his kite string in 1752, which led to his invention of the lightning rod. And it was Franklin also who suspected and proved that storms do not just grow and rage in one locality but move progressively across continents and seas.

No one, even among the ancients, had doubted that great violence occurred in the fully aroused cumulo-nimbus, yet actually measuring the muscle of this Ifrit was another thing again. It remained for the latter days of the airplane for man to penetrate the beating heart of the thundercloud to see what makes it roar.

In the nineteen twenties and thirties with this in mind, many daring pilots, even glidermen, flew and soared straight into thunderclouds and quite a few lived to tell about it — though often with more emotion than objectivity.

Usually their tales went something like this: "I don't know where I went, but it was terrific. I seemed to be thrown up, then down so violently and so often I thought my wings would come off. The rain beat on me in sheets, and the lightning scared me silly! All I could think of was: Am I going to get out of this alive?"

And too often they didn't get out alive. At a glider meeting in the Rhön Mountains just before World War II five Hitler-inspired pilots soared into a huge thunderhead and were whirled upward with horrifying violence. All of them soon jumped for their lives, opening their parachutes as they fell blindly through the turbulent air for fear they might be dashed upon a mountain. But it was a deadly mistake. The mighty updraft filled the parachutes almost to bursting and whooshed the men up like feathers, pelting them with sharp hail as they got into the freezing levels. And they kept on going up till they froze stiff at what must have been at least 30,000 feet and thirty below zero. They became literally human hailstones and may have been blown up and down for a long time before the wrathful Thor was through with them. Only one landed alive and he lost three fingers and most of his face before he got out of the hospital.

Glidermen who fly into thunderstorms nowadays know they are really sticking their necks out, but the coveted updrafts still lure them occasionally. Just the other day a Swiss engineer named René Comte took off in a sleek "buzzard" in South Africa. At 1200 feet over Baragwanath he cut loose his tow line from a Tiger-Moth and headed for Bloemfontein two hundred miles away. South of the course loomed a giant thunderhead with rain at its base and lightning flickering from the dark anvil top.

He couldn't resist the temptation to turn toward the cloud, for he knew it would lift him up to where he could practically dive into Bloemfontein. He realized the danger of course, for he had had six years of soaring in America and the Swiss Alps, but if he succeeded he would win two prizes and perhaps break the South African gliding altitude record of 21,000 feet.

Once in the great cloud he felt his sensitive plane swirling in the black lashing rain, spiraling nose down while being sucked mightily upward into the cold unknown. At 11,000 feet the rain became hail that rattled noisily on his wings. His rate-of-climb indicator froze at 50 feet per second. At 16,000 feet he turned on his oxygen. The thunder in his ears grew louder and louder as he watched his altimeter going "round like the hands of a crazy clock." At 27,000 feet the needle of his sealed barograph reached its limit, but the plane kept on climbing — up inside the very anvil itself. His spine seemed to congeal from the deathlike cold and the shock of the hammering thunder.

As the cloud turned from greenish gray to milky white, suddenly a blinding flash! "The whole cloud lit up," said Comte afterward, "with me inside it. I felt lightning hit the top of my head a sharp blow and run through my hands into the control column. The plane continued flying steady, but I was scared."

He coasted out of the thunderhead at 32,000 feet on a compass course for Bloemfontein — with a new altitude record and a fluttery stomach.

The generally recognized facts about thunderstorm flying by the end of World War II were: (1) flight below the storm usually encounters violent updrafts and downdrafts, heavy rain, hail, and possible lightning strike, (2) flight into a greenish or off-color region invites the same, (3) the blackest part of the storm is safer from lightning but still has plenty of dangerous vertical winds, (4) flying just below the freezing level attracts the most lightning, (5) above it, icing, (6) a thin-looking part of the cloud may be a channel to the other side, but sometimes leads to a dead end with storm all around, even closing in behind, (7) a wide hole with clear sky or land showing through is usually a safe cloud-canyon through which to fly, (8) it is better to pass to the right of the storm in the northern hemisphere, left in the southern, to avoid headwinds, (9) better over it than under it — assuming you are equipped for high flying, (10) twenty thousand feet is the average altitude of greatest danger, but you may have to go three times that high to clear the top.

These rules gave a general idea of thunderstorm manners and the flyer's proper behavior in the great presence. Yet weather men were still very uncertain and curious as to the real nature of the thunder beast. Just how does he suddenly rear up so fiercely? Is there any pattern or order in that wild turbulence inside? Why the cold downdrafts? Whence the hail, the rain?

So in 1946 the United States government organized its Thunderstorm Project to answer these questions once and for all, putting in charge a crack weather man, Horace R. Byers, head of the department of meteorology at the University of Chicago. The Air Force, the Navy, the National Advisory Committee for Aeronautics and the U.S. Weather Bureau all participated and they really put old Thor on the spot.

The first thing Thunderman Byers did was organize a vast three-dimensional network of weather stations to keep continuous tabs on a storm during its whole rampage. Some of the stations were set up aboard a squadron of Northrup Black Widow night fighters piloted by Air Force volunteers. These planes made precise simultaneous instrument flights through thunderclouds at prearranged altitudes, continuously recording temperature, pressure, turbulence, humidity, precipitation, and electrical field. Weather balloons were released from many points at regular intervals, automatically recording similar data. Radar records were kept meantime of the positions of all these moving weather posts, while the ground below was honeycombed over a wide area with fixed stations keeping minute-by-minute recordings of rainfall, wind and the other data required.

Besides all this, long-range radar was used to seek out thunderstorms in advance, measure their development as they approached, and guide the airplanes. Before the days of radar of course there had been no way to keep track of positions of either airplanes or balloons inside a turbulent cloud, so 1946 was about the earliest year that this project could feasibly have been launched.

As might be expected results were not immediate. Thunderstorms had to be waited for, and different kinds of them measured. The hundreds of men assigned to the work spent many trying months in Florida, and again a long session the next year in Ohio examining both thermal thunderstorms (created by updrafts caused by uneven heating of the earth's surface) and mechanical thunderstorms (such as are created when a fast-moving cold air mass wedges its way in under warm air, forcing the latter violently upward). And to some extent they checked also a special kind of mechanical thunderstorm, the orographical (created by updrafts where strong wind has to rise over mountains).

After the data were assembled and the thousands of photographs of the radar 'scopes sorted and the time records filed away, Byers and his thunder staff set about analyzing and digesting it all, adding up the tons of figures and graphs into some understandable conclusions. It took them about three years more before Byers was ready to publish the first results — but the wait was worth it. A new understanding of the most baffling storm of them all has emerged to enlighten the world.

The thunderstorm has turned out to have quite a complex nature, indeed in some ways a kind of animal nature, for it is found to be composed of cells that grow and fuse and multiply, as Byers explains, "in much the same way as the growth of masses of certain kinds of bacteria." Or, if you like the analogy of the cumulus cloud and the tree, the thunderstorm is shaped like a large banyan tree which extends itself by dropping new roots from its branches, which grow into fresh trunks with branches that drop more roots in turn.

The storm begins with a single great cumulus cloud which contains the "mother cell." This cell is at first just a very strong updraft of warm air which rises so fast it penetrates the ceiling that halts ordinary cumulus clouds. That is, instead of cooling itself by expansion as it goes up until it is as cool as the surrounding air, this ferocious updraft rises so fast it gets into cold air faster than it can cool itself. Furthermore its condensation into cloud is so rapid that it actually generates a lot of heat. Just as you feel cold when water is evaporating from your skin and would be warmed by the opposite (condensation) so is the thundercloud. Therefore a kind of chain reaction excites the rising cloud, producing more and more heat relative to surrounding air as the cloud builds up. It is actually a kind of explosion, though much slower than an atomic explosion of course. In this connection it is interesting to realize that the dramatic mushroom bomb cloud is just an artificial form of cumulus which, like any thunderhead,

may eventually start to fray into cirrus fibers after the frigid heights
have flattened its top.

By the time the mother cell has attained a diameter of four
miles or so, its updraft may be boiling skyward at 160 m.p.h. or
more, whirling increasingly outward until its anvil crest is half a
dozen miles long as well as eight or ten miles high. Its main body
may also contain an incipient tornado, though this in most cases
will be a matter of definition to say nothing of being factually
unverifiable. At any rate the cell is now (after ten minutes of
rapid growth) changing from what is called the cumulus stage
into the mature stage. Its rising droplets of condensing moisture,
having passed the freezing level, begin to coalesce with the ice
crystals, forming rain or hail. And when the raindrops or hailstones
have grown too big to be held up by the updraft they start to fall
— first in the weaker parts of the rising cloud, then spreading to
the whole cell — a change of direction at just the height that
effectively forms the flat top of the characteristic anvil, which is
then tapered by the wind to a leeward point.

This downward motion of cool precipitation naturally drags
along a good deal of air with it, creating by air friction a cold
downdraft right in the middle of the hot updraft — specifically
in the center of what corresponds to the eye of the thunder cell.
The ensuing wild battle of vertical winds, hot and cold, is the
secret of the well-known turbulence of the thundercloud: violent
upwinds and downwinds so close together that they can flip an
airplane upside down in a second or break its wings in one mighty
pneumatic bounce.

Even when such an ordeal fails to throw an airplane out of control it has been known to kill or injure persons aboard, not to
mention wrecking valuable equipment. I will never forget having
part of the floor of a C–54 explode in turbulent air one day near
the end of World War II when our hydraulic system blew apart
over the Atlantic — leaving us the ticklish problem of landing
twenty-two seriously wounded soldiers in Newfoundland without
benefit of flaps, landing gear, or brakes.

The cold downdrafts in thunderstorms were not formerly much known as compared to the more obvious updrafts, but it is the cold downdrafts that do most of the damage on the earth. They also eventually win the battle of up against down, with the help of their artillery of hail, snow pellets or rain, steadily increasing in size and strength, squeezing the updrafts, growing more violent as they descend to the gound with their thundering downpour. Then whooshing outward along the earth beyond the rain, these winds often reach 60 or 70 m.p.h., their cold-air mass shaped something like a foot, the toes reaching out several miles ahead of the storm, the heel following close behind.

It is where these cold foot gusts kicking outward from the mother cell meet other winds that new updrafts are started, which grow into new cells — young cumulus children of the mother cell who is passing her prime. The baby cells thus bud forth all around their tiring mother, springing upward in new heat explosions, some so close they fuse with mother or each other, some several miles away. Their cumulus forms shoot up into the freezing levels again, causing fresh condensation into rain and hail — fresh outbursts of lightning and thunder — fresh feet of cold wind.

Here is as good a place as any to point out, in verification of coriolis effect, that as northern thunderstorms approach their maturity the inblowing winds that feed their updrafts turn slowly counterclockwise around the low pressure vortex, while in the later stages of the same storms the downdrafts that nourish the outblowing winds turn clockwise around the newly created high pressure region at the ground. Thus at intermediate stages in most thunderstorms there must normally be two vortexes, one inside the other, simultaneously spiraling (sometimes very slowly) in opposite directions!

Meanwhile as the descending central downpour of rain increases, dragging more and more air with it, the mature stage of the cell (after half an hour) has passed into the dissipating stage which presently culminates in the total cessation of updraft. All that remains of violence now is falling downward to earth, slowly and more slowly. Thus the great thermodynamic engine eventually exhausts itself and the earth beneath is cooled and the barometer rises back toward equilibrium.

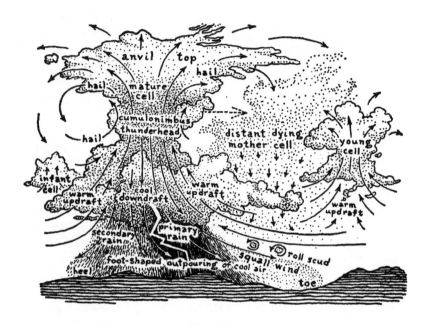

This evolutionary process meanwhile is being repeated in the offspring thunder cells and cloud towers which keep springing up like amebas, generation by generation, each turret rising higher than the last, rolling and slowly subsiding, different cells in different stages of life at any one time — the great cells pouring over the earth together like the plague — the whole "thunderstorm complex" leapfrogging forward cell by cell across the world.

These complex sequences of thermodynamic and coriolis cause and effect (which have their varying parallels in hurricanes, tornadoes, and the circumpolar jet streams) explain in a general way the cloud development and the wind and rain of a thunderstorm.

But what of the thunder and lightning that are the distinguishing features of this familiar yet mysterious storm? What is the electrodynamic basis for the flashing fury around us?

So much research is now going on in this field, with inconclusive and contradictory indications, that it is hard to generalize without risking serious errors — but at least some of the principal facts are becoming clearer and a consensus of scientific opinion is forming.

The sudden upthrust of warm, moist lower air into the shocking cold of the frozen heights is the creative basis for thunder. It is also the prime earthly example of static electricity generated by friction. The furious friction of the clash develops static electricity on a gigantic scale and the electrical potential in turn triggers the lightning and thunder. Thus the flashing might of the thunderstorm is an almost direct consequence of millions of warm water droplets being hurled into comparable masses of brittle ice crystals — colliding with them, rolling over them, here melting them, there being frozen by them into combined pellets of snow, into seeds of potential hail.

The exact proportions of electric charge developed by the many and complex dynamic forces of this battle of heat and cold are still a matter of conjecture. Some investigators think the action of wind against the rain is the principal factor, that it tears off the outer surface of each falling drop like pulling a sweater over a child's head, making a fine negatively charged mist while leaving the main part of the drop positive. Some think that electricity is born to the sky by the bursting of tiny air bubbles in the melting snow or hail. Some hold that the friction of snow crystals splintering in the wind sets up the static charge. Others think that freezing somehow generates potentials in the infant ice, or that it may be the tiny eddies in the slip streams around the falling snow. In reality it may well be all these factors and more that combine to do the work.

In any case huge masses of charged rain droplets and hail and baby snow become sorted into preponderantly positive and negative reservoirs of electrical energy at different parts of the thunderhead, creating between them fields of very great extremes in potential. It is the discharge of energy through such fields upon the sudden breakdown of intervening resistance that we call lightning.

There are nearly similar electrical fields of course extending between clouds and from the clouds to the earth. Normally the positive pole is located high in a cloud, the negative on earth, but sometimes this is reversed; and two parts of the ground adjoining each other may be oppositely charged.

Almost any combination of potentials may happen in the complex, moving thing that is a thunderstorm. Wherever the wind blows the resounding anvil across our sky, an opposite charge in the ground follows directly below it, biding its time like the swain pacing beneath the moonlit balcony — an invisible Thor impatient for his fair Sif of the golden hair.

The mechanism of his eventual strike is one of the most intricate of meteorological phenomena, the heat of his passion rising as high as 50,000° F., his path among the moiling molecules curving crookedly in forks and irregular branches like a tree of fire, a river of wrath between earth and heaven.

It begins with the pressing of an atomic button by a single electron, which triggers what physicists call a "streamer mechanism," which in turn sets off the main charge. Although the whole thing lasts less than a thousandth of a second, it turns out that the procedure is more complicated than the method used by an ancient army in crossing a brook.

If you think of the air between clouds and earth as the brook and the electrons as warriors, the first warrior picks up a stone (another electron) at the edge of the brook and throws it across to the opposite bank. He is immediately joined by many other soldiers who also throw stones (electrons) across the brook, the stones soon forming a sort of jetty (streamer), which grows bigger and extends back toward the men as they continue tossing stones. When the jetty has become a causeway completely bridging the brook, all the warriors charge (like lightning) over it to the other side.

The first stone in this analogy obviously represents the trigger electron that initiates the chain reaction of lightning. It may be any stray electron, such as one dislodged by a cosmic ray, but it will only act as a trigger when the surrounding dry electrical field has a stress of at least "10,000 volts per centimeter."

Advancing from the negative end of the field toward the positive, the trigger electron picks up energy, knocking other electrons out of atoms it collides with billions of times per second, thus setting in motion an immense avalanche of electrons which, like the stones, arrive at the positive side of the field to build the jettylike streamer back across the sky. This streamer is the ionized conducting filament through which the lightning is to flow, and it threads its crooked course up or down the gusty air, sometimes smoothly (the so-called "dart leader" process), sometimes in waves or jerks (the "stepped leader" process) like a brook picking its way among rocks.

Once the streamer is complete (which it may have become in any of innumerable forms and by any of many processes) it instantly releases "a cataclysmic burst of electrons from the negative terminal" which, like the ancient warriors, dash headlong to the opposite bank. These excited electrons literally drill a path right through molecules and atoms in their frenzy, lighting up the whole streamer channel in the great flash that is lightning, incidentally draining energy from the positive terminal of the field as well.

One such stroke of lightning however often does not drain a cloud of enough of its potential, which may immediately recharge from other sources, so that there can be repeated strokes in rapid succession down a single channel. A high-speed camera has actually recorded forty consecutive strokes within the time span of a second — effectively demolishing the legend that "lightning never strikes twice in the same place."

The evidence is that there are slow rhythms of lightning frequency also, each thunderstorm cell having peaks of intensity about every eighteen minutes, which is the average interval between the rise of turrets. As each thunderhead turret thrusts its top upward in turn, rising at about 12 m.p.h. then receding at 8 m.p.h., the whole cloud rotating ponderously, the electrical fields naturally follow suit, successive lightning strokes now tapping higher and higher regions of cloud, now lower and lower, playing up and down the scales of potentiality like the bagpiper of spring.

There must be corresponding rhythms of stroke direction also, the quota of bolts from the blue followed by a proportionate number of bolts from the bowery. One can tell the up or down aim of the flow at a glance by the direction of its branches, just as with a river or a tree. And there are correlations between stroke frequency and height of the anvil, the higher and colder the top of the cloud the faster and louder the thunder.

A whole thunderstorm in perspective of course is really a kind of moving voltaic cell in the gap between the two electrodes of a gigantic spherical condenser, the inner solid sphere of earth separated from the outer ionosphere by the leaky non-conductor of lower atmospheric sky. It used to be thought that the fairly constant negative charge of the earth in respect to the positive charge of the ionosphere (a difference averaging something like 400,000 volts) was the cause of thunderstorms. This gradient is steep enough to make the air around your head 200 volts positive in relation to the ground at your feet, and it continuously induces radioactive gases to escape from the earth to join wandering ions in the high atmosphere in an effort to discharge the difference.

But this perpetual fair-weather discharge has recently been found to be the exact opposite of thunderstorms and a result rather than a cause of their existence. For one C. T. R. Wilson is credited with the new and widely verified discovery that the net continuous current (about 1500 amperes) generated by some five thousand thunderstorm cells believed to be forever roaming the earth's surface (on the average) is just enough to keep ground and sky charged as we find them — that the true role of Thor is, as the ancients believed, a stirrer up of differences instead of a settler of argument, a fomenter of trouble rather than the atmospheric peacemaker some had later deduced him to be.

Thus the gentle joining of radioactive gases and ions can never fully achieve electric equilibrium: the thunderstorms of the world are ever ahead of them, charging heaven and earth in their constant if helter-skelter battles of expression — their marching across the plains of Nebraska in a straight rank three hundred miles wide, their rolling course over Pakistan drinking the humid air of the Brahmaputra, following the river valley to be bloated in the end by the summer updrafts of Tibet.

Is not this ever the way of the thunderstorm, of its lightnings and its angry roar? Its stroke has been measured in length all the way from five hundred feet to nine miles! In thickness, from the equal of a fine wire to more than a foot when it fades from visibility. Its thunder at close range is the explosive crack of shock waves sent out by the lightning channel's few micro-seconds of expansion, waves that have been seen to make a rainbow literally quiver in the sky like a plucked harp string. In the distance its rumble is a blending of reports from sundry segments, repeated strokes, and echoes near and far. Beyond eighteen miles, though it cannot be heard, its reflected flicker of light from over the horizon is seen as "heat lightning," its flash diffused in dense cloud as "sheet lightning."

Some of the sky's lightnings are actually too "slow" to produce thunder, taking as much as a tenth of a second to expand to size — which is even slower than quick human hands can move. Some lightning helps farmers by fertilizing their soil, combining chemically with rain into a worldwide "100 million tons of valuable nitrogen fertilizer every year."

The most powerful single stroke of lightning ever recorded in the United States pointedly hit the University of Pittsburgh's "Cathedral of Learning" on July 31, 1947, charging it with 345,000 amperes or enough current to light 600,000 sixty-watt bulbs for the duration of the flash: 35/1,000,000 of a second.

Very different from such a well-grounded building, however, is an airplane flying high above the earth. If it should become in any way grounded in flight an airplane would suffer greatly from lightning. But I do not know of any case of lightning directly causing an airplane accident. Ninety per cent of the few lightning hits on commercial aircraft, according to the records, have happened at night in maximum turbulence when it was raining or snowing and within 6° F. of the freezing point. These incidents almost always occur between 12,000 and 20,000 feet, where vertical winds are at their strongest, and are generally preceded by St. Elmo's fire.

Saint Elmo, if you will remember, was the beloved Bishop of Formiae in ancient Italy 1650 years ago, whom Mediterranean sailors have ever since been invoking for aid during storms. It was natural to name the corposant after him — that visible discharge of static electricity that is commonly seen "on the tops of the masts and the tips of the spars" at sea before thunderstorms, and in our day playing about the wing tips and propellers of airplanes in soft bluish tongues of light. That this eerie corona is a real omen of lightning is statistically accepted beyond question, and it is now believed to be formed by the glowing passage of billions of electrons quietly discharging their local differences amid the field sources of lightning. It is also known that it can be dangerous in itself for it has been explicitly convicted of causing the explosion of the airship Hindenburg at Lakehurst, N.J., in 1937 by igniting a mixture of valved hydrogen and air as the famous dirigible came in after a successful crossing from Germany.

Probably closely related to St. Elmo's fire is the strange ball lightning that so long has baffled science. I have only seen it once, bouncing slowly along the ground in a thunderstorm downpour, but there are innumerable records of its astonishing doings. I once read a French account of a "fire ball" that in October 1898 appeared in a room in Marseille and advanced toward a small girl sitting on a table with her legs dangling. Rising as it came close, the fiery sphere, surrounded by a glowing haze, circled the terrified child twice before darting up the chimney to explode on the roof with "an appalling crash that shook the whole house."

Years later a similar "ball of fire" was seen to hit the ground in an English village, breaking into two parts, both of which bounded to a nearby roof to enter separate chimneys — evidently a favored route. One part descended into a cellar and exploded, wrecking a valuable chicken brooder, while the other in a different house glided quietly through a room in which a man was reading to a boy. Leaving them both untouched, it burned a small hole in the floor and plunged into a sheepfold below. Several young lambs jumping about were not hurt, but five large sheep were killed one by one. The shepherd's son standing in an open doorway was then astonished to see the glowing object squeeze past him out into a yard and off across a field almost as if it had a mind of its own.

An explanation for this kind of stalled thunderbolt is that it is really not lightning at all but "a creeping corona discharge" that advances along "a relatively intense portion of the electric field." The electric field itself is evidently full of unaccountable wrinkles and irregularities.

Cattle and sheep seem to be particularly vulnerable to most varieties of lightning and there is a recorded case on a Utah mountainside of one bolt killing 835 sheep, evidently because the dry earth offered more resistance than the roundabout route of traveling "from the ground, up one leg, through the moist body, and down another leg . . . "

Small houses are sometimes completely shattered by a thunderbolt, as great trees or chimneys are split by the explosive expansion of the extreme heat, but I heard of one house that was saved by the same lightning that set it afire. After passing through the building and igniting some woodwork, this bolt with a conscience "leaped to a near by fire-alarm box, set it off, and summoned the engines!"

There is a story in Minneapolis of lightning throwing a type-writer up from a table so hard it was imbedded in the ceiling, a case of lightning at sea burning the gold braid off an unpopular mate's uniform, in Argentina of melting a farmer's bedsprings at night so deftly that he sagged to the floor without waking up. And you may have heard of the brewery that got hit in such a skillful manner that the beer was aged and flavored faster than ever before — undoubtedly the earliest case in recorded history of a storm actually brewing.

Of all known kinds of lightning I think the rarest must be the literal "bolt from the blue" or thunderbolt out of a cloudless sky. Like the invisible tornado it has occasionally been known to happen, but your chances of being blitzed by a clear sky are virtually nil. Even your much more likely chances of ultimately being done to death by a thunderstorm in the United States are statistically no greater than one in 365,000 (assuming you are as foolish as the average person), which is only ⅓₅ as likely as being killed by one of the much rarer but deadlier tornadoes.

You might think the former a negligible risk and one you couldn't do much about anyway, but it is really quite possible to improve your prospects significantly. During one five-year period last century, records show that the British Navy lost seventy ships to lightning, mostly by having masts struck at sea, the bolt traveling all the way down to the step, then blasting a hole through the bottom. But today's ships, like modern power lines, airplanes, and many a house, are protected and seldom get hurt by lightning.

Even a man whose work exposes him almost daily to lightning can do something about it for, despite the saying that you will never know it if lightning strikes you, one can sometimes feel the bolt coming and if quick enough take evasive action in time. A lineman I know of in Indiana can testify to this, for he was working on a power-line pole one afternoon in a thunderstorm and suddenly realized his hair was standing on end and that a great magnetic tension was building up in the air all around the pole. Realizing what it meant, he quickly unbuckled his safety belt and threw himself full length upon the nearest cross-arm. Just then the lightning struck the pole and, vaporizing 130 feet of heavy wire, leaped to another pole, and from there to the ground. The lineman was knocked unconscious, but his prompt action had saved his life.

I was surprised when I first learned that hail is much more dangerous than lightning in the sky. This is only too true however, for hail not only needs no grounding to take effect but it can float in treacherous ambush in apparently empty air while awaiting opportunity to dive-bomb its unsuspecting victim at almost any height.

A few years ago an American Airlines plane suffered more than ten thousand dollars worth of damage while flying in clear air within half a mile of a large thundercloud. The pilot had not thought the great white anvil soaring innocently high above his wing tip could endanger him so long as he kept well clear of the actual cloud, but the beautiful canopy and its scarflike fringe had already dispatched a barrage of invisible heavy hail which struck him out of the blue like a volley of golf balls, denting the wings and fuselage so seriously that half the duralumin skin of the airplane had to be replaced.

Hail is born in cumuliform clouds, particularly in thunderclouds. It is the stepson of violence, growing in distinct cycles or steps. It begins when raindrops get caught in such a wild updraft that they are swept up to freezing levels and turned to ice. If they fall to earth right after this they usually melt on the way down, becoming rain again — or if the air is cold enough may land as small hail.

But if they are to be larger they must go through many steps of this kind of growth before they reach earth as hail — many ups and downs in the turbulent engine of thunder. This has been shown by the numerous coats of different kinds of ice found in large hailstones. Each time they fall through the rain cloud they take on a wet coat. Each time they are whisked upward again this wetness freezes into a new coat of ice, which may be clear ice or rime ice depending on the rate of freezing. Clear ice is quick-frozen like the ice cubes in your freezer compartment. But grainy rime ice accumulates slowly like the refrigerator's coat of frost that needs defrosting. It commonly grows in the sky from cloud droplets (not rain) coating a hailstone while it is falling through a supercooled cloud, a cloud that is unfrozen but below freezing temperature — an unstable condition common in clouds above the freezing level and which requires only the passage of a solid object like an airplane to produce ice. Almost any sequence of ice textures may thus clothe the hail, and the longer the vertical wind circulation continues the bigger grow the hailstones, until finally they become too heavy for even the strongest updrafts and fall all the way to the ground.

It is unusual for hail to grow bigger than the size of a grape, but on rare occasions hailstones have been seen bigger than baseballs and weighing more than a pound and a half. In June 1954 hailstones up to "fifteen pounds" were reported during a severe storm in Holland, which seems very unlikely. But a hailstone of lethal heft is known to have killed a cow in Annapolis, Maryland, many years ago. Others have killed people all the way from America to Asia, where an especially disastrous hailstorm accounted for about 200 deaths at Moradabad, India, on April 30, 1888. This one was part of a tornado surrounded by heavy discus hail that suddenly whirled through the town, leaving 230 dead and thousands of injured behind it. Although the tornado itself killed two or three dozen persons by smashing their homes, the great majority of the dead were said to have been beaten down by the giant hailstones which, if they were like some record hail picked up in the wakes of American tornadoes, could have been disk-shaped up to ten inches in diameter and three inches thick at the center. Probably formed while spinning rapidly near the growing vortex of the storm, these flying saucers (usually not more than an inch or two in diameter) are such an accepted accompaniment of tornadoes that some meteorologists theorize that the cooling effect of their dynamic presence may even be a factor in triggering off a twister at the start.

The largest ones fall at well over a hundred miles an hour and must have been cradled in updrafts of equivalent speed to keep them aloft while they were growing. They have been observed to hum in the air, about fifteen feet apart, while smaller stones fall proportionately more slowly, quietly, and closer together — all the way down to the tiniest soft hail or graupel which can descend as gently and as densely as snow.

As the speed and flight pattern of hail must be influenced by its shape, which is created by its adventurous history in the clouds, which again depends partly on its shape, there is a delicate interbalance of nature here at work. And one can get some inkling of its complexities by observing the final form of the most developed hail after it has landed: some of the stones being shaped like acorns, saucers, holeless doughnuts, apples with stems, hourglasses, maces, turtles, fritters, wavy or warted surfaces that look like chunks of peanut brittle or odd half-melted jackstones.

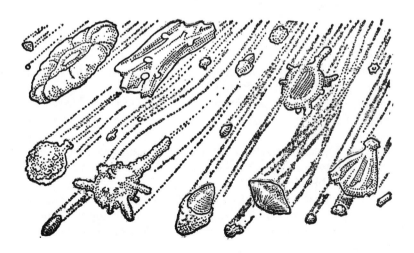

I used to think of clouds as hazy masses of fairly evenly distributed moisture, and I vaguely imagined that when it rained the rain was started by the cloud somehow forcing out its excess water, as you would squeeze a sponge. The truth is rather different.

Rainbirth is a complicated phenomenon that is exceedingly difficult to observe. It is a combination of the slow growth of cloud droplets in humid air and collisions between drops of different sizes or between drops and hail or snow. It is not a mere continuance of the simple saturation process which brings clouds into the world.

A raindrop can be about a million times the size of a cloud droplet which again is larger than an invisible molecule of water vapor by about the same degree. It is an effort therefore to visualize the microscopic flesh structure of the cloud. The tiny droplets that form on dust particles to create a cloud are far apart from each other, actually as far apart in comparison to their size as the earth and the moon. Yet there are so many of them in a cloud that they seem a uniform mass of matter, just as the Milky Way appears to be homogenized rather than a collection of separate stars.

Each cloud droplet may be less than 1/10,000 of an inch in diameter, yet it is floating independently on many millions of bubbling molecules of air like cream on milk, dancing in the sky, ever changing with temperature, pressure, and humidity. As humidity increases or temperature decreases, the size of the droplet grows, more and more moisture condensing on its surface, increasing its weight in relation to surface resistance until the air can no longer hold it up and it accelerates to an appreciable speed of falling.

When the droplet attains to about 1/200 of an inch in diameter it is likely to descend as gentle mist. At 1/50 of an inch it falls as light rain. In falling it is bound to collide with other drops and often ice in some form. If there is little wind and the drops are all of the same size, however, they will fall at about the same speed like cars moving down a highway in file, thus avoiding bumping into one another. In this case the drops do not get very big and

CLEAR AIR
moisture held in
separate molecules
too small to see

descending
ice crystals
of infant snow

rendezvous of
cloud droplets with
the baby snow in
collisions that create
small rain

CLOUD
some of moisture is
condensed into droplets
around dust nuclei

rain growing
by more collisions

condensation level

RAIN
friction of air
limits size of drops
and at same time generates
potential for lightning

the earth receives no more than a drizzle. This is what normally comes from a thin stratus cloud on a calm day.

But when wind currents mix up drops of different sizes so that they fall at different speeds as in a thundercloud, the bigger drops will hit smaller, slower ones while trying to pass them. Thus they will combine together into bigger and bigger drops.

Henry Houghton the meteorologist has gone so far as to figure out that if a drop of mist ¾₀₀ of a millimeter in diameter falls through a cloud full of drops of ⅖₀₀ mm., that in forty-five minutes it will descend 210 feet and grow to ⁵⁄₁₀₀ mm. diameter by picking up water from drops it bumps into. The farther it falls the bigger and faster it will get, steadily accelerating so that in the next forty-five minutes it will fall four times as fast and far, attaining a diameter of ⅒ mm. And in the thirty minutes following it will go a mile and a half more, growing to a full millimeter thick and changing from light into moderate rain.

Bigger raindrops come only by still more collisions, which probably depend on drops of different sizes being stirred together by the wind or by the arrival of hail or snow. Langmuir's law of raindrop collisions shows that "for each drop size there is a minimum size of the larger drop below which no collisions will occur." Thus a drop of less than .045 mm. will never hit a drop of .012 mm. diameter, which will simply follow the air streamline around it, guided perhaps by repelling magnetic forces as well as the inexorable dictates of aerodynamics.

While droplets in a cloud remain small, therefore, they will be fairly stable, retaining their moisture. But the bigger they become the less difference in size is found to be necessary to bring about collisions, so their growth is by geometric progression — a kind of chain reaction that would be almost explosive were it not for the air resistance that finally limits their size and speed.

The biggest known raindrops are slightly less than a quarter inch in diameter — or would be if they were round. Actually they are seldom spherical, nor do they look in the air like the traditional "tear drops" you see in cartoons. High-speed flash photographs show instead that once they have reached falling equili-

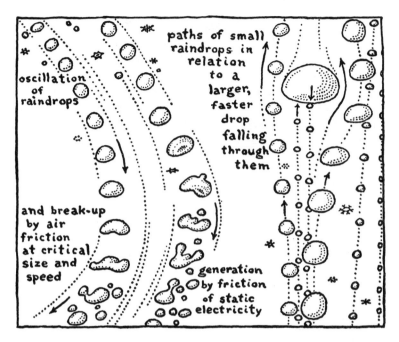

oscillation of raindrops

paths of small raindrops in relation to a larger, faster drop falling through them

and break-up by air friction at critical size and speed

generation by friction of static electricity

brium they are flattened out at the bottom into a modified parachute shape that is the almost exact replica of a hamburger bun. This turns out to be nature's compromise between surface tension, which would keep them perfectly round, and the aerodynamic pressure of passing air which pushes against their bellies and sucks out their flanks to a degree that literally tears them apart if they reach the quarter-inch limit.

It is only while they remain tiny droplets of cloud or fog, therefore, that the aerodynamic pressures stay virtually nil and they float like perfect globes upon the air. For as soon as they start to grow and fall their instability increases geometrically with size, speed, and the air's turbulence until, oscillating more and more wildly from egg to bun to egg to bun shape, the drops become tattered in the uneven wind, perhaps dish- or doughnut-shaped, and irregular pieces begin flying off into their wakes of spray.

This has been found to happen around the airspeed of eighteen miles an hour when friction apparently breaches rain's hydrostatic equation. The discarded pieces meanwhile, being smaller than the main drops, have more air resistance in proportion to their weight, so fall more slowly until by collision they in turn may approach a quarter-inch size again, repeating the cycle.

Thus mercifully rain never falls faster than eighteen miles an hour through the lower air and no matter how numerous the drops they cannot be more than a quarter inch thick. Even when the swift downdrafts in a storm may lash the rain against the ground at seventy miles an hour the rule holds, for the 18 m.p.h. is airspeed not groundspeed and the storm-lashed rain still can move but little faster than the air.

Of all the collisions experienced by rain droplets in the sky the most productive of growth are believed to be collisions with newborn snow or infant hail. This may be because it takes a larger nucleus than dust to hold together a full-size drop of rain. Even in the tropics ice crystals form in cumulus tops and small hail circulates in thunderheads, and these cold nuclei pick up moisture as they flit about the clouds, colliding with droplets of mist or falling rain.

By this means the bigger drops of rain are usually accumulated. Their hearts are made of ice, to be sure, but they are melting hearts that generally dissolve by the time they greet the warm earth. This fleeting ice or graupel (snow pellets) is the normal childhood of heavy rain and it can only come from heavy clouds — clouds tall enough to provide cold collisions — secret rendezvous of snow and rain, of rain and hail, of rain and rain — diphthongs of the drops.

Thus it is evident that hard rain is born of updrafts high in the sky, of muscle aloft — rivers of heat, and the clash of cold — the bitter tears of the wind — the very stuff of thunder. And as this sort of cumulus violence is moody by its nature, the earth beneath cannot but expect her sudden downpours, her rainbow surprises, her victories for Noah and the sons of Noah.

A chimney of hot air puffing upward through a cloud, however, is likely to stop the mightiest of rains from falling, perhaps evaporate it before it reaches the ground as often happens over the Sahara — for indeed much of rain is for the sky alone to see. Or this great flowering puff of heat may carry the rain bodily upward to brandish it in the chill attic of heaven before dashing it later all at once upon our heads.

Such a torrent is called a cloudburst and happens in just that way, the upwind damming the rain with a dike of dry air, balancing it magically aloft in the volatile tub of sky for many precarious minutes before the downwind bursts the bottom out to trigger the deluge.

One day in November 1911 a weather station at Panama recorded a fall of "2.47 inches of rain during three minutes" of severe thunderstorm. Where there is not enough vegetation to absorb it such a cloudburst can be disastrous. I was in Los Angeles recently when a sudden rain drowned twenty persons in the city streets. Pedestrians were swept off their feet by torrential streams amid the traffic and more than one car driving through a flooded dip washed into a deep ditch and overturned, pinning all its occupants under water.

In July 1911 in the Philippines a terrific downpour dumped forty-six inches of rain on the town of Baguio in twenty-four hours, the heaviest measured rainfall for a single day in history. And there are those who think that Noah's great forty-day flood may have taken place near Chirapunji in northeastern India where saturated monsoons have been known to sweat it out with the Himalayas to the tune of 905 inches in a year, most of it concentrated into the two worst months of rainy season.

When you consider that one inch of rainfall on the ground weighs a hundred tons per acre and that 905 inches would make a lake 75 feet deep over everything, you can see rain more nearly from Noah's point of view.

Even to a dispassionate scientist a rain cloud is pretty impressive, the visible moisture in a cubic mile of it weighing as much as a large ocean liner; some estimates going as high as 70,000 tons. And if that cubic mile of cloud should drift over a desert and be evaporated by warm dry air it would disappear, yet the same weight of moisture would still be in that same chunk of sky: many thousands of tons of water floating invisible in the empty blue.

Such changes by evaporation and condensation are going on in the sky all the time. What they amount to really is a spreading out and a gathering together of whatever moisture is present. The cloud, as we have said, holds its water condensed into tiny droplets perhaps a thousandth of an inch in diameter and a fortieth of an inch apart but when the cloud evaporates, this moisture suddenly breaks up into separate molecules and disperses itself evenly throughout the whole space available, becoming thousands of times greater in volume than the condensed droplets alone, and spread out so thin it will not refract light and you can see right through it.

It is as if you were flying at 10,000 feet over a great plain upon which thousands of compact companies of soldiers were gathered, each company composed of a hundred men dressed in white uniforms and standing at attention shoulder to shoulder, the companies two hundred and fifty feet apart in all directions. The dots of condensed white would be visible down there, blending in the distance into a faint but vast cloud of humanity. Yet if, at a signal, all the groups suddenly disbanded into individual men, leaving twenty-five feet between each soldier and the next, the cloud of humanity would literally evaporate into invisibility.

It is in exactly this way that sky clouds evaporate by uncondensation, by the scattering of collected moisture back into its elementary parts. And the same holds true of course in the case of water evaporating from the ocean, or from grass or trees — an almost continuous process everywhere there is air. The average oak tree, I am told, evaporates 180 gallons of water a day while in leaf, and there are calculated to be 16,000,000 tons of water evaporated each second from the whole earth.

The air that absorbs this moisture, far from being burdened as you might think, actually expands and becomes lighter, for water vapor is only five-eighths as dense as dry air — so the water rises faster than the drought, bringing vital raw material right up to the cloud factory levels — great invisible rivers continuously flowing up from the land and sea, dispersing through the sky, condensing and pouring back down again. And rain is more than the wind's tears. It is the blood of the earth — its downward flow moves through arteries out of the thunderheart of the sky, its upward evaporation through veins of air, back to the clouds to be purified anew and undiminished to pump its life to the body of the planet.

The life in the rain blood has of course been recognized the world over, endowed with personality, often deified and prayed to in time of drought by primitive peoples. The rain god Parjanya has been worshiped of old in India, the rain dragon Lung-wong in China, the rain stone Lapis Manalis in Rome, the rain frog in the Americas — human blood spilt to attract the cloud's blood by Australian Mura-muras, by Javanese rainmen — umbrellas raised on elephants at the Indian festival of Teej. It is true too in the eyes of biologists that the clouds are more alive than empty air. The dust cyst dissolves with condensation, the ameba awakes in the mist, and the slumbering air stirs with fresh life amid the rain. Even as the oyster long ago shed acrid tears, underwater tears that drifted upwards and away with the Gulf Stream to add salt to the spray on the bows of the Mauretania, so does the cloud cry down as rain upon the earth.

8. Cold and the Silent Snow

LOOKING OUT on the occasional snow flurries we inevitably encounter in this winter's crossing, I think of my first visit to the earth's ice age. For that is what the Greenland icecap really is: the last large remnant of the most recent ice age that covered the whole northern half of North America and Europe only ten or twelve thousand years ago. Approaching Greenland at 12,000 feet, riding a four-ton cargo of meteorological equipment one morning in 1944, I saw a range of spectacular mountains with a long flat cloud resting on top. It was apparently a very smooth crest cloud like the white "tablecloth" of Table Mountain in South Africa and it lay there snug and still. But when I looked again I suddenly realized that this was really no cloud at all — not even part of the sky but part of the earth. It was the great Greenland icecap! It was the southern tip of that famous shining mattress of ice more than a mile thick and a thousand miles long that staggers the imagination and far outshines the North Pole region itself for sheer bulk and majesty. Beset by the frigid descending fall winds that are an unsung wonder of the world, and continuously weighted down by new snow, this great ice field is expanding ever outward in all directions at a rate which in places reaches 125 feet a day (an inch a minute) — a bed of snow that blankets jagged 10,000-foot mountains so that they are completely smothered from view — great-grandmother of the icebergs which are born daily in its hundred fiords, crashing roughshod from the crumbling childbed glaciers into the oceans to drift downward to the shipping lanes of the earth.

The snow fields were very treacherous to airplanes until radar gave us the absolute altimeter, for it was almost impossible before then to judge distance when flying above that unbroken whiteness. It is a deceptive whiteness — often called the "whiteout" — that sometimes seems to move along with the airplane — sometimes slightly faster, sometimes slower — sometimes appears half a mile below you when it is really fifty feet, and on occasion has been known to rise up in a mad blurry rush till two great white plumes appear on either side of your cockpit and you rock to a sizzling stop, discovering you have flown into the icecap.

In one rare case described to me by Colonel Norman Vaughan, director of Search and Rescue in the North Atlantic in World War II, a plane flew into a fall of fresh feathery snow that stopped it so gently that for several minutes the crew thought they were still flying, although the airspeed needle had quietly swung to zero and they were in reality nestled firmly in snow so deep the steady-cruising propellers had blasted great ten-foot furrows for half a mile and the fuselage was buried almost to the windows.

The boys who pioneered T–3, the 9-mile-long ice island then floating only 250 miles from the North Pole and getting closer, can tell you about the problems of landing on unprepared ice, how they made passes at the island for nearly an hour, bouncing their ski gear from hummock to hummock like a stone skipping on a pond, until finally they knew the contours well enough to risk a landing. That was in March 1952 when Colonel Joe Fletcher's small group of arctic experts started building T–3 into the most northerly range station, weather bureau, and landing field in the world.

Setting up housekeeping in sixty below zero weather calls for special techniques, clear thinking — a realistic understanding of the usually misunderstood arctic. The North Pole, it turns out, is not a land of continual blizzards and snow. It rains there fairly often in summer. All blizzards north of the polar front are local and there is less snowfall than in parts of Virginia. Furthermore it doesn't get as cold there as in dry Siberia or dry Montana, for the water under the North Pole's ice (28° F.) is like a stove in comparison with the atmosphere and warms it correspondingly. And since a heat loss of 80 calories per gram of water is required just to freeze it into ice without lowering its temperature a single degree (which otherwise takes only 1 calorie per gram) most of this great polar stove is actually unfreezable.

If you dress properly in the arctic you will probably notice the cold much less than you would on a windy March day on North Michigan Boulevard in Chicago. People do not catch cold at the North Pole or come down with T.B. or pneumonia, for the germs or viruses that cause these diseases just do not exist up there. Your main polar problem is getting rid of old popular notions about the frozen North.

There are some useful tricks of survival of course at the times when the cold is severe. Frostbite is among the first of arctic dangers, especially to the nose. I froze my nose once when it was more than 60° F. below zero in Siberia so I know the discomfort of having a nose swollen to twice normal size with the skin peeling off like an onion. The Air Lines War Training Institute manual advises that when you find any frozen place on your skin you should take off a glove and press your bare hand to the white, stiff flesh. This will thaw it just enough. The book strongly warns against rubbing a frozen spot, or using snow on it, for that is likely to bruise the brittle frozen skin, leaving a path for infection.

And if you should get caught in an arctic blizzard in the open don't fight against it. Take it the easy way. Sit down and make yourself at home before you get lost or exhausted. Vilhjalmur Stefansson, the famous explorer, tells of an old Eskimo woman who slept out in the open during a rare and bitter three-day storm. She did not try to reach her home near by, realizing she would get lost walking a hundred feet in that blinding snow. She had enough fat on her not to need food either. She just made like a hibernating bear, hollowed out a snow cave and went to sleep. When the blizzard was over she shook herself off and walked home for dinner in fine spirits.

If you get thirsty in the arctic you can use your head equally well and adapt yourself to your surroundings. Instead of looking for drinking water, which is apt to be underneath thick ice, if anywhere, and very expensive in time, work, or fuel for thawing, the arctic manual recommends eating snow. Not wolfing large quantities of it all at once, but nibbling it steadily like a horse grazing. This will not quench an aroused thirst very quickly but can forestall your next thirst indefinitely. You can warm the snow in your hand first and compress it in order to avoid freezing your mouth or stomach.

Insulation is something you should also understand thoroughly if you are going to reason your way out of any problem of freezing. A blanket is not really a source of warmth but merely retards the transfer of heat from your body to the air or vice versa. It will keep a cake of ice cool in July just as effectively as it will keep your body warm in January, and the Arabs actually wear heavy woolen abas which have a cooling effect as long as the desert air is above 99° F. and hotter than their blood.

Animal fur and fat serve as natural blankets for arctic animals, keeping their body heat in. But the smaller the animal the thinner the insulation it is able to carry — which is why little creatures do not survive arctic winters and why you never see mice or insects in the polar regions, nor in fact any mammal smaller than a fox.

Extra food intake of course is a way of counteracting loss of heat in the arctic. But if an animal can't find enough winter food to maintain body heat he has still an interesting alternative. He can set his nerve thermostat of body temperature to a lower, easier level and reduce the load on his insulation. That's what hibernation is all about. It is a combination of needing less and saving more. It is like shifting into overdrive or flying on "maximum range" mixture to conserve fuel and get the most miles out of each gallon.

Unfortunately most humans don't hibernate easily. The story still persists that some of the early Vermont villagers used to force their old people to hibernate in winter to save food, fuel, and care. But it was not accepted by modern medical science that the human body could survive a temperature drop of more than fifteen or twenty degrees below normal until the case of Mrs. Dorothy Mae ("Johnnie") Stevens came to the attention of the world in February 1951.

In case you haven't heard of her, Johnnie was a twenty-three-year-old tough girl from Chicago's South Side who had recently been charged with assault "for almost cutting her husband's ear off." But when she got drunk on a certain bitterly cold February night she just didn't have the strength to drag herself home and stumbled and staggered until she fell unnoticed in a dark alley. When a policeman found her lying there at 7:45 next morning the thermometer read eleven below and Johnnie was frozen solid as ice. She looked like a day-old corpse. Her stomach felt stiff as stone, her jaw was locked tight, and her eyes were crystal hard — "like two glass beads." Reported the cop: "I could've sworn she was dead except all of a sudden she groaned."

At Michael Reese Hospital they couldn't take her temperature right away because regular clinical thermometers don't go low enough. But around 9:30 a laboratory thermometer was found and gave a rectal reading of 64.4° F. — far below what was generally considered fatal.

Doctors crowded into the emergency ward to see the medical miracle of Johnnie, the female ice cake. Staff surgeon Harold

Laufman injected plasma for shock, then two hundred milligrams of cortisone. "I still don't know if it did any good," he said that evening, but Johnnie's temperature rose to 77° F. by 3:30 and was 86° F. at 8 P.M., with pulse and respiration almost normal. Then at last she opened her glassy eyes, let out a sigh flavored with drugs and stale alcohol, and murmured: "I'm cold."

Next morning she was close to normal and her temperature had leveled off at 101° F. She could see perfectly well out of eyes that yesterday had been frozen solid and feeling was satisfactory in all her limbs. Said Dr. Laufman: "This is not frostbite, but a frozen state of animation. I don't know what to call it but a deep freeze."

Could it be that if a human being is frozen quickly enough until even his heart is solid ice that, like quick-frozen meat, his tissues will remain undamaged by the small ice crystals in his flesh cells (unlike the big, slow-growing crystals of frostbite) and he can be thawed out again a year later without ill effects?

There are many mysteries of ice and snow that at the present writing remain unsolved. There are forms of ice that sink in water instead of floating — ices of unnatural densities made by freezing under great pressures in a laboratory. At least six varieties of these strange ices have already been classified. Scientists are doing intensive research in Illinois to find out why snow varies in weight all the way from one to forty pounds a cubic foot. Army engineers are measuring snow's tensile strength, its resistance to bombs, studying which varieties of it can be packed into arctic runways, which should be scraped away. The problems of constructing large buildings on permanently frozen ground, of polar sewage disposal, are already nearing solution, but the design of subzero machinery that can be started, serviced, and operated in the bitterest arctic weather appears to leave quite a bit of room for improvement.

Anyone who has done much cold-weather flying should be familiar with the hazards of frost, even though, like Job, he accepts it as given by "the breath of God." For a thin dainty coating of frost on wings may change the air foil enough on a cold morning to make taking off dangerous if not impossible. And motors have been almost equally vulnerable.

Do you remember the thirty-seven F–84 Thunderjets that rose from the air-force base at Dayton a couple of years ago and roared westward over the Indiana farms? Only ten minutes after take-off, violent calamity struck the formation. Eight of the planes suddenly seemed to burst apart and plummeted to earth to crash in flames.

The F.B.I., called in to investigate what looked like sure sabotage, however soon found the real culprit: ice. Ice had blocked the jet air intakes, strangling the motors until they exploded. And the difficulty was not solved until engineers invented a silicone de-icer made of rubbery stuff like "bouncing putty" that would not crack and could be electrically heated without melting. That is the kind of struggle the arctic imposes on its invaders right down the line.

Ice fog is another danger not easily eliminated. Ice fog is formed not of condensed water droplets like ordinary fog but of microscopic ice crystals that have sublimated from water vapor in the air. Sublimation, or direct freezing of the vapor without its going through the intermediate liquid stage, rarely occurs when the temperature is not at least 20° below zero and in clean air around 50° below. If all air were nearly pure, ice fog would be too scarce to be a problem even in Siberia, but the smoke from a small arctic village or an airport kitchen or even an Alaskan highway is enough to form ice fog on the lee side on almost any nearly calm, cold day or night, and the ice crystals will sparkle like diamond dust in the sun or moonlight as the fog thickens and settles into low spots, often later spilling slowly out over a large area.

At times the balance between ice fog and no ice fog is so delicate that the microscopic nuclei from the exhaust of a single airplane warming up at one end of an arctic runway is enough to transform clear air into dangerous ice fog over a whole airport in ten minutes. At such times a pilot at 6000 feet and twenty miles away may see the airport clearly and approach a runway thinking visibility is unlimited only to discover just before his wheels touch that the air is turning white and low horizontal vision is so reduced he can hardly see the runway in front of him.

This frozen-fog phenomenon is closely akin to the vapor trails that occur almost anywhere in cold air, and which can be made by animals as well as machines. I have heard of wild geese leaving vapor trails high over the Canadian Rockies, and similar trails have been seen behind caribou and reindeer in 60° F. below zero air almost as distinct as those produced by a bomber at 30,000 feet.

Still another danger in polar flying is the supercooling of pure water droplets, which often occurs in a cloud. Purified water in a laboratory has been artificially cooled to as low as 37° F. below zero before freezing, because ice is very reluctant to be born unless microscopic impurities of some sort serve as nuclei to start the crystallization. But once a little ice-coated dust or other foreign matter is allowed to touch such supercooled water the whole mass of the liquid will start freezing instantly by chain reaction. This is how an airplane flying through an innocent-looking supercooled cloud can sometimes ice up with fatal rapidity.

Since degrees of temperature are in reality degrees of relative motion within the atoms there is theoretically a limit to cold at the point where atomic motion ceases altogether. This so-called absolute zero has been calculated as —460° F. and has been nearly reached in laboratory tests, which thus have far exceeded in one spot on earth even the fierce cold of Neptune, Pluto, and the meteorites of outer space. Steel and rubber reduced thus to —456° F. have been found to get as brittle as glass, "strings" of mercury can be tied in knots, oxygen becomes magnetic, and helium turns superfluid and creeps upward in defiance of gravity.

By comparison the modern comfort of life in T–3 as it has been developed since Colonel Fletcher first went there is of course like living in a tropical hotel, even though it is existence based on a floating remnant of the last ice age. The newly discovered arctic ice islands by the way are believed to have been drifting clockwise around the arctic ocean before the perpetual easterly winds perhaps for thousands of years, now skirting Alaska, now the New Siberian Islands and Fridtjof Nansen Land, now brushing the North Pole itself. T–3 for instance drifts about 40° to the right of the wind's track and at about one forty-fifth the wind's speed, going an average distance of nearly one and three fourths miles per day. Some 200 feet thick and many miles long, these floating plateaus may well have been thought to be real land if seen by early explorers. Indeed there is gravel on them, boulders and streams and growing moss, and the icescape is mainly a series of ridges 900 feet apart but only a few inches (sometimes a few feet) high, separated by shallow valleys into which melted snow flows in summer to form dainty finger lakes which freeze solid every autumn.

In the antarctic, I am told, there are even larger ice islands. One in particular was measured as seventy miles long and twenty miles wide or roughly the size and shape of Long Island in New York state, only it was much more rugged of contour, having a vertical height in some places of 2500 feet. Undoubtedly there have been larger ones, and some like floating independent worlds that venture forth upon the cold currents of the earthly seas. I have seen a large lake on one great berg off Greenland that contained a lesser but sizable iceberg floating on it containing a smaller lake on which a still smaller iceberg floated — a world within a world within a world . . . As I watched it from the sky I thought of the bunk in which our engineer lay breathing air asleep on an air mattress in an airplane which itself rested on air.

The line of icebergs drifting south on the cold Labrador current is a beautiful sight as you look down between cumulus clouds, themselves seeming to be heaven's version of the same thing. And they mark the course of that current so definitely 200 miles off Newfoundland that some of the navigators have long since taken to filing their E.T.A.'s by them when coming into Gander from Europe.

We in the air seldom see icebergs or glaciers closely enough to examine their grain, but of course glaciers have their varieties almost like living things. The successive deposits of summer pollen and moss on large ice fields, separated by winter layers of packed snow, form a record of individual history similar to the growth rings of trees, so that by drilling for core samples deep in the ice glaciologists can tell what that glacier was doing in the days of Richard the Lion-Hearted or Caesar. And when the glacier thaws, the "aqueous cement" between the grains melts faster than the hard grains themselves, thus engraving the ice's history in its most legible form, but also incidentally loosening the grains and sculping vertical prisms which soon "rot" and become dangerous, eventually either evaporating or falling into the sea — to disappear irregularly like old newspapers after a series of adventures, while later issues ever flow behind.

The names of these editions of sea ice have always fascinated me, as they give something of the flavor of polar history, of the practical talk of bearded men in adverse arctic circumstances. *Brash ice* is crushed ice that rises less than 2 feet above water, *sludge ice* is in slushy lumps, *slob ice* a thick layer of sludge, *pancake ice* dish-shaped with raised edges, *growlers* hunks from 3 to 7 feet above the sea, *cake ice* less than 10 yards across and flat, *small floes* tabular pieces from 10 yards to ⅒ mile across, *floes* from ⅒ to ½ mile across, *blocky icebergs* with flat tops and steep sides, *pyramidy bergs* pinnacled, winged, twinned, or horny . . . A *silver thaw* is icy coating left by a damp wind, a *snow roller* a windrow of blown snow . . .

Perhaps the loveliest of all sights in the arctic is the mist called sea smoke that sometimes rises up from between cold lily pads of ice, spiraling and respiraling to a great height only to be suddenly cut off by a stratum of warm air. In the antarctic dawn in spring you will see such frost smoke columns rising in pale blue at the edge of the continental pack ice — their tall tops the first to be turned pink by sunrays from below your horizon, the warm color creeping steadily downward to greet the sunrise, then leaping to the distant ice cliffs whose shadows mingle with other wandering veils before the lazy polar sun.

The evolvement of snow, however, must be far and away the most magical of all earth's experience of cold, even though it is close to so many of us. Have you noticed how the first snow flurry in October sometimes looks like a drone of bees searching for a garden or a place to land? How, if there is a breeze, the uncertain fledgling flakes flit upward almost as much as downward, seeming afraid to trust themselves to this cruel dark world of warm rocks and trees and houses?

Snow's real home of course is in our upper sky where one must go upon wings to see it. Up there it is always snowing somewhere and there is always snow — even snow that sleeps, small snow that rests year upon year on the strong blue molecules of sky, snow that never comes down. Spawned in the crystal tail of the white mare, nurtured in the celestial seas of the silver mackerel, these tiny flakes just float and float, shimmering in the sun by day, fluttering now upward to ring the moon, now downward to feed the rain, now northward to doze in arctic silence o'er the pole.

But how are snow flakes born? Whence the ancient treasures of the snow?

Snow in truth springs straight out of the mystic womb of sky where hyperborean winds forcep the molecules of water vapor into sublimated birth. For snow birth is literally sublime. It generally occurs unseen in the great secret heights where the conditions of cold most favor the transition from vapor to solid without becoming liquid on the way.

Sublimation of water vapor can happen, as we have said, only when it is colder than about 20° F. below zero. In very clean upper air it has to be nearly 60° F. below or colder. An invisible particle of salt or dust or maybe a dry spore floats amid vapor and suddenly, like the mystery of life, becomes the heart of a new crystal, a fertilized ovum of potentiality, the beginning of a snowstorm.

Some scientists think that such snow germs can be born spontaneously without any foreign nucleus at all, but it is hard to prove. In any case the tiny crystal grows symmetrically in free air with magical wonder. Even when born wrapped in a cloud, the evidence is that it springs direct from the clear vapor between the condensed droplets, moving freely between them like a comet between the stars, growing with the stuff it passes. For infant snow feeds on supercooled clouds like a suckling babe on its mother, drawing the moisture not direct but by evaporating it from the droplets and then sublimating it to its crystal self. This magical process occurs because the "vapor pressure" of supercooled water is higher than that of ice at the same temperature, so that H_2O vapor drifts like a microscopic wind down pressure gradients from higher to lower areas, from decadent water to nascent ice, nourishing the seeds of winter, nursing the baby snow in its wild blue cradle of sky.

The snow baby is never pampered, however, nor allowed to become a spoiled child. It is raised oh so strictly under the prim "law of crystal lattices," which explains hexagonal symmetry: 2 atoms of hydrogen plus 1 atom of oxygen make 3 atoms that form a molecule of H_2O with a basic triangular tendency that develops into the hexagon — an innate waltz-time attitude toward the world of white and the water crystal, three on three, six on six — air and cloud and snow. It is true that a mysterious cubic or four-sided rhombohedral ice has recently been discovered that seems somehow to defy the law of H_2O crystallization, but until science explains it we must consider it just an anomaly in the hexagonal world of snow.

Starting as a submicroscopic three-dimensional triangle or hollow prism, the normal ice seed always shoots out crystal ice buds at angles of 60° in any direction, solidifying water vapor as it finds it, grabbing molecules as they come, three at a time, half a dozen at a clip. Rapidly the prism thus becomes the axle or hub of a three- or six-sided wheel, which may assume any shape so long as it repeats its pattern to the tune of three. Some turn into hourglasses, scrolls, pyramids, crosses. In high cirrus clouds which are cold and dry the hub usually remains as a bluish cylinder or hollow bullet with minor branches growing only slowly, the whole retain-

"cubic" forms   common hexangular and triangular forms

some basic forms of snow crystals which grow and combine in the sky, becoming snowflakes that may eventually reach the earth

ing a compact prismatic or hexagonal spool-like form. But in warmer, moister air or lower clouds it will grow faster, the hub alone remaining short while the six spokes at each end develop complicated barbs and barbules, forming a thin, flat double wheel of wondrous lateral symmetry, occasionally 12-spoked, slowly combining into a solid, greenish disk, sometimes a hexagonal whiskey glass or a jackstone shape which may be also lacy or star-pointed.

The five commonest snow spool motifs are said to suggest the needle, feather, tree, cup, and plate, but all these varied snow types repeatedly fold their crystals around the air as they grow, thereby creating minute hollow tubes which appear as delicate systems of dark dots, rods, and branching lines under the microscope. So individual and charmingly imaginative are these markings and shapes inside a snowflake that you can almost see the merry snow angels up there falling over themselves thinking up new designs for these most exquisite creations of heaven, no two of which have ever been found quite alike.

Though the lateral symmetry of a snow crystal is often as perfect as is a well-made wheel, the two ends of the hub (as in the wheel) are almost always of different sizes, which gives the whole the semblance of a tiny parachute, sometimes a double parachute. And this crystal parachute is functional, for the flake always falls with the hub's small end downward, leaving it slightly convex upward. Some kinds even grow spicules converging downward like the shroud lines of parachutes which, if the flake falls long enough through moist air, meet at a bottom point and eventually fill the enclosed space with crystalline structure, creating the pellet known as graupel.

In one way or another all of these crystals spin and spiral as they parachute down the sky, now rising on the wind's whim, now settling in its lull — ever changing or growing with the passing invisible vapor, their very shape a perfect record of their journey from the cirrus kingdom, their little spicate branches by their pattern preserving their history of the layers of moisture and temperature through which they have traveled. The main branches grow faster in the more saturated layers of sky while the lesser twigs sprout in the drier spells, eventually whole colonies of related limbs from many sources making up one mature crystal, a sort of patriarchal system arrayed around the six sons of the single common ancestor still seated in his central throne.

There is a whole world in this tiny skyborn gem, you see, and it gathers sound waves and creates magnetic forces of its own as it floats, even broadcasting dainty music like a purring newborn kitten from its own radiolike sending station as if to tell the big world below of things it never dreamed — if only, if only it could hear and understand.

Like most of the sky's snow, which never comes to earth at all,

even the few flakes destined to reach the ground linger inter-
minably on their downward journey — in some cases taking weeks
or months on the way, seldom less than many hours. Their start,
as with infant rain, is very slow. It is only after the single crystals
have grown big enough to have reasonable chances of colliding
with each other that they begin to make noticeable downward
progress, collecting gradually into double and triple parachutes,
capturing splinters from passing damaged flakes, building colonies
of spools and spicules and outwardly irregular tree masses, and
finally the great soggy conglomerations we see in heavy flurries,
which may reach more than an inch in diameter by the time they
come to rest on earth.

As you may have noticed, these falling snowflakes spiral in a
number of different ways. Some float almost straight down without
turning. Some spin rapidly like propellers. Some twist clockwise;
others counterclockwise. Some rotate alternately one way then

the other, a few with a flapping motion like a wounded bird or a falling leaf — each a unit of graceful individual expression until its dance is cut impersonally short by the ground.

Delicate and ephemeral as snow often is and beautiful its silent fall, its collective mass is not always just a sweet frosting on the cake of earth, for it can strangle New York City's transportation system in half a night. In Alpine villages it intermittently spells sudden death by avalanche — sometimes the billowing loose-snow avalanche, sometimes the deadly slab-snow avalanche in which a whole mountainside crust of snow may slide in one huge piece. Even its breath, the avalanche wind, has taken its victims by the score.

During the terrible week end of January 18, 1951, the avalanche winds in the Alps sneezed away dozens of small houses, hurling some of them for hundreds of yards. In one house where a child was asleep in an upper bedroom the wind blew the roof off so violently that the suction swept the child's bed up and out onto a snowbank. The child awoke unhurt in the snow while the whole house was crushed and everyone else in the family killed.

Avalanches can also strike so suddenly that when you are driving a car you don't even hear the last-minute rumblings when the snow is on its way and it is already too late. On December 22, 1952, the air blast from an avalanche roaring down Arlberg Pass in Austria blew a bus full of skiers off a high bridge, killing twenty-three of the thirty-one passengers.

Of such is the record of errant snow. And even in its gentler moods snow's feats can be prodigious. Sixty inches once fell in a single day at Giant Forest, California, and 884 inches (74 feet) in one winter at Tamarack, California. In Calumet, Michigan, which might be called a home of snow, it snowed daily for fifty-one consecutive days from November 1950 to January 1951.

Heavy snowfalls are often very hard to predict for they depend on complex combinations of factors in the impulsive snow factories of the sky. One of the few generalities to be made is that the heaviest snowfalls usually come when the wind has had a long fetch over water or when its veering so matches the movement of the storm center that the precipitation sector of the storm is held over one spot a long time.

It might be appropriate to end this interlude about earthly winter with mention of snow's curious similarity to feathers. This similarity is particularly noticeable with the large multiple flakes whose many crystals seem to be held together after collision in flight by a microscopic zipper action. The fine hexagonal crystals indeed are comparable to barbules and barbicels in that they hook into each other, I've noticed, with a grip strong enough to turn a snow-swept chicken-wire fence into a solid mat of snow resembling a feathered wall, to bridge the gap between swaying clotheslines a foot apart and lock them into a single system, or even to balance such a tonnage of weight on delicate telephone wires that the foot-thick poles holding them up break and collapse to the ground.

Like feathers, snow also makes fine insulation, and the primitive snow-block igloo is one of the world's best-insulated houses. When light fluffy snow later falls and covers the blocks the insulation value increases greatly, however, for like rock wool or fiber glass, ice crystals that entrap air in innumerable tiny cells have a marvelous power to prevent the passage of heat. I once measured the temperature of the ground under a foot of feathery snow and found it 44° F. warmer than the air above. And a scientist testing the reflective power of snow discovered that it could mirror as much as ninety per cent of bright sunshine.

This downy stuff may be literally the flesh of the lower cirrus clouds that somehow got sucked downward and fluttered long enough in very dry air to reach the earth. At any rate its crystals are lacelike and hollow and the snow they make is virtually nothing but air. One part water to twenty parts of air makes a light snow, but some gossamerlike snow tested in Finland was found to contain as little as one part water to three hundred parts of air. That must have been ghosty stuff indeed for twenty-five feet of of it would melt down into only one inch of water!

Heat is not the only thing stopped by this wonderful insulation either for, like the feathers of owls, it is about equally effective in dampening sound. Its hair-fine filaments of hollow crystal not only fold up air in cells but reflect the sound waves back and forth until they cancel and fade below audibility.

As the swooping owl absorbs more sound than he makes, therefore, so do the feathers of snow impose a silence on the earth. They even make the blind man blinder by destroying his subconscious sonar sensitivity, by blotting up his footfalls, his voice, his breath, so their faint familiar echoes do not reach his navigating ears. Snow in effect seems to turn the world, like Ascalaphus, into a kind of peaceful white owl, seasonally pluming and repluming her dusty breast with the purest of crystal down.

9. The Wine of Weather

IN A ROUTINE CHECK of my instruments at 01:00 G.M.T. I noticed that the temperature had suddenly risen about six degrees to +8° F. And I could no longer see any stars. The difference in altimeter readings showed a corresponding increase in barometric pressure, indicating a stronger drift to the left.

What did these things add up to?

Until the last quarter century they would not have suggested much more than a warm southerly wind with perhaps its hint of an early spring. But now the implications were vastly greater. In fact they had taken on a whole new dimension. For it was quite obvious we had just passed a warm front. All the evidence was there on the instruments, with the high overcast to verify it.

"What's the weather going to do?" a voice at my elbow asked. It was Co-pilot Dropford returning from the cabin with his customary two paper cups of coffee: one for himself, one for the captain.

"Just a weak warm front," I replied. "A little air up from Spain. Maybe a shower. But it won't last long."

"'S'all right with me so long as there's no more ice," said he, swinging back into his seat just forward of my own.

There was nothing unusual in this exchange of comments on the weather, for talk of fronts and air masses is by now long since common among people who fly. A realistic concept of weather is so plainly life and death to us of the clouds that we have naturally adopted the jargon of meteorologists and tried to fathom all their great new discoveries.

In some ways, I suppose, it is easier for us than the weather men to see the truth of weather, because we know it more with our eyes than with our minds: we see it with a bird's perspective, flying alternately above and up to our eyes in it. Almost at once do we view the approaching storm and the rainbow behind it.

We see the sky change with the seasons too, for autumn clouds change color and wither in their way just as leaves on a tree, and the secret roots and the cambium flow of spring have their counterparts on high. New clouds appear as summer approaches and, like foliage, clouds cover more of the sky in warm weather than in cold. This bears a relation of course to the interconnection between weather and vegetation, for not only does moisture in the air affect soil and the growth of plants but also the state of vegetation reflects back upon evaporation and the humidity of the air. Even animals add to this influence, inhaling oxygen exhaled by the trees, exhaling carbon dioxide to be absorbed by the flowers, playing their little share in the total metabolism of the atmosphere.

But what of the new basic weather concepts that are beginning to affect our daily speech, and where did they come from? What is the matter with Ben Franklin's old discovery that weather just rolls along, hitting Philadelphia this evening, New York at midnight, Boston at dawn?

The trouble with the old weather ideas that prevailed until the age of flying came into its own after World War I is that they were two-dimensional. They took into consideration latitude and longitude and vast areas of land and sea but ignored the third dimension of height and the volume and shape of the masses of air that move about the earth.

The principal discoverer of the modern air-mass concept was the great Norwegian physicist, Vilhelm Bjerknes. Standing up there amid the mountains near the very top of the world, he saw something that others had missed. He conceived the simple truth that the weather moves around the earth in great waves thousands of miles apart. Using small free balloons that carry instruments and checking them with airplane reports, he proved that air in the sky circulates in distinct chunks or masses with definite boundaries which have now come to be known as fronts. He made people realize that they are like fish in an aquarium tank with an attendant (God) to change their water (air) at regular intervals, that a complete fresh bath of air literally engulfs our temperate world every few days.

Before Bjerknes, people assumed that air was just air and, like well-stirred soup, that all parts of it blended imperceptibly into one another to make a homogeneous broth of sky. That theory seemed reasonable enough except that it could not explain how a warm, soggy, misty night would suddenly change to a cold clear, crisp dawn, or why winter always comes in jerks: three days cold and clear, two days damp and thawing, one day of snow followed by five days cold and clear, three days cloudy and warm, two days cold and clear . . .

Of course God might just as easily have arranged the weather so that cool seasons blended gradually into warm. But how much more imaginative and exciting and maddening and educational to have made it as we find it — all arranged in clear-cut patterns and moving irregular shapes that we have had to rack our brains to learn the meaning of!

Now that Bjerknes has opened the gate, of course, it all seems basically clear, even obvious. That warm, soggy, misty air did not change miraculously into cold, clear, crisp air. It simply moved a hundred miles further east and was replaced by new air of a different kind.

But how come the air is arranged in packages of different sorts? What are these airs like? Where do they hail from and whither are they bound?

You know many of them from daily experience: from looking through them, sniffing them, breathing them.

Take the common clear, cool, dry air of the northern and eastern parts of America. It is brisk and bracing and feels newly washed, spiced with spruce and pine and crisp as snow. It should be exactly that way for it has just arrived from Canada where it drifted slowly for weeks among snow-capped mountains over dry northern plains and evergreen forests and cold sparkling lakes. That particular brand of air is called by weather men Polar Canadian or Polar Continental. It sweeps down over the Dakotas and the Great Lakes to New York and New England in intermittent waves, cold and clear and dry from the ground up to the thin stratosphere — waves that may be two or three thousand miles and a full week from crest to crest — waves containing fifty million cubic miles of air in one chunk.

Now what about the air that is between those waves of Polar Canadian air? That is the familiar warm, steamy brand of air that comes in on a southwest wind with a flavor of the Gulf of Mexico and sultry tropical thunderstorms. The weather men label that Tropical Gulf or Tropical Maritime air, for it is fresh from the Spanish Main or the shores of Texas and Louisiana. As it sweeps up the Mississippi Valley between the cold waves, men pull off their wool shirts and long underwear, buds appear on the trees, and the birds flit about with thoughts of mating.

Besides these two best-known American airs, there is the Polar Pacific air that comes from Siberia, picking up moisture off the Aleutians and bringing rain to Seattle. There is the Polar Atlantic air that descends on Nova Scotia and New England as a nor'easter bringing cold rain and the salty tang of the Grand Banks. There is the Tropical Pacific air out of the South Seas that means sunshine in Southern California, and the dry Tropical Continental air off the hot deserts of Mexico and Arizona that blows the sonora northward in summer and may threaten a new dust bowl in Kansas.

Airs, like wines, can be recognized by their taste, color, and quality — by all sorts of subtle manifestations of character. Some airs are milky and mild, some glassy green, some clear as crystal. Every combination of humidity and warmth, of dryness and coolth, is found in some one of the earth's airs. And each has also its own quality of life, sheds its own light, produces its own dew or frost or halos around the moon, has its own distinctive way of moving, its particular treatment of clouds and smoke.

Connoisseurs can often tell a brand of air by one glance at the smoke pouring from a chimney. Smoke is perhaps the most sensitive of signs in the material world. In still, sultry air it will creep lazily forth, in lively, cold air it will bubble and boil, in hurricane air it will be whisked to leeward in wild streamers, in inverted air it will float neatly in layers. Like a cat's tail the very angle and wave motion of the mounting appendage expresses character and mood. Each wisp, each peristaltic furrow flows out as a kind of writing, a nephic soul script that only those who think to the rhythms of the wind can begin to understand.

Sometimes the outward dress of the air changes as it moves over the countryside so that it is hard to recognize where it came from. Tropical Maritime air for example, when it sweeps northward across the United States in winter, leaves Florida like a sparkling summer morning. But over the cold hills of Tennessee and Kentucky it starts condensing so that it arrives at Detroit a dark drizzling mass, and hats and mouths turn down at the corners as people look upon the dismal winter day. One might liken it to a girl in a blue silk bathing suit who puts on an old brown overcoat when coming north. Although she looks very different now she is really still the same girl.

However, not only may a *single* air mass dress oppositely in different kinds of country: a *single* country may influence *different* air masses to dress just as oppositely. An example of this might be a stretch of flat Iowa cornbelt thawing in spring. As a wave of cold Polar Canadian air pours over it, it feels warm to the bottom level of the wave which, as it heats, begins to expand, becomes bottom-light and unstable until rising columns of it sprout into vertical puffs of cumulus cloud and moil upward into the paths of airliners whose passengers soon feel queasy and complain about the bumpy weather. But to a following wave of hot Tropical Maritime air that same Iowa farmland feels chilly and the lower level of hot air cools off instead of warming, contracts to become bottom-heavy and stable, leaving the whole air mass floating comfortably in nice horizontal layers of stratus and alto-stratus cloud, while air passengers can sleep all the way to Denver.

This kind of difference is what keeps weather from being simple and weather forecasters from sleeping nights. The combined and changing factors of temperature, humidity, pressure, and motion over irregular land and sea produce all the kinds of clouds and weather in the world: from the eerie stillness of the arctic where often neither vertical nor horizontal cloud is seen to the dramatic celaje cloudscapes of Guatemala where flat-lens clouds commonly float among giant cumulus, complete stability and peace right next door to explosive uncertainty!

The weather men seek to keep perpetual track of all these goings on in the sky by measuring what factors they can with instruments, some of them dating back to very primitive times. The hygrometer, which measures humidity by the expansion and contraction of human hair, may have been inspired by American Indians who had a saying "When the hair turns damp in the scalp house look out for rain." The thermometer is a result of one of Galileo's mercurial experiments; the barometer the brainchild of Torricelli, first human to stake his reputation on the reality of air.

The greatest of the newer instruments are the basic radiosonde and the now widely used radar. The little radiosonde balloons already are climbing the skies to check upper air over much of the world by day and through the dead of night. They carry small boxes containing a miniature radio attached to a thermometer and simple moisture meter suspended from a five-foot balloon — man-made questionmarks that rise humbly toward heaven as if to inquire of God His will for today and tomorrow.

The answer comes back by theodolite and by an ethereal radio signal chattering steadily for the hour it takes the balloon to reach the stratosphere and burst. It tells the trained weather man what kind of clouds are forming up there, at what height they are, which way they are developing, and the speed and direction of the wind.

By such and sundry educated probings with a little slide-rule thermodynamics, the weather office maps the sky and is learning within reasonable limits what to expect over desert or sea or forest or arctic ice. It has discovered that the hottest and coldest parts of the earth are respectively far from the equator and the poles: the official heat record 134° F. in the shade in Death Valley, California, 36° North Latitude, until it was beaten recently by 136° F. in Azizia, Libya, at 25° North; the official northern hemisphere record for cold —93° F. (unofficially —108° in 1938!) at Oimyakon, Siberia, at only 63° North Latitude or parallel with mid-Sweden.

They say that a noticeable difference between temperatures above and below —100° F. is that when it gets down to about 100° below, horses' heads start to freeze and it becomes risky to let them stand out-of-doors. Their frozen breath may also become a problem and I have seen a Siberian pony standing in a railroad station on the Trans-Siberian in midwinter with an icicle literally reaching from his nose to the ground so that he could have leaned on it.

Perhaps more surprising than surface differences is the fact that at the altitude of twelve miles it averages fifty degrees colder over the equator than over the poles where the warmer stratosphere begins only five miles up. The extreme spread at the surface, however, is actually as great as the difference between freezing and boiling, between ice and steam (Oimyakon is said to have had it as high as +104° F. in summer), and it is mainly nature's effort to equalize or balance this disparity of at least 212° (at most about 250°) that drives the winds and makes the weather.

Trends of long-term change of course are recorded as well as the daily reports, for meteorologists cannot forget that explorers in frozen Antarctica have found tree trunks eighteen inches in diameter and coal seams obviously the remains of an ancient forest, while in central India and central Africa, two of the hottest regions on earth, are extensive evidences of glaciers. Some suspect that the present wide disparity between steaming tropics and frozen poles is a passing abnormality that will largely disappear in the next few thousand years.

They pay attention to cloudiness all over the earth and have discovered that on the average the sea is cloudier than the land, the oceanic southern hemisphere cloudier than the drier northern, the whole sky slightly more than half covered with clouds, the fewest of which are in the horse latitudes, and most in the polar frontal areas where the large majority of the world's people live.

Like the sea, however, the clouds are a friendly stabilizing in-fluence on temperature, for moisture heats or cools more slowly than dry air. So cloudy days and cloudy summers are cooler, while cloudy nights and winters are warmer.

In order to forecast weather many things are thus taken into consideration: behaviour of clouds, temperature, humidity, pres-sure . . . But the single most essential factor is now recognized to be the air mass. One must know its nature and reactions to the country, and most especially its boundaries, the seams of the at-mosphere, the fronts that mark the end of one air mass and the beginning of another.

For these drifting, twisting sky seams are where the most significant weather is found, and recognizing them and analyzing their behaviour is the main work of the modern meteorologist. This is called frontal analysis. It is the greatest part of Vilhelm Bjerknes' gift to the world.

Fronts are pretty easy to spot, once you know what you're looking for. They are a sudden change of air bringing a distinct rise or drop in temperature, a wind shift, different humidity, and a new aspect to the whole sky. In an hour from the ground — or in five minutes' flying — you will see the low soggy clouds disperse and the dull gray shroud overhead change to clear, cool blue. It seldom takes much longer for a cold front to pass.

Often the actual air boundary is drawn for you in a line of clouds straight across the entire visible world. It may be a row of thunderstorms, a line squall with roll scud clouds scooting like freight rollers close to the ground before it, or just a slight cumulus demarcation. When flying you will certainly notice the drop on your thermometer, the swing in your driftmeter, and the radically changing clues of wind.

Since cold air is denser and heavier than warm air, a moving mass of cold air naturally hugs the ground — and it moves forward at first underneath the warmer air it is replacing, prying it up and pushing it back as you might raise an old board with your boot and kick it away. A cold front cross section, like the cold air under a thunderstorm, is in fact shaped almost exactly like a boot, the rounded toe rising perhaps twenty thousand feet high, followed by a wedgelike foot sloping gradually up to forty thousand feet and more.

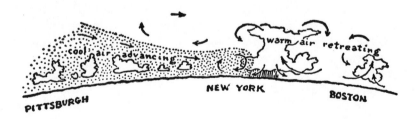

An hour or so before the toe of cold air arrives at any one spot, the clouds there can feel the warm air rising and shying away from the approaching boot. Their nervous motion at this time is like a bunch of horses before a prairie fire — the fire of rising heat bubbles disturbed by pressure. Otherwise there isn't much warning. The air feels as warm and moist as ever, the wind still mostly south.

Then it strikes! Big cumulus clouds appear to the northwest — feminine cumulus thunderheads with beautiful, treacherous curves. They may look light and gay up top, but will turn out to be darker and more threatening in the middle. In summer they are spiced with lightning.

This rolling bank of clouds is the actual forward edge of the advancing cold air, the toe of the boot — held back a little by scuffing friction at the ground but bulging forward angrily to kick the warm air up and away. At the moment of impact there is sudden rain, often a cloudburst, the cold shock condensing the moisture far beyond the air's capacity to hold it. Then the full mass of cold air surges in from the northwest in gusts. Sometimes it is a squall vicious enough to tear shingles from roofs, topple trees, or flip taxiing airplanes over on their backs.

In a half hour the hurly-burly is done, the rain stopping, the Dutchman's breeches showing blue. The front is passed. The new air mass has swallowed the whole sky and you can reasonably expect "air mass weather" for a while — at least weather characteristic of this particular kind of air mass until some new front announces another change of air.

The next front could be another one still colder, but it is five times more likely to be a warm one, bringing Tropical Maritime air of some sort. Warm fronts are easier to forecast because they send messengers days ahead of themselves, envoys of high flying cirrus to tip off weather men, farmers, or sailors. This the source of the adage: "Mare's tails and mackerel scales make lofty ships carry low sails."

As warm air is light, the shape of a warm front is very different from the heavy scuffing boot of the cold front. Instead of coming in low, its leading edge rides high and is shaped in cross-section like a ski — the long light ski of a jumper landing: the forward end of the ski well off the ground, the trailing end just touching.

This warm-front sky ski is a thousand miles long, two or three times as long as the cold-front boot. Its forward curved top over Boston is made of curly cirrus clouds 30,000 feet high, feathers of snow appropriate to skiing. Along its straight length is the usual sequence of descending clouds: cirro-stratus the milk cloud at 20,000 feet over Pittsburgh, alto-stratus the sheet cloud at 12,000 feet over Columbus, nimbo-stratus the drizzle cloud at 5000 feet over Indianapolis in a mood to drag its feet there with light rain for several days, possibly mist or fog.

As indicated in the aphorism "Rain long foretold, long last; short notice, soon past," the easy warm bath of the warm front is a long-acoming, long-agoing, lackadaisical affair — in contrast to the short and snappy cold shower of the cold front. When its soggy clouds finally break up, the wind will be found to have swung toward the south and the weather will persist warm and humid — until the next air mass arrives.

And so goes the air-mass cycle — cold and dry, warm and humid, cold and dry, colder and drier, warm and dry, cold and damp, warm and humid, cold and dry . . . There is a rhythm to it — certainly a repetition, if somewhat irregular. The great air waves come along in an unending procession. They don't all hit the same spots and are of very different shapes and sizes — their storms sometimes misleading like the instability line of squalls that often precedes a cold mass at ground level by many hours, their fronts sometimes almost unrecognizably weak or washed out or straggling — just as waves of water or waves of birds flying or waves of trees in a forest. But they keep on coming, following natural laws, until you can learn to understand them, to anticipate them some.

It is a little as though you were a snail clinging to a rock at the edge of the sea where the surf was coming in so that you were under water about as often as out. Each wave would hit you a little differently, some bigger, some smaller, some foamier, some saltier, some spaced far apart, some close upon the one before.

It would be next to impossible to predict reliably whether you would be in water or air at exactly one minute hence — yet you'd have a pretty good idea of the situation of five seconds hence, maybe ten seconds hence. That is how it is with the weather man: he can see the waves coming plainly enough, but telling exactly when, how, and where they will strike is another thing again.

The United States Weather Bureau with some five hundred stations, no doubt the best equipped and most extensive synoptic meteorological organization in the world, is said to attain only about eighty-five per cent accuracy of forecast. To a wave of air three thousand miles wide, the U.S. Weather Bureau bears just about the same relation as a bunch of snails to an ocean wave.

The motive force behind both kinds of waves is the same: the sun's heat and the earth's motion. Chapter 5 told of the basic wind circulation of the earth in which heated tropical air rises and flows poleward to replace cold, settling polar air being sucked equatorward to replace rising tropical air flowing poleward . . . This general flow, however, is immensely complicated by the coriolis force of the earth's turning and the wrinkles of the world's skin: the monsoon effect of summer sea winds and winter land winds, the barriers of mountains, the up and down drafts over gulfs and plains.

And amid all this complex dynamic flowing of winds, of doldrums and horse latitudes, one of the great meteorological discoveries was made about the year 1917: the polar front. Although four out of every five persons on earth lives on a polar front, no one had realized it or comprehended the front until the genius of Bjerknes brought it to light. The polar front is the superfront or permanent zone of warm and cold fronts. It is the main traffic intersection between warmed tropical air flowing north and cooled polar air flowing south. It is where the low pressure storms roll counterclockwise between the clockwise-turning high-pressure masses, like ball bearings between wheels in an engine. It is the great crossroads of the sky — to some extent a social circle, a mixing hall, or a prize ring. Bjerknes called it a front because this belt of continuous conflict between different airs reminded him of the battlefronts of the great war that was still going on.

In tne Southern Hemisphere where west winds can blow clean around the world without obstruction between the Andes and Antarctica, the polar front is fairly simple and confines itself largely to the uninhabited band of the graybeards and the albatross between south latitudes 50° and 60°.

But in the Northern Hemisphere, which is interspersed with the eggbeater action of jagged Rocky Mountains, Greenland's icecap, Norwegian fiords, and the Himalayas, the story is different. Here the polar front doesn't go just through the Bering Sea, Hudson Bay, and so on around the subarctic world but swashes and splashes over the whole temperate zone from Mexico to Alaska, from Arabia to Norway. Of course semi-tropical places such as Florida and Egypt and Formosa are beyond the reach of most of the waves. They are like seabirds sitting on a cliff: they get only an occasional lash of spray from the huge combers that march steadily across the northern United States and Canada, northern Europe, Siberia and Japan. The crests of these main waves average about three thousand miles apart, so that it takes only six of them to ring the earth at latitude 50°, but there are smaller wavelets corrugating the surfaces of the big waves, a mere thousand miles or so apart, often overtaking each other (occluded fronts), often curling at their crests (large storm areas) like whitecaps on the sea, reaching too high for stability, breaking and dissolving into islands of foam (dwindling rain areas). These are the assorted, squirming little cold and warm fronts we've been describing that hit Chicago and Berlin and Tokyo two or three times a week. They are the minor waves of the air ocean.

Like all weather, polar front waves move somewhat with the sun, marching closer to the Arctic Circle in summer, licking the Tropic of Cancer in winter, parading endlessly eastward around the earth — here fading, there reappearing — their troughs and crests bringing alternately snow and buds to half the world.

Until the Norwegian school explained that the belt of surface collision between north-moving tropical air and south-moving polar air was bound to have waves moving along it, the confused, swirling low-pressure areas and high-pressure spots drifting across the weather maps made little sense to anyone. But now at last we have an answer; modern meteorology has arrived, and it has been proved that any surface between moving fluids of different densities is certain to be more or less wavy, just as the sea has waves between the heavy liquid below and the lighter fluid of air above. So the light tropical air whips up waves in the heavier polar air next to it, and our weather progresses in barometric lows and complicated spiral tongues of moisture and warmth — as it has for hundreds of millions of years — on and on and on.

Just how far and fast a single air-pressure wave can continue as a recognizable entity is shown by the fact that the weather men spotted a tiny ripple on the polar front at Havre, Montana, on February 23, 1925, and watched it grow into a giant wave of low pressure, a winter storm swirling steadily eastward, out across the North Atlantic past Iceland to Britain and the Baltic Sea. For a full month they traced it — all the way across Siberia and the North Pacific to Alaska and Canada, past its starting point and on again to the Gulf of St. Lawrence where it melted into another and larger wave on March 23. In twenty-eight days this individual wave of weather had traveled 21,379 miles at an average speed of 32 m.p.h.

Such waves are born just as are waves of the sea: by some minor irregularity of pressure, perhaps caused by a small island as in George Stewart's *Storm*, maybe by invisible radiation, or a wind deflecting from a hill or canyon, or any combination of the ever changing reactions between gases, liquids, and solids in this throbbing, breathing world. From a minor ripple with a poleward crest, the wave grows into a counterclockwise curlicue of low pressure spreading over ten states. As the winds blow their spiral around it, the more southerly winds suck northward the warm tropical airs while the northerly winds pull the polar cold south. That is how the two air masses get locked in their whirling storm of combat, the cold air bulging southward in great convex curves enveloping and undercutting a slimmer tongue of warm air that reaches almost to the heart of the vortex.

Often the advancing boot of low polar air overtakes the light ski of the warm front, closing in and fusing with the other cold wave retreating ahead of it at the ground, so that the northern crest of the warm air is forced upward and retreats southward or is cut off. This is the occluded front and its complexities were completely baffling before Bjerknes explained air masses. They are still puz-

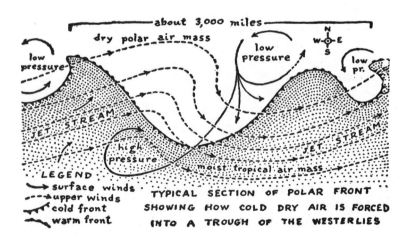

LEGEND
→ surface winds
---→ upper winds
⌃⌃ cold front
⌒⌒ warm front

TYPICAL SECTION OF POLAR FRONT SHOWING HOW COLD DRY AIR IS FORCED INTO A TROUGH OF THE WESTERLIES

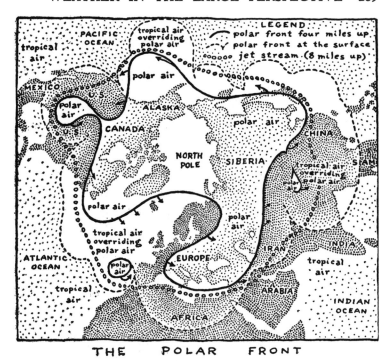

THE   POLAR   FRONT

zliug enough, though more is being learned about them every day, and more about the invisible upper winds, the hidden ringmasters who crack the secret whips of command.

The jet stream of circumpolar vortex, already described as the major wind of the world, is seen in the largest perspective as the dominant factor in all regional heat waves or cold waves that pass over the temperate earth. Even the 10,000,000,000 tons of air that twice a year roll across the equator from summer to winter are guided by its changing courses, and it is becoming increasingly important in long-range forecasting as it pulls lower air along in the friction of its wake. Whether it circles the planet in three days of January or in ten days of July, its eddies whirl outward and downward for weeks as cyclonic rains and blizzards, sub-eddies in turn as thunderstorms, and in some cases sub-sub-eddying tornadoes or waterspouts. And associated with it are such newly discovered phenomena as the tropical cold storms that form six miles high and a thousand miles in diameter near the equator — massive disturbances that never come down to earth at all.

If knowledge of the jet stream and the ionosphere above it is the beginning of a greater science of weather, now still as infantile as Keplerian astronomy, there is also a lesser science of weather called microclimatology. This has to do with local atmospheric conditions at airports and on farms, and small-scale weather in general. Orchardists study it to circumvent frost, florists use it to create optimum climates in their greenhouses, manufacturers and air-conditioning engineers, foresters and highway experts keep close tabs on it.

Barnyard climate affecting the health of cattle, pigs, and chickens can be improved by architectural design taking into consideration sun slant, drafts, humidity, insulation . . . Stripping moss off arctic ground in Siberia has enabled the summer sun to thaw large areas deep enough to grow vegetables. Building small windbreaks and mulching as a general farming practice has affected the climate of whole regions, helped turn dust bowls into gardens. Even anthills and furrows have their warm, dry sides and their cool, moist sides — each rock its little climatic divide, its significant pattern of pressure areas.

Pressure is an aspect of weather that should be especially considered because it not only helps us keep track of the moving storm areas (usually associated with low pressure and the falling barometer) but is a clue also to such seemingly unrelated phenomena as volcanoes, earthquakes, explosions, tides, swells, and the capacity of wells.

Average or standard sea level pressure is 29.92 inches of mercury, which means that in a large U-shaped tube half filled with mercury, one end sealed up to preserve a vacuum between it and the mercury, the other end open, the air pressing in the open end on an average day will force the level of mercury on that side 29.92 inches lower than the other and airless level. That's the classic barometer invented by Torricelli, and it demonstrates the weight and substance of air, which can also be measured in bars or millibars (1013.2 mbs. standard pressure at sea level) as is now universal practice.

To give yourself some realistic idea of what hefty stuff air is, just remember that the air in a cube-shaped room thirty feet on each side weighs one full ton, just like a ton of coal. Every square foot of the earth's surface holds up more than a ton of air, which you can imagine as a column a foot thick rising invisibly as high as air is air.

Of course the only reason this column a hundred miles high or so doesn't weigh much more is that the air gets rapidly thinner and lighter as it goes up. But, logically enough, it also gets thicker and heavier as it goes down. In fact air weighs quite a bit more in places hundreds of feet below sea level like Death Valley, and somebody figured out that if miners should dig a mine thirty-five miles straight down they would have trouble keeping track of their shoring lumber, for the boards would float around on the dense air like driftwood on the sea. If the mine were much deeper than that the miners themselves would start to float and the whole project might take on the dreamy atmosphere of the deep sea.

The sensitive relationship between weather and slight changes on the barometer is shown by the fact that the lowest sea-level pressure ever officially recorded on earth was 26.35 inches of mercury on the Florida keys, September 2, 1935. That was less than twelve per cent below normal, yet it took a hurricane to restore the atmosphere to balance again.

Perhaps some otherwise unexplained incidents in history could be caused in part by the psychological effect of low atmospheric pressure, for it has been statistically proved that when the glass is low more accidents occur, more suicide attempts, more crimes, more lovers' quarrels, more babies are born, more packages left in buses, more gloves forgotten, more dogs gone astray.

Temperature and humidity undoubtedly also play their part. In the Bank of England, for instance, they used to have a rule that the important files be locked up during dense fogs because of the mysterious errors that occurred then. Examination marks have been found to be lowest in hot humid weather. Crimes of passion reach a peak in July and August, liquor in summer is more intoxicating, ponderous reading more difficult, memory more slippery.

Someone has even worked out a relationship between changes of air masses and the state of the body, concluding that cold fronts cause contraction of blood vessels, spasms, improved metabolism, and biochemical reduction; warm fronts the opposite.

In recent years research has been made on the relationship between air pressure and earthquakes or volcanic eruptions, and there seems good reason to believe that the rapid decrease of air pressure against the ground at the passing of a storm center is likely to trigger off any faults in the earth's crust then under severe strain and close to the point of snapping.

During the pre-dawn hours of Saturday morning, September 1, 1923, for example, squalls and cloudbursts from a typhoon swept past the central island of Japan, but the skies had hardly cleared before noon when Yokohama and Tokyo were suddenly struck by the most devastating earthquake recorded in history. More than half a million homes were completely destroyed that day and a hundred thousand people crushed or burned to death. Later calculations indicated that a deep fault had snapped just offshore under Sagami Bay, very likely triggered by the unusual reduction of the pressure overhead.

In the first week of December 1951, to take a more modern

example, a typhoon whirled northward through the East Indies. As its lowest pressure passed over Hibokhibok, this volcano blew its cap and the explosion was repeated four times with tremendous violence in the next three days. Although the usual lava did not pour from the mountain, white-hot boulders and clinkers were thrown for miles up into the black clouds and fell sizzling over wide areas amid the torrential rains that were handmaidens of the storm. And with each new explosion came a scorching air wave of hot concussion almost like an atomic blast that uprooted jungles and flattened buildings, its sudden heat in some places literally roasting men and animals to death in their tracks.

We were not brought up to think in terms of such explosion weather, but a meteorologist named Charles L. Hosler of Penn State has pretty well proved its existence, even in connection with mine disasters. Carefully comparing weather records with forty-one major coal mine explosions he noticed that in all but one case a sharp drop in barometric pressure took place before the blast. Usually the actual explosion occurred a day after the passing of the lowest pressure, an indication, he reasoned, that that much time was needed for the reduced pressure to suck enough gas out of the coal to create an explosive mixture.

Country people sometimes tell about the rising of streams and wells before a storm, and their stories are supported by the same pressure evidence. And accounts of premonitory wind groanings and whistlings heard in "blow wells" just before a hurricane have their similar scientific explanation in the fact that the abruptly decreasing external pressure encourages any air trapped in the ground to escape at just that time.

This type of phenomenon of course not only shows the extent to which the solid earth breathes the sky, but helps us on the flight deck to visualize the ramifications of pressure and its associated influences on wind and temperature, on cloud and weather. Our rules of thumb and our notebooks are full of it. Our minds swim with vague memories of Boyle's Law, Charles' Law, of the dry lapse rate and the laws of gases. We recall that: "When passing through any weather front in the northern hemisphere, your drift will always change toward the left; oppositely in the southern hemisphere. When flying from a high barometric area toward a low, your pressure altimeter will read higher than you are; from a low toward a high, the opposite. When climbing, the wind may be expected to increase and veer (change direction clockwise) in the northern hemisphere, to increase and back (change counterclockwise) in the southern . . . "

It is all rather confusing at first, but it digests into sense when you give it thought and time: "Tropical Maritime air in the south creates ground fog just before sunrise, and patches of it may blanket wide areas for two or three hours. . . Dry Polar Canadian air blowing down over New England in summer is very clear but extremely bumpy . . . Polar Continental air that is moist and bottom-light in winter from passing over the warmth of the Great Lakes is apt to be triggered by the Appalachians into turbulence, letting fall dense snow flurries or rain squalls . . . "

From my window before the wing I can see at last a little logic in it all. I think I can really see weather in its three dimensions. The cold front hits me like a slanting wall of ice. I watch the rain descending in waves and see the thermometer of outside air drop sharply, the pressure altimeter rising. There is hardly room for doubt as to what is actually going on.

I can see fairly clearly now that rain and snow do not ride in on the wings of a storm as I used to think, but are born locally, sired by the arriving air mass upon its nuptial clash with the retreating maternal air. I can realize why the deserts are generally on the lee sides of great rain-catching mountains. I can guess something of ground temperature miles below by the look of train smoke mixed with steam, which billows out more fully when the air is sharp. Far overhead the blueness of the sky measures for me its transparency, telling of its recent travels. In the distance that odd saucer of smoke over Mexico City with a few fluff clouds above it looking like soapsuds on wash water is obviously a stratum of warm air between layers of cool.

Even some of the ancient aphorisms take on new sense now.

Those swallows dipping low before the rain are catching bugs that can't fly high because of the burden of unusual humidity on their wings. The same must hold for swarming bees and wasps. And the damp air preceding rain naturally sets the frogs to croaking as well as putting a halo around sun and moon and settling the particles of smoke to turn it back to earth. If the drain can be smelt before the storm it is the low pressure releasing gases, and the same low pressure could conceivably explain premonitory creaking bones or corns that ache on the eve of a hurricane.

Seeing the great waves of weather roll by from our new height and speed and knowledge makes me think sometimes of those science movies of sprouting flowers in which hours are condensed into seconds and you are given a God's-eye view of the green shoots literally popping out of the soil and dancing in the sun as their petals and leaves unfold in search of light and fulfillment.

The same treatment may be applied to speeding up slow developments in geology, astronomy, economics, and it has already been used seriously by meteorologists in studying cloud movement.

One such time-lapse movie, for instance, proved to weather students that most cumulus clouds are continuously curling over — rolling so slowly that their true motion had not been comprehended before. Speeded-up thunderheads on the screen were revealed to have a new majesty of explosive rhythm, the successive cumulus towers shooting up at their appointed intervals like puffs of smoke from a steam locomotive, and a steady forward turning of each cloud mass upon the axis of its invisible lower air circulation like a series of great wheels rolling inexorably across the sky.

When we can extend this time-lapse to the dimensions of whole continents of space and several days of time, the larger picture will be a movie version of the kind of still photograph taken from the V-2 rockets a hundred miles up, in which cloud formations often look like white caps on the sea and circular storms mere bubblings of the continental cauldron. In profile on such a scale a warm front a thousand miles long will sweep forward as a single dark wing behind silvery cirrus feathers. The curved isobar lines drawn on a pressure map will appear in motion as oil on flowing water. Flooded rivers and snow left on the mountains will be just faint cloud footprints, tiny clues of precipitation.

Upon the arrival of real space flying, meteorological television will be shot from heights above five hundred miles. Eventually the whole sunlit polar front will be televised simultaneously from many points in the spherical sky and the hemispheric picture projected in time-lapse motion to aid the long-range forecaster. The application of tempo, the fourth dimension, will thus have turned the clouds into modern sky glyphs every educated man can read.

The present daily weather map is of course little more than a laborious creation. When I worked in a weather office we used to have half a dozen ticker tapes going all the time, bringing in weather information in code from all over the world: radiosonde reports, pilot balloon winds for different altitudes, hourly estimates from airliners, reports from freighters at sea, regular weather ships, and lonely stations on islands and mountains and deserts everywhere. For many hours we would copy the more pertinent facts down on the blank map in figures and symbols: the exact time of the report, the barometric pressure, and little flags to show the direction and velocity of the local winds.

When enough information was thus assembled, the isobar lines of equal pressure would be drawn in and the cold and warm fronts outlined across them, giving the map graphic meaning. But this process can be tedious and frustrating. It requires the same kind of sensitive, creative effort as drawing a portrait of a person you have heard described but have never seen. The isobaric lines at first are completely tentative — a hint here, a brief stroke there, averaged from the tape. Like an archeologist recreating a skeleton from a piece of jawbone and a rib, we reconstruct by educated imagination the gaunt pressure bones of the sky, the graceful spiral courses of the winds.

This creative effort is actually going on perpetually in thousands of weather bureaus all over the world. Even above the clouds in airliners it is done — for any navigator worth his salt is able to make a weather map in flight. His information may be provincial — just his own observations and routine reports from nearby stations or passing airplanes — but it can save him valuable time, even help him find his way in an emergency. Knowing the correct barometric pressure where he is and the contour of the corresponding isobar on the weather map, he has a pressure line of position all plotted, somewhere along which he should be. Probably very few navigators actually use pressure lines in this way, but knowing how can increase their confidence — and in some unforeseen emergency make all the difference.

The weather room is where pilots and navigators get perspective on the atmosphere just before taking off into it. A series of weather maps of the world is in fact a rather exalting spectacle, permitting one a glimpse through a sort of keyhole of the sky. Clouds and continents are spread out like playing cards from outer space.

At Gander in Newfoundland, for instance — the first city in the world to grow up almost wholly on the nourishment of flight — the weather men can show you African weather, Swedish weather, U.S. weather, Greenland weather, Scottish weather, Icelandic, Bermudian, Azorian, even North Pole weather. You get a sense of detachment about the world there. Each man's "weather" is so to speak tailor-made to fit his needs. If you are to take off at midnight, you may be informed casually, "We'll have your weather for you at ten o'clock, sir." It sounds like Saint Christopher speaking to the Angel Gabriel.

Your personal "weather" is handed to you as a neat folder containing at least two large maps. One is a pressure map of isobars and fronts, a bird's-eye view of the world you plan to fly over as it looks from high overhead. The other a cross-section of your course looking horizontally from the side, showing the cloud systems expected en route each at its reported position and height, with symbols in color showing icing conditions, rain or snow or lightning, and the freezing level as a dividing line. With figures for winds in every zone at different altitudes, temperatures, and ceiling and visibility at the terminals, you have the main facts at your fingertips. It should help you keep out of trouble.

But the truth is that there is still a sad dearth of weather information — especially from certain vast areas in which no one lives and airplanes seldom penetrate. All too often the pressure ridges and troughs have moved beyond the realization of the weather office, the wind has radically changed, and conditions are not what the reports have led us to expect.

I remember that the forecast given out at Lagens Field in the Azores during World War II was once so far off that five westbound freight planes arrived at Bermuda more than an hour and a half late while others had to turn back to the Azores.

On another occasion a Bermuda-bound plane got such a surprise tail wind that it overshot that island altogether and barely managed a forced landing in North Carolina.

Rapid closing in of weather in a congested area like New York can be very serious when not forecast accurately. If you were living there in the winter of 1947 you may remember the case of the four-motored American Airlines plane that took off from LaGuardia airport at dusk bound for Los Angeles with twenty-one passengers aboard. The pilot, J. E. Booth, was unable to make his scheduled landing at Washington because of bad weather, so he turned around to try Baltimore, which was reported open. But before he got there, Baltimore also had its ceiling fall below the allowed limits, and Philadelphia likewise folded before he could land. So he returned all the way to New York, only to hear from the La-Guardia tower of heavy snow flurries which had just closed up that airport tight.

As nothing closer was reported available, Booth now headed through the night sky for Westover Field in Massachusetts, but on discovering he had only twenty minutes' gas left turned again, requesting emergency clearance at LaGuardia. When he got down to five minutes' fuel and still couldn't find LaGuardia he requested a radio fix of position. A minute later he saw water below through a hole in the clouds — then a beach. He dropped flares and could just see a park and a level causeway, so he circled and came in to land. Being unable to get more than an occasional glimpse in the darkness and snowy air he overshot, bounced through some scrub grass at the end of the causeway, and luckily came to rest on the sand of Cedar Beach (next to Jones Beach), Long Island. Although he was cut on the head himself, all his passengers were safe.

But the same unpredicted blanket of snow and sleet that had descended on the area for 250 miles around New York that night had trapped another plane bound from Miami to New York. This one, not so lucky, crashed in New Jersey — its co-pilot and two passengers killed, and nearly everyone else aboard seriously injured.

One of the very best examples of what can happen even when the forecast is reasonably good is the crash at Laramie, Wyoming, on October 17, 1946. Perhaps with some justification in past experience, the pilot in this case took his weather forecast with an overdose of salt and made his own decisions in defiance of regulations.

Flying a DC–3 with thirteen aboard he ran into thick weather during an unscheduled flight from Oakland, California, to Newark, New Jersey. He had planned to refuel in Cheyenne but learned by radio that the airports in both Cheyenne and Denver were closed because of very low ceilings and poor visibility. So he turned to Laramie. He was told that Laramie also was below minimum safe weather conditions, but he evidently got a little panicky at the way the soup was thickening up over a wide area and decided to try landing at Laramie anyway.

Of course he should have asked for information as to other airports with above minimum conditions, for he still had two hours' fuel and could easily have flown into Nebraska, South Dakota, Kansas, or even back to Utah. But he seemed to regard Laramie as his only hope and doggedly let down toward the Laramie field.

He came out of the cloud bank at 400 feet above ground but it was snowing and he could see only a few hundred yards ahead of him. The more he circled around trying to get lined up with a runway the less time he had left in which to go elsewhere, so the more desperate he became. As he circled he repeatedly lost sight of the runway he was aiming for and the snow seemed to get thicker each minute. Finally in a frantic attempt to keep a runway in sight long enough to land on it he made a very sharp turn about 200 feet off the ground, banking until his wings were almost vertical. In this position a plane is apt to lose altitude rapidly, and before the pilot realized it one of his wing tips struck the ground and the plane was whipped into a blinding crash.

That was all. There were no survivors.

On Wings of
Mystery

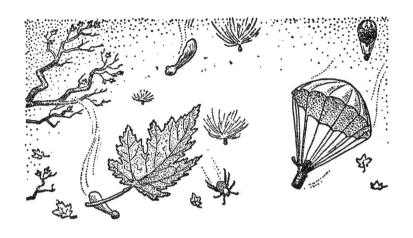

10. Floating on Air

THE SKY has not been easy to explore. Even as I look out my round window at 11,000 feet, I realize that the lower air is about eight hundred times lighter than the water that is the lightest medium below it. Yet many times it has been invaded by beings heavier than itself. For again and again has life risen up from the gentle earth and the sea to dare to fly. And five times it has amply succeeded.

After the very early passive launchings of pollen and spores and tufted seeds came the winged insects nearly a billion years ago in the earth's first active conquest of the air. Second, the ancient pterodactyls and other flying reptiles. Third, the birds. Fourth, the bats. Fifth, man.

Although man's great victory has come largely in my own half lifetime, it is already complete enough to be accepted casually by many professional flyers. I personally find it hard to share their carefree forgetfulness of the meaning of flight. Perhaps it is from having spent so many years entirely on the ground between flying jobs that the sky still slaps me fresh in the face at every take-off.

279

It hit me especially hard one night while climbing over San Francisco Bay into the vast moonlit Pacific Ocean of the air with a load of human blood for Korea. I sensed anew then the boldness of this upper world of the future that we are just managing to peek at through its slightly opened door.

Casual as they are, the flying men of today have a rashness of spirit that I feel in my every bone as I slant upward over the sparkling cable-car hills of the gold-rush city. Of course the men of last century were bold too in their way, but they were dealing with the homely things they knew: marlin spikes and axes and muzzle-loading guns, cross-trees and whales and the great waves of the ancient deep. Today the instruments we use and invent are so strange their strangeness alone is frightening, and the very waves of our ocean have scarce begun to be understood.

It is plain that life on earth has suddenly quickened. One generation has leapt off a horse's back and through the sonic wall. Life moves naturally upward in a spiral, but here the spiral is bent strangely, before continuing its accelerating, buoyant course. It is the way of things important to life. It is irregular, not entirely predictable, but continuing: the motion of air under wings that hold up airplanes and birds, the flow of blood, the breath of consciousness, the growth of stars, even the prophetic revelations of God.

It was the Persian poet, Firdausi, in the eleventh century who wrote of an early human attempt at flying by the eccentric Shah Kai Kaoos who built himself a unique craft shaped like a four-poster bed. Being better versed in falconry than mechanics, Kai Kaoos harnessed four eagles for motive power, one at each corner. To get his engines to lift he placed raw meat above them on the tops of the sharpened posts. Firdausi reported that the Shah managed to get this contraption off the ground but had trouble synchronizing his motors and soon had to make a forced landing in the desert from which he was rescued only with the greatest difficulty.

The medieval windmill was another precursor of human flight, providing a close model of the modern four-bladed, square-edged propeller — almost as prenatal human growth reviews human evolution.

The idea of using hot air or gas as a lifting agent seems to have come to many persons during the last four centuries. Leonardo da Vinci is credited with having once made some wafer-thin figures of wax which he filled with hot air and launched into the sky on the occasion of Pope Leo X's coronation.

The Jesuit, Francisco de Lana, designed an aerial sailing ship in 1670 with four copper vacuum spheres to lift it. His theory of buoyancy was remarkably advanced but perhaps he realized that his vacuum spheres could not be both thin enough for lightness and thick enough to withstand the inward pressure of the air, for he never tried to build it.

A few years later in 1709, however, another Jesuit, Bartholomeu de Gusmão, actually sent up a small hot-air balloon and designed a large airship on the hot-air principal which might well have carried him aloft had he had faith or fortune enough to execute his ideas.

In those days the feminine principle of passive, rotund, floating flight was even less understood than the bird-inspired masculine concept of active, flapping flight — yet it was destined to come to glorious fulfillment both soon and suddenly in 1783. That was the famous year when two French brothers in the paper-making craft noticed how a fire wafts pieces of paper upward on its hot clouds of smoke, and they tried filling a paper bag full of the same kind of smoke to see if it would rise too.

It did. Even better than they had expected! And so Joseph and Etienne Montgolfier got started in ballooning. They looked up Priestley's famous treatise on air, and made bigger and bigger bags of hot smoke until on June 5 of that year, feeling confident at last that they had hold of a real discovery, they put on a public ascension before a thousand spectators in the market place of their home town of Annonay, near Lyons.

This first full-size balloon was made of linen and paper, 105 feet in circumference and buttoned together in gores. The Montgolfiers built a fire of straw and wool under it, filling it quickly with thick yellow smoke. Then they cut the cords and it rose impressively for several thousand feet, landing ten minutes later about a mile and a half away.

This demonstration by the Montgolfiers made a tremendous sensation and within a week was the talk of all Europe. The Paris Academy straightaway commissioned its physicist, J. A. C. Charles, to investigate. Professor Charles may have assumed that the balloon's inventors utilized Cavendish's recent discovery of hydrogen, then popularly known as "inflammable air," for he quickly designed his own idea of a hydrogen balloon and had one made thirteen feet in diameter which he set up on the Champ de Mars before a crowd composed largely of "philosophers, officials, students, and loiterers" on August 27. Although it rained that day, the balloon rose on schedule and disappeared into the low clouds. A wag among the open-mouthed spectators just then turned to the aged American ambassador standing near him and asked "Of what use is a balloon, Mr. Franklin?"

Replied the inventor of the lightning rod, "Of what use, sir, is a new-born baby?"

An hour later some peasants near Gonesse saw a strange globe miraculously descend from the clouds and bounce upon a field. Frightened but fascinated, they gathered around the mysterious buoyant object. When one jabbed it with his pitchfork it hissed forth a dangerous smell, so the others all joined in killing the evil creature with spades and scythes. When nothing remained but shreds, the corpse was dragged off tied to the tail of a horse.

Meanwhile the Montgolfier brothers had come to Paris to demonstrate their hot-air balloon to the Academy. They built a new and fancy one with colorful decorations and pictures on it, which ascended successfully on September 12. By this time people were talking about human travel by balloon, but no one had yet volunteered to try it, so on September 19 the Montgolfiers sent up a large balloon carrying a sheep, cock, and duck to see if life could survive way up there in the unknown.

After the barnyard delegation landed safely a new balloon was built for human passengers and the king wanted to send up two criminals for the first flight, but Pilâtre de Rozier, curator of the Royal Museum of Natural History, persuaded His Majesty that the privilege of being the first human to fly was too rare an honor to waste on a convict, so he and the Marquis d'Arlandes were given the chance. During November they cautiously experimented in the new balloon while it was tethered and at last on November 21 were cut loose on the world's first free human flight!

This momentous event went off smoothly and the balloon rose some 500 feet and drifted five miles over the Bois de Boulogne in plain sight of hundreds of cheering people.

From this date ballooning was accepted throughout the Western world, and Professor Charles completed the first hydrogen balloon of almost modern form in time to take off on December 1 from the Tuileries with a fellow balloon maker named Roberts. This remarkable craft, launched in 1783, still the birth year of ballooning, was complete with rubberized fabric, a net to support the basket, top valve, ballast, and a barometric altimeter. Charles flew all the way to Nesle that time, twenty-seven miles.

Only a year later a balloon crossed the English Channel from Dover to the forest of Guînes in France. Jean-Pierre Blanchard was the first, and among the greatest, of aerial showmen. A "petulant little fellow" around five feet two inches tall and "well suited for vapourish regions," he made the first ascents in America and in many European countries, and was determined to be the first man to fly the channel. Not having much money, however, he persuaded an American physician, Dr. John Jeffries, to finance the trip. But he tried desperately to prevent the doctor from accompanying him and diluting the glory. He pretended the balloon was not big enough to support them both and secretly wore a lead-lined belt to prove it.

His unpleasant argument with Jeffries was patched up only at the last moment by the Governor of Dover Castle as the two men took off from the white cliffs on January 7, 1785. Their interesting cargo included a barometer (for reading height), a compass, anchors, flags, cork life jackets, thirty pounds of ballast, a packet of pamphlets, a bottle of brandy, biscuits, apples, and the latest in aerial navigation equipment: a large rudder, two big silk-covered sky oars, and Blanchard's famous "moulinet" — a hand-operated revolving fan, which was the first big step upward in the windmill's evolution into the propeller.

They got away safely on a fine northwesterly breeze, but the crossing proved a hair-raising adventure. Evidently the sky was full of cumulus clouds with strong updrafts beneath them and downdrafts between, for the balloon kept rising and falling with bewildering inconsistency until the two men were at their wits' end. One can imagine what the uncontrolled Blanchard muttered to his companion every time the balloon started downward toward the sea. As the balloon moved with the air rather than through it, the rudder was entirely useless, and the oars and moulinet were ridiculously unwieldy and ineffective under the great sluggish hulk of the hydrogen bag.

They had not reached halfway before all the ballast was gone and they had to jettison the anchors, the rudder, oars, moulinet, even the brandy, in order to stay in the air. Just off the French coast the situation looked so desperate that both men, after relieving themselves, started removing their clothes and the panicky Blanchard had just tossed overboard his trousers with a dramatic gesture when an unexpected updraft raised the balloon so high that he nearly froze before they finally descended into the trees twelve miles beyond the coast. The car of the balloon can be seen today in the Calais Museum.

The original Montgolfière or hot-air balloon was within two years almost entirely supplanted by the superior Charlière or hydrogen balloon and ballooning became a widely practiced sport. To what lengths impetuous Frenchmen carried ballooning in the decades that followed cannot be better illustrated than by the duel fought on May 3, 1808, when two emotional gentlemen of Paris blazed away at each other with blunderbusses while drifting in balloons half a mile above the Tuileries Gardens.

Probably the biggest part in history played by balloons was during the siege of Paris in 1870–71 when sixty-six of them evacuated about a hundred important persons, nine tons of mail, and four hundred homing pigeons from the city. At first the balloons took off by day but when a few were nearly shot down by Prussian bullets and shells, night departures became more common. Fifty-nine of these balloons actually succeeded in landing in friendly territory, five fell into enemy hands, and the remaining two were presumed lost at sea. The zeppelins of World War I later also evolved from balloons but balloons have since then, despite their increasing use in meteorology and air-raid defense, faded in importance relative to the airplane.

Before the epic story of the airplane, however, we must take up another earlier invention that developed almost simultaneously with the balloon: the parachute, a natural vehicle of passive flight.

So natural is the parachute in fact that not only have seeds and spores resorted to its principle but many animals have adopted either it or its companion principle of gliding, obviously the prelude to active flight.

The insects were earth's first real flyers, most of them — especially the very small ones — using the parachute idea about as much as the wing to stay aloft. Their very minuteness has made that inevitable for the same reason that the surface of any small object is greater in proportion to its weight (more parachutelike) than that of a larger object of similar shape and material.

You can figure this out mathematically on the basis of simple dimensions. As surface has only two dimensions and weight (like volume) three, so the relationship between surface and weight is proportionately as the square to the cube. Thus a creature loses more weight than surface as he becomes smaller, and it is its *relatively* great surface that gives the little ant enough air resistance to parachute safely any distance. Large beetles can do fairly well in parachuting too. Even a mouse can drop from an airplane without much risk of injury. A rat, however, is usually knocked out. A dog is killed. A man is broken. A horse splashes. An elephant disintegrates.

For this reason specialization in the form of a parachute is unnecessary to any animal smaller than a mouse. But many animals only a little bigger have adopted them in varying degrees from the Malayan umbrella lizard or draco, with his gorgeously colored folding parasol made of fine membrane stretched over actual ribs, to the Bornean glider snakes which can suck their bellies against their backbones and float from tree to tree like ribbons on the wind.

The first human to design a parachute seems to have been the versatile Leonardo about A.D. 1500, but the only actual use for parachutes after his time was in the popular "umbrella dance" often put on by court entertainers who amused their royal patrons with tremendous leaps made possible by big umbrellas attached to their belts.

It was not until the birth year of the balloon, 1783, that the real parachute became an independently proven possibility. In that year Sebastian Lenormand made himself the first full-fledged parachute and jumped with it from the tower of Montpellier Observatory in France. He landed safely but seems to have regarded his apparatus as nothing more than a new means of escaping from fires in tall buildings.

Showman J. P. Blanchard was the first person to use a parachute in a drop from a balloon. In 1785 he released one from several thousand feet up containing a dog in the basket beneath it. The dog barked on the way down and landed unharmed. Blanchard still felt uneasy about trying the parachute himself but finally did so eight years later. His primitive parachute either was too small for his weight or swayed very violently for Blanchard hit the ground so hard he broke his leg.

The real father of the parachute is generally considered to be André Jacques Garnerin who had plenty of time to design parachutes while serving a prison sentence in Budapest. Shortly after his release he made his first drop over Paris in 1797, followed by many more descents in other parts of France and England. His 'chutes oscillated so violently that he would get actively seasick on the way down and usually arrived in no condition to appreciate the raucous enthusiam of the cheering crowds who wanted to carry him triumphantly on their shoulders.

Garnerin's parachutes were like huge beach umbrellas with a basket hanging below similar to a balloon's car. They were made of canvas about the same size as modern parachutes but inevitably heavier and they must have hit the ground much harder.

The first life saved by parachute was that of a Polish aeronaut named Jordaki Kuparento whose poorly made hot air balloon caught fire over Warsaw in 1808. Luckily he had a parachute aboard, got it opened up in time, and managed to drop to safety.

A few years later Garnerin's niece, Eliza Garnerin, was the first woman parachutist. But there was still a lot of basic experimenting to be done before the parachute would achieve its present perfection, and one of the wide-eyed young spectators of Garnerin's first descent in London, Robert Cocking, was the first to be killed in an attempt to improve on it.

Parachutes were brought into common use by German aviators during the last few months of World War I while the Allied flyers still considered them too bulky and heavy to be worthwhile except in the case of observation balloons which often were shot down several times daily.

But just after the war the seat-pack type of 'chute was generally adopted for its efficiency, weighing only eighteen pounds and replacing the seat cushion so that it carried the aviator instead of the aviator carrying it. More than 1500 experimental jumps were made at the end of the war in perfecting this invention, while literally millions of descents have been made since then in working out the exact parachute procedures used today.

The parachute schools now teach students such long-proven lessons as the headlong dive from open cockpit planes for getting one's head and shoulders away fast. And that after you jump it's important to wait before pulling your ripcord until you have lost your forward speed — especially if you jumped out of a plane traveling several hundred miles an hour, which may well be enough to tear your parachute apart or jerk the harness clean off you. Contrary to what you might think, your speed through the air just after jumping is almost certainly decreasing rather than increasing — for at least several seconds — and the faster your plane was moving the more certainly this is true.

The modern manuals explain that you should not dive with your knees drawn up because that makes you somersault and when you pull the ripcord while somersaulting the lift webs are apt to yank up between your knees, causing you to descend hanging upside down and probably painfully. A British pamphlet says, "a very good view of the ground is at once obtained but the position is extremely uncomfortable, definitely undignified, and you may even lose things out of your pockets."

The American Naval Manual thoughtfully adds: "If one of those things in your pocket happens to be your address book, you'll bewilder the farmer who picks it up and also leave yourself with nothing to do at night but go to the movies. That's hard on your eyes."

Some think that the opening of a parachute after falling for a mile or so must be a terrific jerk but the modern 'chutes have built-in shock absorbers to make your whole ride more comfortable.

The silk or nylon canopy is woven loosely enough so that some of the air flows right through it and the remaining trapped air has just enough resistance to slow you up like an automobile with brakes applied, which is much gentler than hitting a stone wall.

The serious swaying that bothered Garnerin and Blanchard so much is virtually impossible in a modern 'chute, and even if you should find yourself swinging a little you can easily eliminate it by pulling on the shroud lines, spilling air out of one side or the other of your canopy. You can change your angle and speed of descent that way too, thus controlling to an important degree where you are going to land.

You should of course have a fair amount of time to work on your landing on the way down. Once it opens, your parachute slows your falling speed to about twenty feet a second — depending on your weight and the density of the air.

The manuals advise jumping from above 1000 feet, and consider it very dangerous to bail out from less than 250 feet. However, a few lucky lads have gotten away with it under desperate circumstances at around 100 feet, which can be taken as the absolute limit below which it's a better bet to stick with your falling aircraft even if it's full of dynamite and heading for a cliff.

In general the higher you are when you jump the better your chances — that is, up to 20,000 feet or so, depending on the conditions of weather and air. Jumps have been made from much higher without ill effects, but above 30,000 feet the shortage of oxygen becomes a problem of first importance. Special oxygen masks and even heated pressure suits are now being used in stratospheric parachuting.

Which brings up the interesting question of the effect a jump has on a man, physically and mentally. Since men are not birds and have not evolved gradually into the sky life, are they apt to get panicky, dizzy, or faint in falling and thus fail to pull the rip

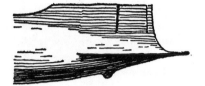

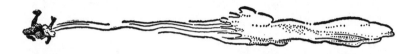

cord? Does the rush of air ever impair their senses and make it difficult for them to see and hear? In short, how does it actually feel to make a parachute jump?

No one appears to have answered this question with more exactitude than Captain Harry Armstrong who, as director of the Air Corps' physiological research laboratory at Dayton, Ohio, once made a delayed-opening drop especially for the purpose of observing his sensations and reactions. Jumping at 2200 feet, he allowed himself to fall for 1200 feet — most of the way plummeting end over end at what he later calculated as 119 miles an hour — before pulling the cord.

His published report says that:

> during the few seconds preceding the jump the predominant mental factors were fear and excitement . . . Throughout the free fall all conscious mental processes seemed normal. As soon as the airplane was cleared, fear and excitement disappeared . . .
>
> Perception of an auditory nature may or may not have been impaired. While twelve airplanes were in close proximity . . . no airplane noise can be recalled. Also it was expected that the rush of air past the ears would produce considerable sound, yet none was noted. . .
>
> Visual perception was normal . . .

For the first second of fall there was a horizontal velocity of about 175 feet a second, and a vertical acceleration downward . . . At the same time there was a tumbling motion of the body, making a complete revolution in about two seconds. Of these motions . . . the only one recognized was rotation of the body . . . During the third and fourth seconds the eyes were voluntarily closed, and during that time all sense of motion was lost . . . The sensation was that of being suspended at rest in midair. When the eyes were opened, which was at an altitude of about 1,900 feet, and the ground again sighted . . . there was for the first time a definite sensation of falling. This . . . increased rapidly.

There was none of the empty or "gone" feeling in the abdomen so common in elevators and in airplanes. The eyes, although unprotected from the high wind blast, were not irritated . . . Breathing was even, regular, and undisturbed.

The last phenomenon . . . has to do with skin sensibility and was a result of the increased air pressure on the lower surface of the body. It consists of that force which restricts terminal velocity to 119 m.p.h. instead of infinity, and appears in consciousness as a very gentle, evenly distributed, generalized, superficial pressure on the surface of the body toward the earth. The nearest possible similar earthly experience is that of being lowered gently into a great bed of softest down.

That is a scientific description of the benign feeling of support given by the empty sky as you fall steadily at terminal velocity — at the fixed speed your body attains after its accelerating (or decelerating) resistance to the air has reached final equilibrium with gravity. It is a kind of peaceful balance of nature long known to bugs but just recently discovered by man.

With falling parachutists while their 'chutes remain unopened, this velocity is believed to be always within the range of 100 to 150 m.p.h., varying only with altitude, weight, and shape of costume. It is actually quite a comfortable speed for riding on air and the fact of its harmlessness to a human was dramatically demonstrated a few years after Armstrong by a Russian flyer who dropped from a height of 26,575 feet to 650 feet before pulling his rip cord. The sheer fall of five miles took two minutes and twenty seconds — time long enough for any good surface runner to run consider-ably more than half a mile.

It requires a maximum of only nine seconds to reach terminal velocity after jumping, during which time you have dropped some-thing over three hundred feet. But it is interesting to reflect that stunt divers have survived jumps off the Golden Gate Bridge at about that height and must have hit the water when falling at very little less than terminal velocity. Which is an indication that it is not necessarily all over for a parachutist whose 'chute does not open when he is over water.

Further evidence of what the human body can withstand came in a recent Air Force shock test in which Lieutenant Colonel John P. Stapp successfully "took 46.8 Gs for .008 seconds." At the mo-ment of impact he weighed about four tons and was absorbing a shock "equivalent to running an automobile into a solid brick wall at 120 m.p.h."

During World War II, I heard of a case of an airman forced to jump from several thousand feet over the ocean without a 'chute, and he successfully withstood the impact and was picked up little the worse for his adventure.

This may even happen on dry land when some factor is present to brake the shock: a steep hillside at just the right angle or heavy trees or a wooden roof with the exact amount of give. A very un-usual case was the fall of a brawny pitboy named Charlie Arter who was walking along a mine field in South Yorkshire, England, a few years ago. A swirl of dust momentarily blinded him and he stepped toward the edge of a shaft.

Two miners behind him shouted, but it was too late: Charlie's foot was going down in empty air. He clawed desperately at the edge as he fell and his frantic screams echoed hollowly out of the yawning pit. The miners froze in horror. It was certain death — the shaft 1554 feet deep with a bottom of solid rock!

But part way down, Charlie overtook an elevator making a swift descent with a full load of miners. By that time he was falling nearly a hundred miles an hour and the elevator perhaps seventy. He landed feet first on the cage roof, rode easily the rest of the way down, and walked off unharmed at the bottom!

The prize fall of all history, I think, must go to British R.A.F. Sergeant N. S. Alkemade who was tail gunner in a Lancaster bomber over the Ruhr one night in March of 1944 when the big plane was hit by enemy fire. A fuel tank exploded, suddenly shooting flaming gasoline down almost the whole length of the fuselage. As he felt the plane heel over out of control, Alkemade reached for his 'chute which he had left hanging on a rack. He was horrified to find it a mass of fire. What could he do? The 'chute was obviously too far gone to be usable even if he could smother the rising flames. His boots were already beginning to burn. He decided to jump anyway, preferring sudden death on the ground to being roasted alive in the sky. This is it, he thought as he yanked open a sizzling hot door and dove into black space 18,000 feet from the ground — three and a half miles straight up!

That's all he could remember until he awoke to see a small patch of stars overhead. Was he dead? He turned his head and moved his arms. His head throbbed and his back pained sharply. He felt cold and damp and noticed he was lying in snow and underbrush three feet deep in a dense fir forest. Slowly he moved his legs and raised himself and tried to sit up.

His boots were gone, his flying suit in shreds. He looked up and down incredulously. Large broken branches above his head showed where he had plummeted into the big trees before crashing through at reduced speed to the wonderful mattress of snow where he had rested deep and protected from the wind for three hours!

When he was eventually carried into a village the Nazi soldiers who took him prisoner scoffed at his story. But higher German authorities organized a thorough investigation which resulted in Alkemade's being given a unique certificate, signed by a British colonel, attesting to the fact that he had actually fallen 18,000 feet without a parachute and lived.

11. Of Feather and Wing

THERE MAY COME a day when men, through long controlled genetics, have adapted their bodies in size and shape to gliding or flying. I don't see much sign of it yet as I glance at my fellow crew members at work around me, sitting, writing figures into forms like so many bookkeepers. Yet more remarkable things have already happened in the world to less intelligent creatures.

You may have heard of the archaeopteryx, the first known bird in the world, who lived some hundred million years ago and is thought to have evolved from much more ancient birdy reptiles called pseudosuchians. A lot of archeological work has been done digging up and sleuthing out the clumsy early flyers and giving them such top-heavy names as ptychozoon, archaeornis, hesperornis, pterodactyl, pteranodon, rhamphorhynchus . . . The earliest of them evidently learned to fly by being such ambitious lizards that they took to leaping about the trees for food, gliding and parachuting more and more until their descendants' bodies actually attained the power of flight.

As one might guess, those which got their hind legs hitched to their wings, such as the flying squirrels and cobegos, didn't turn out half as well as the ones that kept their hind legs entirely free for walking and clutching. The bats in fact are the only hind-leg flyers who have really checked out in the sky, but inevitably bats are limited in take-off ability, having to hang upside down and drop into the air from above in order to get up flying speed. The archaeopteryx on the other hand became a kind of feathered lizard which could fly with its front limbs alone and had the essentials of a bird, including feet with forward and hind claws, a bill, and real wings. Its long lizard tail with twenty vertebrae had feathers in pairs sticking out both sides. It was a true pre-bird.

Some of these bird pioneers appear to have specialized entirely in ground running and hopping about the lower limbs of trees, some in the shady middle level of the jungle, some in the sunshine of the treetops, others in swamps, grasslands, rocky cliffs, and the open sea. One of them, the great pteranodon, had a crest of paper-thin bone protruding backward behind its skull, a kind of vertical fin in the air. Its wingspread was twenty-five feet (twice that of the albatross) but it weighed only thirty pounds. Its bones were hollow and it was practically tailless, with batlike claws on all four limbs which it probably used for catching fish as well as climbing rocks and trees.

Of the birds that we see flying successfully around us every day, it is important to remember that they are only the surviving ten per cent or so of much larger numbers that hatch from eggs, who in turn represent far less than one per cent of all that would be hatched if the extinct birds survived in their former numbers. In other words, our present birds are a very select bunch, being actually only the top-flight athletes from among the few hardy survivors of the multitude of struggling pioneers. They are truly champions who have won the flying tournament of evolution by their prodigious feats of soaring, of diving at terrific speed, plunging deep into the sea, or fighting in the air.

Can you imagine any better example of divine creative accomplishment than the consummate flying machine that is a bird? The skeleton, very flexible and strong, is also largely pneumatic — especially in the bigger birds. The beak, skull, feet, and all other bones of a 25-pound pelican have been found to weigh but 23 ounces. Yet the flesh too is pneumatic and in some species there are air sacs around viscera, muscles, and, where balance and stream-lining permit, fairly large areas immediately under the skin. The lungs are not just single cavities as with mammals but whole series of chambers around the main breathing tubes, connected also with all the air sacs of the body including the hollow bones. Thus the air of the sky literally permeates the bird, flesh and bone alike, and aerates it entire. And the circulation of sky through the whole bird acts as a radiator or cooling system of the flying machine, expelling excess humidity and heat as well as exchanging carbon dioxide for oxygen at a feverish rate.

This air-conditioning system is no mere luxury to a bird but vitally necessary to its souped-up vitality. Flight demands greater intensity of effort than does any other means of animal locomo-tion and so a bird's heart beats many times per second, its breath-ing is correspondingly rapid, and its blood has more red corpuscles per ounce than any other creature. As would be expected of a high-speed engine, the bird's temperature is high: a heron's 105.8°, a duck's 109.1°, and a swift's 111.2°.

Fuel consumption is so great that most birds have a kind of carburetor called a crop for straining and preparing their food be-fore it is injected into the combustion cylinders of the stomach and intestines, and the speed of peristaltic motion is prodigious. You may have heard of the young robin who ate fourteen feet of earthworm the first day after leaving the nest, or the house wren who was recorded feeding its young 1217 times between dawn and dusk. Young crows have been known to eat more than their own weight in food per day, and an adolescent chickadee was checked eating over 5500 cankerworm eggs daily for a week.

The main flying motors fed by this bird fuel are the pectoral muscles, the greater of which pulls down the wing against the air to drive the bird upward and onward, while the lesser hoists the wing back up again, pulling from below by means of an ingenious block and tackle tendon. This extraordinary halyard which passes through a lubricated pulley hole at the shoulder is necessary be-cause the heaviest muscles must be kept at the bottom of the bird so it will not fly top-heavy.

Just as its motor may weigh half of a small airplane, the powerful wing muscles of a pigeon have been found to weigh half the whole bird. These pectorals, by the way, are the solid white meat attached to the breastbone or keel, a location insuring the lowest possible center of gravity — just forward of such other low-slung ballast as gizzard and liver, and well below the very light lungs and air sacs.

If you want to see the ultimate in vertebrate flexibility you must examine a bird's neck. More pliant than a snake, it enables the beak to reach any part of the body with ease and balances the whole bird in flight. Even the stocky little sparrow has twice as many vertebra in its neck as the tallest giraffe: fourteen for the sparrow, seven for the giraffe.

The most distinctive feature of all in a bird, of course, is its feathers, the lightest things in the world for their size and toughness. The tensile strength of cobwebs is great but feathers are stronger in proportion in many more ways, not to mention being springy and flexible. They serve simultaneously as propellers, wings, ailerons, rudders, shingles, and winter underwear — practically the basic equipment of an airport. They also form a colorful fluid vestment that is changed several times a year, now serving as camouflage against an enemy, now advertising the owner's charms to a prospective mate. Feathers are the known descendants of fish scales and the cousins of teeth, whiskers, and toenails. Their descendants in turn may be as wonderful and as far beyond feathers as feathers are beyond scales — only God can know yet.

The growth of a feather is like the unfoldment of some kinds of flowers and ferns. Tiny moist blades of cells appear on the young bird, splitting lengthwise into hairlike strands which dry apart into silky filaments which in the mass are known as down. At the roots of the down lie other sets of cells which, as the bird grows older, push the down from its sockets. These are the real feathers and when the down rubs off they appear as little blue-gray sheaths which may be likened to rolled-up umbrellas or furled sails.

Each of these sheaths is actually an instrument of almost unimaginable potentiality and at the right moment it suddenly pops open — revealing in a few hours feathers that unfold into smaller feathers that unfold again and again. Each main shaft or quill sprouts forth some 600 dowls or barbs on either side to form the familiar vane of the feather. But each of the 1200 barbs in turn puts out about 800 smaller barbs called barbules each of which again produces a score or two of tiny hooks known as barbicels. The complete interwoven mesh of one feather thus contains some thirty million barbicels, and a whole bird normally is

encased in several hundred billion tiny clinging barbicels.

It is hard for the human mind to take in the intricacy of this microscopic weaving that is a feather. There is nothing chemical about it. It is entirely mechanical. If you pull the feather vane apart in your fingers it offers outraged resistance: you can imagine the hundreds of barbules and thousands of barbicels at that particular spot struggling to remain hooked together. And even after being torn the feather has amazing recuperative power. Just placing the split barbs together again and stroking them lengthwise a few times is sufficient to rehook enough barbicels to restore the feather to working efficiency — by nature's own zipper action.

The feather webbing is so fine that few air molecules can get through it and it is ideal material for gripping the sky. In a sense the feather is as much kith to sky as kin to bird, for by a paradox the bird does not really live until its feathers are dead. No sooner is a feather full grown than the opening at the base of the quill closes, blood ceases to flow, and it becomes sealed off from life. The bird's body does not lose track of it, however, for as often as a feather comes loose from a living bird, a new one grows in its place.

Did you ever notice how similar are a feather and a sail? The quill, though it can be bent double without breaking, is stiff enough for a mast. The forward or cutting vane is narrow as a trimmed jib, the aft or lee vane wide like a mainsail. The barbs correspond to the bamboo lugs of a Chinese junk, strengthening the sail, enabling it to withstand the full typhoon of flight. The primary feathers of some sea ducks, however, can be as jibless as catboats, having virtually no vane forward of the quill which thus itself becomes the leading edge. The cross-section of such a feather is rather like an airplane wing and highly efficient in lift.

Besides its individual qualities a feather is a perfect part of a whole, its shaft curved to blend exactly into the pattern of the wing, its shape to fit the slipstream of the sky. Like roof tiles feathers are arranged in overlapping rows, the forward part of the bird corresponding to the top of the roof. Which explains why birds do not feel right unless they are facing the weather, why when they turn to leeward the wind blows against their grain letting the rain soak through to the skin just as shingles reversed will funnel the wet into the house instead of shedding it away.

Different feathers naturally have different functions and shapes. The wing-tip feathers are called the primaries, usually ten in number, and serve to propel the bird. These grow out of what corresponds to the bird's hand.

The forearm feathers nearer the body are the secondaries, twelve to fourteen of them — they mainly support the bird — while the upper arm tertiaries or tertial feathers fair in the secondaries with the body and stabilize the bird in the air.

The tail feathers average about fourteen, overlapping from the center outwards, but they vary so much in different birds that hardly any generalization can be made about them. They are rooted in a pincushionlike muscle mound, the pope's nose, which in some species has been found to house more than a thousand individual feather muscles, each capable of moving one feather in one direction.

One might think that as a bird moults, shedding feathers from once to three times a year, the uneven loss would sometimes set the bird off balance in flight. But nature provides that at least the important primary feathers drop off exactly in pairs, one from the right wing with the corresponding feather from the left wing, waiting then for two new feathers to replace them before moulting the next pair — a technique that developed as a kind of preview in history of the regular 100-hour and 1000-hour overhauls we give our airliners.

If feathers are important to birds they are not without place also in the affairs of men, as witness the American Indian use of the feather as a badge or service ribbon: an eagle primary with red spot denoting an enemy killed, a notched feather a throat cut, a split vane an honorable wound received. Besides such as Byron's "grey goose quill" in literature and Audubon's nibs from trumpeter swans in art, we must remember that the American Declaration of Independence was signed with the feather of a wild, free bird — presumably a bald eagle — despite Benjamin Franklin's regret that the award of the emblem had to go to one who is "generally poor and often very lousy."

In the latter connection it may be worth pointing out that the feather, for all its efficiency and ethereal association, is by no means immune from living reminders of its mundane origin. The scientists have at the present writing identified 25,542 different species of lice that eat feathers. As only 8531 species of birds have been identified, there are now an average of three species of lice specializing in each kind of bird — with the scientists (God bless them) still at work.

This parasitism is thought likely to have been developing since long before the archaeopteryx and today it is extremely rare to find a bird entirely free from lice while some have thousands of many different kinds, not to mention fleas, ticks, mites, flies, worms, flukes, nematodes, and less common parasites. One louse species feeds exclusively on the tears of swifts.

As you delve deeper into the study of such things you may travel from one fascinating world to a smaller one, thence to one still smaller — discovering that within the bodies of fleas that live under the feathers of birds are mites which themselves house various microbes which again are the traveling homes of submicroscopic viruses. . . . And all the while the feathered bird flies unsuspecting through the sky, a blithe spirit that on closer scrutiny becomes a zooming zoo.

When Leonardo da Vinci and later Otto Lilienthal and the French glider pioneers studied birds in order to learn the principles of flight, their concentration naturally was focused on the motions of wings and tail. But these movements turned out to be so fast, complex, and subtle that their analysis was extremely difficult. Even today much remains to be learned of them.

One of the first facts revealed by close observation and the high-speed camera was that wings do not simply flap up and down. Nor do they row the bird ahead like oars. The actual motion is more that of sculling a boat or screwing it ahead by propeller action, a kind of figure-eight movement.

A bird's "hand" (outer wing) is longer than the rest of its "arm" (wing) but it has almost as complete control over it as a man has. It is true that two of the original "fingers" have fused into one and the others have disappeared, but the big primary feathers have replaced them so completely that it has gained many more digits and muscles than it lost. It can twist its "hand" to any position, spread its ten primaries, waggle or twiddle them, shrug its shoulders, even clap its "hands" together behind its head and in front of its breast. That is why wing motion is so complex, variable, and hard to comprehend.

The powerful downstroke that obviously lifts and propels the bird also is a forward stroke, so much so that the wings often touch each other in front of the breast and almost always come close at take-off and climb. Many people have trouble understanding this fact proven by the camera until they reflect that it is likewise forward motion of the airplane wing that generates lift. Just as a sculling oar or a propeller drives a boat ahead by moving at right angles to the boat's motion, so does the force of the bird's wing resolve itself into a nearly perpendicular component.

Even the wing's upstroke plays its part in driving the bird upward and onward — for the same reason. This quick flip of recovery takes half the time of the downstroke and has much less power, but is still part of the sculling motion that is almost peristaltic — like a fish in the sea or a snake in the grass — probably closest of all to the rotor screw action of a moving helicopter: forward and down, backward and up and around.

A fuller understanding of this marvel can be gained by careful study of photographs taken at very high speed, flashed in slow mo-

tion on a screen or strangely frozen in stills. The pliable feathers at
the wing's tip and trailing edge are then seen to bend according to
the changing pressures, revealing how the air is moving.

The downstroke plainly compresses them tightly upon each
other the whole length of the outstretched wing, each feather grabbing its full hold of air, while the upstroke, lifting first the "wrist"
then the half-folded wing, swivels the feathers apart like slats in a
venetian blind to let the air slip by. It is an automatic, selective
process, probably nature's most graceful and intricate valve action,
the different movements overlapping and blending smoothly, the
"wrists" half up before the wing tips stop descending, the "fore-
arms" pressing down while the tips are yet rising. The convexity
of the wing's upper surface and the concavity of its lower of course
aid in this alternate gripping and slipping of the air — this compression of sky into a buoyant cushion below the wing while an
intermittent vacuum sucks from above — this consummate re-
ciprocal flapping that pelicans accomplish twice a second, quail
twenty times, and hummingbirds two hundred times!

If the ability to swivel wing feathers in flying rhythm is a step toward our variable-pitch propeller, the hummingbird goes a step beyond it. In addition to swiveling his feathers he can turn his wings literally upsidedown without diminishing their speed and fly straight up or backward.

If the anti-stall slots that some modern airplanes have in their wings reduce the danger of mushing in a climb, the eagles, vultures, cranes, and other large birds have an even more efficient control of air flow in their emarginated primaries which automatically bend upward and forward in separated fingers to smooth out the burbles and maintain the differences of pressure above and below their wings. Many species also elevate their winglets or thumb feathers as an additional anti-stall device.

Birds are clearly way ahead of the airplane in aileron or roll control and some, like ravens and roller pigeons, close their wings to make snap rolls just for fun or courting. And the same bird superiority holds in the case of flaps which brake the air to reduce speed in landing, the birds fanning out their tails for this purpose as well as their wings. Web footed birds such as geese usually steer and brake with their feet also, and inflect their long necks like the bow paddle of a canoe to aid in steering and balancing.

The tail is of course intended primarily for steering — steering up and down as well as to right and left. Some birds with efficient tails can loop the loop, fly upside down or do backward somersaults like the tumbler pigeon. Small-tailed birds such as ducks are handicapped by not being able to make any kind of sharp turns in the air, though their tails steer well enough in water and in slapping the waves on take-off from water. The male whidah bird has such a long tail that on a dewy morning he actually cannot get off the ground until the sun has evaporated the extra weight from his trailer.

The variety of bird tails never ends, nor does its multiplicity of functions. Furled to a mere stick or fanned out 180° and skewed to any angle, tails serve for everything from a stabilizing fin to a parachute, from a flag to a crutch.

Man cannot hope to match the bird in sensitivity of flying control mainly because he usually has to think air or read it off instruments while the bird just feels air everywhere on his feathers and skin. This is not to say, however, that the bird is a faultless flyer. Birds make plenty of mistakes — even forced landings! Not a few are killed in crashes. Usually bird slip-ups happen so fast they go unnoticed. But when you get a chance to watch a flight of birds coming in to land in slow-motion movies you can see them correcting their errors by last-moment flips of tail or by dragging a foot like a boy on a sled. If a landing bird discovers he lowered his "flaps" too soon he still can ease off these air brakes by raising his wings so that his secondaries spill wind, his primary feathers remaining in position for lateral or aileron control. Buzzards do something almost similar called a "double dip" to correct a stall. But lots of times excited birds do not notice their mistakes soon enough and lose flying speed while trying to climb too steeply, or fall into a spin from tight turns or from simply misjudging the wind. Once they have ceased making headway they tumble downward just as surely as a stalled airplane.

I saw a heron one day muff a landing in a tree, stall, and fall to the ground, breaking his leg. This is particularly apt to happen to heavy birds like ducks when they are tired. Sometimes ducks lose half a pound on a long migratory flight and are so exhausted on letting down that they splash head over heels into the water and cannot take off again for hours.

The energy required of a heavy bird at take-off of course is very great. It has been estimated at five times normal cruising energy. Many birds, like the swan, need a runway in addition to the most furious beating of wings to get up enough speed to leave the ground. Others like the coot are lighter but low-powered and take off like a 1915 scout plane missing on three cylinders. All birds naturally take off against the wind for the same reason that an airplane does: to gain airspeed which is obviously more significant than groundspeed at take-off time. You have surely noticed that birds feeding by the lee roadside will often take off across the path of an approaching car, actually tempting death to gain the wind's help.

Heavy birds that dwell on cliffs of course have the advantage of being able to make a catapult take-off, dropping into a steep glide until they build up flying speed — but again they must beware of landing some place where this needed gravitational asset is not available. The penalty for lack of such foresight can well be death.

I heard of a loon that made the mistake of alighting on a small pond set amid a forest of tall pines. When he wanted to take off an hour later he found himself stymied. He could not climb steeply enough to clear the trees or turn sharply enough to spiral out. He was seen thrashing along over the water, whipping the waves with his wings to get under way, even pedaling at the water desperately with his webbed feet before getting into the air. He almost made it a couple of times but also nearly got killed crashing into the big trees, then plowing back through the underbrush on his sprained wishbone. Finally he had to give up. But this particular loon was lucky. After four frustrated days in his pond jail a very strong wind came up and enabled him to take off and climb so steeply against it that he just brushed between the treetops and was free!

A very different and special capacity is required in bird formation flight or mass maneuvering. Did you ever see a puff of smoke blowing against the wind? I did — but it turned out to be a tight flock of thousands of small birds. When you get close enough to watch a large flight of starlings feeding on a field you wonder how each bird can so completely lose its individuality as to become part of that smooth, flowing mass. Sometimes the flock moves like a great wheel, individual birds alighting and rising progressively as parts of the rhythm of the rim. Now it rolls as a coach on the highroad, now with uneven grace like a tongue of sea fog folding over and over.

Sandpipers, plover, turnstones, sanderlings, and other small shore birds are all expert in this sort of flying which seems to depend on extreme quickness of eye and a speed of selfless response not equaled elsewhere in nature — not among its counterparts in the hoofed animals of the plains, not even among the mysterious schools of the deep sea where whales and the lesser fish have been seen to dive in wonderful co-ordination miles apart. No one knows exactly how this amazing unity of action is accomplished or why. It may depend on much more than visual contact. It may be a part of one of the seams of life where the individual is granted a pretaste of absorption into a greater order of consciousness, far above and beyond his own little being.

When birds migrate they often fly in V formation and for the same reason that the Air Force does. It is the simplest way to follow a leader in the sky while keeping out of his wash and retaining good vision. Birds instinctively do it, peeling off from one heading to another and sometimes chasing after man-made gliders. They even have been seen pursuing power planes until they were unable to keep up with them. I know of a glider pilot who was followed for half an hour by a young seagull who copied his every maneuver: figure-eights, vertical turns, spins, loops. It was only after the glider led the gull into a vertical dive for three thousand feet which blew most of the bird's feathers off that it realized it had been a little too gullible and left off the chase.

Lots of birds, far from feeling jealous of human trespassing in their ancient territory, seem to get such a kick out of airplanes that they hang around airports just like human kids watching the big ones take off and land. At Los Angeles International Airport I used to see a meadowlark regularly sitting on the tails of our big C-54s parked on the ramp. He was a ratty little thing and looked spattered with oil from too much fooling around the hangars, but how he could sing! One day he was sitting on the radio antenna near the tail as one of the planes was being started up preparatory for take-off. The first engine's roar seemed to give him the greatest pleasure as he swayed on the rigamaroo in the sudden blast of wind, and he sang through the starting of the second and third motors. But when the last propeller turned over and caught and began to growl he cocked his head in anticipation and then flew to the tail of another airplane.

Another time a kingbird actually remained sitting on the tail of a Constellation for about a third of its take-off run, seeming to revel in the torrent of air until it blew him tit over tippet into the sky. And many a time I've seen seagulls at the big Travis Air Base near San Francisco flapping nonchalantly among the huge ten-engined B-36 bombers while their motors were being run up. The smoke whipping from the jets in four straight lines past the tail accompanied by that soul-shaking roar would have been enough to stampede a herd of elephants but the seagulls often flew right into the tornado just for fun. When the full blast struck them they would simply disappear, only to turn up a few seconds later a quarter mile downwind, apparently having enjoyed the experience as much as a boy running through a hose or doing the shoot th'shoots into the swimming hole — even coming around eager-eyed for more.

Of all birds the hawks have probably contributed most toward teaching man to fly — through their example of soaring over the zones of the earth where most men live. But how they accomplish their miracle has been discovered only a little at a time over long periods.

Lord Kelvin, once questioned about soaring, replied, "That which puzzled Solomon puzzles me also."

Sir George Cayley around 1810 did better by working out a specific problem. He concluded that a rook whose weight is about a pound for each square foot of its wing area would be able to glide horizontally as long as it could maintain a speed of at least twenty-five miles an hour. What could enable it to keep up that speed, however, he did not pretend to know.

A partial answer was revealed long afterward by a study of gulls circling close to the sea in autumn and winter, times of year when the relative warmth of the water often produces updrafts in which birds can soar indefinitely. Even in a fresh breeze when these warm columns of air are blown over to leeward until they lie almost flat upon the waves, the gulls have been observed soaring buoyantly along the invisible wind seams — gliding magically upwind upon a continuous fountain of air where two counter-rotating columns adjoin.

But when they cannot thus coast "downhill" in air flowing "uphill," neither on thermal nor deflected updrafts, soaring birds somehow still manage to stay aloft on almost motionless wings — traveling at high speed as often against the wind as with it. A mission of the French scientist, Idrac, to the South Seas last century to solve the mystery of the albatross determined that this largest of soaring birds flies at the high average speed of forty-nine miles an hour. When soaring close to the waves and losing altitude, reported Idrac, the albatross uses his remaining speed to gain height If he can rise only four or five times his wingspread of about eleven

feet he usually gets into an air stratum fifty feet up where the wind is blowing three times as strongly as at the surface, thus giving him an extra boost just as a kite will be sent upward by a gust of wind.

The theory of this eventually expanded into one of the first real explanations of why birds soar in circles: since surface friction reduces wind speed at lower altitudes, the bird soars against the wind aiming slightly uphill to take advantage of higher wind velocity as he goes up, giving him the kite boost by *horizontal* shearing (by differences of wind speed at different horizontal levels). But as forward speed eventually falls off because of the climb, he turns away from the wind and coasts slightly downhill to leeward, again getting a boost from his increase in airspeed as the tail wind decreases — then into the wind once more, and so on round and round.

The principles of "static soaring" — soaring on rising air currents — have been worked out in detail mainly during the last twenty-five years as sail-plane pilots have experimented with thermal currents over sun-baked fields or up the windward slopes of hills or cold fronts. But only more recently has "dynamic soaring" come into use by man: this more difficult since it depends on the sudden variations of wind speed in gusty air to impart the kite boost by *vertical* shearing (by differences of wind speed in different vertical planes), relying of course on the pilot to be heading to windward at each increase of wind and to leeward at each decrease, a rhythm that can be irregular to the point of inscrutability.

All of these discoveries have helped explain how birds can glide on motionless wings against the wind, for it became clear that gravity is to the bird as the keel is to the sailboat or the kite string to the kite. All three hold the moving object firm against being blown to leeward, each in its own way.

The form of the wing is obviously another basic factor in flying effectiveness and birds have adopted a great variety of special shapes just as have the airplane designers after them. There are the narrow, pointed wings of the fast and strong flyers: the falcons and swallows, the swifts and hummingbirds . . . There are the bent-wrist wings of the fast gliders like the nighthawk; the broad, fingered wings of the slow soarers, the red-shouldered and red-tailed hawks . . . the short, rounded wings of the woodland darters: grouse, quail, the small sparrows and finches . . .

Gulls and albatrosses also have narrow, pointed wings, theirs however adapted specially to long-range gliding and soaring over the open ocean. The albatross in fact, so perfectly geared to the air that he cannot fold his lengthy wing restfully inside his flank feathers when on ground or sea, is thought to stretch out in sleep while actually on the wing — dozing aloft, even as some of us, but literally in his own feather bed upon the sky.

Little by little the factors of wing efficiency have resolved them-selves into the separate relationships or dimensions of the wing, specifically: its aspect ratio or the proportion between its length and breadth, its degree of bluntness or pointedness, its camber or curvature fore and aft, its horizontalness or dihedral angle in rela-tion to the other wing, its slotting or spacing of primaries (if any), its degree of sweepback, its fairing or smoothness of surface, its thickness, its flexibility, and innumerable minor points.

Aspect ratio in birds averages around three to one. That is, their wings are generally about three times as long as they are wide. The albatross exceeds 5:1. Airplanes sometimes reach 7:1, and sailplanes as high as 18:1. Theoretically the higher the ratio the greater the lift but practically a limit comes when the wing gets so long and narrow that it may break in gusty air. And of course soaring birds have many considerations besides flying that affect their shape: things like catching food, preening their feathers, folding their wings, laying eggs, raising a family. Thus sailplanes, built solely for soaring, have a distinct advantage over the bird who must also be somebody's uncle or grandmother.

The camber or arching of the average bird's wing has been found to average around 13:1. That means the amplitude or con-vexity of the curve is one thirteenth of the breadth of the wing at the point of deepest arching. Slower birds may have a deeper camber of 10:1, the fastest are shallower, around 15:1. The Wright brothers' first glider had a camber of 22:1. As you get into fast air-plane wings, camber tends to flatten out until the wing is about equally convex top and bottom. On the newest and very hottest supersonic jobs, the wing or fin is shaved down to the flatness and thinness of a razor blade.

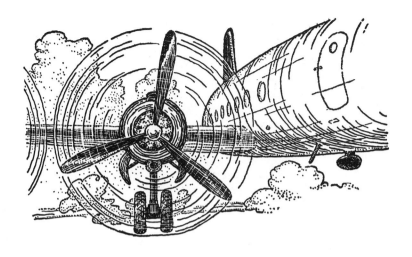

12. Trying Out the Pinions of Man

WE ON THE FLIGHT DECK have become so accustomed to the vibration of four engines that it almost cancels out in the brain. Sometimes I can imagine we are aboard a giant glider coasting effortlessly across the unknown world of night — pioneers of future flight that has not yet wholly unleashed itself from the fetter of earthbound ideas.

Perhaps there comes then an inkling of how Otto Lilienthal must have felt as he studied birds with German thoroughness in the 1870's and '80's and tried with great persistence to translate their secrets into human science. Leonardo long before had designed a flying machine with wings fitted to stirrups and pulleys so that they could be rowed like oars, and in the nineteenth century a whole series of attempts was made to unlock the secret of flight — from Sir George Cayley's propellers to Henson's 25-horsepower steam plane in the 1840's which could not get off the ground.

Lilienthal at first had tried sticks of palisander wood as pinions for his ten-foot wings, the barbs on these "quills" being large goose primaries sewn on tape and fastened to the sticks. He had figured a man of 160 pounds would need wings twenty feet in total span. But a few minutes of diligent but ineffective flapping convinced him that he would also need pectoral muscles correspondingly large: somewhere around four feet thick on his chest. All too clearly statues and paintings of dainty angels flitting aloft bore no relation to the problem of human flight under conditions of earthly gravity.

So Lilienthal tried a different approach. He shifted his attention to soaring birds and built gliders with rigid wings and hawklike tails, and he actually got off the ground in them — gliding downhill into the wind, sometimes for many seconds before his feet touched again.

All during the eighteen-eighties and in the nineties he kept at it, experimenting, methodically trying out wings of different aspect ratios and cambers and shapes. He wrote tables of pressures and got out a book: *Bird Flight as the Basis of the Art of Flying*. He steered by shifting his weight, sliding to right and left on the frame. In all he made more than two thousand glides in safety (evidently few longer than about twenty seconds) until one windy day, August 9, 1896, a sudden gust flipped his glider over, sending it into a sideways dive out of control. When they picked him up, forty-nine-year-old Otto Lilienthal was breathing his last and just managed to gasp out in stiff German syllables: "Sacrifices must be paid for."

Among all the men who shared the dream of flight it would have

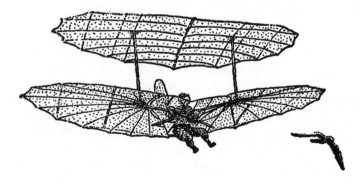

been difficult in the year 1900 for the most discerning scholar to have foretold what sort of inventor would be the first actually to penetrate the secret of the birds, to crack the ancient mystery wide open beyond any doubt. Certainly there was nothing to attract particular attention to two bicycle mechanics in Dayton, Ohio, named Wilbur and Orville Wright. Aged thirty-three and twenty-nine years respectively, they were the youngest sons of Bishop Milton Wright of the United Brethren Church.

It is true that both boys had a good deal of mechanical aptitude. They had built a calculating machine that could multiply as well as add, a home telegraph, a typewriter "more simplified than any in existence," hundreds of bicycles including the popular "Wright Special" for $18 retail, the first "balloon tires," and a printing press made with a buggy top mounted on a gravestone which got them into the newspaper business as a means of keeping the press from lying idle.

But such examples of ingenuity were not rare in a pioneering nation, especially in the exciting new age of bicycles on tires, of express trains and ocean liners, of horseless carriages — yes, and gliding machines. God alone knew what wonder might be coming next. Anything could happen, and often did — such as the bishop's arrival home one afternoon with a toy flying machine that buzzed to the ceiling. Invented by an ingenious Frenchman named Alphonse Penaud, who originated the elastic-band motor, this double-propellered helicopter immediately fired the imagination of the young Wrights. They wasted no time in putting together a number of model planes and after the death of their hero, Otto Lilienthal, at last tackled the question of why wasn't there some better way to keep a glider on an even keel than having the pilot slide his body back and forth?

With a wonderful mixture of caution and boldness they built first an experimental five-foot kite to try out Wilbur's idea of warpable wings, the ancestor of ailerons. Then, making a pilgrimage to the wind at Kitty Hawk, North Carolina, on the basis of the Weather Bureau's figures of an average velocity of fifteen miles an hour there year in year out, they constructed their first "man-carrying" glider. It weighed just fifty-two pounds and cost fifteen dollars, mostly for spruce spars, ash ribs, and sixty yards of white French sateen cotton sewn to dimensions on sister Katherine's sewing machine.

Though the mosquitoes rose out of the marsh grass on hot still nights so thick that the boys more than once thought of packing up for home and the wind was maddeningly fickle, one day a gale, the next three a doldrum, they somehow never quite quit. A mark of their collectively independent genius was their homemade box of wind, an eighteen-inch starch box fitted with a glass top that became what was probably the first wind tunnel in history and which showed them for the first time that the vacuum above a wing is at least as important as the pressure below in generating the lift essential to flight.

The story of their patient efforts and quiet success with a homemade twin-propellered plane in December 1903 is now too familiar to need repeating — even though it was so astounding at the time that almost no one believed it for several years.

As the twentieth century went into its second decade many new names sprang up in aviation — Farman, Blériot, Paulhan, Ferber, Curtiss, Esnault-Peltrie, Delagrange — and the world was wrenching itself out of its ruts trying to adjust to the wing and the propeller and all their ramifications in speed, distance, and dimension.

Blériot had flown the English Channel in 1909. The next year Paulhan made an altitude record of 4150 feet over Los Angeles and won the *Daily Mail* prize of £10,000 by flying from London to Manchester. In 1911 a prize of $50,000 was offered the winner of an air race across America, coast to coast, an idea so bold that even Orville Wright was moved to remark: "They are attempting the impossible. The machine has not been made that can do it."

Yet it was quickly demonstrated that Orville did not know the wonder of his own works. The trans-America race was won by Calbraith Rodgers who had learned to fly at the Wright School in Dayton, soloing after only ninety minutes of instruction. It was said he judged the smoothness of a landing by whether or not it knocked the ashes off his cigar.

The appearance of the several planes that showed up for the start was not much different from the Kitty Hawk original: biplanes with guy wires all over them, chain-driven propellers, warping cords that had to be worked with the shoulders, ski skids out front and bike wheels beneath. The actual flying time of Rodgers' plane, the *Vin Fiz*, was three days and ten hours between New York and Pasadena, but this was spread over a period of forty-nine days and sixty-nine different landing places as Rodgers fought his way westward, spending six times as many hours repairing his machine as flying it. The whole plane was literally rebuilt four times during the race and the only original parts of it that got to California were its vertical rudder and its drip pan.

A sample Rodgers' problem was his battle with a big eagle that chased the *Vin Fiz* for twenty miles near Waco, Texas, diving at it again and again, clawing the rudder and breaking several wires. To Rodgers it seemed a case of jealous rivalry between the old king of the air and a younger, bigger challenger — a kind of mad defense in desperation like the Indian attacks on the invading wagon trains that had so recently ended on the ground below.

For some time afterward many people retained their doubts as to whether the airplane was here to stay, their attitude fittingly expressed by a black aborigine in Australia who asked, "Can the airplane see?"

"No," said the mechanic at the air field. "It's not an animal. It's a machine."

"Well, if it's blind," continued the blackfellow, "it's not much good, is it?"

Teaching mankind the true nature of flying was to be a long process, often exciting, often tedious, sometimes painful. It was to be done by men who tinkered with engines all night in cold barns, by visionaries in cow pastures, by army and navy volunteers preparing for the unimaginable sky battles of World War I.

I myself began flying in the twenties and got my first licenses as a pilot in 1935. But even then the airplane was a fairly flimsy affair, held together by wooden spars, doped cloth, struts, and wires. The machine I first soloed weighed two hundred pounds less than the Wrights' 1903 power plane at Kitty Hawk, had only half as many cylinders and but a single propeller. It could be lifted up by the tail and rolled like a wheel barrow. It would land in still air at 35 m.p.h. or in a normal wind around 25 m.p.h., often leveling off so slow that it would have been possible to jump out just before the wheels touched without injury.

Although in those days the average training time before flying solo had been increased from a couple of hours to six or eight, it was still largely a practical preparation with a minimum of theoretical understanding of why and how. I remember that the girl flyer who soloed just after me was unable to explain how the rudder worked. She didn't know whether her hands or feet moved it, nor why — yet she could fly quite well, without thinking, like a bird.

Today, on the other hand, the theory side of flight is coming at last into pretty sharp focus. More than 15,000 shapes have been tested in wind tunnels to date. Even Bernoulli's theorem that a flow of air (of any fluid) creates a definite suction around it is becoming fairly well understood, as is the "Magnus effect" that explains the curving baseball and aspects of the whirl of helicopters and hurricanes; and differential calculus, now common college fare, the study of speed and shape and change.

Lots of mere passengers in airliners have come to feel safer when flying fast than slow, to sleep better high than low — both symptoms of a conditioned instinct that was unknown among humanity before the airplane. Strange but true, people are gaining confidence in the slippery, wallowy air, recognizing it as not just a nothing but a real something with mass and muscle to hold you up. They are coming to realize that a wing is more than a beautiful example of streamlining — that it is quite physically a deflector that pushes and pulls air downward. The engineers of course have helped by devising elaborate ways of making the slipstream visible so they can more closely see the whirls of air above and below the wing, the burbling glip behind each wing tip, and the extended wake wimpling and eddying downward for miles after the airplane — these four flows together comprising the "closed system" of total wing circulation. And imaginative air passengers everywhere are more and more expressing themselves as able to forget their connection with their familiar earthscape in favor of the invisible wind above it.

If all this reflects the conquest of gravity in the public mind, it is only part of aviation's accomplishment. Complete control of motion in the air is something further and the steps toward it have been demonstrated in such advances as wing slots, flaps, variable-pitch propellers, the helicopter, the automatic pilot, and the fool-proof airplane.

The latter of course was designed to be unstallable for the benefit of the common fallible pilot and it worked by putting him figuratively in handcuffs, denying him some of the airplane's control which had been locked instead into the machine itself. This self-control of an airplane is called inherent stability. It was an important objective of the Wright brothers and has been further developed since. It means building an airplane that "wants" to fly, that refuses to get upset, that will balance itself in the air like a ship at sea and does not have to be kept right side up by its pilot.

All proper airplanes have a good measure of this built-in inherent will of their own. The principle is everyday stuff. You can lean back in your seat, let go the stick, and twiddle your thumbs as you wish and she will fly on — even correcting herself after tipping in a gust or wallowing in a downdraft. I remember once piloting a small Aeronca across Lake Michigan in bicycle fashion, "no hands," turning it to right and left simply by leaning my body to right and left, bowing forward to descend, bending back to climb. It was easy as pie — mile after mile. I even did figure-eights.

And every now and then you hear of someone leaving an airplane unattended with its engine running on some field until it starts moving by itself, pilotless. Usually it just chases its tail around the airport but once in a while one will go straight and pick up enough speed to take off, perhaps even clear the trees and fly calmly around the sky for hours until its tanks are dry. And when the engine quits it does not stall nor lose control, but gently noses down into a glide, perhaps even lands safely in a field.

The difference between a passenger today and twenty-five years ago is striking. Ruth Elder and Amelia Earhart became world figures by flying the Atlantic as passengers, yet today ten thousand passengers may cross it in a day in hundreds of airliners without even patting each other mentally on the back. The change has come because ocean flying suddenly shifted during World War II from something apparently hazardous to the safest kind of flying there is — so safe that, as this is written, not a single paying air passenger has yet lost his life on the high seas! The mountains along the coasts and inland have accounted for many but the ocean itself has a record remarkable mainly for its forbearance.

How come? The big new airports are what did it. The finances of war built long runways in many places on the coasts of the world's oceans, and on the strategic islands, making it possible for the first time for land planes to take off with really heavy cargoes of payload and fuel. Without big loads ocean flying obviously could not be either profitable or safe. But wheels could lift off much more weight than seaplane hulls which are held back by the buffeting friction of waves — so the boat-bottomed clippers had to go, even though they had been the first ocean airliners. It was a change as practical as it was paradoxical and it altered the world's thinking overnight.

I remember that in May 1940 when I was sent hurrying to Europe as a war correspondent, the only way I could get there fast was by catching the lonely Pan American clipper which took off from Flushing Bay, New York, once a week for Lisbon with what passengers could be squeezed in after the mail. In those days the success of the Atlantic operation depended entirely on the fact that this flying boat "carried its own airport on its bottom." Yet only three years later I was practically swallowed up in the dozens of daily ocean flights by land planes of the U.S. Air Transport Command that had already turned the oceans into routine extensions of the continental airways.

You might think the danger of a water landing would have held back the land planes at least in the very early days. But on the contrary almost all the pioneer ocean flyers, including Lindbergh, used land planes — because these were the best bet for getting into the air with enough fuel to make the distance. There were no feasible seaplanes then available anyhow outside the Navy. Besides, anyone optimistic enough to think he could fly the Atlantic would certainly be convinced he would find just the gust of wind needed for clearing all obstructions at the departure spot, inevitably some such sporting proposition as the saucer at Harbour Grace, Newfoundland, or the slanty sand beach of Old Orchard, Maine.

As for coming down on the sea, when that ugly thought came to mind at all, wasn't it as easy to rationalize getting picked up from a land plane with wings buoyed by ping-pong balls as from a seaplane with its hull splitting apart under the battering waves?

The decision to use four engines was another factor in trimming the seas to present size. Why not two, or three, or five motors on ocean spanning planes? Or six? Why four?

The answer: four is just many enough for safety, just few enough for economy. Fact is: engines sometimes quit. Wolfgang Langewiesche, the test pilot and expositor extraordinary of flying, has analyzed it clearly. He says "the odds that a single engine will get you across the Atlantic are about 500 to 1." This was good enough for Lindbergh but if the airlines had no better a batting average they would be losing a ship to the drink every couple of days.

Two engines are a big improvement, says Langewiesche. "The chance that two independent engines should happen to quit in the same hour is 1:25,000,000." Since a good twin-motored plane is able to fly on either engine alone, a million average flying days would see it forced down only once with dead engines. That bet sold the DC–3 to the domestic airlines and has kept them in business ever since. When you are flying over land, even a forced landing is not so serious with the nearest airport at most forty-five minutes away (by law) when the first engine stops, still nearer should the second quit, and downhill all the way.

But over the ocean where there are no landing places two engines just aren't enough. Forty-five minutes is one thing; four or five hours another. The trouble is, explains Langewiesche, two engines in the same airplane can't be wholly independent. Not only may the same flaw be in the second engine, which probably has a fairly similar history, but when the first one dies it literally tosses its burden to the second, heaping this on top of the load already there, regardless. This means the plane is forced to limp, fly slightly sideways, increase drag, slow down. As the lone laboring engine gets hot and you open its cowl flaps the drag gets worse, the speed still slower, fuel consumption higher, strain greater, new breakdowns more likely.

What it adds up to in some situations is that, since you actually may not get there if either engine quits, starting with two quittable engines gives you two chances of failure instead of only one if you had (like Lindbergh) used a single-engined plane in the first place!

Trimotor planes are hardly considered at all these days, probably because they would certainly be unable to survive a double engine failure and in any case would put a plane out of balance unless one motor were located in the fuselage where room is scarce and complications best avoided.

Four engines are the least that can really do the job — and they do it so well that there is no percentage in spending money on more. It has been calculated that each engine quits about once in 6000 hours on the average. And when that happens the other three engines can carry on without any appreciable difference — except in the minds of those aboard. In fact any two engines can drag you home in a pinch.

A flight engineer friend of mine who had nursed four engines back and forth between New York and Stockholm once a fortnight for four years told me he had lost an engine only twice in all that time — which works out close to average. Others, including Langewiesche and the designers, agree on the figures. On my own first ocean flight as a navigator, one engine quit cold right in the middle of the South Atlantic — but I had it happen only one other time in the next two years. And on each occasion the other three engines brought us in nicely.

Airplane motors really are more rugged than most people think, even in this age of intricate specialization. The other day a mechanic opened up a sick cylinder in a C–54 engine that had just landed on Wake Island and found the source of its trouble: a spanner wrench carelessly left inside. By figuring back to the last time that cylinder had been worked on, it developed that the airplane had flown for 700 hours, making twenty transpacific crossings between San Francisco and Tokyo, with a wrench inside a working cylinder unnoticed!

Of course on rare occasions a second engine will quit before the four-motored plane has reached base on three engines. But with all the hundreds of planes continuously in the air over the oceans this has happened only about once a year — and the plane always manages to make it somehow. At least nearly always.

A freak exception was a case in which one engine quit over a hot desert. Then a second and finally a third under the increased load and undiminished heat. But that was a new type of plane, unfamiliar to the maintenance mechanics — not a case that is likely to be repeated.

About the most startling thing that can happen in a four-motored plane is to have all four motors stop at once. That has happened twice in my own experience — but fortunately forced landings were avoided both times. The four engines are virtually independent of each other, outside of fuel supply and the pilot's mind — and sure enough both these factors were responsible on each occasion. We were not totally out of gas but one of the pilots had left a valve closed in the feed line by mistake, until the sudden sputter of four engines followed by deathly silence woke him in a hurry! Though I was busy checking our position for the S O S each time of whining, crescendoed descent, I'll never forget the expression of quiet horror on the pilots' faces.

Despite such nerve-straining episodes, any well-tried four-engined airplane is safe for ocean flying. Without hesitation I'll bet my life it will fly as long as the engines get their fuel. A legion of men have been betting their lives on this every day since World War II and who can think of anyone who lost his bet? One cannot deny that it may happen someday — but so may you be hit by a meteorite.

Another fascinating problem analyzed by Langewiesche is the old "engineering curse" that they used to say limited the airplane's range, sort of naturally, to about 750 miles. This was all too true for any size of airplane. It would take about two thirds of the total lift to hold the plane up in the air. Of the final third, at least half would have to be fuel — say four or five hours worth — leaving the remainder for payload which was the real reason for flying. That last sixth quite literally had to pay for everything, being as vital to the airplane as a checkbook to the Aga Khan. If you wanted to fly more than 1000 miles you could do it of course, as did Lindbergh, but you would have to give up payload for fuel. From the viewpoint of an airline stockholder you might as well go back to wearing snowshoes.

What then was the solution? Size of plane? No. Bigger airplanes need bigger fuel tanks and bigger, beefier engines — almost in proportion — and longer runways.

Lightness? No. Lightness reduces strength.

Power? Speed? No. Fuel consumption rises proportionately. You can't get along with an economy-size engine built just for long range either, because it wouldn't have enough power to clear the trees on take-off. Like the pelican, the airplane just doesn't have much margin in getting off the ground.

The answer turned out to be streamlining. Of course the rudimentary streamlining was done in the first couple of decades of flying: eliminating struts, cowling the engine, retracting the landing gear. But the airplane even in its DC-3 heyday was still a rough diamond with protruding rivets and airscoops and angular windshields and humpy fuselage. Polishing that stuff into a slick article made all the difference at 200 m.p.h. and upwards. The ultimate in streamlining efficiency is probably the flying wing at moderate speeds and the rocket at high speeds. The sureness of their coming can be measured in the benefits already gained, in the fact that it takes only a quarter as much propeller thrust, pound for pound, to pull a modern sky liner through the air as it did to pull a strut and wire biplane in 1920. Did you know that by just smoothing out the DC–3-type riveted skin the designers added four paying passengers to each Atlantic crossing?

Thus the engineering curse is solved by smoothness, by a purer slipperiness that lets the airplane slide ahead faster through the sticky air, lets each pound of gasoline drive it farther, leaves more room for payload, stretches the range two or three fold.

Still another index of airplane efficiency is wing loading: weight in relation to lifting surface. A light airplane with big wings naturally is easily maneuvered, slow flying, safe as a butterfly; while a heavy one with small wings flies fast and straight, lands "hot" like a duck.

The Wrights had to be in the butterfly class, their wing loading two and one half pounds per square foot. But the airlines, needing to carry as much and as fast as possible, now reach about seventy pounds per square foot — a ponderable difference which is symptomatic of the increasing competitive pressure to load stuff on regardless of the consequences in hotter landing speeds and bigger airports required.

Maximum-load laws now therefore have to be enforced in the interests of public safety and common sense. Many operators, it is true, have demonstrated that you can greatly overload an airplane and get away with it for a while — like some of the early transatlantic flyers — but in doing so your margins of safety are inescapably reduced: your take-off run is longer, your climb harder, your engines hotter, your landings faster, you are more apt to buckle your landing gear or snap your wings and if anything goes wrong it will be harder to stay up or stretch your glide to shore. If you put a ball and chain on an eagle and make him fly you will notice the same thing. Flying will no longer be a pleasure but a job.

Notwithstanding, cargoes have grown rapidly bigger and more complex until today everything from tropical fish to atomic artillery is carried by air freight. I remember the load of 197 monkeys we picked up in London once, flying them to New York — the stench so strong it made your head swim. Other cargoes have been pleasanter: wounded soldiers, race horses, German war brides, sausage skins, pilgrims to Mecca, a rare white square-lipped rhinoceros from Zululand, and pregnant Syrian women who were racing the stork to America to have their babies born U.S. citizens. Some of these cargoes have put crew members on their mettle in unexpected ways: like the radioman who was called upon to round up a Siamese elephant that went off its nut in mid-Pacific and tried to jump out a window; or the engineer who fetched hot water in proper movie style when an expectant Iraqi mother felt birth cramps during a thunder squall but turned out to be as puzzled as she as to what to do with the water next.

Flying men as a class, solving their complex problems, seem to be among the more broad-minded of humans — particularly the older captains. This is understandable, for there are few but have flown 10,000 hours and more — much of it through the remote byways of the world. Is not Christendom just one alley of their bailiwick; the lands of Buddha, Moses, Zoroaster, and Mohammed but full familiar to their eyes — even much of the wide kingdom of Baha'u'llah? Certainly neither spiritualism nor dark occultism are strangers to them, nor the petty superstitions that long have been the wont of seafarers. Of a truth flying crewmen are the harbingers in mind as well as body of the great new age of voyaging, the three-dimensional mariners of the new earth. And they are accustomed to drifting from the employ of one company to another, like professional baseball players, according to the for-

tunes of intercontinental deals or war contracts. Former Pan Am
men are now working for TWA or American or Seaboard — Transocean men for United, Northwestern men for the Flying Tigers —
comrades all and most of them carrying in their flight bags thick
manuals of data gleaned from other companies, some wearing the
shirts of their competitors, many carrying briefcases with outdated
names stamped in gold.

The chances and dangers of flying are of course their daily fare
and the occasional brushes with disaster their natural spice of life.

Young as airplanes still are, very few of them fall apart in the
air any more. In fact the only proven case I know in the past ten
years of a major airline tragedy laid to this cause was the Martin 202
that snapped a wing panel fitting over Minnesota in a thunderstorm in 1948; killing all thirty-seven persons aboard.

Of course there are occasional cases of airliners diving into the
ground for no known reason, which could be structural failure —
like the C–54 that crashed near Bainbridge, Maryland, in the
spring of 1947. Bound for Miami, it was flying at 4000 feet, only
thirty-seven minutes out of Newark, when two Civil Aeronautics
Board officials in another airplane saw it begin a gradual dive which
got steeper and steeper, soon becoming vertical, then beyond the
vertical until it approached the ground at terrific speed partly
upside down — its fifty-three passengers and crew by then falling
against the roof in what must have been a horrifying apprehension
a few seconds before their instantaneous death.

The fastest things moving on an airplane are its propellers.
Propellers therefore invite trouble more than the slower parts.
Sometimes also this source of danger is so remote from its consequences that diagnosis is difficult. Thus when a Florida-bound
airliner in 1948 was suddenly shaken by a loud bang at 22,000 feet,
followed by severe vibration and depressurization of the cabin, no
one knew just what was the matter — not even after a pilot

noticed that parts of the No. 3 engine were dropping off and its propeller already gone. Only minutes later was it discovered that a purser had been killed in the galley by a propeller blade that had knifed through the fuselage, letting the sealed air escape.

Another time as a DC–4 approached a landing field in Michigan a similar noise was heard, followed by violent shaking. Then a pilot discovered a fire in his No. 1 engine and saw that both No. 1 and No. 2 propellers had disappeared. Only careful investigation later on the ground revealed that some mysterious internal breakage in the No. 2 engine had made its crankshaft lock, shearing off its propeller which flew into the No. 1 propeller, breaking that in turn and sending it hurtling through the edge of the left wing.

Such tendencies of propellers, even if rare, have disturbed the dreams of more than one crew member trying to sleep in flight. Some of us have gone so far as to wonder: could it be for the very purpose of reducing our temptation to snooze that the C–54's bunks have been located exactly where a thrown blade could slice a sleeper in two?

When reversible-pitch propellers became common after World War II another danger appeared: if a propeller should inadvertently become reversed in flight the airplane is apt to be thrown out of control, a typical instance being the Martin 202 which suffered this very mishap over Minnesota in 1950 and spun downward turning to the right until its right wing hit the ground, cartwheeling it violently and killing all aboard.

Collisions between airplanes are about as common as collisions between ships at sea, despite the airplane's advantage of an extra dimension to dodge in. But air collisions have proved definitely the more disastrous for obvious reasons. Even the airlines, flying their different courses at carefully assigned separated altitudes, have their collisions — most often near airports where congestion is greatest, where climbing and descending planes must somewhere pass each other in altitude.

The recent collision between two C–54 airliners over the Oakland range station is a fair example. Both planes were heading approximately eastward and therefore could legally use the same "odd thousand" feet of altitude as they crossed the range. Somehow the Oakland tower failed to inform them of each other's presence, and again the improbable happened as they hit blindly at 3000 feet directly above the station, one slicing off the entire tail section of the other, sending the remainder spinning downwards out of control to crash on a highway, involving also a truck and two cars which were unable to duck the flaming debris.

One might think that anyone unlucky enough to be in the tail of a plane cut in two by collision would have no chance without a parachute, but I heard of a tail gunner who proved otherwise in World War II. What appeared to this unsuspecting fellow as rather prolonged evasive action by his pilot during a sky battle was eventually revealed to his consciousness as the natural "falling leaf" gyrations of his tail assembly after the rest of the bomber had flown on for several minutes without it. Yet the wild tail turned out to have some fair gliding qualities of its own and actually made a passable crash landing in a forest that left the gunner more amazed than hurt.

Less blest was an airliner full of Delta Airline company officials that was just landing at Muscogee Airport in Georgia when a private plane also landed unseen squarely on top of it. The airliner was still a few feet off the ground and, feeling his tail being forced down, its pilot applied his throttle and zoomed upward again to about 150 feet, dragging the smaller plane along like a dragonfly its mate — whereupon both stalled, and crashed to the ground, killing all occupants.

Collisions with birds for some strange reason are getting less frequent in spite of the fact that airplanes are becoming faster and more numerous. Perhaps the feathered flyers are getting better adapted to the competition begun at Kitty Hawk, for although they used to wreck more than an airplane a year and actually killed several of their big rivals, mostly by flying straight through windshields into the pilots' faces, the Civil Aeronautics Board records only three bird collisions since World War II (involving a buzzard, a small duck, and a pair of seagulls) none of which injured anyone or wrecked an airplane.

Collisions with electric wires occur fairly often and airplanes usually survive them but the collision record is not so good with trees — still worse with solid ground.

However, there have been cases when an airplane hit a mountain hard enough to bend propeller blades and damage landing gear and yet bounced back into the air to arrive safely at its destination. I heard of a veteran flyer who even did this on purpose under desperate circumstances and got away with it. This hot pilot had just had a few after-lunch drinks in Fairbanks, Alaska, and, as a result, was ordered by his supervisor to postpone his flight to Juneau until the morning. However, he staggered out to his plane and took off, swooping wildly over the big gold dredges in a nearby swamp. On the way to Juneau he overheard a radio message from Fairbanks ordering his arrest on landing at Juneau. He would have decided then to avoid the place except that his fuel supply was no longer sufficient to take him elsewhere.

Continuing on, as he approached the airport at Juneau he noticed the posse of men with shotguns and rifles waiting. But he was in no mood to give in easily and he had a fertile imagination. So he swooped dramatically upon a gravelly ridge three quarters of a mile from the airport and bounced on it hard with his wheels, kicking up a cloud of dust, then disappeared over the other side, giving the impression he had crashed. While the posse rushed up the slope to view the remains, he circled quietly in the valley beyond to give them time to get there, then flew around and landed on the airport, refueled quickly and took off for Seattle.

Some of the worst accidents have occurred when a pilot stalled in attempting to clear an obstacle. In a few cases he cleared it but crashed from the resulting stall, and generally such disasters have had contributing complications like engine failure or bad weather. The worst I know of happened to an American Airlines DC–6 flying from New York to Mexico City in November 1949. Three hours before arrival at Dallas, its engine No. 1 backfired so persistently it was feathered and the flight continued on three engines. Approaching the Dallas airport, Captain Clarence Lord decided not to restart No. 1, nor did he bother to transfer the excess fuel left in No. 1 main tank which had made the left wing some 1400 pounds heavier than the right. As he maneuvered rather late to line up with a runway, making a flat S skidding turn, No. 4 sputtered and he asked the flight engineer quickly to put the booster pump to it. Now the big plane with only two engines working properly was sinking fast as it skidded in the air so Lord had to apply a good deal more throttle to clear buildings before the beginning of the runway. He got his nose up all right but at that moment No. 4 forced by its booster overspeeded, sending the lopsided plane into a mushing left bank — heading it way off the runway and toward a big hangar.

Lord realized then he couldn't make the runway so he applied full throttle and decided to go around for a fresh approach. "Gear and flaps up!" he shouted. The first officer jerked the gear lever, raising all landing wheels again, but he forgot the flaps — and so the plane, still short in power, did not pick up the airspeed it needed to climb. Vainly the captain raised its nose in a final desperate attempt to clear the buildings, but it continued to mush into a stall.

"We are really in trouble now," muttered Lord as he tried to squeeze the quavering plane between a hangar and an office looming in front of him. With a splintering crash both wings struck the buildings and the fuselage hurtled downward between. Witnesses said that after the crash there was a moment of silence in the big plane, then "screams, prayers, and pitiful moans." Flames sprang up almost instantly, followed by explosions, which engulfed the two damaged buildings and blazed "two hundred feet in the air." Somehow Captain Lord, two other crew members, and fifteen passengers clambered free of the wreck, but twenty-eight more were burned beyond recognition in what was headlined as the "WORST AIR DISASTER IN TEXAS HISTORY."

Like the birds, all pilots misjudge landings more or less. The only reason landing accidents don't happen much more often is the saving combination of wide and long runways, flexible shockproof landing gear, and last-minute corrections by the pilot. Even with all this, landing accidents are by far the most common of flying mishaps. It is hard to cite any typical example from among the undershootings, overshootings, skewshootings, and other common errors, but the case of the DC-3 that overshot at Burlington, Vermont, in September 1948 is as good as any. He came in a little high and fast, perhaps his flaps were not all the way down, and his wheels didn't touch the runway till about half way along it. If the pavement had been dry his brakes probably would have stopped him, but the wheels skidded so obviously that he knew he would overrun the runway if he couldn't get back into the air. In the instant of decision he chose the air — perhaps the flyer's acquired instinctive trust in his wings again — but in this case he overestimated his speed or his power of acceleration (as many a bird has done) and his throttles couldn't pull the plane ahead fast enough to get it up in time. It bounced along for 300 feet beyond the runway, struck a mound and a grove of trees that whipped it violently to the left, twisting it into an unsalvageable heap in the brush.

Take-off mistakes, while less frequent, are more serious than landing ones as a rule because airplanes take off by straining to utmost speed. A case in point was the C-46 pilot taking off at Seattle who had a power failure in his left engine just as his wheels were about to leave the runway. He instinctively closed the throttles on both engines to stop, but then almost immediately, realizing he couldn't stop in time, redecided to take off and applied full power. Unfortunately the sputtering left engine did not clear itself out as he hoped and he couldn't get off soon enough. The plane hit a power line, then pitched downward into a cluster of small houses, killing two passengers and one person in a house, seriously injuring ten others, besides minor cuts, bruises, and burns to the dozens more who were either in the plane or involved in the crash and fire.

Of course other factors than power failure can botch a take-off:

too much weight, for example, or too little density of the air. On hot days sometimes the air expands to such lightness and thinness that much greater speed and longer runways are necessary to get off the ground. And cockpit complications may at any time arise.

A pilot at Anchorage, Alaska, would have got off with his sixteen passengers all right if he had had three hands, but while he moved his throttle hand to the trim-tab wheel to correct a veer to the left into soft snow, his co-pilot neglected to keep the throttles fully advanced and just after leaving the ground the reduced power stalled the plane into what they jokingly used to call a Chinese landing: "one wing low" — in this case low enough to dip into the snow so that the plane was dragged sideways back to earth and crumpled beyond salvaging.

There are lots of warning lights, bells, horns, and other devices in modern airplanes to tip off the pilots when gas is dangerously low, airspeed too slow, wheels not locked down for landing, a door not properly shut . . . But still the main reliance is inevitably on human alertness to avoid trouble. Anyway there is a limit to how many gadgets you can cram into a cockpit and leave peace of mind enough to fly.

Taking the matter of doors not properly shut, it may seem minor but it is deadly serious. For a door swinging out in the slipstream at 200 knots becomes a rudder or an elevator and, not being controllable from the pilot's seat, may throw the airplane into a spin or a buffeting vibration that cannot be corrected in time. This actually happened to a DC–3 near New Milford, New Jersey, in 1948, and to a Constellation near Richmond, Virginia, in 1951, both of which crashed.

An airplane door can also be a death trap of another kind. Every year people accidentally fall out of airplanes to their deaths in a way that suggests treacherous door suction. In April 1949, for instance, passengers in a DC–3 flying the Alaska coast felt a cold draft, and a co-pilot who tried to fasten a blanket over the leaky door accidentally opened it and was swished into space. In February 1950 as a big Pan-American Boeing let down toward New

York a steward investigated what seemed to be a loose door and it also suddenly opened, catapulting him into the sky over Long Island. In June 1950 and again in March 1951 it happened to pilots checking doors. Even a passenger seated several feet from a door was sucked out on July 27, 1952, when the main hatch of a pressurized Pan-American B–377 opened near Rio de Janeiro with an explosive blast of decompression.

And so it goes. The causes of air accidents range all the way from playfulness to panic with the biggest factor usually just human carelessness or poor judgment — often fatigue and boredom contributing.

It may have been boredom that led an American Airlines captain to playfulness one October day in 1947 while flying a C–54 with 49 passengers near El Paso. At any rate he was sitting on the removable "jump seat" behind the regular pilot seat to let another captain get C–54 experience when, without either of the men at the controls knowing it, he quietly moved the gust lock to the closed position, thus making the rear elevators immovable. The nose started to rise and the guest captain moved his controls to nose down position to correct this. Seeing no effect, he moved them still further to offset the strange tail heaviness. Then just as he seemed about to catch on to the game, the captain in the jump seat released the gust lock — expecting the resulting down flip of the elevators to send the airplane into a sudden dip that would momentarily startle his friends. But instead the column had been pushed to such extreme dive position that the big airplane started into a wild downward outside loop that threw even the jump seat captain into the air and in a few seconds the ship was actually upside down with the horror-stricken passengers hurled upward and banging their heads against the roof. Somehow the co-pilot managed to roll the plane out to the left until it was on an even keel whereupon they descended to El Paso airport to attend to the thirty-four injured and assess the damage to the plane itself, described by investigators as "substantial."

Among the commonest pilot errors are raising landing gear a little too soon on take-off or forgetting to lower it for landing. One DC–3 had its propellers bent from digging into the runway after the co-pilot had raised the gear just before the wheels were off, yet it stayed in the air, its pilot unaware of the damage until arrival at its destination 350 miles away. Two C–46 pilots on the other hand recently made a surprise belly landing at Washington National Airport because they were so distracted checking the right engine's fuel flow meter during the approach that they clean forgot their gear was *not* already down.

It hardly needs repeating that the littlest things often make the biggest difference in flying — even the interpretation of a gesture or a phrase in conversation between crew mates of long acquaintance. One recent accident was traced to a pilot's pointing to the landing gear lights which the co-pilot unthinkingly took to be an order to raise the gear — in this case too soon. In another accident at the pilot's command, "Pull 'em up!" the co-pilot had raised the flaps instead of the intended landing wheels.

A recent survey into the sources of pilot errors came up with the conclusion that an even 50 per cent of them were "substitution errors": slips resulting from inability to unlearn old habits or substitute new ones quickly enough when new types of airplanes replaced old ones, bringing with them "better" and more complicated gadgets and controls. Another 18 per cent were "adjustment errors": mistakes such as closing the wrong switch. Another 18 per cent: "forgetting errors." And the remaining 14 per cent divided between "reversal errors," unintentional activation of some device or control, and difficulty in reaching something.

The very real problems of the modern pilot can hardly be appreciated without seeing him at work, without studying the basic instruments in the mechanical, electrical jungle that is the cockpit.

The number of dials and handles and buttons that must be within his reach has grown so large that for twenty years and more they have covered not only all the walls, the ceiling, and most of the floor but special hummocks of them rise up from his feet, irregular boxes and levers, not to overlook that weird growth called the pedestal between the pilots' seats which contains so many throttle and other control knobs that it looks like a Christmas tree, each series of handles a different color to aid the pilot (who has been checked for color blindness) as he darts his fingers this way and that as if to pluck grapes in an unpruned vineyard.

Seeing the crew preparing for take-off in any modern airliner is akin to witnessing a symphony orchestra tuning up for a concert. Each man has his check list of so many vital items that he couldn't possibly trust his memory alone — and the pilot's check list normally contains between thirty and a hundred. First there is the "Before Starting Engines" list: check (1) drift meter "caged," (2) landing gear lever "full down" and "latched," (3) landing gear up-latch lever "unlatched," (4) emergency landing gear extension lever to "up" (open), (5) hydraulic pressure (1800 lbs. minimum), (6) emergency brake pressure (1000 lbs. ± 50), (7) automatic pilot hydraulic pressure valve "off," (8) hydraulic hand pump bypass valve "closed," (9) battery switch "cart battery," (10) instrument switch "on," (11) navigation lights "on" (night) "off" (day), (12) wing de-icers "off," (13) propeller anti-icers "off," (14) generators "off," (15) ignition switches "off," (16) pitot heaters "off," (17) . . . and on and on.

And then there are the "Before Take-off" check list, the "After Take-off and During Climb" list, the lists for "Cruising," "Before Landing," "After Landing," and "Securing the Airplane."

Along with all this checking inside the airplane of course there must be a nearly continuous checking outside as well — visually during take-off, landing, and between if conditions permit — otherwise mostly by radio, especially when in congested areas.

Here, for sample, is what a pilot is up against as he approaches Chicago from New York on a busy winter day. The visibility is fair at Chicago but A.T.C. (Air Traffic Control) has stacked up the incoming planes anyway, just to be on the safe side — that is, each has been ordered to circle at a different altitude till its turn to land, each new arrival being added at the top, each clearance to land removing another plane from the bottom, all descending in altitude at the same time, step by step working their way to earth.

Light ice has been reported over Toledo, and there is some radio skip with the usual static. The pilot tries to report over Goshen, 100 miles east of Chicago, using his assigned number: Flight 422. He hears in his earphones: "422 from Chicago clearance. A.T.C. clears 422 to . . . squeal, bzzz-zz . . . 6099 at 4000 . . . squeak . . ." There must be two planes on the same frequency, he thinks. " . . . Stand by 6099 . . . 207 from Detroit clearance. Stand by, Cleveland. Report each thousand feet on descent . . . Stand by, Cleveland. South Bend from 644. Changing over . . . 644 from South Bend. Changing over. South Bend altimeter 2978 squeal . . . Chicago from 311, I can't hold any longer. I'm low on gas. Give me clearance to Joliet or some place. Tell airways . . . squeal, squeal . . . leaving thweee thousand feeee-e bzzzzzzzzz . . . "

The co-pilot has a try at it. "Chicago from 422," he says. "Stand by 422," replies the radio; "355 from Springfield squeal . . . "

"Best not try to bust in now," says the captain. "311 is in trouble and there'll be more in trouble soon."

"But Cap, we need a clearance. We haven't got any authority to be here."

"Never mind, bud. Remember the one thing that saved A.T.C. from folding up years ago was that God always packs such a hell of a lot of room into three dimensions."

The radio continues: "Detroit from Chicago, when was 181 over Tecumseh? . . . Chicago from Detroit, over Tecumseh at 44 at 5000 . . . Detroit from Chicago, okay, 44 at 9000 . . . No, no. Five — two, three, four, five . . . Cleveland from 192, cleared at 6000? Thought we were cleared to let down to four. Going back up . . .

Stand by 192 . . . no, NO, two, three, four, FIVE . . .well, we're down to five now and . . . "

That's the way it always is when traffic and weather get together. They can put more airplanes into the air easy enough, but more radio channels is another thing. There are just so many frequency bands in existence. Emergencies get little special attention, and guessing is vital to success. Avoidance of collisions around big cities is inevitably left to chance at times.

In this case the pilot had to allow two extra hours for holding over Chicago, plus time for missed approaches. Two hours on instruments in the overcast, blind, always turning, turning . . . After half an hour the pilot was picking his ear and running his fingers through his hair. His eyes were getting tired. He wanted to look up something in the procedure book but decided not to. It was too dark to read without lights, and if you turned up the lights you couldn't see outside — not even after it was dark again until your eyes had taken time to adjust.

When a hypnotist goes to work on a subject he puts him in a comfortable chair in a darkened room and makes him look steadily at a lighted object while listening to a monotonous musical tone. That's exactly what happens to pilots on instruments. They sit comfortably in the darkened cockpit gazing fixedly at luminous dials, reading quivering needles of light, with all the while the buzzing of the radio range in their ears — a perfect set-up for hypnotic sleep!

Is it any wonder that pilots sometimes forget what beam they are on, take the wrong reciprocals, or start their let-down a half minute too soon? If bad luck should add to this a needle dial that is 30° off, an automatic loop that has taken to telling lies, a leak in the hydraulic system that controls the flaps, landing gear, and brakes, some freezing mist on the windshield, or a burned out landing light — things that happen every day — the preponderance of the factors of disaster can easily develop beyond any practical hope of resistance.

Even as we take necessary measures for safety against these

dangers we have to beware safety's own saturation point. We must remember that 3510 pounds of lifesaving devices can become an anchor of death and forty-six flashing red lights, buzzers, horns, bells, and radio traffic signals may ultimately arouse only a craving for paper dolls. Like Pyrrhus, we now hear the captains crying " . . . another such victory and we are lost!"

There is ground for hope of remedying this pilots' dilemma, however, for an organization called the Air Navigation Board has been set up by the United States government charged and authorized to solve the whole complex problem of flight traffic in co-ordination with all similar agencies everywhere. Radio engineers, traffic engineers, and human engineers are already at work on it, keeping their plans flexible enough to adopt useful future inventions, yet steadfastly progressing toward a basic permanent arrangement that promises to be as simple, foolproof and efficient as is possible to man.

This ultimate common system of air navigation and traffic control is scheduled to include the recently instituted omni-range radio direction setup which already tells flying crews their exact direction from two or more known range points. But as soon as the new DME (distance-measuring equipment) is in full use only one range point will be essential at a time, for the combined equipment, to be known as OBD (omni-bearing distance), will continuously inform the pilot or navigator exactly how far away he is as well as his precise direction from the range, thus effectively pinpointing his position. In addition the plane's altitude and individual identification will be continuously available to the control towers by automatic transponder installed in the plane to reply to radio code queries, just as its exact latitude and longitude position are already available by radar. Thus traffic control officers will be able to check all aircraft in their areas at will, helping lost planes locate themselves in emergencies, directing individual flights through traffic with the simplest of spoken clearances on private frequencies: "proceed," "hold," "go left," "go up," "go down" — keeping a constant flow control to and from runways, spacing the landings at least thirty seconds apart on each strip, allowing the jet liners to take off and climb swiftly to economical jet altitudes while the propeller craft are assigned to the slower-piston stratas in the lower sky.

By that time two-way traffic will not be separated by altitude alone but by horizontal track as well, and perhaps slight separations in track will also divide planes following close upon one another like cars on a six-lane highway. This course precision, now impossible except by impractical visual methods, will become easy when the automatic course line computer is standard equipment in a few years. This is a simple device that makes geometric computations electrically, giving the pilot his exact true course at all times. It must be tuned, however, to OBD for guidance, hence its delayed appearance pending completion of ground equipment.

To top off the future pilot's composure in traffic he will have before him a maplike screen on which will be projected pips of light representing not only his own position but those of other craft, enabling him to monitor the traffic situation continuously and check navigation by eyesight in the densest cloud. In so called "blind" landings he will also have the latest refinements of the instrument landing system (ILS) with precision-approach radar (descended from World War II's ground-control approach to supplement ILS if need be) and, should he come out of the overcast before landing, approach lights directing his eyes to the glide path and runway with graduated intersecting beams.

Inside the cockpit the jungle will be more orderly by then too — more standardized, probably simpler, though it will take an expert to realize it. That is the main province of the human engineers: to match up men and machines for optimum practicability. Their work in effect must cut short the slow threshing of evolution which in ages past solved comparable problems for the flying insects, perfected the gyrotronic sense organs of flies (vibrating "haltere" rods behind each wing), the airspeed meters of locusts, the bank indicators of dragonflies, the bees' system of celestial navigation . . . Human tactual discrimination, they observe, requires at least six inches between controls that are in front of the pilot within easy reach, or a foot of separation at his side, behind, or above him. Confusion of these controls can be reduced also by making them of distinctive shapes as well as colors, by standardizing their positions, aligning them for easy comparison, and making their functions normal: forward always meaning on or more, numbers always increasing clockwise about a dial . . . Graphs can usually be replaced by tables, which take less concentration. And so forth.

Elimination of everything unessential is a big load off the crew's brains. When the flight engineer wants to check whether his battery generators are working he used to have to read a dial needle pointing to numbers of amperes of charge or discharge. In future he will only see a green or red light indicating "yes" or "no." With fifty such indicators shorn of their wool, the crew will be spared much of the dangerous excess information from which they have long had to select, abstract, interpolate, extrapolate, derive, and ignore — sometimes literally to the point of death. The airplane will enter a new phase of progress.

Right now of course about the most definite thing to be said about the airplane's first half century is that it has grown so amazingly in muscle. It is a fledgling that has already outdistanced our thundering locomotive in horsepower and humbled our dauntless battleship in potency of destruction. Although we have not even completely recovered from the shock of its birth, its adolescent accomplishments are piling up at a rate to confound us.

Can you remember Admiral Byrd's flights to the poles? The gallant struggle to conquer the oceans? It is hard to sort it all out in the mind — almost futile to try to recover more than a glimpse here and there.

It was in September 1941 that I met Squadron Leader J. H. Thompson of the R.A.F., having come to hear his story of capturing a German U-boat: the first time in history an airplane single-handed had forced an undersea craft to surrender. I can remember how he sat there telling of the low rain clouds and stormy seas that had given his British Hudson (land patrol plane) the advantage of surprise as it flew that day low off the Hebrides patrolling the convoy lanes — how his second pilot had startled him by suddenly yelling: "There's a U-boat! And very handy."

The submarine, true enough, was only three hundred yards away but obviously submerging fast. Thompson sized the situation up as a case of getting there first. Turning sharply he made a straight run at it, dropping a hasty stick of bombs. Looking back during his tight climbing turn he could see the white columns of water rising. Then up popped the U-boat again.

Thompson immediately attacked a second time, letting go with all his machine guns, his wireless operator manning the "belly gun" while his "second" took photographs. Then a third run at the sub as its hatch opened and a dozen Nazis emerged in yellow life jackets, obviously in no mood to fight.

Just after his fourth attack the Germans huddled in panic and one of them waved a white handkerchief, then another raised a white board. By this time there were nearly forty of them clustered around the spray-swept conning tower — and Thompson ceased fire, wirelessed the news to the nearest surface craft, and started circling around his captive about fifty feet above the sea to await help. Of course he had to keep his guns ready so the enemy could not pull any tricks such as a crash dive or setting up a deck gun — and his strongest recollection after the long circling vigil's successful conclusion was of a very stiff neck!

One doesn't usually think of airplanes as being capable, like ancient frigates, of ramming each other and surviving it. Yet something very suggestive of certain tactics in falconry was used by Pilot Officer Kenneth William Mackenzie in a desperate fight over the English Channel during the aerial Battle of Britain in 1941, which not only earned him the Distinguished Flying Cross but was undoubtedly one of the strangest uses to which flying machines have ever been put.

Mackenzie, a young Irishman from Belfast, had just made a series of forays on high-flying groups of Messerschmitts over Folkstone when one of the German planes, probably slightly damaged, went into a steep dive toward the sea and headed back in the direction of the coast of France. Mackenzie turned his Hurricane after it, flashing out of the bright sunshine at 28,000 feet into the light mist below. After a short burst from his guns at the fleeing Nazi the Irishman ran out of ammunition. But he was determined not to let his enemy escape — even if he had to lick him with his fists.

Flying alongside the German, Mackenzie saw him gripping his control column as though hypnotized. The Nazi glanced up out of the corner of his eye at his opponent, then turned back to his instrument board, flying doggedly on without any attempt to attack or evade the Hurricane.

Next time the German glanced his way Mackenzie waved him down to ditch in the channel. But he paid no heed. They were flying then at 180 m.p.h. about 100 feet from the waves. Climbing a little, the Irishman sideslipped right under the German and up on the other side. The Messerschmitt held exactly to its course. Then Mackenzie repeated the maneuver, while the Nazi flew rigidly on, glancing up only occasionally and glassily ignoring the imperative signals to go down.

"It was exactly as though he was hypnotized," the Irish officer said later. "I didn't know what to do. I climbed to about 800 feet and put out my undercarriage, thinking to take his tail off with it, but I found I had not enough airspeed to do him any harm, so I pulled up the undercarriage.

"At that time we were flying within 80 or 100 feet of the sea and I could just see the French coast. Then the idea occurred to me that I might knock his tail off with my wing. I flew on his port side just above him and came up until the end of my wing was just over his tail plane. Then I gave a huge amount of right aileron which brought my starboard wing slap down on his port tail plane. At once I saw the tip of my wing fly off up into the air while his tail plane collapsed and he simply dived straight into the sea and never reappeared."

Mackenzie was lucky that only three feet of his own wing tip broke off cleanly without affecting the aileron, and also that the two Messerschmitts that attacked him on his way home didn't quite kill him with the hail of bullets and cannon shell they sprayed into his defenseless machine as it dodged desperately about, barely dragging its tail over a white Folkestone cliff in a trail of smoke to belly land in a field 300 yards from the edge.

Probably the most amazing feat of all yet accomplished in flying — and one that should have aroused the envy of the birds — was the jet rescue of a blacked-out flyer in the Korean war in 1951 by two other airplanes literally using their wings as crutches to help him home. It happened on November 16 to Captain John Paladino of North Little Rock, Arkansas, who was roaring back at 500 m.p.h. in his single-place Republic F–84 from a raid on North Korean railroads inside MIG Alley. Luckily for him he had two good friends flying in the same formation at 32,000 feet when suddenly his oxygen supply failed and he faded into unconsciousness.

"I was flight leader that day," recalled Paladino talking to correspondents afterwards, "and we were returning from a routine job. There was another flight of eighty-fours on their way home ahead of us, so I started to lead mine out of the way. You never know it when you're not getting enough oxygen; in fact you feel wonderful — sort of rocked, like on vodka. Your co-ordination and reasoning are off a little, but you feel right up to par. That's how I felt, until it was too late to do anything about it. The first I knew I was in trouble was when I lost my vision. The instruments went hazy and I couldn't see the flight ahead of us. That's all I remember."

"I saw John turn," said Captain Jack Miller, his wing man, picking up the story, "and I figured he was going to make a regular three-sixty turn to let the other boys get ahead. But he only got through about ninety degrees when he suddenly went into a steep dive to the left. I thought maybe he was practicing evasive action or something. After he'd gone down a few thousand feet his plane did a 'pitch-up.' That means it went through the speed of sound and then, because of a characteristic of the plane, suddenly nosed up into a climb. I still thought he was just fooling around. Then he fell off into another steep dive, this time to the right. He did another pitch-up and went into another climb. After he had climbed a few thousand feet he stalled again, only this time he straightened out on a level course at about thirty thousand. I noticed that he was a few degrees off course, but I still thought he was okay."

"I radioed Paladino," said Lieutenant Wood McArthur, his other wing man who by now suspected something was wrong. "I said, 'Fox Leader, this is Fox Two. Are you all right?' And he answered, 'Yes, I'm okay.' He sounded quite normal and his plane was leveling off all right. I caught up with him and noticed he was tugging at his oxygen mask. I told him to throttle back for the descent home. He didn't do it, so I radioed him again and this time he slowed down."

"I pulled alongside too," said Miller, "and we went along like that for a while. Then I noticed that John's head was resting against the canopy. Then all of a sudden he slumped forward. We knew right away what was wrong. I radioed him, 'Fox Leader, Fox Three. Are you all right?' He didn't answer and I called Fox Two (McArthur) and told him I thought Johnny had passed out. I told Woody to pull up in front of him and try to shake him awake with the blast from his tail. Woody started to. Then we decided that might send Johnny into a bad spin, so we pulled back. 'Woody,' I said, 'put your wing under his wing and I'll put mine under his other wing and we'll keep him level until he comes to.' Just as we got into position John fell off into a steep left turn towards Woody so I radioed Woody to catch him. 'Roger, I got him,' he said. Woody pushed him a little too hard and he rolled over onto me. We did that twice. The second time was not as bad as the first and he began to straighten out."

While making these difficult maneuvers of "catching" their fallen comrade of course neither Miller's nor McArthur's wing actually touched Paladino's wing. It was the stiff cushions of air flowing over the wing tips at 400 m.p.h. that actually supported Paladino just as the cushions of air inside parachute canopies support parachutists drifting down the sky. "If John had been conscious and had exerted all his strength to keep his plane level," explained Miller, "I could probably have banged my wing against his, but it would have taken all my strength on the stick to break through the air flowing around his wing."

From then on all Miller and McArthur had to do was use their flying skill to keep their wings under Paladino's, carefully guiding his plane downward toward breathable air, making sure he didn't fall into a spin which might let him crash before he could regain consciousness. When they got to 15,000 feet the two wing men could see Paladino's head nodding and they both radioed to him: "Wake up, Johnny! Wake up, wake up! Hey, Johnny!"

Paladino did not answer but soon Miller saw him tilt his head back and he told him to switch his oxygen feed to 100 per cent. Paladino could not remember it afterward but in his half consciousness he responded enough to twist the valve part way. Then at 13,500 feet his eyes opened and he snapped awake. He was breathing fairly dense air now besides what little extra oxygen his apparatus supplied.

After he landed Paladino's face was a deep purple and he had a fierce headache, but he was happy to be alive after his 100-mile 15 minute ride through the valley of the shadow at better than half the speed of sound — snatched from Icarus by a maneuver unprecedented in the history of flight!

When Captain Miller was asked where he got his idea, he replied simply: "Well, we used to touch the wings of our fighters in Europe. Sometimes when a pilot's bombs got hung up someone nudged them loose for him. And I guess every pilot is always thinking up there of all the crazy things that might happen some day. I know I've often thought that if I ever got into trouble it sure would be nice if two other guys could carry me home."

Checking over all the stories of air exploits of the past fifty years, stories that go on and on, it is hard to think of anything possible to wings that has not already happened somewhere or at least been tried. What the airplane itself has turned into overnight, as if by its own momentum, is alone enough to make the mind pop.

Did you realize that our ordinary run-of-the-mill bombers already have wing spans as long as a city block in New York, or big enough to cover two huge 120-foot barns placed end to end, each capable of housing eighty cows? Their fins already reach five stories high; their power is that of fifteen thousand turboed horses. They can lift 150,000 pounds seven miles up and fly it 5000 miles in twelve hours, and the new ones now being built will cost more than $4,000,000 apiece.

After they land they are towed into drydock-like hangars by wheeled tugs just as marine liners are maneuvered into a harbor by tugboats. They are worked over with a meticulousness suggested by the report that their top engineers get longer training than surgeons. Inspectors inspect their inspectors. Adjustments to their automatic pilots are made under microscopes. Their propellers are balanced so exactly that laying a paper match on one blade will turn that blade downwards.

The same precision goes into all the new planes — into the flexible B–47 stratojets that literally flap their wings through arcs of eighteen feet at the tips, into the new pogo planes that stand erect on their tails, into the secret atomic ships, the ram-jet heli-copters, the three-phase rockets and the supersonic athodyds. Air-planes no longer need grow old: virtually every bit of them is re-built like the *Vin Fiz* at regular overhaul periods, improved parts substituted for outdated ones. Airplanes actually grow young by their own unique brand of immortality.

That is one of the significant wonders of this creation of man that still looks, when dismantled, so much like a plucked bird, its unhinged flaps and ailerons lying about like feathers in a nest, its cowling segments scattered like symbolic eggshells. What the fledgling will be when full grown no man can say. It is now just reaching through the portals of free space. "Why, if the Soul can fling the Dust aside, and naked on the Air of Heaven ride," should it balk at any stratum or zone or sound or orbit? Its bonds to earth lie conquered in eggshells on the hangar floor. It is immortal.

13. Music in the Air

AS I FLY I can't help but hear the sky moving around me — around the airplane. We all hear it subconsciously most of the time, that enduring moan just audible beneath the engines' roar. Akin to the lower ocean's thunder of rushing foam, the sky's tongue is a volatile organ of its own, a characteristic voice that inflects with each rising wrinkle of wind, each purling fold of air.

It is the music of flight — a tone compounded of propeller grist, strut stutter, the flit of wing and tail, the aeolian humming of antenna wires, the gentle snurling of aileron and elevator and rudder . . . The whole slipstream is in it — that graceful, unseen flame, that flowing song that rollicks over our surfaces and out behind, curling and rolling, mewing and mumbling — mile on mile on mile.

There are words to the song too, words to the wise who understand them — words of joy and the feel of the air, informative words about the eddies you cannot see, about airspeed and air density — stern words warning of the death that lurks below.

The Wright brothers used to tell how fast they were flying

partly by the audible swish of the air past their wings, by the gentle humming of their wires. In some small airplanes this sound may still be the only airspeed indicator and its pitch a reliable clue: the higher the key the greater the velocity, any considerable drop in the scale being a warning of danger — of stalling which will be followed by a bigger drop on a different and harder scale.

In one little airplane I used to fly the humming struck a soothing harmony at cruising speed which soon seeped into my consciousness till I could never forget it. Testing the sound with a tuning fork one day I found its chord A♭. But when my nose got too high and the speed fell off, the pitch rapidly sank to G and G♭. That was mushing, a gentle reminder. If I did not immediately correct the trouble the airplane's key might sink to F, a note warning to "Beware of stalling!" At E the pitch would finally shout, "Hold everything. This is it. You're out of control!"

Some pilots used to say that the descending scale of successive warnings seemed to play "Nearer, My God, to Thee." Langewiesche tells how the burbling air before a stall would start a strange flutter like someone rapping on the cabin roof: "Hey, you, that's about It." Whatever the melody, the song of flight always has words for those who hear. Even in a sail plane where it is only a faint hissing, or in a rocket where it is a shriek, it is a language all good flyers hearken to — for their lives depend on it.

The same is true in lesser degree of engine sounds, particularly the synchronization of four motors. Often you see a pilot walk slowly aft on the flight deck, stopping here to count the beats between two of the throbbing tones, crouching there with head cocked as he inclines an educated ear to the pitch of No. 4. A few steps into the bunk room, a step back — ah! There! It sounds better now. He returns then to the cockpit like a piano tuner, delicately adjusting the mixture handles and throttle knobs. Does Jascha Heifetz take more pains tuning his Stradivarius?

The place where sky music gets strongest of all, I guess, is at velocities near and above the speed of sound. This is because of the nature of sound itself, of air compressibility. It is a clue as to why the flight pioneers had such trouble in passing the "sound barrier" in speed — even as to why they considered it a barrier.

Sound of course is nothing more than waves of pressure created by vibration or shock. These waves do not move like ripples traveling the length of a loose rope, perpendicularly (lengthwise) to the (sideways) motion of the rope. Instead they move parallel or in the same direction as the motion of the medium they are in: toward and away from their own source. In other words particles of air transmitting sound vibrate in parallel waves of alternating supernormal and subnormal pressure.

These waves in fact are the sound. And they travel not only through air but through any substance — and the solider the faster. They move at four miles a second through the hard steel of a railroad track, at slightly less than a mile a second through the softer medium of water, at only about 1100 feet per second through the extreme softness of air. They are a milder form of the shock waves caused by explosion blasts and move at the same speed.

I remember when I was in Dover, England, in September 1940 while Hitler was trying to soften up the Channel ports, we used to watch the batteries of guns on the French coast firing across. From the instant of seeing the guns flash we would count 58 seconds then duck, for we knew by experience that the shells took between 59 and 60 seconds to cross the intervening twenty-odd miles. However, the sound of the guns took 20 seconds longer than the shells to travel through the air and 35 seconds less time than the shells to move through the water. The weird result was that 24 seconds after each battery fired we would hear first a faint boom (the guns' report coming out of the water) followed in 35 seconds by the sudden Bwhommmmm of the shells exploding as they hit the ground near by. It was only after all this that our ears received through the air the delayed sound of the shells approaching — in reverse of course — which lasted 20 seconds and ended with the distant original boom of the guns finally arriving again at the tail end of the long procession through the sky. The whining decrescendo of the shells' delayed approach-in-reverse thus gave us a vivid sense of time's illusion, for it was just as if the shells' past were catching up with their present through an invisible celestial phonograph running backwards.

Temperature is another factor affecting the speed of sound, warmer substances transmitting the pressure waves faster than cooler ones. This fact explains why you can usually hear better and further at night than in the daytime. It is not just because of the stillness of the night but more the cooling off of the air close to the ground relative to the upper layers. For once the lower air is cooler than the higher, the bottoms of all sound waves moving through it are retarded, thereby bending the waves toward the earth in the same manner that a caterpillar tractor is steered toward the left by retarding its left track.

All of these characteristics of sound, of course, affect flight — flight of birds, airplanes, bullets, rocks, rockets, of anything — even if some of the things are thrown or shot rather than flown. For sound is a symptom of the air-flow pattern around any object, a pattern which in turn is the key to flight — that same secret of the birds that Wilbur and Orville discovered half a century ago.

In the case of an airplane wing, as the Wrights knew, the sound it makes in flying depends on the speed of the air flow, the amount and shape of the suction above and the pressure below it, the waves and eddies before and behind it. In other words, its music is nothing less than the total pattern of the slipstream. And this pattern may be very gentle and quiet — the suction that holds up an airliner's wing is less per square millimeter than that made by a child sucking lemonade through a straw — or it may have the screaming violence of a white-hot meteor ramming its trajectory down the atmosphere at forty miles a second. Flight sound has a far wider range than any ear can hear and a potent significance that can both warn of trouble from stalling and show the way through the sonic wall in either direction.

To understand this mysterious, almost hypothetical, barrier that tried the wits and courage of thousands of pioneers for the best of a decade, we must visualize what is going on upstream from a wing as well as downstream and all around, especially the faint but definite waves of pressure and suction that are continuously advancing ahead of it in the sky, probing forward like long-range ethereal whiskers to enable the air to feel the wing's approach and start flowing into its pattern before the wing itself arrives.

This invisible run-ahead of pressure impulses in front of the airplane is akin to the shaping of swells to windward of an island and it occurs with the speed of sound: 760 m.p.h. in average sea-level air. In slow planes it naturally extends far ahead — at least as many miles ahead as you can hear the airplane coming. The sky is thus preparing itself, shaping its molecules to accept the approaching wing long before it can be certain it will ever get there. In faster planes flying around 500 to 600 m.p.h. the run-ahead extends only a little way forward because the airplane is almost keeping up with its sound and the relative run-ahead speed is only the difference between the speeds of sound and of the airplane.

But when an airplane has stepped up its speed to mach 1, the varying actual speed of sound, the run-ahead ceases entirely and the air-flow pattern of pressures changes so radically that the very principles of wing lift are altered. What was a smooth efficient wing becomes in effect a crude club that has no lift and stalls in the sky. Its bow wave of air, unable to outspeed the airplane that now equals it in velocity, can no longer escape to disperse its energy but is locked against the machine streaking across the heavens while its pressure builds up with terrifying rapidity, sending the subsonic-type unprepared wing into a convulsion of vibration that usually either breaks it apart or stalls the whole airplane earthward out of control. This phenomenon of explosive compressibility of air is called a shock wave and is virtually the same thing as the initial outward air blast from an exploding bomb! Riding such a power wave and even prodding it into greater pressures is what in effect the sonic airplane does — therein building its own dilemma by ramming virgin air that has not felt its approach nor had time to shape itself to facilitate its passage. If the speeds of plane and sound are indeed exactly balanced the shock wave can amazingly stand stationary upon the wing — invisible, unimaginable, a still photograph of shock blast in material form through which air is continuously flowing at 700-odd miles an hour yet the pressure of which may be 15 pounds per square inch at one spot and only 5 pounds less than an inch away.

mach 1.4   mach 1.   mach .6

PROGRESSIVE   SOUND-SHOCK   WAVES

You have heard of the daring test pilots who cracked this sonic barrier and ultimately conquered it. They did it not in one grand swoop but by a long, deliberate process like a chick pecking stubbornly at the inside of an egg until, after gradually weakening it, the shell falls apart to reveal a new world.

Those who first touched the crux of the problem probably were just a little too full of beans for their better judgment. Perhaps they had to be. Test Pilot Langewiesche has described his conception of the first nearly supersonic dive. A young fighter pilot seven miles high one day doing close to 400 m.p.h. with no urgent business decided to try the thrill of a high-speed dive. So he winged over, aimed his nose straight down and opened her up wide, feeling the tingling wonder of speed unreined, the crescendo of the scale: 450 . . . 500 . . . 550 . . . 600 . . .

Since airplanes are made for stability, this one tended to lift its nose again, to come back to level flight and reduce its excess speed, but the pilot firmly held the stick forward enforcing his will like a cow puncher breaking a broom-tail bronc. Soon he thought he was going faster than any man ever had who lived to

tell it — and probably he was. The idea might have been useful
as a hint. Could he hold on any longer? Should he? Before he
had time to decide, the winged bronco went strangely tame
under his hand. With a shudder and a buck the plane ceased
resisting his pressure on the stick and became ominously *willing*
to dive. Its roar dwindled into a soft, mushy sound and its nose
was sucked downward as if in a maelstrom. The invisible pattern
of pressures around it had changed from the known into the unknown.

Apprehensive, the pilot pulled back on the stick to start leveling
off — but the ship did not answer. It was as if the elevators were
slapping impotently in a vacuum. By then the plane was plunging
a mile every five seconds, and as the horrified young man still
tugged frantically at his stick the machine screamed into a hillside
like a bullet — and exploded in a high white flame.

Runaway dives of this sort happened every now and then in the
early nineteen-forties and no one knew just what had gone wrong.
Sometimes the planes spun or wobbled or skipped like a stone on
a pond. People on the earth sometimes said the tail must have
broken or the pilot had had one too many. But in a few cases the
pilot was able to describe the awful nose heaviness and the ber-
serk controls over his radio just before he crashed. Many scraps of
real evidence were thus collected, carefully preserved and examined.

By the end of World War II it was widely recognized that new
aircraft designs would be necessary to cope with speeds approaching the sonic wall and tests would have to be made to supply data
for the designers. Tremendous supersonic wind tunnels were
speedily engineered and built. Then, as the designers worked
out each new experimental high-speed model — often by art as
much as science — the test pilots tried them out, actually proved
them in the sky.

It is hard to imagine a more soul-straining project or to think of another occasion short of war when dozens of highly trained pilots have given their lives in a cause as hazardous and significant. Once each man reached 700-odd m.p.h. and lost control he had no chance. The powerful slipstream pressures at that velocity made it out of the question for him to think of bailing out.

Yet the sacrifice in human lives and the millions of dollars spent recording and analyzing and testing the facts inevitably bore fruit for the rest of humanity. Month by month the tabulated records of strain gauges and photorecorders pieced together a vision of a new world of speed. Several test pilots who saw white fog over their wings while pulling out of dives at more than 600 m.p.h. revealed that the passing sky is forced to expand so sharply around mach .8 that even normal, warm, dry air can be refrigerated into condensation — a new version of the vapor trail. Puzzled engineers had to allow for the fact that when the airplane as a whole is flying just below mach 1 parts of its slipstream (usually just above the wing) are already going faster than mach 1. They remembered of course that for a similar discrepancy the whole development of high-speed flying had had to await perfection of the jet engine: because spinning propellers, inevitably moving faster than the wing behind them, were always being nullified by their own sonic barrier of compressibility before they could pull the airplane itself even nearly that fast.

When you hear the familiar yowl of an airliner taking off you hear indeed the sonic wall being nudged by its propeller tips whirling close to mach 1. A million windowpanes being scored by glass cutters in unison is what it sounds like. And it means that the air just doesn't have the resilience to get out of the way in time. It demonstrates that the propeller tips have topped their limit of effectiveness, that any increase in r.p.m. will not add to their pulling power, may even reduce it with distorted pressures as when their shape has been altered by a coat of ice.

No doubt it was such new-learned behavior of the propeller slipstream that brought out the modern square-cut windmill blade — and earthbound developments like General Electric's new slicing machine that revolves at 65,000 r.p.m.! The rim of this circular blade purposefully moves faster than sound to form a cutting edge of compressed air so sharp that it slices hard metals into sheets two millionths of an inch thick — yet the blade itself never gets dull for only the air edge that it keeps recreating touches the work and that edge has diamondlike teethlets of unimaginable thinness that are in reality supersonic jet streams of invisible air molecules.

By the time such wonders of man-moved air were revealed to us, of course, the little jet and rocket-pushed pioneer planes like the Bell X–1 and the Douglas Skyrocket had already showed the world the way beyond mach 1 in 1947 and thereafter. The engineers and the test pilots had licked the galloping shock waves of the "transsonic zone" by a combination of thinner wings and a blitz passage past the danger range. The supersonic wind tunnels had taught them how to slice air at speeds too hot for plowing, and they had knifed their way through to what was then believed to be "the smoothness and peacefulness of supersonic flight."

The world beyond sound, however, has not yet turned out to be a less mixed blessing than the trouble-bound adagio world we were born into. Almost the first things the bulletlike superships met beyond the barrier were such sobering phenomena as supersonic yaw and the friction roast.

Pilot Bill Bridgeman, one of the dauntless pioneers of the sonic zone, says that rocket flights start out peacefully enough. When his Skyrocket is dropped from the belly of its mother B–29 at 35,000 feet the feeling is like descending quietly in an elevator. Even after he kicks on his rocket motors and feels the steady surge of acceleration there is hardly any sensation of speed. The slender plane responds "like a little queen" to his lightest touch. When the airspeed indicator reaches 600 he noses upward into a steep climb, thus keeping her under mach 1 until she reaches the thin upper plains where really high speed is as natural as it is essential. Slanting toward the sun in an arrogant 200-mile arc he quickly attains such an altitude that the surrounding near-vacuum can no longer support the Skyrocket below the speed of sound.

So he bends over to a flatter angle of ascent and lets the speed rapidly build up — straight through the transsonic zone. There is naturally a bit of buffeting near mach 1 but the ping-pong ball molecules at fifteen miles above the earth are so far apart that they do not seriously kick his knife-blade surfaces and he goes rapidly on to high supersonic speed. As he told it himself on one occasion, "she usually comes over the fence pretty hot, but goes on light as a feather."

Far below him meanwhile the mountains melt and flatten into prairies and the dark blue sky above deepens toward a sterile black that brings out Venus and Jupiter and the brighter stars. By this time, although she still feels as if sitting almost still up there in space, the Skyrocket is actually moving at more than twice the speed of a bullet from a Colt .45. If Bill in fact could now fire a shot backward behind his plane the bullet would still move forward toward him at a greater velocity than if it were fired straight at him by a man standing stationary in the sky behind his tail. The amazing truth in other words is that no man could be hit at Bill's speed by any stationary gun fired from any position except forward of his beam.

As for general comfort Bill feels remarkably at home in his strange silent super-world where even the external moan of wings is swept behind too fast to reach his ears and all he can hear is what travels internally through the trapped air of his cockpit. His clothing and oxygen gear are somewhat confining, but he has grown fairly used to that. His refrigerator so far has been able to keep friction heat from becoming seriously oppressive. If he could continue this almost dreamy ride at 1000 m.p.h., Bridgeman would be able to relax and enjoy it as no doubt we all will in a few years, but his job is to test the highest speeds now possible, to put his Skyrocket on her mettle, to push his trained consciousness into the unknown. So he must open up his rocket throttle wider, ever wider — he must fly faster, faster, faster — more dangerously —

still more dangerously . . . fast as she will go!

One day when he was really letting her out under the dim day stars Bill felt for the first time a strange yawing motion that swerved the Skyrocket gently at first to the right, then the left, then the right . . . "Then I was in for it. Suddenly the yawing began to get violent. If I had thought it would get as bad as it did, I would have cut the power. But things happened too fast and I was too late."

The plane acted like a car with a wheel coming off. It swung in terrifying swoops and spirals like a mad thing over the sky. Its plunges increased in rapidity until they were so fast Bridgeman's expert hand on the controls could not keep up with them and he was afraid if he tried to correct one swerve he might be just late enough to make the next one worse. While the sleek ship zig-zagged out of control at a speed never before reached by mortal man, Bill strained every nerve to catch the rhythm of its oscillation. Counting "1-2-3-4, 1-2-3-4 . . ." over and over, he just managed to come in on the first beat of each measure and each yaw with enough elevator and aileron to offset it somewhat — he hoped.

"It didn't take muscle," he said afterward. "It took concentration. I never concentrated so hard in my life."

Although it seemed a long time it was probably less than half a minute before the Skyrocket had slowed down enough to really ease its swaying. Fortunately she was still of one piece, but Bill Bridgeman had had plenty enough experimenting for that day. "I was scared as hell," he explained to a reporter next morning, "but not until I got back on the ground."

Skyrocket designer Ed Heinemann immediately went over the yaw symptoms with him in detail and considered the shock wave changes in the regions of mach 1.5, 2, 2.5 . . . Since the trailing control surfaces of craft outflying sound cannot propagate their effects on the air forward to the leading edges they are limited when it comes to damping out a yaw. Therefore it might be necessary to build controls that would activate the leading edges also. Or would it be better to work up a gyroscopic "yaw damper," a kind of automatic pilot to apprehend incipient yaws in time to

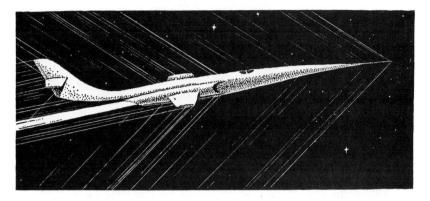

countercontrol them? Of course this would add at least another fallible "black box" to the awesome gadget array which already makes up the Skyrocket's precocious brain and high-strung nervous system. Would it be worth it?

Neither Heinemann nor Bridgeman warmed up to this black-box approach. It seemed too much like adding a fire escape to a house instead of building it of fireproof materials in the first place. So Ed went back to his drawing board to see what he could do about a whole-moving wing, something that Leonardo had once had in mind, later Wilbur and Orville Wright — something that might yet become a practical answer.

Meanwhile other engineers worked on other angles such as reducing shock waves by decreasing the frontal area of the airplane, shaving the fuselage down, perhaps right down to one slender blade, a flying wing. This idea naturally leads toward having the pilot fly lying down — as the Wrights did at Kitty Hawk — so that he makes possible the minimum thickness of the fat leading edge presented to the sticky high-speed air.

Still other engineers developed the perforated wing which may soon become standard on large subsonic planes as well as supersonic. This works by sucking outside air into the interior of the wing to increase control of the slipstream's "boundary layer" that sticks like invisible molasses to the plane surfaces. Left to itself, this capricious layer of air may grow many inches thick and boil with turbulent eddies to build up serious friction and heat, but the perforations suck away the incipient eddies before they can develop, preserving a smooth laminar flow that ideally remains less than an inch from the skin surface everywhere and has already been proven to have increased wing efficiency as much as seventy per cent.

For passenger transport of course supersonic planes will have to increase in size, and the problem of what large shape will best preserve laminar flow at their speeds is pointing toward the full-scale fin-winged rocket as an optimum vehicle above mach 2. But what of mach 5, mach 10? Time will be the pudding.

Certainly our present intensive research is widening in that direction, taking on an amazing scope. New alloys are being tested for heat "creep," the tendency for metal to soften and stretch as friction raises skin temperatures into the hundreds of degrees; and for speed "flutter," a destructive vibration likely to start somewhere around mach 2; and for resistance to raindrops which become bullets at supersonic speeds. Guided missiles already are navigating by radar and television, even by mechanized celestial observation. Their fins with razor-thin diamond-shaped cross-sections steer, roll, or lift them just as if they were airplanes. Some have ram-jet motors for thin-air stratospheric travel. Some have futuristic rocket motors for vacuous ionospheric routes.

These "birds" (as missile men call them) take off with an indescribable sound that is the combination of a bone-shaking roar and the scream of a thousand angry eagles. Even higher in pitch is the accompanying ultrasonic vibration that, witnesses say, seems to press directly upon the brain, bypassing the ears entirely.

Once they are off, the birds are out of sight in a blinding flash and must be followed by telescope, telecamera, radar, radio, television . . . Most fascinating to me of these automatic reports is the audible tone that is recorded on magnetic tape as broadcast from the missile's instruments: an eerie kind of symphony in which altimeters, thermometers, airspeed indicators, cosmic-ray counters, all express themselves musically together. First you hear the quiet harmony of the bird at rest on its launching platform, the tones, deep and shrill, of its continuous-reporting instruments, like skirling bagpipes. And mingled in this drone the intermittent-reporting instruments: the tinkling cosmic glockenspiels, the magnetic harps.

When the missile is fired of course the music changes. The cello thermometers bow up the scale as combustion heat rises. The bassoons of pressure grow more insistent. The tinkling melody is joined by the strained dissonances of the control fins struggling to keep the bird aimed straight. Over-all vibration is heard as a guttural growl, rhythmic rolling of the missile a recurrent groan.

It is only when the slender craft has risen free of the earth's atmosphere that the discords fade. In the vacuum of space there is no air to roll it, no external vibration at all. The fins completely relax in nothingness. The bird's song changes from minor to major harmony, exulting in its new freedom, singing among the asteroids.

The rocket and the missile reports are but examples of a universal attribute of music. Music is everywhere matter is — particularly in air. Music is vibration in harmony, wave motion in tempo, melody in rhythm. A man's cheek is resonant inside with modulated song, or in an extreme wind it can flutter outside like a flag in the sky — a hymn of mortal flesh, a quavering stave of psalmody. Do not arias of blended male and female voices purl in the air like the joining of rills in a stream, a folding in and over of harmonious currents to a common end? What is that scrimshaw on the still pond but the written notes of a summer breeze? Is that peep in the nest aught but the voice of instinct calling from inside the egg?

The roof of our C-54 sometimes leaks when it rains, a homely problem accompanied by the melodious tattoo of wet bullets on duralumin: music in rain — in blood, in nerves, in heartbeats. Sometimes this rhythmic percussion turns our cockpit into a sky womb from which, even as the unborn babe, we hear the thunder of intestinal rumblings, the rale winds, equatorial flatulation, borborygmi of polar fronts.

In World War II we could tell when bombs were headed our way by the doppler differences in crescendo as they accelerated toward the ground. The slower the crescendo, the farther away the bomb was headed. If a bomb was coming right for you its crescendo was so steep you hardly got any warning at all, as I discovered that September day in 1940 when a 550-pounder knocked me out of a fifth floor hotel room in Dover down to the rubble of the street!

Each thing in creation has its key in the musical scale — each pitot and spar vibrates to its own — each vertebra, each tibia, each thumb, each brain.

When our pigeons fly across the barnyard their wings flap in F, the key of pigeon flight in nature's scale — fugue of feathers, *timbre des barbules*. When the cat meows to the vacuum cleaner's whine I've noticed she hits middle C exactly in tune with the machine.

Does each tree also have its natural note? Each house, each bridge, each bedspring, each cloud? And is the wind other than the staff on which these notes are written? Was Pythagoras mistaken when he saw music in the movement of the spheres?

You may have heard the trackwalker's waltz, the hummed or whistled melody in 1-2-3 by which railroad section hands keep time as they step along the ties. It is cousin to the little tune Jack Dempsey used to hum in the prize ring to aid the cadence of his metered jabs — and to Bill Bridgeman's antidote to the supersonic yaw. When a coryphee moves gracefully through an intricate *enchainement* of ballet steps, entrechats, fouettes, and attitudes her mind is seldom conscious of muscular sequence, for she has a kind of automatic pilot set to cover her accustomed course — and music is its brain. Like the plowman we all sometimes lean a little on the uphill furrow. Even as in the air we bank to avoid the skid.

The limitations of earthly music are not yet known, nor of course is anything appreciable understood about music beyond the air. Even up where the air gets slightly thin, music takes on unfamiliar forms, new problems. A pilot I know who likes to play the accordion in flight is often reluctant to climb above 10,000 feet, even to catch favorable winds, because his squeeze box begins to labor and wheeze up there. It is reported that Sir Edmund Hillary and Tenzing the Sherpa who first reached the top of Mount Everest could not whistle with awe at the view, for it is impossible to whistle above 25,000 feet. Quite as definitely the angels cannot be whistled at either, except pretty low ones. And for the same reason a young man I know of with an audible watchlike tick in his head, caused by a palate spasm, hates high altitudes because the reduced pressure ends his ticking, leaving him feeling like a stopped clock.

Are these things clues to the matchless range of Yma Sumac's voice, she the four-octave nightingale of the Andes? Can it be doubted that the range of altitudes of her mountain heritage is related to the range of pitch of her singing — perhaps an octave gained per 5000 feet of acclimation? And what of the strange aural paradox of the giraffe who has the highest and longest of throats but the feeblest of voices?

The answers to more than a few mysteries of sound can surely be found in the upper regions, for not only does atmospheric temperature affect the speed and direction of air-pressure waves but also the wind warps them and things like dust and humidity and electricity all have their subtle influence. The so-called acoustic horizon, for instance, is an elusive, moody line at the extreme range of audibility. Beyond it may lie a band of diatonic doldrums in which the spent sound waves stagger from hill to cloud to hill all wrinkled, effete and unnoticed.

The acoustic foreground, on the other hand, is alive with younger, clearer waves, more than strong enough to be heard — yet here again all mixed up with eccentric eddies and improbable echoes, often to the point of inscrutability. If such complexities could be sorted out, as probably they will be one day by selective tuning, they would no doubt diagnose many a haunted house or other acoustical mystery. A friend of mine heard the exciting sound of running water on the desert near his home in Southern California but could not locate the source. Dozens of hydraulic engineers tried over a period of years and failed to solve his mystery, which never made itself heard except in rare wet and cloudy weather — until finally he traced the sound to a rain-time brook a mile away whose exotic gurgles were being deflected back to earth by an inversion consisting of warm air over low clouds.

Earthly noise is normally bent upward by the retarding effect of cold upper air (usually around 65° below zero, ten miles up) which helps turn loud explosions into silence on earth within a very few miles. But in the high ozonosphere about thirty miles up, the air is quite hot (around 170°) and accelerates the portions of sound waves that reach it, in effect bending (or refracting) them back to earth and creating a secondary sound or echo beyond the silence — this a kind of sonar version of the radarlike echoes off the ionospheric layers so important to radio.

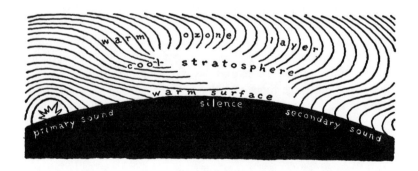

Sometimes there are several such zones of silence arranged in strange patterns, sometimes no sound-sheltered region at all. It depends on the distribution of the thermal layers and probably on the amount of ions currently being absorbed in the ozone stratum. The upper winds influence it too, the prevailing easterly winds in summer, and the westerly winter winds above twenty miles.

The most interesting and best-documented illustration of this I know of was the atomic explosion set off in Nevada on February 2, 1951, which sent out a shock and sound wave that a mile away jumped the air pressure from its usual 15 pounds per square inch up to 23 pounds, then let it spring down to 12 pounds before returning to normal. A combination of strong upper winds and a temperature inversion made the loud report skip over the earth like a flat stone on water, eleven miles to a bounce. Las Vegas was sixty-six miles away and the sound took just over five minutes to get there, arriving on its sixth bounce with enough force to break "many windows."

Serious study of sound-wave travel over long distances began exactly at the close of the Victorian age, having been brought to the attention of scientists by the striking news that people 70 miles away could hear the dead queen's funeral guns plainly while no one in the 30- to 40-mile range heard a thing. This odd fact of course does not jibe with convincing reports that large numbers of people heard the explosion of Krakatoa from all distances up to about 3000 miles — perhaps due to an extreme inversion at the time. But it does correspond to later phenomena in World War I when the thunder of cannonading was often heard in England when it did not reach much nearer places in Belgium and France.

By that time of course sound waves were pretty well understood and had been photographed. They also had been seen by the beholders watching the eruption of Vesuvius in 1906. At each fresh volcanic explosion in fact, it was reported, many witnesses saw a thin ring of light flash upward and outward from the crater like a ripple from a stone dropped into a pond. Professor A. Perret, the distinguished authority on volcanoes who was among them, had promptly pointed out the phenomenon, explaining that the sound wave of compressed air was visible because thick air refracts light more than thin air.

When similar "flashing arcs" were seen regularly at the firing of big World War I guns ten years later, history seemed to have proven that Shakespeare was a better prophet than he knew when he put into *A Midsummer Night's Dream* the jesting line, "You must understand he goes but to see a noise that he heard."

Acoustic engineers have ever since been comparing sound waves to other wave motions that fill the physical world: water waves, wind waves, light waves, radio waves, magnetic waves, heat waves, smell waves, nerve waves, weather waves, volcanic waves, waves of emotion, waves of evolution, pulsations of vegetation, throbbings of stars . . . Waves of great storm areas, they explain, are remarkably like sound waves on a huge scale for these barometric crests and troughs of air parading around the polar fronts are also waves of compression and rarefaction that move at a fairly constant pace. Their shape, like the timbre of sound waves, is molded by temperature and reflections and physical surroundings as, for example, the northeast-southwest elongation of northern storm fronts in conformance with the familiar NE–SW coastlines of North America and Asia from which they take flight across the great oceans.

It is evident that wave motion is an extremely complex thing, for almost every wave has elements of others in it. This is shown by the ripples and swells that mingle with ocean waves like overtones and partials on the bowed violin string. It is revealed in the unpredictable tornado and the unseasonable rain, in the famous tide-rip "roosts" of Scotland where waves of different sizes and origins clash at belligerent angles, in such varied "cross sea" phenomena as the throbbing of deep organ notes, the iridescent colors of floating oil, the confusion of homing pigeons, and the twinkling of stars.

Subaudible sound, an octave or so below the piano, is now being used to fetch weather information from much higher in the sky than radiosonde balloons have ever reached. Like Queen Victoria's funeral guns, carefully controlled explosions of TNT send out shock waves (mostly inaudible) which curve away from the earth only to be deflected back by the upper warmth, enabling special artillery-spotter-type microphones to hear and record the sounds 14 minutes and 160 miles from their source — sounds too low in pitch for human ears but which, analyzed on paper tape, give valuable clues about stratospheric winds and high atmospheric temperatures. Meteorologists are already using these long waves in forecasting and missile men eagerly check them before firing their high altitude rockets.

Ultrasonic sound, too high-pitched for our ears, seems to have an even bigger future than subsonic sound for, believe it or not, we humans have already passed the mice and bats in its development. An American scientist named S. Young White built an ultrasonic siren shortly after World War II powerful enough to set paper afire and paralyze human beings. Similar ultrasonic sound has since then successfully boiled water, cooked steak, dissolved kidney stones, cured arthritis and migraine headaches, massaged sore backs, killed mosquitoes, bacteria and rats, dusted a room, eliminated smoke, changed fog into rain, cracked crude oil into gasoline, and cleaned and sterilized clothes in a portable "Electro-Sonic" washing machine that has been on the market since 1952.

In a fairy story read to me as a child I vaguely remember some favored character boiling water by crying "Boil, boil" over the pot. It was fiction of course, but since fact has now largely caught up with fiction the method may make more sense than anyone then realized. Wasn't it an acoustic engineer who recently calculated that if you could say to water "Boil, boil, boil . . . " for 20,000 years it would actually boil — assuming it could be kept from evaporating in the meantime? And a slightly better if no easier way, I believe the engineer added, would be to persuade 35,000,000 people to cry "Boil" at the water at the same instant, thereby immediately raising its temperature to 212° F. Today a steel siren in fact boils water by this same principle — only saving many man-hours of work by utilizing modern knowledge of resonance and compression.

The effect of ultra-sound on animals, whose bodies are four fifths water, can be of course much like boiling too. Rats and other furry animals are thus killed easily because the high-speed pressure waves of sound quickly raise their temperature to a point where body proteins coagulate. Humans, however, without fur insulation, have such good skin ventilation that they can stand much more powerful waves.

This is just as well for aircraft carrier crews in the Navy where jet engines now scream so loud on the narrow landing decks that medical men have been forced to the realization that they may soon have serious losses unless they quickly catch up on research into ultrasonic nerve disorders. Already many of the new crewmen exposed to jet afterburner noise for the first time on flat-tops, I've heard, are seized with a combination of pain, deafness, and unreasoning fright. One jittery lad, seeing no escape from the strange ultrasonic pain, confided afterwards that he just wanted to roll himself "into as small a ball as possible."

One thing researchers have so far found is that the average man entering a sound field of 120 decibels (partly ultrasonic as is common near jet tail pipes) feels an acute burning where his fingers touch each other. His ears and nose get painfully hot and if he opens his mouth his nasal passages start to resonate like panpipes. Some victims have said they could see only vague blurs through their waltzing eyeballs while their neck muscles twanged like plucked lutes and their knees became jelly. It may well be that nerve connections are shaken loose by the rabid waves, thus producing the temporary paralysis.

Perhaps the piezo-crystal nature of our hearing stems from the simple vibration resonance of some primitive crystal structure in every cell. If so, our whole bodies must be amplifiers of a sort, may be akin to snowflakes with their delicate crystalline skeletons that play inaudible tinkly tunes on our hearts.

I know a chemistry professor who has transposed the vibration rates of the elements down many octaves until they can be played on a piano as musical tones. The compound for water, H_2O, is a real kind of chord — even though it doesn't exactly match the diatonic intervals or fit into the mood of Offenbach's "Barcarolle."

Something almost parallel may be done with the basso profundo melodies of earthquakes, the rhythms of the days and moons and seasons, the climates and pressure patterns. Indeed clouds are clearly a kind of cosmic score sent to earth from outer space, from the sun and stars, their costume music often transposable in weather offices for our daily enlightenment.

No two storms can be quite the same, nor any sunrise like another. Even as the gestures of the trees and the dances of the saplings are never ending, so the patterns of the heavens make sequence in their depth and variety. So too a counterpoint in the playing of lightning, a reverberation of deep thunder, a sad, soft piping in the lofty cirrus sky.

14. Magnetism of the Sphere

AS I MUSE upon the cloud plains beneath my starboard wing and see the halo of the moon, and the glow of St. Elmo's fire on our propellers, I think of the minds of other mortals near me who are witness to these sights. What does Pilot Blake Cloud see in the salmon dawn? Does our engineer from Texas reckon the source of thunder? Will radioman Ernie Silvers wonder at the birth of snow?

"Look at the sun," says Blake. "It's in the wrong direction. Look how blue it is at the edges. It doesn't look real — must be a sun dog. I think that's what they call a parhelion. I've heard it comes from reflections off snow floating faintly in the air."

Even the greatest minds, in describing what they see of mystery in the world, have confessed the feeble power of their human comprehension before it, attempting only the beginning of awareness of the all.

To see what they see, one can try virtually any corner of nature's estate. And vision will not be limited by what is looked at so much as by the mind behind the eye that sees it. With my mind's eye therefore I testify to the mystery of the world: a shooting star, a girl before her mirror, an old clock's story, the passing of a cloud, the weight of gold on the balance wheel of commerce. The eye is verily more critical than what it looks upon. For what avails it to sweep the sky or wash the window if the eye be not clean?

I know the aspect of the mystery is not really greater in air than in water or land or fire, but somehow the contrasts with time and things of the day's work pluck my life strings more sweetly in air. The supernal continuum of mists and stars, creatures and places and things aloft is somehow stepped up. It seems easier up here to keep off the rutted streets of narrow vision and to steer my imagination out any window I choose — downward or upward — inward, awayward — even if for no better reason than just to see how far it will go.

I am writing of the world of free air and freer thoughts — of the ocean that has a bottom but no top — of the wind's way and the cloud's way and the way of the bird and the shrouded night — of the sound wave and the light wave and the howl of vibrant electrons tuned to the unearthly note of the cat's soul, the magnetic pole.

Cats have an affinity for magnetism, I hear, and they are certainly a tradition as generators of static electricity. I have a feeling too that thunderstorms disturb them emotionally because of their feline sensitivity to the pull of Faraday's magnetic lines of force. Which may explain also why they feel so surely the potentiality for lightning building up in their vicinity, enabling them in some reported cases to escape to a more neutral spot before the fatal strike.

Could there be a further and less understood connection between magnetism and the mind as exemplified in the telepathy of cats, and in the geomagnetic field which pervades our entire world with the evident fullness of a universal mind? All too clearly his individual subconsciousness may allow a man to be afraid of all cats simply because he was startled one night thirty years ago by a particular cat which has now been dead for a quarter of a century.

Pondering these things, I check my navigation instruments once more and write down the corrected facts in my log. "Time: 02:46. True airspeed: 194 kts. Average groundspeed: 180 kts. Temperature: + 4°. Altitude: 11,000. Course: 92°. Wind: 160° at 25 kts. Compass heading: 120°. Magnetic variation: 20° W. Magnetic deviation 2° E."

We are now about an hour off the coast of Ireland, and I think of Donegal Bay, the gray rocks of Achill and the brown bogs and patchy green fields beyond, where I once lived for a month in a family of sixteen children in Swinford, County Mayo. Perhaps I can feel faintly the geomagnetic favor of Connemara's stones. At any rate it will be good to be over land again, and I am glad we have our reserve fuel in view of what we wasted in the unforeseen affair of the ice.

"How about a radio bearing?" I ask Ernie Silvers sitting next to me. "I have no stars and we've been on dead reckoning for nearly four hundred miles now. We need a QTE from Prestwick or some place to the south." A QTE is radio code for a bearing on an airplane taken from a station. It is created by telepathic sensitivity to the unseen Hertzian electromagnetic waves that gird the earth — cousins of light, outriders of immortality.

"Okay, I'll try Prestwick," says Ernie. "I guess we're close enough now." He throws a switch, tunes in, and takes hold of his key to tap out a message: "5SJ (Prestwick) 5SJ V (from) CHUN (abbreviation for Chocolate Uncle, code name of airplane No. 896) CHUN, K (go ahead.)" Code is usually found more understandable than voice when the radio must reach outward as far as four hundred miles.

In Scotland, still two hours away, Flying Officer Anthony Tweedle sits in the control room at Prestwick. Most of us know him by sight from our intermittent meetings in the dining and lounge rooms at the big Scottish air base. Once I played chess with him while grounded in Prestwick on a foggy afternoon. He is pink-cheeked, slim, and affects a type of fluffy mustache common among those who wear the dusty blue of the Royal Air Force.

It is 02:51 Greenwich Mean Time on this inky black morning

of February sixth when Tweedle hears Silvers' message crackle into his head phones. Immediately he keys his perfunctory reply: "CHUN V 5SJ K."

Ernie Silvers then asks: "5SJ V CHUN INT (request) QTE (true bearing on me)."

Responds Tweedle: "CHUN V 5SJ INT QTG (press down your key)."

Ernie holds down his key for thirty seconds: "—————— V CHUN K."

Whereupon Tweedle records the reading of his sensitive radio compass needle as it points to the source of the distant hum: "262°." He relays this to Silvers as "QTE 262 A (class of dependability of bearing) 0252 (Greenwich Mean Time)."

After tapping out final acknowledgement to Prestwick, Ernie Silvers hands me a slip of paper reading: "QTE, first class — 262° on Prestwick at 0252 G.M.T."

"Thanks, Ernie."

It is about now that I notice a few stars winking through the murk. Providential, I decide. Just in time for a fix.

I climb quickly upon my astral stool, set my octant for Alioth in mid-Dipper and start the mechanism. The star sways gently beside the luminous bubble as I collimate it, turning the knob to the right, the left, the right again — holding the bubble's equilibrium like a cyclist coasting down a smooth-paved road. Although at one point Alioth blinks out behind clouds, it reappears in a few seconds — soon enough to save my reading. At two minutes the mechanism stops, I look at my watch, mark the time and altitude, rewind the octant, and start shooting red Antares of Scorpio to the south.

By 3:08 I have plotted the Alioth line of position on my chart, running north and south, and the Antares line running northwest and southeast. So all I need to add is the radio bearing (NE and SW) from Prestwick to make a complete three-line fix, each line corrected for time. The QTE I measure with my protractor at Prestwick, correcting its angle for the distortion of the mercator projection of the chart, and draw the line westward across the Bloody Foreland of Ireland, just as the radio waves carried the signals, until the line meets the two star lines near 54° 30′ North, 13° 00′ West. I remember also to correct the radio bearing line for its passage down the northern Irish coast — because it is true that coast lines tend to bend radio waves a little, and this tendency must be compensated by good judgment in plotting. My final correction is to move the whole fix about three miles to the right (south) to allow for coriolis, the centrifugal force of the earth's turning.

With the resulting radio-celestial fix I recalculate our ground-speed and make a new estimate of our time of arrival over Nutts Corner range station near Belfast and then Prestwick. This information I pass on to Captain Cloud: "ETA Nutts 04:10, ETA Prestwick 05:06."

Thinking of the radio miracle which has helped make this prophecy, it is a wonder to me that so much practical advantage has already been taken of the earth's mysterious waves and forces and fields about which we know so little. I like to recall the ancient Chinese word for magnet, which is translated as "the stone that loves." For ancients in many countries, and some people today, attribute a soul or a libido to lodestone whose breath "penetrates secretly and with velocity" to draw iron "even as amber attracts mustard seeds."

This naturally magnetic iron ore, magnetite (composed mainly of the oxide Fe_3O_4), indeed appeared to have qualities of spirit which fitted priestly ritual, abetted witch doctors, and gave a patient resolution to the north-pointing needle. There is evidence that the Chinese had won over this strange and steadfast magic with a compass of twenty-four divisions as early as the fifth century, that the Finns and Lapps used a floating needle on their Baltic voyages in A.D. 1000, and the Vikings probably soon after.

But it was not until some five centuries later that men began to realize the nature of geomagnetism, that the single-minded needle might be seeking coition with part of the earth itself rather than with the aloof lodestar, Polaris. The Roman edition of Ptolemy's Geography, published in 1508, pictures the magnetic

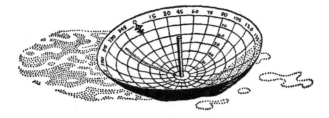

pole as a mountain rising out of the sea north of Greenland. And William Gilbert, who was a contemporary of William Shakespeare, founded the science of terrestrial magnetism on the publication of his great *De Magnete* in 1600, in which he calls the spherical lodestone a *terrella* or "little earth" and in rhetorical elaboration likens its magnetic "effluvia" to gravity and the soul stuff of our world which "that she may not perish in various ways, and be brought to confusion, turns herself about by magnetic and primary virtue."

Although much closer to our own times there have been those who, like Franz Anton Mesmer, experimented with drawing the "magnetic fluid out of diseased portions of the human body to effect a cure," and some who still hold that the magnetic field is a kind of aura that surrounds all life and is visible to the clairvoyant, science has recently managed to collect a few crumbs of generally accepted truth about magnetism on earth.

Gilbert's inspiration that the earth is a great ball of lodestone, a super-magnet, just does not fit the facts of interior terrestrial heat (which is too high for magnetism) and slow irregular changes (that do not occur in magnets). Rather is geomagnetism like an invisible field surrounding a flowing electric current, a river which mysteriously erodes its banks, slowly cutting this way and that in an inscrutable pattern of circulation. No actual magnetic poles are to be found on the earth's surface, and even the interior ones which must exist are so moody and ill-defined that their main importance to navigators is the fact that compasses become completely aimless near them, and radios produce overmuch of the voice of frying bacon. Were it not for the Pfund sky compass (that measures the position of the hidden sun by its rays above the horizon) or the new "grid navigation" system (that supplants the narrowing longitude of polar regions), or radar or the gyro-compass, navigators would be hard put to find their way across the starless, sunless arctic regions where continuous twilight and the dearth of magnetic and radio aid have compounded many a fatality.

That there really are internal poles of magnetic flow somewhere, however, is shown by the places on earth where magnetic lines of force rise vertically out of the earth, pointing inevitably to their mystic focal roots below. The north magnetic pole thus wanders slowly under the region of Prince of Wales Island, Canada, and its southern counterpart beneath latitude 73° S., longitude 156° E. in Antarctica. Even though Admiral Byrd went to that part of Antarctica, compass in hand, to check it a few years ago and found the pole definitely not at home, magneticians still are confident that it lurks somewhere below the general vicinity — at least most of the time.

With the understanding of magnetic forces so close to the plinth of navigational science, a navigator is bound almost constantly to engage the unknown, especially in his basic dead reckoning. Like Columbus, every time he looks at his compass he must fend with magnetism. He must make a precise allowance for the fact that the north magnetic pole is some 1350 miles from the north geographic pole. This correction factor, measured in degrees east or west of true north, he knows as "variation."

Isogonic lines, along which the variation is constant, are printed on all navigation charts and they stripe the globe's entire surface in graceful abstruse curves, flowing toward the magnetic poles like spindrift to the Norway maelstrom. The two lines of zero variation, for instance, which are of special attraction to navigators, extend from each magnetic pole to the opposite geographic pole, swooping wildly over the earth's land areas, avoiding the oceans with a strange aversion, passing through all seven continents and veering far afield to touch the areas of densest population. One heads southeast from the north magnetic pole, passing between Detroit and Chicago, down through the industrial United States, across the West Indies and the heart of South America, grazing Buenos Aires on its way. The other goes northwest from the south magnetic pole across Australia to the Dutch East Indies where, curving to the right through the Malay States, Siam, and Indo-China, it swings left around Japan in a great loop like the seam on a baseball, returning southwestward across China, Tibet, Mount Everest, and India between Karachi and Bombay, thence to the horn of Africa and, curving northward, through Egypt and central Europe to the north pole.

No one knows why these mysterious curves of magnetic equilibrium (on which the compass actually points to the true geographic north) cleave so consistently to the habitats of man, including navigators on their days off. Yet they not only exhibit a human bias now but are increasing it with each passing year. For the charts of annual variation change show that the "no variation" line in the United States is moving closer to the crowded northeastern seaboard, in Europe closer to teeming Germany and Italy, and in the Orient closer to Japan and the densely packed Chinese coastal plain.

In places the isogonic lines are moving at the rate of a degree (of variation) every three years, yet in some others no motion at all has been detected. And there are four magnetic neutral spots in the world where the "no motion" lines cross the "no variation" lines, where the local inhabitants can permanently assume their compasses are pointing exactly to the true geographical pole. These favored points, (1) Lake Michigan, (2) the Bahama Islands, (3) Asmara by the Red Sea, (4) a place in the Pacific Ocean near Japan, are not free of dip, however, which is the tendency of a compass needle to tip from the horizontal as it lines itself up with the magnetic lines. Asmara, being closest to the magnetic equator, is probably almost dipless, but the valuable maximum horizontal component of magnetic force at the equator steadily fades to a useless nothing at the poles, thereby making all compass navigation relatively unreliable in high magnetic latitudes where the needle becomes more and more easily seduced by any local furculum or passing magnetic fancy.

An example of such an anomaly is Port Snettisham, Alaska, where some subterranean dynamo of mesmeric backwash is trying to twist the local isogons into a kind of subpolar eddy. Another such tarnhelm is off Jussaro Island in the Baltic and credited with several shipwrecks, while the one of greatest feck of all, at Kursk, south of Moscow, causes a fixed reversal of the compass of almost 180° over a wide area.

While anomalies of this sort do not seem to move at all, magnetic observatories have detected a slow general flow to the west among all foci of magnetic change, suggesting a dynamo-like circulation of molten magnetite within the earth — a slight lagging behind our planetary rotation perhaps because of a tendency to be attracted by the moon or sun, a tidal flux that in effect amounts to a mild magnetic trade wind.

Another indication that the earth's crust acts as the armature of a huge irregular dynamo is the evidence of the rocks. Particles of magnetic ore in silt settling like a perpetual slow-motion snowstorm upon the ocean floors have been found to line themselves up like tiny compass needles to match the earth's polarity. Once solidified into rock strata, however, they become permanent lithographic pages of history, reliable records of magnetic conditions at the time they were formed. And such "rocks of ages" now indicate that "the earth's magnetic field has shifted radically since two hundred million years ago." The only alternative, say the scientists, would have to be that the continents themselves have become totally realigned.

At the opposite extreme from such profound changes in macro-magnetism are the local components of compass distraction inside the body of the airplane, a complex of micromagnetic forces which can be no less troublesome to the navigator in luring his needle from its purpose. The sum of the latter forces is known as "deviation" and both the corrections — variation and deviation — must obviously be applied to any magnetic compass reading to find the direction of true north.

This factor of deviation, however, is far more painful to the navigator than the vicissitudes of the great magnetic poles which other men have already set down for him on his charts. Deviation is different every time you fly, and it is definitely out of step with evolution. In the days of wooden whalers and clippers, deviation could be logically attributed to the iron spikes in the ship's sides and sometimes to the broken-down blacksmiths among the crew. But the Industrial Revolution almost literally exploded the last plausibility of such argument.

Today there are a hundred thousand pieces of metal alloy and moving parts of unknown magnetic power in the airplane which have to be averaged out by pelorus (a kind of non-magnetic compass for taking visual bearings on sun, stars, or the ground) at the start of each flight, particularly when the cargo has been changed. Who under heaven can divine the extent of this multitudinous traffic of uncountable influences — some pushing, some squeezing, some twisting east, some yanking south?

I doubt not that a few unexplained mountain crashes of off-course planes could be laid to deviation's door. Certainly an electric exposure meter nesting in the unwary captain's pocket might skew north to north-northwest in polar latitudes and, if uncorrected, whisper "A Dios" to five tons of top-priority freight, a million dollars of airplane, or a hundred human lives.

The basic sources of magnetism in the world are still among the great unknowns that Einstein and his protégés are trying to fathom along with gravity and other aspects of mass and energy. Magnetism appears fundamental to all matter, for evidence of it has been found everywhere from the nuclei of atoms (where it is measured in "nuclear magnetons") to the most distant galaxies in the sky (where presumably it eventually will be estimated in "galactic magnetons"). And all these systems of matter spin on their private axes and move on their individual orbits — protons expressing their magnetic moments as separately from electrons as stars from their planets, as mesons from neutrinos or photons from gravitons.

Each order of matter seems to be profoundly stirred by the deployment of its ultimate parts into the parallel alignments of magnetism. A metal bar, for instance, undergoes a small but measurable motion when magnetized, as the orbits of its electrons fall into mysterious synchronization, a harmony we can deduce but not yet understand. The earth in its turn literally glows with ionic excitement each time it receives a dose of magnetism from the sun, the glow becoming visible as "northern (or southern) lights" about twenty-five hours after an observed eruption or storm on the sun.

The relationship between these sun spots and magnetic disturbances on earth is already proven beyond question by records of more than one hundred years, so that magnetic observatories now confidently predict electric turmoil in our world when they see the whirling hurricanes of ions lashing outward from the sun at 600 miles a second — invisible tongues of our paternal star speaking to us in atomic language that we cannot evade, showering us with hydrogenic breath until we cannot even understand our own words.

An example of such solar hurly-burly was the famous magnetic storm of Easter Sunday, March 24, 1940, which started all over the earth at 14:00 Greenwich time. At that hour most radio broadcasts suddenly ceased to get across, wired communication became unintelligible, and surprisingly even a number of electric power systems in the United States and Canada went out of order. A message came through on multiplex teletype as follows: GOVE AND EAETER GREETNNGS LROM AGLWGRA CZMGOPBWQQ8TP)ZLQP . . . A telephone conversation between two rapturous persons who thought they were speaking in boudoir privacy somehow got transposed onto a radio program which was heard for one weird minute by several millions. A difference in potential of 800 volts in the earth's electric flow was recorded between New York City and Binghamton, New York, a gradient of 5.7 volts per mile.

When this sort of thing tends to repeat itself in a rhythm of 27 days (the period of the sun's rotation) and again every 11.2 years (the cycle of sunspot maximums) it leaves little doubt as to whence the trouble comes. The less obvious question of just how the fiery electrons crumple the smooth ionization levels of our atmosphere and turn magnetic equilibrium into bubbling pandemonium is hard to answer, but is being investigated from many angles including spectroscopy, astronomy and (surprisingly) astrology.

Several years ago the Radio Corporation of America assigned an engineer who was also an amateur astronomer to figure out how to predict magnetic storms and he has come up with a promising theory that "configurations" of the planets are associated with both sunspots and magnetic storms. Configurations occur when two or more planets make angles of 0°, 90°, or 180° between the lines connecting them with the sun. The more and bigger the planets involved in a configuration, it appears, the worse the resulting storm. The great magnetic storm of July 1946, for example, came when our two biggest planets, Jupiter and Saturn, were in near configuration with the earth while three others (Mercury, Venus, and Mars) assumed a supplementary "critical relationship." Although not all configurations coincide with storms, serious radio disturbances have been recorded ten times as often on configuration days as elsewhen.

To an astrologer this must seem wholly expectable and the new evidence that the sun is pouring ions from its fire into the mysterious magnetic circulation of our entire world at the behest of the planets when stationed in certain "houses" can surely be assimilated into the plausibility of the horoscope — or, for that matter, the eternal harmonic of the spheres.

Study of aurora light and analysis of its refracted colors is just another way of looking at the same great mystery of this earthly existence. As we fly regularly from Iceland to Greenland to Labrador or Newfoundland in our weekly rounds, we follow for thousands of miles the belt of most intense auroral visibility, which continues westward across Hudson Bay, Alaska, the Barents Sea and North Cape to Iceland again. The official average is 243 auroras a year at this magnetic latitude, two nights in every three.

But you don't have to be a researcher to grasp something of the significance of the almost continuous drama we behold here. You can see what it is by its very shape, night after night after night. Almost every time I step into the astrodome on the Iceland-Greenland run I am awed by the auroral majesty above me, by tremendous shapes — green, white, and yellowish pink — arching over the northern horizon and moving stiffly across the heavens on an alarming scale.

Many are narrow crystalline forms that seem to knife their way between the stars. Some are fat, bold, pulsing creatures with fingers of cold flame palping ponderously from their waving limbs. One minute may see the Milky Way completely hidden behind a drifting lavendar veil while in the next the veil is suddenly swept aside by a great gloved hand. Sometimes a stealthy serpentine band that reminds me of the fabulous Siberian snow snake slithers silently out of the north only to be attacked by a flaming raylike dagger, perhaps just in time for a troupe of pale green ghouls to frighten them both away.

The concentric green arcs and rayed bands of course are clearly part of the great oval ring of ionized light created by the entrance of the sun's hydrogen-spray particles into the geomagnetic funnel of our northern sky. Sometimes when we are far enough north to be near the magnetic zenith the parallel rays converging in perspective hundreds of miles up form the rare "corona," which may appear directly overhead as a great yellow wheel with spokes, a pink tiara, or perhaps a sunburst crown of golden light.

More often the aurora just flickers irregularly about the northern half of the sky as though we were lying on a rug of air around the corner from a blazing fire (the hidden sun) watching the firelight dancing upon the ceiling of stars. When I reflect that some of the rays of that strange light have been measured by triangulation to be more than 600 miles up and no part of it ever found lower than 35 miles, the majesty of the aurora becomes almost too much for the mind to encompass.

Astronomers, however, look upon the phenomenon as just a local example of ionic friction: the collision of solar hydrogen with earthly outer atmosphere — gas against gas — ion into ion. To them the auroras are kinds of earth tails comparable to (but different from) comet tails pushed outward from our host planet by the "pressure" of sun energy: wreathes of incandescent solar breath now revealed by the spectroscope to be ever present on earth even though normally invisible to the unaided eye — double hydrogen-oxygen torches of life. As viewed from outer space the northern and southern auroral belts must look like two glowing polar collars on the night face of the earth, perhaps at maximum like twin Saturnine rings, and actually illumined by the principle of the neon tube, their main control switch hidden in the mysterious depths of the sun.

At the exact ring centers there is relatively little auroral activity (about as much as in New York), for these are the calm cores of the ionic funnels, the eyes of hydrogen hurricanes, the geomagnetic poles. These ends of the geomagnetic axis of the earth, by the way, are not the same as the magnetic poles, being only 12° off our geographical axis while the magnetic poles are some 20° away. Our north geomagnetic pole happens to be very near the great new polar air base of Thule in northwestern Greenland, the dead center of the aurora borealis and roughly halfway between the north magnetic pole and the true (geographic) north pole. The north magnetic pole, on the other hand, is definable as the place where the earth's lines of northern magnetic force *vertically* intersect the earth's surface. For some unknown reason this region of verticality is now six hundred miles southwest of the geomagnetic pole at Thule, potent northern end of the axial core of the dynamo of earth.

If it is difficult to visualize even a beginning of the mysterious magnetic workings of our world, one might gain perspective by recalling what the northern lights have meant to mankind in the historical past, the interpretations sometimes being more colorful than the spectacle itself. According to the Books of Maccabees a rare and spectacular aurora foretold the sacking of Jerusalem by Titus Vespasian, before which "there were seen horsemen running in the air, in gilded raiment, and armed with spears, like bands of soldiers . . . with the shakings of shields, and the multitude of men in helmets, with drawn swords, and casting of darts, and glittering of golden armour, and of harnesses of all sorts."

In later centuries the Norsemen have traditionally seen fierce Valkyries riding the pulsating auroral rays above their arctic fiords, and American Indians the glow of fires of northern medicine men making stew of their captives.

It is said that a gory band of light in the sky above Rome early in March, 44 B.C., foretold the death of Julius Caesar. Another brilliant red display in 1170 just after the murder of Thomas à Becket was attributed to the blood of the martyr going up to heaven; while the Irish in 1854 beheld a similar divine reflection of the blood-drenched ground at Balaklava.

Aristotle's famous De Meteoris is unique in antiquity for describing a flamelike aurora as being "purple, red, or blue" which, in the light of modern auroral research, suggests it to have been one of the ray types which seldom show up as low as two hundred miles from the earth, and are virtually unheard of in the magnetic latitude of Greece.

Professor Carl Störmer's recent classifications made in his native Norway show that the common lower forms of aurora (60 to 100 miles up) appear as arcs and bands generally apple-green, on rare occasions flowing like breaking waves with emerald flashes between the pale crests. And it is only the very highest ray types (reaching sometimes 600 miles into lingering sunlight) that turn into mysterious curtains of gray-violet like celestial shrouds stirring in a silent wind. Through spectroscopic analysis it has been shown that the bright red and yellowish-green aurora colors are given off largely by collisions with oxygen atoms at the lower levels, while the orange-red, blue, and violet colors come from ionization of nitrogen molecules higher up.

Most people who see the auroral drama only occasionally hardly have a chance to realize that there is order in its orgy for the patient observer — that, as with a thunderstorm, when you take the time to study out the known causes and effects, you will see an understandable pattern there that follows a sequence almost as plain as in a continuous movie. Of course few people watch it long enough to notice this pattern, and they may find themselves coming in at almost any part of the show. Twilight may have raised the curtain past the climax or the first act may not begin until after midnight.

The complete regular program of northern lights commences with a whitish glow. This presently becomes a rising arc which brightens, usually turning yellowish or greenish and breaking into separate parts or cloudlike shapes that wax and wane. The northern boundary (bottom edge unless you are looking from near the north pole) is usually well defined. It lies exactly parallel to the lines of geomagnetic latitude. And when it is very bright the arc normally turns reddish at the bottom and splinters into rays — a smooth curve with searchlight beams diverging from the top. Next the even arch becomes wavy and serpentine, thickening into a rayed blue band and eventually forming the curtains that billow into great flowing folds a thousand miles apart. These tend to move gradually overhead, spreading southward as horseshoe-shaped bands and complicated draperies, with sometimes a corona of rays converging at the zenith, or spider web patterns throbbing slowly to a visual crystalline melody.

At midnight the aurora may appear more to the south than north as successive pulsations of light arise in the southwestern sky to flash eastward, fading into the southeastern horizon. At our distance a rotating sunbeam should sweep by the earth's surface at about 250 miles a second which, sure enough, checks out to be almost precisely the speed of the flashing pulses. Is this the reflection on our elected planet so long foretold by the tent maker's son:

> We are no other than a moving row
> Of magic shadow-shapes that come and go
> Round with the sun-illumined lantern held
> In midnight by the Master of the Show?

Of course many irregularities or sideshows appear along with the main auroral dance, especially when interesting clouds are abroad upon the sky. Cirrus wisps easily refract the ionic glitter and sometimes low-lying fog or smoke reflects it, making it appear much lower than it really is. Besides that, astronomers say that about one fifth of the light of the normal night sky is a kind of faint non-polar aurora or side dish of the sun's main course of hydrogen particles. Some scientists have called this a "self luminescence of the upper atmospheric gases." It is the diffuse green glow over the whole earth that creates our permanent "earth tail" of excited oxygen atoms under the never-ending barrage of ultraviolet hydrogen.

Still another component of the night's light results from a slow chemical recombination, at about 600 miles up, of atoms and molecules separated by sunlight above our air screen during the daylight hours. This process that begins at every gloaming all over the earthly skies, clear and cloudy alike, may well be described as an actual physical reconstruction of the night.

The whole material of our world apparently is to some degree in process of reconstruction constantly. This is expressed by such varied laws as the conservation of energy and Hoyle's new theory of a spontaneously regenerating universe. And there seems little doubt that some sort of metabolism holds sway in the world as a whole as within the bodies of its creatures. A snowflake broadcasts energy in electromagnetism even as it melts in descent; a raindrop primes the engine of thunder as it blows apart in the wind; a meteor frantically flares forth its thermodynamic soul as it rams the fierce furnace of earthly air; high-tension wires on high-flying airplanes put out strange electrical radiations that combine oxygen atoms into ozone, replacing one form of energy with another — balancing the eternal equations of this incomprehensible world.

The electromotive force, such as arises when tides of ions play across magnetic lines, like the bowing of violin strings, has its counterpart in the human brain and nerve cords where comparable vibrations create "brain waves" that can be tuned in on, measured and interpreted by man. The electroencephalograph for instance records the brain's tides and weird melodies: the alpha rhythm "resembling a scanning device," the delta wave's "billowy rhythm of sleep," the theta rhythm evoked by repulsion and disappointment, the kappa waves that are most active when cerebral "wheels are grinding" in a conscious effort to remember.

Can it be of less ultimate meaning that epilepsy is being successfully treated as "a temporary electrical storm in the brain," a cross-circuit of billions of neurones? Or insignificant that smell is transmitted by an amplitude modulation (AM) system while most other sensory perceptions reach the brain centers by the static-free frequency modulation (FM) system — firm evidence that the mysterious ocean of thought is alive both with hidden waves and different types of current?

If brain waves are so individual that they can be analysed like a kind of subconscious or "automatic" handwriting, who knows but what they will in some cases show responsiveness to faint stimuli like the geomagnetic field. A great deal of evidence has in fact been collected suggesting that some wonderful but still unrecognized organ of both bird and mammalian bodies can do this very thing, enabling homing pigeons and displaced cats to find their way home for hundreds of unfamiliar miles. Come to think of it, there may be no creatures entirely free of this directional sense for it is known among fish, reptiles, insects, humans (especially primitive ones), and probably all vertebrates in varying degrees. Scottish stags exported to New Zealand have even been found far out at sea, swimming confidently northward — "heading, oblivious of certain death, across the width of the world for their native Scottish hills!"

Most famous of all bumps of locality of course are those possessed by the migrating birds which, far more than the monarch butterfly, the arctic lemming, or the moray eel, find their way almost literally from pole to pole. Some of these have even been observed to go hundreds of miles out of their way in what looks like true "pressure-pattern flying," riding the spring south winds and fall north gales right around the spiraling pressure areas that cross our world, saving whole days of flight time on the bounteous wings of air.

Whose guiding hand directs these sage spirits? What secret navigation needle points the way as they rise wheeling in great questioning circles waiting, waiting for that inner bias of direction? How can the murres of Alaska dive straight through dense sea fog to their lonely island rookeries? What urge brings the penguins of Little America unerring thousands of miles north to Argentina and Brazil — slowly swimming through the sea? Is it like the gathering of lightning that polarizes the cat, this pull of far places and future seasons?

There are probably many kinds of clues that activate the navigational instincts of birds and animals, but the most definitely proved ones are celestial: the sight of the sun by day and the stars by night. In the 1950s in Freiburg, Germany, for example, a research ornithologist named E. G. F. Sauer took about a hundred eggs of several warbler species that fly at night and are known to migrate in autumn from northern Europe to southern Africa and experimented to find out if the birds might be learning celestial navigation from their parents or other birds. He hatched the eggs one spring in separate, soundproof boxes and raised the chicks in complete isolation so that they never knew the existence of other birds, the sun, moon or the stars until fully grown. Then at navigation time in September he let them see the night sky for the first time. Although screens kept them from flying, they obviously wanted to fly and Sauer noticed that they consistently aligned themselves in the correct direction of their migration routes except when clouds obscured the stars.

Next he placed them, one by one, in a special planetarium so that each bird could see only artificial stars while being monitored by a trained observer from below who recorded the exact direction in which the bird headed while fluttering its wings and trying to fly. And Sauer was delighted to find that the birds responded to the planetarium's tiny lights exactly as if they were real stars, the garden warblers instinctively heading "southwest" toward "Spain, Morocco and West Africa" and the lesser whitethroats "southeast" toward "Greece, Egypt and East Africa" just as their respective ancestors had done for millions of years. He checked all his birds in this way and even gave them course problems to test their navigation senses. For example, he confronted some of them with a starry sky that looked exactly as it would have looked at that moment if they had been in Siberia, to which they reacted by heading westward to get back on course. Then he arranged the sky to look as if they were in America and again saw them turn to get back on course, this time eastward, both responses confirming the bird's extraordinary navigation instinct.

Of course it was an instinct almost certainly inherited through some sort of species memory of the patterns of the "fixed" stars imprinted in the cells of the visual areas of the birds' brains and handed down for millions of generations through the genes in the egg. You may wonder, since the stars are not really fixed but rather drifting continuously about on their remote and inscrutable orbits, how the birds' genes could keep up with their motions. But just remember that the stars are so remote, their apparent motions are extremely slow and that genes, like other body parts, metabolize and change, and they would only need to adjust slightly in a thousand generations to enable their host birds to recognize the star constellations, even as men today still see the belt and sword of Orion essentially as did Aristarchos in the third century B.C. Thus when the migrating warbler sees Cassiopeia's Chair overhead of a September evening, he feels not only reassured by the familiar pattern but impelled to head southward toward the beckoning Square of Pegasus. And his happens to be a dynamic memory, incorporating and compensating for the clocklike rotation of the sky (relative to the turning earth) as he feels the instinctive urge to veer more and more to the left of Pegasus (at the rate of 15° every hour) as the night wears on—an inner genetic drive that somehow pervades his mind and body straight out of the egg, a mysterious impulse geared to the rolling planet of which he is in very truth a part.

A different and human example of the influence of mysterious things on navigation occurred about ten years ago to a navigator friend of mine named Willie Leveen. Willie was inadvertently cast in the leading role in a living nightmare over the British Isles one stormy night near the end of World War II. His was a true-life adventure which may well take its proper place in history as a modern navigation classic.

Willie had been my radio instructor in the last months of 1943 and he had served American Airlines as a crack radio operator during most of the war. He had learned navigation only in the early months of 1944. The occasion of his great adventure was his fifth transoceanic trip as a navigator, under the Air Transport Command, when he was flying a cargo of "eighteen American generals" from the Azores to Prestwick. The Battle of the Bulge was less than a month away and this heavy helping of high brass was just returning from a final conference with General Marshall at the Pentagon.

Willie's weather folder showed a severe cold front approaching Britain from the west but it was not due to hit Scotland for at least an hour after the plane's arrival there, so he was not particularly concerned. The long afternoon dragged on uneventfully until the sun, seen withershins from the airplane, swiftly settled into the western ocean. Then suddenly night closed down like an eyelid upon the seeing earth, Ireland was still three hours away and, as the first stars appeared, Willie could see a dense cloud bank far ahead — the rear of the cold front.

Knowing that he had little time left in which to get a celestial position, he quickly picked out several well-dispersed stars and shot himself a good four-star fix. The position showed the airplane practically on course and substantiated his 1:05 A.M. ETA on Prestwick.

By the time Willie had worked out the fix it was nearly ten o'clock and the airplane had entered the cloud bank. There was now nothing left to navigate with but the radio and dead reckoning. The flight was still going according to plan, however, and neither Willie nor his pilot, Captain Daniel L. Boone, had any apprehension of serious trouble. One of the generals sitting in the passengers' cabin was amusing himself by keeping track of the headings of the airplane, aided by his own pocket compass and watch. The airplane was a Douglas C–54 and her code name was Great Joy Queen.

After about an hour Willie got a radio bearing from the range station at Valley, in northern Wales. It gave him a line of position that plotted at right angles to his course, an indication of ground-speed. But Willie didn't rate it of much value because radio could not be relied on at two hundred miles out, and besides, the line, if correct, showed that Great Joy Queen must have slowed down to an almost absurd degree.

As the next hour passed, Willie kept expecting better radio reception, but neither he nor his radioman could raise a thing. They couldn't even get Valley any more. "Mighty strange," thought Willie. "Could the radio be on the blink?" Not likely, as all three radios on board acted the same. An eerie loneliness came over Willie as he looked out into the black nothingness beyond the windows, and heard only the sound of sizzling fat in his ear phones.

He leaned over Captain Boone's shoulder: "We still can't get a thing on the radio, Dan. All I've got is dead reckoning. Do you think we could climb out of this soup and get a star shot?"

"Not a chance, Willie," said Boone. "This cumulus stuff goes way up. Better stick to D.R. and keep trying the radio."

So Willie kept to his original flight plan, using dead reckoning, guessing the wind from the weather folder carried all the way from the Azores. He also kept at the radio. He worked the command set while the radio man worked the liaison set. Between them they tried the automatic radio compasses too, even the loop. They tried everything. But, as Willie said afterward, "no dice."

Landfall had been estimated for about 12:00 P.M., so after midnight Willie assumed Ireland was below. What else could he do? And when the time came, according to flight plan and dead reckoning, he made the turn over the range station at Nutts Corner, heading northeast for Prestwick. Of course he had no check as to whether he really was anywhere near Nutts Corner, but when you don't know something in such a case you have to assume something. It's at least a hypothesis until proven or disproven — for you can't stop and ponder when you're moving at 180 knots.

As the Queen flew northeastward toward a hypothetical Prestwick, and still no radio, Willie wondered what to do next. He had long since passed his point of no return, so there was no chance of going back to the Azores. His alternate destination of Valley was still a possibility but without radio would be no easier to find than Prestwick.

Should he try to descend under the clouds and find Prestwick visually? No. With only a vague idea of where he was and no knowledge of whether there was any room between clouds and earth, descending blindly down into mountainous Scotland would be almost as sensible as diving out an office window in New York City in hopes of landing in a haystack.

Then what about going up? It offered small hope and would use a lot of gasoline, but men in dire straits must grasp for anything. Willie again put it to Boone.

"No," said the captain. "There must be something you can get on the radio. Radio's our best bet for getting down, Willie. Even a three-star fix can't show us the way down through this soup — but radio can."

So Willie and his radioman twirled the knobs some more. Was there any station at all on the air? Evidently not one . . . No. Nothing. No — yes, there was one. But it was hard to tell whether it was a voice or dots and dashes. Then it was gone. The static sounded like a crackling fire. For millions of miles outward toward the sun the unseen sky was filled with hydrogen ions whipping downward upon the earth, playing hob with magnetic stability around both temperate zones. Scotland was almost in the band of maximum disturbance.

Willie switched on the radio compass again, tuned to Prestwick. The dead needle started breathing, twitched, and moved. Then it reversed itself, wavered and spun around three times . . .

Willie wished he had radar aboard. Radar might just have worked in a time like this. What a help it would have been to get a radar reflection back from the ground, to feel out those craggy Scottish hills a little. But the lesson of Job, "Speak to the earth, and it shall teach thee," had not yet been learned by this flying boxcar.

Nor was there yet any loran on this four-engined sky horse — loran, the new visual radio that since World War II has widely simplified long-range navigation, permitting quick fixes of position by electronic measurements of micro-second intervals between pairs of synchronized stations.

Willie wasted no thought yearning for this fluoroscopic magic that was already enabling other navigators to home in on special loran charts of hyperbolas in many colors — this ballet of the pine needles, of shimmering sky waves, subsea grass and green fire, of storms and snakes and music and lightning standing still. He knew that he couldn't have gotten a fix on the best loran set in the world under the magnetic pandemonium now enveloping his world. Loran was too new, too delicate, too tricky still — and anyhow he didn't have it.

So, "What about it, Dan?" asked Willie once more. "Want to go up? Not a prayer on the radio."

"Let's try the Irish Sea," said Captain Boone. "That's right here somewhere to the west of us. It would be pretty safe to let down there to a couple of thousand feet and maybe we can get on contact and see our way into Prestwick."

"All right," said Willie. "Better fly two-seventy. I don't like this much."

Boone adjusted the throttle knobs and started letting down, turning to a course of 270°. Willie watched anxiously.

Down and down — ... 8000 feet . . . 5000 feet . . . 3000 feet . . . 2000 . . . 1500 . . . Finally Boone leveled off, but still there was no bottom to the clouds

"You win, Willie," he said. "I guess we have no choice now."

He set his throttles for a long climb. Presently all the men adjusted their oxygen masks and opened the valves for higher altitude. Willie and the radio man kept their ear phones on, kept trying everything in the book — but heard only the wail of the unknown void around them, the unearthly howl of outraged electrons flying from the sun. And the altimeter needle moved slowly upwards: 15,000 feet . . . 16,000 . . . 17,000 . . .

After a long half hour Great Joy Queen was getting close to her ceiling, and still in the clouds which seemed to have no end. The needle read 25,200 feet and the big plane was beginning to mush. There was hardly enough air to hold her up, but somehow she managed to claw her way among the molecules of nitrogen still a little   higher — 25,400 — and   a   little   higher — 25,500 . . . 25,550 . . .

Willie was beside himself with anxiety, and consciously appealed to what divine powers there might be in the great unknown vastness above and all around. Could he have a peek at a star? Just a few seconds of a star? Just one little star. Any star would do. Anything would do, please God.

As Dan Boone labored toward the last inch of ceiling, Willie's gray eyes scanned the dark nothingness out of the astrodome — wistfully, pleadingly, desperately. Was there a light anywhere? A whisper of a star? Now was the crucial time. Now, God.

What was that over there to the east? The frost on the dome? Willie rubbed the frozen breath with his sleeve. And there was still something light up there: the moon!

Ah! Willie thanked God in his heart as he reached for his octant and swung it toward the hazy glow of light. It was the full moon. It was dim and vague but strangely big — as big as a parson's barn — almost too big. The sky was still deep in clouds but now and then Willie could see its roundness clear enough to shoot. He quickly removed his oxygen mask to clear his face for the eyepiece.

"Hold her steady, Dan," he called as he balanced the silver bubble and pressed his trigger on the moon. It was the most difficult shot Willie had ever made — and the most fraught with consequence. The angle twisted his neck and he was cold. Besides, he could hardly make out the moon's limb and he had to keep rubbing the frost off the Plexiglas every fifteen seconds, the while dancing on his little stool. He didn't have the traditional electric hair dryer for cooking the frost off the dome. He just rubbed with one hand, desperately. Without oxygen, his breath came in short gasps.

Somehow he managed it, and as Boone started descending again Willie figured and plotted a moon line. But as his fingers drew the line Willie's eyes widened with amazement. The line was mostly off the map. It ran north and south and put the plane somewhere just off the coast of Norway!

"Dan, do a one-eighty turn and let down," gasped Willie. He half expected Boone to question his wild request, but Boone promptly banked the plane into a complete reversal of direction and the Queen was headed southwest, presumably back across the North Sea toward Britain again. "We must be in one hell of a west wind," muttered Willie.

When he was asked later by investigators why he accepted that single implausible moon shot as accurate, Willie replied, "It was all I had had to go by in more than four hours. What else could I believe?"

Fortunate it was for the war and at least two dozen lives that Willie had that much confidence in himself, and that Boone trusted him too — for fate was figuring close that night, and there were only a couple hours of gasoline left.

As the plane descended steadily toward what Willie presumed was the North Sea, Boone throttled down his engines to save every possible drop of fuel. He put her on maximum range. That is the slow overdrive prop and throttle setting of lean mixture (more air and less gas) originated by Pan American, with Lindbergh as advisor, for just such an emergency. It means flying just slow enough to squeeze as many miles out of each gallon as you can without mushing.

The plan was to try to get below the clouds and the strong winds while over the sea where it would be reasonably safe to descend that low. To do this Willie had to bet the lives of all on board on his moon shot. The war in France might also feel the consequences. He had to wager everything on coming down to the sea rather than into rugged Norway, Scotland, or the Orkney Isles.

Down, down they went. When the altimeter showed 500 feet, anxiety became intense. If over land, this altitude could easily be

disastrous — and Willie could not even judge the accuracy of the altimeters because he had received no barometric correction since the Azores.

At "400 feet" a grayness appeared in the black below. The sea! Willie relaxed a little. Boone leveled off at 200 feet where he could avoid the full force of the evident headwinds of higher levels. Willie gazed anxiously at the water. He thought he could see huge white caps: a gale blowing from the west.

Consulting with Boone, Willie had determined to fly west until the British coast appeared, then fly along the coast in an attempt to recognize some locality and, if possible, find a landing field. Meanwhile the flight clerk and engineer were making preparation for possible landing in the sea. Life rafts were dragged forth and Mae West jackets handed to all the generals. It is interesting to think of the comments that must have come from the brass as they were being assigned individually to rafts. Of that, alas, I have no record.

After a half hour Boone suddenly cried, "Land!" He banked to the right and headed up the coast. All the crew looked eagerly at the dim outline of the shore and Willie tried to match it with some part of his map. It was tantalizing. He could not recognize anything, nor tell whether the coast was England, Scotland, the Shetlands, or even something else. Willie felt cold shivers in his bones.

Soon realizing the unlikelihood of identifying the blacked-out coast in time to do any good, Willie decided it would be better to go inland in search of airfields and possible radio contact. So he got Boone to turn west, and they agreed to fly inland for thirty minutes. If they could not discover anything useful in that time they would return to the coast. By then, they figured, the fuel tanks would be about empty. They planned in the end to ditch in the ocean as close to land as possible in hopes of being able to make the shore in their rubber rafts against the gale blowing out to sea.

As they flew west Willie and the radio man continued trying everything in the book on their radios, desperately seeking even the faintest recognizable response. And Willie peered ahead at the same time over Boone's shoulder watching the murky landscape below for a light or a city, a railroad line, a highway, a lake — any clue.

At one point Willie suddenly saw a high hill approaching dead ahead. It was so close he was sure they would crash. He braced himself frantically as Boone zoomed upward and the "hill" burst all around them! It was a black cloud — and in four seconds they were out again on the other side. Hard on the nerves, this.

Every now and then Willie would look at the radio compass — just in case it should settle down and come to the point. It was still spinning now and wavering except when passing through clouds, he noticed. Sometimes large cumulus clouds have enough current in them to activate the radio compass and thunderstorms have been known to masquerade as range stations. So he watched and checked and waited for identification — and listened — and looked some more.

What was that whine in the headphones? Was it Scotland or Norway or Russia? Willie could not decide whether the radio sounded more like bagpipes or Tchaikowsky's Chinese dance. It would have been funny if only it had not been so serious.

When the allotted thirty minutes were nearly gone, the radioman suddenly shouted, "Prestwick! I've got Prestwick!" It was now 4:30 A.M. and this was the first radio contact made in five and a half hours. The sputtering code sang forth as in the Psalm: "He spake to them in the cloudy pillar." Willie prayed it would not prove too late.

The radioman tapped out a request for position. A couple of minutes passed while Prestwick control and other co-ordinated stations took simultaneous bearings on the airplane; then the position was given in exact latitude and longitude.

Willie scribbled it down frantically: "3° 35′ W., 53° 20′ N."

"Dan," he shouted, "do a one-eighty. We're headed for Ireland.

We're over the Irish Sea near Liverpool."

Willie had to think hard. He knew where he was at last, but there was so little gas left that it seemed out of the question to try to reach Prestwick. Some nearer field would have to be found. But the radio was still scarcely usable and very uncertain.

As the Queen approached land again Willie racked his brains for ideas. He remembered vaguely having heard of an emergency radio system the R.A.F. used for helping disabled bombers find their way home. It was known by the code name of "Darkee." It was the emergency Darkee System, but how could Willie find it? What was the frequency?

Willie found himself praying again. "Dear God, we need You still." There was not a minute to lose. And to Willie's amazement an answer popped into his head at once: 4220 kilocycles. "It came straight from the Lord," he told me afterward.

Willie's fingers twirled the knobs to 4220 and held down the microphone button: "Darkee, Darkee, Darkee — "

He got an answer: "This is Darkee! Circle. Circle. We are tracking you . . . Now we have you. Fly one-twenty degrees. We will give you further instructions. Altimeter setting is 29.31. Highest obstruction four hundred feet."

Willie leaned over Boone's shoulder as Boone flew the course of 120°. He corrected the altimeters to 29.31 for existing barometric pressure, and Boone kept the Queen at 600 feet. It was so dark that scarcely anything of the landscape below could be seen and often it was obscured by fog or low clouds. Time went by . . . fifteen minutes . . . twenty minutes . . .

Just when Willie was beginning to expect splutters from the engines as the fuel tanks went dry, Darkee said: "Make a three-sixty turn. You are over the field. Let down to five hundred feet."

Boone did as he was told, but could see nothing of the ground. "Darkee, we are still in solid clouds," he reported.

"Then go down to four hundred," said Darkee.

When even that failed to reveal the ground, Darkee urged, "Three hundred feet, but very carefully."

Again Boone crept downward, feeling his way with eyes now on the altimeter, now on the blackness beyond the windshield. When the needle read 300, the clouds remained as impenetrable as ever.

"Still can't see you, Darkee."

"I can hear you plainly," said Darkee. "You are south of the tower now, about two miles. Fly thirty degrees. That will bring you over the tower."

Boone banked quickly until his compass showed 30°. In less than a minute Darkee said, "Now you are exactly above me. Circle to the right and let down to two hundred feet."

Boone nosed downward again and at 200 feet saw what seemed to be an opening in the murk. Venturing to 150 feet he could dimly make out the ground at times, but no sign of an airport.

"Where is the runway, Darkee? Will you shoot off a flare for us?"

A beautiful green flame rocketed into the sky from almost directly below.

"We are right over you, Darkee, but can't see any runway."

"The runway is below you now. Circle and land! You will see it. Circle and land!

As Boone circled desperately once more, Willie noticed that the fuel gauges read zero. Still no runway in sight. Long afterward Boone was to write me: "When I think about it I get a sick feeling in the pit of my stomach."

"We are going to land anyway," cried Boone. "Give us all the lights you've got, Darkee. We are out of gas. We have no choice."

Just then there was a sputter from number four engine and it quickly died. Boone circled to the left — descending — apprehensively searching. Suddenly two lines of lights appeared below. The runway! By some strange quirk of mind Darkee had forgotten in his excitement to turn on the lights until now. Skillfully swinging around to line up with the runway, Daniel Boone put her gear down and brought the Queen in on three engines, easing her steeply into the little field, an R.A.F. fighter base. The wheels touched, bounced. She was rolling fast and the runway was short. The brakes squealed and smoked and Boone pulled his emergency bottle, a hydraulic device that locks the brakes — something to be used only under desperate circumstances.

When the big plane finally screeched to rest at the very end of the runway, Boone swung her around to taxi to the ramp. It was only then that Willie noticed that number three engine was also dead. And by the ramp the other two engines had started to sputter. The tanks were dry. They had landed in the little town of Downham Market, eighty miles north of London.

When I last saw Willie a few months ago, he was just out of the hospital after a nearly fatal accident in which his car was hit by a big grocery truck. He had broken a leg and an arm, several ribs, fractured his skull badly and, as in the adventure over Britain, had escaped only with the skin of his soul.

As we walked across Union Square in New York City to lunch I noticed Willie would not venture a foot from the curb until the lights were indubitably in our favor. "I'm not taking any chances," said Willie reverently. "God has always pulled me through the pinches, and I'm not gonna put undue strain on our relations."

15. Beyond the Rainbow

SOMETIMES I FEEL a strange exhilaration up here which seems to come from something beyond the mere stimulus of flying. It is a feeling of belonging to the sky I fly, of owning and being owned — if only for a moment — by the air I breathe. It is akin to the well known claim of the swallow: each bird staking out his personal bug-strewn slice of heaven, his inviolate property of the blue.

Even though we cannot stop up here, not even stop to think, but must snatch what ideas and dreams we may on the wing, we do take fleeting possession of much airy territory. It is ephemeral to be sure, like all possession, we to it and it to us, yet the substance of it is vast in scope, unlimited in potentiality, teeming with stimulation, and its every kilo-acre is incontestibly ours to use while we can — to drink in, to snuff up, to sort and savor and exhale, to void to the void again.

This transitory quality of the atmosphere is parcel of change in a rapid volatile realm. By the time the next fellow roars along, the sky is not the sky we knew. Literally the elements of it, the nitrogen and oxygen, the ozone and krypton, have moved off and re-arranged themselves. Even the light rays from the sun are re-distributed, refracted, rediffused.

More than most things of the sky, rainbows seem to be pecu-liarly our own. And, as if to prove it, they follow us through the sky instead of dropping behind like clouds and vapor trails — almost as if they were of the mind rather than the body. This is true of many optical effects of course, but of nothing more than the rare and lovely rainbows and mist bows, the coronas and halos we see so often in the humid sky.

Have you ever beheld the Glory or Ulloa's rind, which is known in the Alps as "the spectre of the Brocken?" It is the ultimate rainbow, a complete set of circles of spectral colors known only to those who fly or to mountaineers. We see it moving against cloud layers below us when rain is on our shady side. It seems to bend and wave through fleeing empty air. It is as different from the common terrestrial rainbow that forms an arch as the full moon is different from the one-day crescent. Like an elusive color target it speeds in concentric circles along the flanks of clouds on the opposite side from the sun, matching our pace, weaving and dancing in perfect time with our shadow — the small shadow of the airplane remaining constantly in the exact illuminated center of the Glory.

I think the central aura of this spectacle was named the Glory by Samuel Taylor Coleridge who described the spectre of the Brocken as "an image with a glory round its head," for its resem-blance to ecclesiastical pictures of holy persons has been remarked by many and interpreted by not a few as a vision of divine portent.

The flowing whitish corona about the seer's shadow in the center has the interesting quality of appearing closer than its surrounding rainbows or mistbows, and may well be really nearer on the average — even though rainbows on the ground have been measured as close as six feet from the viewer. The rainbow dimensions of greatest certainty seem to be the angles between the primary and secondary bows and the anti-solar point, which is the center of the observer's own shadow directly opposite the sun.

It is just 42° from the anti-solar point to the main (primary) rainbow, which can be defined as that cone surface (apparently a circle) in which all the rain drops are at the best angle both to reflect and refract sunlight toward your eye at the cone's apex. The rainbow in other words has as great a depth as the extent of the rain and it therefore exists more in a direction than in a location. This is so literally true that each eye actually sees its own separate three-dimensional rainbow, and I have clearly seen two such conic bows (right and left) in the spray of a hose in a sunny garden.

The spectral hues of all rainbows of course result from natural white sunlight's being composed of various wave lengths of unequal refrangibility which refract at slightly different angles, becoming bands of red, orange, yellow, green, blue, and violet light like Easter eggs sorted by an egg grader. As if it were not wonderful enough to have this happen at the anti-solar angle of 42° where the light reflects once off the back of each falling drop of rain, passing through the lenslike water in coming and going, it happens also where the light bounces twice off the back surface — in this case hitting your eye at the anti-solar angle of 51°. That is the explanation for the secondary rainbow, fainter than the first and 9° further from your anti-solar shadow — which puts it outside the main bow in our sky, or above it as seen from the ground where

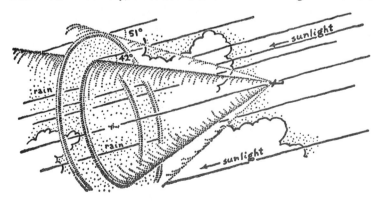

the anti-solar point is below the horizon. Half a degree is about as close as one can figure these effects because the sun source of light is not a single point but has a diameter of 31' of arc.

Between these two best-known rainbows of 42° and 51° I notice the sky is definitely darker than elsewhere, which is said to result from the fact that rain drops in that 9° band are not so placed that their diffuse extra light can reach your eye, this light reflecting mostly inside the first bow and outside the second, the two bows opposite each other as in a mirror with their red edges facing.

Other wonderful bows sometimes appear also from our favored flight deck as the filtered sunshine bounces less simply off the raindrops' various surfaces, both front and back, to the limit of diminishing returns. The shy third and fourth bows arise on the sunward side of the sky, the rare and feeble fifth bow outside the second bow, and little supernumerary bows adjoining each at its violet edge according to the amount of atmospheric diffraction.

Rainbows naturally vary in color balance and character as well as direction, for the condition of the atmosphere modulates the light waves that make them. The size of rain drops affects them so directly that a meteorologist with training in spectroscopy can tell by the distribution of colors exactly how big the rain and how fast it is falling. Big drops (.04 — .10 inches diameter) make predominantly red rainbows with bright violet and green lines but faint blue; smaller drops produce less red; very small drops (.002 inches) make a rainbow with a distinct white stripe. Mist-bows, reflected off still smaller drops, pale down through solid white toward transparency in the dim fogbow which retains only the faintest orange and bluish edges, while the microscopic droplets of pure cloud flesh (.0001 inches) will not support any rainbow at all.

The experts also study the polarization of rainbow light, which is considerable, and an eminent mathematician appropriately named Airy (Sir George Biddell Airy, British astronomer royal) derived from rainbow refraction theory a century ago the famous rainbow integral $A = c \int_0^\infty \cos \frac{\pi}{2} (u^3 - zu) du$ which, for my money, is obviously better suited to remaining a divine recipe for rainbows than to being analyzed as a secular equation in optical calculus.

Since all major rainbows must stay near the anti-solar point opposite the sun they cannot normally show themselves in midday while the sun is high, but are confined to early morning and late afternoon except in high latitudes. This came to me vividly during my frequent visits to Hawaii while flying the transpacific airlift to Japan in the Korean war, for rainbows are almost continuous among some of the humid windward slopes of these islands. Here Iris, shy rainbow goddess, can be seen arising daily full-blown at dawn, blushing among the mists in her hemi-girth, lingering about the northwestern sky for more than three hours of gradual subsidence as the sun swings high — reappearing in mid-afternoon to adorn the recurrent tropic showers until she turns red again at sundown.

If Iris holds sway by day in such a favored rainbow haunt, it is Hecate who takes her place at dusk — Hecate, pale goddess of nightly apparitions, proprietress of the ghostly moonbow, of halos round the lune, of moon pillars, mock moons, and coronas about both moon and planets.

The dewbow is still another kind of rainbow — apparently horizontal — a special spectrum of the sunrise built of reflections from dew on airplane wings or on the ground. It lies upon the surface not as a circle but an optic hyperbola, all of it still 42° from the anti-solar point which is above it, and becoming an ellipse of decreasing elongation as the rising sun tilts the anti-solar point deeper and deeper, ending with the dew's evaporation.

Optically dew is small, stationary rain for it remains in drops rather than becoming a wetness of the surface. It actually does not quite touch wing or grass but floats on air molecules for, unless disturbed, there is always a thin film of air between each dewdrop and any solid surface on which it rests. Thus these tiny liquid jewels act as suspended sun mirrors, collectively a kind of afterglow on earth of the stars of the recent night, a nadir reflection of zenith splendor. When I look at them keenly with half closed eyes at sunrise I can see the stars twinkling over again upon our dewy wings. Every hue of the celestial kingdom is there: the sapphire of Rigel, the amber yellow of Capella and the deep rubies of Mars and Betelgeux mingled with the diamond purity of Vega and Sirius. And these tiny worlds are as truly children of the great sun as all the planets and moons above us, for as the sun lights them to my morning eyes so does the heat of his jealousy evaporate them away again from their fleeting glory.

The same might be said of sparkling new-fallen snow, but here there is the difference that as the dewbow forms at 42° like the rainbow, the terrestrial snow correspondingly emulates its own flying brothers aloft. Snow crystals in the air naturally cannot produce a rainbow, which is born of rain, but instead create the quite different-looking halos refracted from solid ice particles. Their common large whitish ring around sun or moon is the 22° halo which appears through the milky cirro-stratus or other ice clouds at a radius of 22° from the sun, refracted through the 60° prism edges of the crystals. It is only on much rarer occasions that the faint outer secondary halo can be seen with its radius of 46° after refraction through the 90° end corners of the same crystals. Both halos of course are slightly iridescent with inner edges red, outer edges blue, depending on the sizes and shapes and behaviour of their crystals which, as I said of the snow, make stronger greener colors if plate-shaped and paler bluer ones when they take the form of columns.

There seems no limit to either the wonders or the complications of such optics of the heavens which extend all the way from entopic coronas originating in the viewer's eye to green suns seen through misty steam, from parhelic crosses and tangential arcs to the dogs of sundogs, from blue 120° paranthelions to oblique silver moon pillars made by snow flakes spinning slantwise on the wind. It is indeed difficult to see really new sights up here. But it is probably easier for us than for less-pioneering older generations who had even greater handicaps in sorting the new from the known — if likely more mental ones than physical. The corona around the eclipsed sun, for example, was scarcely noticed before 1842. Every year I hear stories about sights not noticed before and often muse upon the much we must still be missing that our grand-children will be excitedly talking about in the year 2000, things that (if we could but know) may be already somehow symbolic, like a blindman's eye or, God permitting, an intra-atomic vision fashioned of sympathetic astroplasm.

Upon each passing rain I know my whole sky must be quite literally full of rainbow, overflowing with reds and greens and violets everywhere at once. I calculate this in my brain. Yet my eyes see only the colors that are aimed from particular conic sur-faces at the exact angles to hit my mortal gaze while the sun and I hold that momentary disciplined relationship. The rest is all for the eyes of others or for God's alone. It escapes my body senses. And so my total rainbow remains subjective: a personal contract between my outer mind and the great sun or perhaps, in broader perspective, thinking of the whole sky and all people, it is become a kind of covenant of color with a celestial being.

Thus, before I know it, it has outsped me — gone into a shape far beyond my own, something outside the genes of the earth and the sky and the fullness thereof. And I remember it is written in Genesis that in the ancient days just after the great flood had subsided God spake unto Noah and to his sons with him, saying: "I do set my bow in the cloud, and it shall be for a token of a covenant between me and the earth . . . And I will look upon it, that I may remember the everlasting covenant between God and every living creature of all flesh that is upon the earth."

This revelation of the covenant appears ofttimes before me at the close of summer rain. No matter where I fly over sea or land I feel its colors haunting me like the eternal melodies of David.

For frequently and quite literally I take his "wings of the morning" and dwell in the outermost skirts of the sky, and even there the hues of the covenant reach warmly forth to bolster me.

Am I wrong in supposing divine revelations to be written in just such figures of the heavens? Is not the sunset a message from its heavenly creator, and the courting of eagles a code for the human spirit? Could the five-fold rainbow be any less than a hint of the supreme glory beyond?

If the shepherds of the earth have gleaned something of the message of the stars, should not we watchers in the pastures of the clouds see even deeper into ultimate truth? What is gravity to the fly inside a bottle being waved about by a flight engineer in an airplane? How does the problem of navigation feel to the least mole?

You are just beginning to learn perspective when you discover that it is not alone the railroad train that moves: that the railroad track moves also. Have you ever considered that when a man tastes a potato, the potato also tastes the man? Or if to the flower the bee is a messenger of love, to the bee the flower is a fountain of life? In the Lord's house are many mansions — and each is another unto its own.

The modern era in physics began about 1895 when the idea of substance in the material world gave way to the idea of behavior. A new perspective appeared in the world. Matter, which had seemed to be composed of particles, began to give "contrary" evidence of being made up of mysterious wave motions. Was matter really made of solid bits of something? Or just intangible waves of energy? Or was the atom built on what Eddington later was to call "wavicles," mysterious particles that vibrated like waves?

Physicists today are still wrestling with these basic questions. If matter is made of particles, what are particles made of? If an electron is nothing but a charge of electricity, what is electricity: stuff, or energy, or imagination? Is it tangible or intangible, acute or obtuse, concrete or abstract? Is it more than a dream of consciousness that creates its own existence? Is it some mysterious essence of the time-space continuum? Or is our limited notion of time or space too meager an abstraction? Does the revolution of an electron in its orbit around a proton actually consume an atomic year?

The old-fashioned Euclidean "space of common sense" has irretrievably exploded into Riemannian geometry (of multidimensional space) and all sorts of new mathematical concepts from Veblen's geometry of spinors to Boolean and lattice algebras and the calculus of variations. These imaginative methods of thinking tend to increase at the same time that light, gravity, time, energy and electromagnetic phenomena are being synthesized into a single generalized theory, even though Einstein and Eddington do not think brain to brain as to what kind of new geometry is best for the job. Mathematics in their minds seems to be reaching below logic toward the more basic authority of feeling, becoming less of a science and more of an art. Einstein "dislikes" certain trains of thought even though they are logical, while Eddington frankly admits the most advanced and profound mathematical choices are basically "a matter of taste." Sir James Jeans, expressing it still another way, declares the ultimate nature of the universe to be "mental" — which is at least a goodly step toward uniting science with religion.

Since it seems unlikely, in the nature of man's finite existence on a physical earth, that we will here be able technically to define matter except in terms of itself, probably a non-technical metaphysical explanation is the best to hope for. After all it would be hard to prove that matter is more than a palpable symbol of the inscrutability that God intends for a primary world. Could it be that matter really exists solely to clothe our toddling thoughts, to define time and space, to educate us in finite things as preparation for the infinite? Should we look upon the Milky Way (or the atom) as just a visible piece of God's imagination — a kind of divine handwriting upon the blackboard of space like that which some favorite teacher once wrote for us in chalk to symbolize a world of maturity we had yet to learn to imagine?

If we conceive this "tangible" universe as a materialized projection of the universal mind we can think of its purpose ultimately identified as our first spiritual lesson. Perhaps then in a new dimension of perspective the mountain below will loom largest as a symbol of strength, of stability. The cloud may exemplify flexibility and imagination. While perhaps the rainbow will stand for purity or beauty — examples all of spiritual qualities in the little soul school of earth.

What are the limits of strength or beauty in this earth world, in this human shade of living? Clearly we cannot know — yet. But the hints we find in faith and music, in love and glimpses of glory promise much more beyond the mortal veil than we could possibly absorb here. Here the dainty capacity of our infantile souls requires that they be sheltered not only against the alluring opportunities outside the eggshell of death but also from the full present sufferings of other souls still on earth. In fact even our own subjective joys and pains, for good reason, have a very restricted range in our present consciousnesses and, once gone, are not normally permitted to linger in our cerebral reservoirs of memory strongly enough to warp our judgment.

In the larger view our first five senses are but crude tools indeed. I suppose they could be considered spiritual rattles or psychic teddy bears of this astral nursery, yet they have the important function of teaching us a wide variety of elementary lessons. Bumping one's head against the rim of the astrodome is certainly a cogent way to learn cause and effect. So is an airmailed letter from a loved one on the eve of suicide. And the aural sensations incident to composing a nocturne are more soul-stretching than one might dream until he has tried it.

In an effort to project ourselves toward our ultimate imagination, our eventual soul sight, we may reasonably attempt to sense the first simple dimensions of God. We must realize of course that, by the very definition of His name, we cannot possibly fathom

Him entire. Probably not His billionth part nor, mathematically speaking, even $1/N^{nth}$ of His N^{nth} degree. But yet logic and faith and humility and imagination and reverence may give us a sometime gleanth.

God could not be restricted to a preconceived limitation of experience, to having to be only one consciousness or personality at a time, or even to having to enter our supposed time-space relativity at all.

From the deepest perspective could it not be possible then that we ourselves — you and I — are an actual part of God's experience, a small yet significant part — that He feels and knows eternally through our senses, our lives, our aspirations, our sacrifices, our creations, along with all such everywhere, everywhen? Which of His prophets has not said as much? For God could not logically be the true Creator unless creatures existed. Even our own small creations in turn then could be looked upon as inevitable sub-reflections of His creatorship. Collectively we are surely some sort of aspect of total divinity, just as the universe is not only God's physical body (His material manifestation) but a vital frame of reference like the white of this page that imparts to these black letters their readability.

Trying to fathom such profundities here in the moving heavens necessarily involves a new perspective on time. For if God's experience, essentially complete and therefore past in respect to Him, is also our experience, it is just as surely incomplete and therefore present in respect to us. In other words, even without overstepping the explored confines of our mortal time-space continuum, God's ancient suffering can be our present living, and our temporary pains and doubts and struggles and slow evolutions a vital jot of His eternal almightiness.

I used to think of the passage of time as a steady motion, harnessed to the constant speed of rotation of the earth and its revolutions around the sun. But up here I am coming to see it as not constant but accelerating. Assuredly clock time as known to children and geographers is an elementary, finite truth, but that can hardly be all that the human mind and spirit are capable of, even in this present life. Time already seems to me more realistically an explosion of the finite into the infinite, an acceleration in which visible outer space symbolizes the past accelerating outward into the present, and deducible subatomic inner space the present accelerating toward the future. As outer space expands at its accelerating velocity it reaches unknowability when its outward rate overtakes the speed of light and its light can no longer come to our material eyes. Beyond that lies only imagination and the great mystery of things outside our definable material universe. So also with time and its dimensions above our mortal span, beyond the few billion years of physical measurability on our astronomical clock.

I cannot any longer even think that time actually begins and ends. Or life. Or love. We have heard that the babe begins at the ignition point, called conception. But look closely at it and you will have trouble finding the instant of beginning. Surely God knew of the little life before sperm found ovum.

Is it not truth to say that life merely changes, grows? Each life is a fusion or synthesis of preceding life in a continuous kinetic process that is materially and spiritually interconnected with all life and all creation. Are you physically more than a temporary assemblage of cells, a momentary meeting of molecules? Surely time is of your mortal essence.

Yet since time has no proven existence apart from the sequence of events (events in the mechanisms of clocks, in the evolutions of stars . . .) all God has to do to change or end time is to change or end the sequence of events. And that is just what He seems to be doing — as it looks from here. By a great but little appreciated natural law He is steadily accelerating time (relative to consciousness) toward simultaneity, toward the infinite.

Hardly any fully grown person can have failed to notice that each year (on the average) goes by a little faster than the one before. This obviously must be because each additional year is a smaller portion of our total experience. It is also by way of being a natural device of growth and education, for how else could the newborn baby find time enough to take everything in? What clearer introduction to his first year than a leisurely taste of a long second, a slow drinking in of a full minute, then a whole event-filled hour, building up to a day, a week, a month — gradually demonstrating the larger and larger meaning of time? Space too, the same way: an easy inch, a big foot, a long yard . . . an interminable mile . . .

Things naturally seem static to a year-old baby. To him Mother is just Mother. She is always the same: never was different, never will be different. Or so it seems. He has not lived long enough to notice much change in anything or anybody. A year to him naturally feels a lifetime. A year literally is his lifetime — to date.

When a man arrives at the age of eighty, on the other hand, the clock has grown to be moving very fast by comparison. Nothing is static any more. His old friends are dying almost every day. New children sprout into adults like spring flowers. Strange buildings pop up like mushrooms. A whole year to him now actually consumes less conscious time than did five days when he was one year old. A year has become scarcely more than one per cent of his total memory.

If you can project your mind beyond death, imagine now how time must fly for a man who has lived a million years. If the same acceleration has continued, a year by then will have been reduced to a mere one millionth part of his total experience, the equivalent of thirty-one seconds to the one-year-old. Babies will grow to manhood in ten minutes and die of old age before breakfast.

Ultimately, as the natural law prevails, whole generations will pass like flashes of lightning. Eons will drift by like time-lapse movies of civilization on the march, evolution evolving before your eyes. Birth and death will merge into a simultaneous whole and time itself will reveal at last its full stature as a dimension of development while total experience will blossom easily from the finite into the increasingly-imaginable perspectives of infinity.

Although the real purpose of clock time, our current finite time (which will ultimately be relegated to a spicy epoch of deep antiquity), thus seems to be to give us beginners a chance to sort out our experiences while learning them, we do not have to lose the minute as we gain the hour. Nor let go the year to grasp the century. I can actually read a chapter of the book of life now in the same number of clock hours it took me to read a single sentence in my childhood, yet I think I understand most sentences of that chapter much better than I understood the single sentence I struggled with of yore. So the acceleration of the years need not take away comprehension or appreciation. Quite the reverse. I am rash enough to predict that when you and I are a billion earth years old and a finite century unrolls in a twinkle, we will still have ample "time" to take in every minute of every year. We will feel then what we can barely deduce now: that time is just as relative a dimension as space, with width and depth as well as length. We will know that the fore and aft ends of our present ancient earthly ships were truly prophetic of these added dimensions because, seen from a river bridge under which the ship is passing, these parts come be"fore" and "aft"er in point of time. And as the ship's forward space is past in time (from the bridge) her backward space is still ahead in the future.

Wasn't it a historian who wrote a few years ago that, of the first century A.D., history remembers but twenty-seven names? And only a few more in the entire first millenium! Even though "new" ancient names have probably been dug up since, in the conscious records of man how certain it is that you and I are destined to oblivion! Even as leaves on the tree or as cells in the body.

What profits us then to wager for glory on earth, for renown between year X and year Y on the time clock? To the understanding of infinity any hour is zero. For infinity divided by a number (of hours, years, centuries) remains imperturbably infinity.

Undoubtedly the day will come, and rather sooner than we think, when our spiritual maturity will be glad our bodies have been left behind — those childish toys that were becoming anchors to hold back our deepening experience. Most of us will need to be old in years, perhaps outside death's shell, to have gained that much perspective of our mortal limitations — yet sooner or later it will come to us all. It may be our first great realization beyond the grave. We will then awake from the dream of finite time-space into a totally different order of comprehension. Perhaps our minds will drift outward from our outmoded cerebrums like magnetic fields escaping an unplugged electronic computer, permitting us to recognize at a thought other souls we have known before.

Supposed psychic evidence, accepted by even such a renowned physicist as Sir Oliver Lodge, suggests that all deceit and superficiality are filtered out by the veil of death so that transcended beings no longer have such distractions as advertising or flattery and can go forward untempted by either fat checks or slim waists into a spiritual companionship and endeavor where both the rewards and surroundings are superior to anything known under the mortal sky.

More generally accepted by science, however, is the growing realization that, since matter remains unprovable, elusive, and largely theoretical, life itself consists mainly in the tuning in for a time of the appropriate harmonics among the atoms. This is to say that out of the myriads of vibrations and waves everywhere, some few in some mysterious manner tune in on certain combinations of organic carbon molecules, giving them the magic lease we sense as life. Such an ephemeral pattern of orbits thus becomes the protoplasm of an earwig, a lily, a bird, a man. It grows into physical being, a meeting place of ideas, a U.N. of consciousness. Yet what is its essence? What makes it alive? Being a group of cells temporarily assembled, it is in a curious way suggestive of a radio. Radio-like, it responds to mysterious and remote stimuli, perhaps expressing itself extravagantly for a few years, ending in a sudden breakdown of parts which cuts it off from its source of power so that it turns cold and silent unto "death."

Does a snowflake with its faint electromagnetic aura thus tune in on the carbon of human flesh: twirling its lacy dial to call Carbon 6 — 66 ring 3? Can the impulses in nerves be compared to the discharges of lightning in the sky? Muscles to towering clouds, blood to warm rain, breath to the wind?

It seems silly that men down there greet birth with smiles, with cigar passings and congratulations, while death brings forth only frustration, crepe and remorse. All because growth is considered good while decay is bad and unhealthy, something to fight against to the inevitable, the bitter, bitter end.

Do they forget that decay begins at conception if not before? That decay is the smell of the rose, the flame of the maple in October, and the inseparable partner of growth, both being vital to life?

Perhaps their blindness to a healthy and beautiful death is necessary to their own growth, the sowing of the larger soul. Who knows the true worth of waste and war and greed, of misplaced trust and fanatic love? Let folly live that spirit may be born. Is the population of cells that is I more than a whirlpool of vibration, an intersection of waves, a magnetic storm, the breath of a star? Is oxygen part of this body it passes through? Does the sky itself sing the song of life?

Death is not the reverse of life, but its unfolding — a sometime equalizer of growth and decay.

For those who see from the distances in the sky death can be a time of release, even a messenger of joy, an inner lifting of the spirit toward the greater firmament outside. I sometimes think I can hear the empyreal essence speaking out of a purple dawn — the seraph of poetry in us all, behind our laughter and our tears, singing to animals in the hills, to the birds resting on the autumn wind, to all of us creatures of the slow kindergarten earth.

What is He saying? What are the lessons of the physical life? Is there any answer we can point to up here? Down there?

The reality of earth to finite eyes seems destined to the shape of enigma, the eternal paradox of truth — a hierarchy scaled from minor contradictions to major mysteries, the full significance of

which can be divined ultimately only by spiritual maturity.

Consider the contrariness of the world, the trivial and tragic wonder of natural things. The moon appears bigger when it is further off, at the far horizon. The hot sun is nearer to us (who live in the northern hemisphere) in winter than in summer. Caruso, now dead, is singing to generations still unborn. A dynamo has been designed and built with the aid of the imaginary number $\sqrt{-1}$.

Wallowing along at a languid hundred and seventy knots at our thought-engendering altitude, I feel ofttimes as if I were back in the crosstrees of my youth, my weather eye upon the soft horizon, musing on the mirror-illusion of this mortal world where day is balanced against night, male against female, land against sea, flow against ebb. It was the budding of new paradox then. It appears the flowering of mature mystery now. For what are positive and negative electricity but symbols of the enduring challenge and response of history? How do we weigh good and evil but according to their lasting fruits: Abel and Cain, Abraham and Nimrod, Moses and Pharaoh, Christ and Caiaphas, Mohammed and Abu Sofian, Baha'u'llah and Yahya?

I learn that the material in space, including stars and planets, is spread more thinly on the average than the highest vacuum that can be created on earth. Yet this unearthly emptiness contains all the matter there is — all the stuff of all the worlds. What substance then or import in the vacuous ocean of truth has the mortal earth? Or you? Or I?

As a man does not become a parachutist without jumping into the open sky, and nations cannot create a world government without letting go some real sovereignty, so we will never attain the greater world of the spirit until we release our clutch on the material of earth. Is our mother thus a fetter to be put out of mind?

Paradox, ever paradox. As ye give your life ye gain it — the *Liebestod* — the nirvana: the letting go, the breathing out that ye may breathe in again and live, the decay of the flesh that ye may burst the egg of darkness.

All the little lessons are here before our eyes. If you would shield yourself with mortal armor, observe the limitations of the turtle and the lobster. If you prefer a liquid body to avoid being pinched in the door or stuck with a dagger, consider the jellyfish. If you would regenerate yourself to get back an amputated leg or arm, consult the angle worm. If you would learn patience, control, design, study the spider. Even navigation is taught here by methods more advanced than man's — by the migrating birds of the sky, by the homing fish in the deep. And what better than the stars as object lessons in perspective — than birth for exercise in humility — than death for a seminar in giving?

As if to remind me that the sky over Belfast was still part of the mortal world, our left wing dipped just noticeably as we turned the corner to let down over the North Channel, heading for the Firth of Clyde. It was 04:08 G.M.T. Soon we would land by Orangefield Castle at the Prestwick Air Base. Blake Cloud drank the last of his cold coffee, set the cup back on the pedestal where the spoon purred in quiet sympathy with our four throttled engines.

As I checked my instruments again, recorded 460 gallons of fuel remaining, and tried to catch up on my log, I noticed we were descending through a flat sheet of silky alto-stratus cloud like a prairie of snow yet so thin I could see below it the flamfoo of moonshine upon the restless waters around Ailsa Craig. The sight of the tall lonely Scottish rock was reassuring, even with the full wind upon it — perhaps, more truly, *because* of the wind.

It was a pale incorporeal wind that seemed to penetrate the earth and every breathing thing upon the face of the earth — blowing as it has blown through all memory and song. I could feel it bearing the body of the airplane within its own body, gently yawing, softly rocking the babe of man safe inside his mother sky — while everywhere the embracing lullaby of wind swept on, coming from we know not where, going we know not whence — inexorable, aloof, of a mind apart.

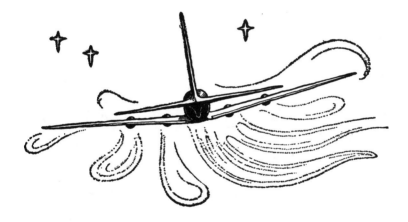

and sound, 248–49; of owl, 249; section
of chapter on, 297–301; illustration of,
297, 298; magical detail of, 297–99;
slipstream of, 299–300; specialization of,
300; overhaul of, 300; in the affairs of
men, 300–1; creatures who live in, 301;
aerodynamics of, 302–4; variable pitch
of, 304; assembled by Lilienthal for his
flapping plane, 313; flaps and ailerons
compared to, 349; fugue of, 364. *See
also* Bird, Insulation, Flight, Streamlining

Fish, as aids to navigator, 29; located
from the sky, 118; motion compared with
that of bird, 302; co-ordination of, 307;
homing of, 422

Fletcher, Colonel Joseph, 233–34, 239–40

Flight, plan of, 71–72, 109, 394–95; level of
future, 109; view of earth during, 99–100,
110–119; errors in 61–62, 68–69, 73–74,
76–82, 84, 108, 120–21, 172–73, 173–74,
205–6, 221, 233, 275–76, 284–85, 287, 305
306, 308, 314; of gossamer spider, 176–77;
meaning of sensed anew, 280; early
attempts at, 280–83; first balloons, 281–
85; first human, 283; principles of buoyancy, 286; terminal velocity, 291–92;
chapter on birds, 294–312; feathers,
297–301; aerodynamics of bird, 302–4;
bird errors, 305, 306, 308; bird formation
maneuvering, 307–8; taught by hawks,
309; aided by air columns, 309; illustration of albatross on wind seam, 310;
theory of circular soaring, 310; static
and dynamic soaring 310–11; shapes of
bird wings, 311–12; attempts of Leonardo,
Cayley, Henson, 313; Lilienthal's attempts, 313–14; of Wright brothers, 316;
first race across America, 316–17; first
solo, 318; modern theory of, 318; public
acceptance of, 317–19; improvements
in modern airplane, 320; transoceanic,
321, 322–26; factors of long-range success,
321–26; why four engines over ocean,
322–23; old "engineering curse," 325–26;
cargo problems, 327; propeller problems,
328–29; collisions, 329–31; the stall,
304–5, 320; 331–32; landing accidents,
332–33; take-off accidents, 333–34; dangerous doors, 334–35; accidents from
carelessness, 335–36; pilot problems,
336–40; sample flight, 338–39; saturation
of safety, 340; hope in better organization, 340–42; amazing accomplishments
of, 342–48; voice of the slipstream, 350–
51; pressure waves ahead of flying wing,
354; shock wave explained, 354–55;
supersonic flying, 358–60; supersonic
slipstream problems, 360–62; guided
missiles, 362–63. *See also* Navigation,
Slipstream, Soaring

Floki, Norse navigator, 40

Flyer. *See* Airman, Navigator

Fog, similar to alto-stratus cloud, 186;
explained, 196–200; deadly, 198–99;
illustrated, 199; from the air, 200; ice
fog, 238–39; sea or frost smoke, 241–42;
from condensation near speed of sound,
357. *See also* Clouds, Condensation

Francisco de Lana, 281

Franklin, Benjamin, on ocean temperatures,
29–30; on lightning and storms, 205, 251;
on balloon, 282; on the bald eagle, 301

Frobisher, Sir Martin, 53

Front, upper cold front factor in tornadoes,
145; frontal analysis, 257–66; illustrations
of, 258, 260, 264, 265; cold, 258–59, 270;
warm, 259–60, 271; polar front, 261–66;
effect of on health, 268. *See also* Weather,
Air

Frost, arctic danger, 234; hazard to flying,
238–39; frost smoke, 241–42. *See also*
Cold, Ice, Snow

Gale. *See* Wind, Hurricane

Galileo Galilei, 53

Gander, Newfoundland, 273

Garnerin, André Jacques and Eliza, 287

Gatty, Harold, navigator, 23; acknowledg-
ment to, viii

Gilbert, William, 377

Gliding, 176; how altitude is gained, 190–91;
as means of investigating wind and
storm, 195, 205–7; adventure with seagull, 307–8; aided by air columns and
wind seams, 309–10; soaring, 310–11;
wing shapes, 311–12; experiments by
Lilienthal, 314; success in by the Wright
brothers, 315–16. *See also* Soaring,
Flight

God, examples of creation, 191, 295; revelations of, 280; prophets of, listed, 327, 421;
and Willie Leveen, 397–98, 402, 404;
on rainbow, 411; His imagination, 413–14;
first dimensions of, 414–15; we are part
of His experience, 415; what is He saying,
420

God, moon, 19; sun, 31; sailor, 33; of thunder, 205, 206, 214, 217; of rain, 231

Goddess, sun, 18, 19; Iris of the rainbow,
409; Hecate of nightly apparitions, 409

Gravity, problems of, 104–7. *See also*
Buoyancy, Settling, Coriolis force, Earth

Greek, navigation history, 34–38; lack of
sense of progress, 56; winds, 121–25, 132

Greenland, visited by Pytheas, 35, 37;
pilotage problem over, 61–62; ice cap
described, 232–33; on belt of intense
auroral visibility, 384; geomagnetic
pole, 386. *See also* Arctic, Eskimos

Greenwich, England, prime meridian of
earth, 90; G.M.T. (Greenwich Mean
Time), 250, 374, 375; basis of mid-west
section lines, 118

Groundspeed, 67, 71; example of use of,
77–78; where easy to measure, 118. *See
also* Airspeed, Speed, Navigation